Textpattern Solutions: PHP-Based Content Management Made Easy

Kevin Potts, Robert Sable, and Nathan Smith
with Mary Fredborg and Cody Lindley

friendsof

DESIGNER TO DESIGNER™

an Apress® company

Textpattern Solutions: PHP-Based Content Management Made Easy

ISBN-13 (pbk): 978-1-59059-832-0

ISBN-10 (pbk): 1-59059-832-6

Printed and bound in the United States of America 9 8 7 6 5 4 3 2 1

Trademarked names may appear in this book. Rather than use a trademark symbol with every occurrence of a trademarked name, we use the names only in an editorial fashion and to the benefit of the trademark owner, with no intention of infringement of the trademark.

Distributed to the book trade worldwide by Springer-Verlag New York, Inc., 233 Spring Street, 6th Floor, New York, NY 10013. Phone 1-800-SPRINGER, fax 201-348-4505, e-mail orders-ny@springer-sbm.com, or visit www.springeronline.com.

For information on translations, please contact Apress directly at 2560 Ninth Street, Suite 219, Berkeley, CA 94710. Phone 510-549-5930, fax 510-549-5939, e-mail info@apress.com, or visit www.apress.com.

The information in this book is distributed on an "as is" basis, without warranty. Although every precaution has been taken in the preparation of this work, neither the author(s) nor Apress shall have any liability to any person or entity with respect to any loss or damage caused or alleged to be caused directly or indirectly by the information contained in this work.

The source code for this book is freely available to readers at www.friendsofed.com in the Downloads section.

Credits

Lead Editors
Chris Mills, Matthew Moodie

Technical Reviewer
Mary Fredborg

Editorial Board
Steve Anglin, Ewan Buckingham,
Gary Cornell, Jason Gilmore,
Jonathan Gennick, Jonathan Hassell,
James Huddleston, Chris Mills,
Matthew Moodie, Jeff Pepper,
Dominic Shakeshaft, Matt Wade

Project Manager
Richard Dal Porto

Copy Edit Manager
Nicole Flores

Copy Editor
Nancy Sixsmith

Assistant Production Director
Kari Brooks-Copony

Production Editor
Ellie Fountain

Compositors
Dina Quan and Darryl Keck

Artist
April Milne

Proofreaders
Paulette McGee and Elizabeth Berry

Indexer
Julie Grady

Interior and Cover Designer
Kurt Krames

Manufacturing Director
Tom Debolski

This book is dedicated to my beautiful wife and children, who have often wondered why the heck writing a book takes so darn long. They have offered nothing but the kindest support and blessed respite, and despite my agonizing over formatting inconsistencies and code accuracy, were there at the end of the day to remind me of the most important things in my life. To my children: I'm sorry the plot and characters do not make for engaging bedtime reading. (I tried to work in some fire trucks and princesses, but the editors said it "wasn't relevant.") To my wife: you could not have been a more patient, loving partner. I love you all very much.

Kevin Potts

I would like to dedicate this book to my beautiful wife, Joci. I never imagined that I would meet someone so caring and supportive to spend my life with. Thank you, Joci, for everything that you are and everything that you make me. I love you.

Rob Sable

I would like to dedicate this book to my wife, who has stood by me throughout my meandering pursuit of job satisfaction and outlets for creativity. Thank you for listening to my ranting about funky code acronyms and encouraging me even when I cannot seem to make sense of it all. I love you more than words can express. You are the world to me.

Nathan Smith

CONTENTS AT A GLANCE

PART FOUR: EXTENDING TEXTPATTERN

PART FIVE: TEXTPATTERN SITE EXAMPLES

PART SIX: APPENDIXES

CONTENTS

PART ONE: GETTING STARTED

PART TWO: THE TEXTPATTERN INTERFACE

PART THREE: CUSTOMIZING TEXTPATTERN

Chapter 6: The Textpattern Model 151

Chapter 7: Creating the Content: Categories and Articles 161

Chapter 8: Customizing the Presentation: Sections, Pages, Forms, and Style. 181

Chapter 16: Case Study: PopularWeddingFavors.com 337

PART SIX: APPENDIXES

FOREWORD

When I first discovered Textpattern in 2004, I was looking for a flexible CMS that could not only power my blog but also power my whole site, especially the portfolio. I fell in love with the Textpattern XML style template tags, clean administration interface, and sheer speed and flexibility. I keep trying other alternatives, but always come back to Textpattern. To my mind, no other system can compete with its flexibility and the strength of its community.

I use it not only to power my site (www.hicksdesign.co.uk) and side projects such as Pimp My Camino (http://pimpmycamino.com), but also to power sites for my clients, including The Forgiveness Project (www.theforgivenessproject.com) and Open Doors (http://student. opendoorsuk.org). Even the most technophobic clients enjoy using Textpattern's un-intimidating administration panel to update their sites. Designers love it because they can easily set up and manage sites by themselves, inputting any content and displaying it where they want, the way they want. Everyone wins.

However, one thing that Textpattern has always lacked is a printed manual—a physical guide and reference work that also demonstrates how it can be used for everything from personal blogs to ecommerce sites. Fortunately, Kevin Potts, Robert Sable, Nathan Smith, Mary Fredborg, and Cody Lindley have more than filled that need, and you now hold the result! *Textpattern Solutions: PHP-Based Content Management Made Easy* is an excellent guide, taking you from installation, to advanced uses of Textpattern with global variables, to writing your own plugins. There is something here for all levels of users and would-be users to glean and enjoy. It's already a permanent feature of my desk!

Jon Hicks, *Hicksdesign*

ABOUT THE AUTHORS

Kevin Potts has been working on the Web since the mid-1990s, having started his career designing his first employer's website with Netscape and Notepad. He has spent the bulk of his design career working as a print designer and web developer, and is now the creative director of a large Midwestern software company. Coupled with years of freelancing and agency work, Kevin has created dozens of websites for businesses of all sizes in an array of industries. He started using Textpattern in 2004 as a blogging tool for graphicpush.com, where he still writes about the business of design and life as a creative team manager.

Nathan Smith is a goofy guy who enjoys practicing and preaching web standards. While attending Asbury Theological Seminary, he initially picked up Textpattern to build a website that could be easily updated by the staff at his church, and that led to a full-time career in web development. Nathan works as an Information Architect/Interface Designer at Geniant and writes semiregularly at sonspring.com and godbit.com. He has been described by family and friends as mildly amusing, but he is really quite dull.

Robert Sable has more than ten years of experience designing and developing web-based applications for small businesses up to Fortune 50 companies. Rob recognized the power and flexibility of Textpattern from its early gamma releases. He has published more than 20 Textpattern plugins and numerous tutorials on his website at www.wilshireone.com. Rob also provides custom software development services using Textpattern as a development frame-work. He lives with his wife, Joci, in Copley, Ohio, which is located between Akron and Cleveland. Rob and Joci love to travel together and continue to find new and exciting places to visit. Rob was born and raised in the Cleveland area and continues to be a painfully dedi-cated Cleveland sports fan.

Mary Fredborg is a member of the Textpattern development team (http://team.textpattern.com). For more than ten years she's been involved in various aspects of web development and remains keenly interested in learning new methods and technologies, as well as refining her existing knowledge and skills. These days you can often find Mary work-ing on Textpattern itself, creating new plugins for it and providing technical support for users of varying levels of experience. She lives in Alberta, Canada with her amusingly crazy dog, who also happens to think the same of Mary.

Cody Lindley is a Senior Software Engineer for SuperValu, working out of Boise, Idaho. When he is not working with client-side technologies, Flash, or interaction design, he spends time with his wife and son, enjoying a simple lifestyle in the Northwest. Cody has a passion for Christian theology and takes great pleasure in learning and studying God's word. His work and ongoing ramblings can be found at codylindley.com.

ACKNOWLEDGMENTS

We want to acknowledge the innumerable hours of thankless work that goes into making Textpattern such a great system. The core developers have built an open-source solution that rivals many of the retail options out there, and their altruism has made possible the book you are now reading. If not for the efforts of these people, there would be no Textpattern: Dean Allen, Mary Fredborg, Pedro Palazón, Alex Shiels, and Sencer Yurdagül. We the authors tip our hats to you, and collectively look forward to where Textpattern is heading in the future.

We also want to acknowledge the dedicated editors of this book for their patience in dealing with us as inexperienced authors. friends of ED/Apress has been a great company to write for. Special thanks to the foED/Apress crew: Chris Mills, Richard Dal Porto, Matthew Moodie, Ellie Fountain, and Nancy Sixsmith. Last but not least, an incredible debt of gratitude is owed to our technical reviewer, Mary Fredborg, who has provided us with the guidance and expert input that only a core Textpattern developer can provide.

Cody, Kevin, Rob, and Nathan

INTRODUCTION

Salutations, brave reader, and welcome to *Textpattern Solutions: PHP-Based Content Management Made Easy*. Since you have this book in hand, it is a safe assumption that you are interested in the content-management system (CMS) called Textpattern. Perhaps you have heard about how its tag syntax resembles XHTML or the ease with which you can build custom templates. Maybe you are looking to switch from some other proprietary platform with restrictive licensing or just want an intuitive online text editor to use for writing and displaying a journal or blog. Whatever the motivation, it is our sincere desire that this book serve you well as both reference and tutorial, guiding you along the path to streamlined website development and maintenance with Textpattern.

Learning something new can often be a daunting task, especially when you endeavor to accomplish it alone. Hopefully this text will find a ready place on your shelf or desktop, providing simple solutions to otherwise seemingly complicated or obscure situations. Each one of this book's authors has traversed the meandering road of open-source content management, arriving at Textpattern as a powerful tool to assist in rapid site development. The book you are now reading is one that we wanted to have when we first learned to use this system. It is the result of a labor of love for a methodology that has made our lives easier. We hope that our combined knowledge will benefit you by saving the time and frustration of scouring the Internet for tips and tutorials, putting all that information at your fingertips.

Book structure

This book is divided into 17 chapters and 2 appendixes. It is obviously not a mystery novel, so feel free to skip around without fear of ruining some gripping plot (the butler did it). In fact, by the time you are done reading, Textpattern will probably be so familiar to you that none of it should seem esoteric. The chapters can be read straight through sequentially to learn things step by step, or the book can be used more as an encyclopedia to look up specific information once you have a handle on the basics.

Chapter 1 is pretty straightforward and covers the background and community behind Textpattern. Some of the more notable Textpattern sites are mentioned to give you some inspiration as you conjure up ideas for your own project. Also, the GPL and MIT licensing models are compared and explained, which is good for those who like to use software knowing that it truly is open source and free of restrictions or fees. After all, everybody loves free stuff, right?

Chapter 2 shows you how to create a local testing environment by installing Textpattern on your own computer running Windows or Mac OS X. Since the components that power Textpattern are all freely available, they have been made to run on just about any operating system. No matter which type of setup you prefer, we've got you covered. Simply flip to the set of instructions that pertain to you and follow along accordingly.

Chapter 3 pertains to the admin section, in which you can check site diagnostics, create and manage user accounts, and check visitor logs. You can also edit a number of preferences, such as changing the site's time zone or tweaking the way your site is syndicated to external sources. This is also where you'll go to install extra third-party plugins, which then enable you to use Textpattern in new and inventive ways. If you want to migrate from another publishing platform, such as Blogger or Movable Type, there is even an import function that converts those older posts to a usable Textpattern format.

Chapter 4 covers the content section of Textpattern. Here you are introduced to the text formatting syntax called Textile, and you can begin to write basic articles. You'll learn how to arrange your site into sections and categories, as well as incorporate images and file uploads into your content. The chapter also covers how to use the links area for times when you want to call attention to something on the Web but are too lazy to write an article about it.

Chapter 5 is all about presentation, which actually happens to be much more than just looking good. You'll dig into making different site sections, associating them with page templates, and controlling their appearance using the Cascading Style Sheets (CSS) style editor. Some basics of the CSS visual presentation language are covered, as well as a few caveats to consider when coding your layout. You'll also look at TXP forms and see how they can make life a lot easier by reusing chunks of code throughout a site.

Chapter 6 dives into the world of semantics, and you'll learn the importance of properly marking up a document based on its meaning. We'll discuss the multiple layers of web development—including the content, structure, presentation, and behavioral layers—and how those four work together within the Textpattern system. You'll understand why Textpattern is explicit in its separation of content and structure, and how those two aspects are eventually woven together.

Chapter 7 explains how categories and articles work together as the primary axis for the Content tab, and how they can be used to organize your articles in associative ways. For instance, an article about a vacation to Europe could be categorized in both vacation and Europe. This way, other vacations could be grouped within the vacation category, and a different article about a business trip to Europe could be grouped in that category while not necessarily having anything to do with a vacation. You'll navigate the finer points of both pieces of the TXP puzzle, including URL structure, different status levels, and the power of keywords; and you'll tackle the management of other content: links, images, and files.

Chapter 8 explores the Presentation tab in depth. You'll learn about the symbiotic relationship between sections, pages, and forms, and how they work together with your site's content. Using a band's website as an example, we'll break down how to develop a template step by step, from moving a raw HTML file into the Textpattern system, to outsourcing pieces of code into different forms, to editing those forms with Textpattern tags for pulling in dynamic content. In addition, we'll discuss the fundamentals of pages and sections, the options available for each, and how they work together to produce full templates for housing content. At the end of the chapter, you'll know how an entire home page is constructed in Textpattern.

Chapter 9 takes the concepts from Chapter 8 and applies them to several real-world examples. We'll discuss further the relationship between articles, sections, pages, and forms; and how they work in tandem to produce web pages. You'll learn about building a page of static content, an archive page for blog posts, a contact page, and a photo gallery. By the end of this chapter, you'll see how the core building blocks of Textpattern produce different types of content while using the same basic principles.

Chapter 10 addresses comments, some of the trickier parts of any Textpattern site. They tend to be more difficult to control than other parts of a site, but you'll learn about the numerous options and tags (as well as a virtual library of plugins) that Textpattern provides to customize them on a very granular level. Additionally, you'll get the hang of managing comments for those occasions in which pesky visitors might leave feedback that is less than welcome: whiners, spammers, and trolls—oh my.

Chapter 11 gets into more advanced territory. Starting with a few fundamental reminders, you'll learn two different ways to create customized error messages, methods for building a search box and customized search results, and finally adding dynamic metadata to all pages of your site. You'll explore some more esoteric functionality, including custom fields, keywords, more conditional statements, and several specialized tags.

Chapter 12 revisits how to make use of custom fields. Since custom fields can be whatever you want, they enable you to tailor the way things work. You can use them to build extra conditional logic into pages. You'll also learn how to use custom fields to sort articles according to criteria that you create, instead of just by date or category. You'll also look at using plugins to enable unlimited custom fields instead of the default number of ten. This unlocks much more potential, such as *tagging*, which has become quite popular on many social networking sites, enabling users to help categorize content.

Chapter 13 looks at several of the more popular and powerful Textpattern plugins. One plugin enables you to easily create an email contact form, while others can help you style the look of article comments. There is even one that enables advanced users to run SQL queries directly against the MySQL database or do an easy one-click backup of an entire site. Needless to say, this chapter will really broaden your horizons as to how extensible Textpattern can be.

Chapter 14 tests your PHP knowledge by showing you how to write a plugin. You'll explore the scenarios in which you might need to write your own plugins: if the basic Textpattern capabilities cannot handle a particular need and if others have not already addressed it with plugins of their own. The plugin architecture is explained, and you'll get a feel for the steps necessary to take an idea and make it a reusable chunk of code that others can benefit from.

Chapter 15 covers a multiauthor website. We'll show you how to create different tiers of users, with varying levels of privileges. This is useful when you want authors to be able to contribute to a site, while not necessarily letting them have authority over its entirety.

Chapter 16 shows how to use a few of the plugins covered earlier to create an ecommerce website. You'll learn about the benefits of using Textpattern to create ecommerce sites and how to use sections, categories, and articles to create an online catalog. We'll also show you how custom coded components can be incorporated into your site to offer shopping cart functions and payment system integration.

Chapter 17 describes case studies of a real live site: a start-to-finish walkthrough of the steps involved in creating a restaurant review site for a large city. By the end of this chapter, you'll have a solid understanding of how to go beyond what Textpattern offers, writing your own code to integrate directly into the system.

Appendix A is a tag reference with brief examples of how each Textpattern tag can be used. Appendix B is an extended list of commonly used helper functions and global variables from the Textpattern source that plugin authors can use when writing plugins.

Necessities

To follow along with the localized examples in this book, you need a computer with an Internet connection running Windows or Mac OS X. You might also want a graphics program of some sort. We prefer either Adobe Photoshop or Fireworks, but other free alternatives, such as GIMP (www.gimp.org) work just fine. Designers tend to be fussy about their preferred imaging software, and we certainly aren't looking to pick any fights. Our examples might vary, but we encourage you to use that with which you are familiar.

The rest of the components for this book can be downloaded and configured as needed (for example, Apache, PHP, and MySQL). To get a live site running, you need at least a shared web hosting service, of course. Because of the myriad of hosting companies and their varying options, we cannot possibly cover every scenario. We do, however, walk you through using some of the common configurations that are available by default for many web hosting environments.

To make things easier, all the custom code examples covered in this book can be downloaded from the friends of ED website: http://friendsofed.com/. You can type everything out manually if you feel so inclined, but to save time we recommend that you go to the website and navigate to the corresponding code download for this book. You can also check the publisher's site for any errata that might pop up, on the off chance that we have actually made any mistakes (hey, it could happen).

Layout conventions

To keep this book as clear and easy to follow as possible, the following text conventions are used throughout.

Important words or concepts are normally highlighted on the first appearance in **bold type**.

Code is presented in `fixed-width` font.

New or changed code is normally presented in **`bold fixed-width font`**.

Pseudocode and variable input are written in *`italic fixed-width font`*.

Menu commands are written in the form Menu ➤ Submenu ➤ Submenu.

Where I want to draw your attention to something, I've highlighted it like this:

> *Ahem, don't say I didn't warn you.*

Sometimes code won't fit on a single line in a book. Where this happens, I use an arrow like this: ➥.

```
This is a very, very long section of code that should be written all ➥
on the same line without a break.
```

PART ONE **GETTING STARTED**

1 SETTING THE STAGE

When reading any good book, there is always an engrossing first chapter that grabs your attention and beckons you to read more. While this book might not be of the suspenseful thriller genre, hopefully it will whet your whistle and get you excited about the possibilities of Textpattern (TXP). You will learn a bit about how it came to be and what the future holds in store. You will also take a look at some of the highly trafficked TXP sites out there, examining how each has chosen to implement the system.

What is Textpattern?

Ask any seasoned web developer about which tools to use for a job, and you will probably hear the same response: "It depends." Some designers swear by Photoshop; others prefer Fireworks. Many people use the Windows operating system, though some might opt for Linux or a Mac. Similar to many situations in life, the best way to find a solution is to first define the problem. So, let's evaluate whether Textpattern is right for you. The official site defines Textpattern as "A free, flexible, elegant, easy-to-use content management system [CMS] for all kinds of websites, even weblogs."[1]

Catchy as it might sound, that bit of prose does not fully encapsulate the power of TXP. Before you learn more about what TXP can do, let's first identify what it is not. Think of it as appraising a piece of property. Many systems are like prefabricated homes, in which you can change only minor details. To do anything more requires quite a bit of remodeling. Using TXP can be likened to finding a vacant lot with only a foundation (albeit a very *good* one) and constructing the rest of house on your own. Depicted in Figure 1-1 is the default look and feel for Textpattern as it appears without any extra customization. Looks can be deceiving, though, for under this nondescript veneer is a powerful engine ready to be harnessed and directed.

Since Textpattern is quite diverse in what it can handle, a brief list of examples helps demonstrate the scope of what can be done with it. It can be used to run a web-based personal journal, referred to as a **weblog** (or **blog** for short). Of course, there are already a variety of services out there, such as Blogger[2] or LiveJournal,[3] that enable someone to set up a blog. However, Textpattern gives you the leeway to choose a host of your choice instead of relying on a shared service. What also sets it apart from the crowd is the capability to manage more complex newspaper-style or multiauthor community sites.

One such site is UX Magazine, a prominent online publication focused on improving web-based user experience (see Figure 1-2). Another is the Godbit Project,[4] which is geared toward helping churches make better use of the Web (this will be discussed in Chapter 16).

---

1. www.textpattern.com
2. www.blogger.com
3. www.livejournal.com
4. www.godbit.com

1

Figure 1-1. Textpattern default

Figure 1-2. www.uxmag.com

Textpattern has even been used to power extremely high-traffic websites such as PvP Online (see Figure 1-3), a web cartoon about video games that is also published in print by Image Comics (best known for *Spawn*). The PvP site gets more than 15 million page views per month.

Figure 1-3. www.pvponline.com

Needless to say, Textpattern is a highly versatile and very capable system. For people who simply want a quick blog without much customization, a fully featured CMS can seem like overkill. However, for those willing to put in a little extra effort, the flexibility of tailor-fitting TXP to meet your exact specifications can be very rewarding. If you are up to it, proceed with confidence that by the time you finish this book you will be able to use TXP for just about any web project imaginable.

A noble history

Textpattern is the brainchild of Dean Allen, who has described himself as the "world's slowest control freak." He did so when referring to the delay between the initial concept screenshots of Textpattern in July 2001 and the first stable release in August 2005. His humorously self-deprecating assessment does not really do him justice. Dean can be described instead as being both altruistic and an entrepreneurial businessman. He got his start working in the printing business as a typographer, art director, and noted book designer. From there, he became increasingly interested in the Web as a publishing platform, which eventually led to the Textpattern CMS.

Dean has also built up quite a successful web hosting company named TextDrive.[5] In November 2005, TextDrive merged with the collaborative technology company called Joyent[6] and now has quite a bit of influence in the world of web development. TextDrive hosts several high-profile websites, such as A List Apart,[7] which is arguably the most popular publication on web design and development. It also contributes to other open-source initiatives by enabling people it hosts to specify to which project they want a portion of their money given. This does not mean any additional cost for the customer, but simply gives back to those systems that TextDrive actively supports.

Ever since the inception of Textpattern, it has been made available to the public at no charge. Because of this (and the consistent commitment to quality with which TXP development has been approached), there has been a rapid uptake by designers and developers using it. Many deploy TXP to run not only their own personal sites but also their clients' projects. It has grown into a robust website management tool, powering everything from simple blogs to online commerce, even being used to run the campaign website of Ted Kennedy, the United States Senator from Massachusetts. Kennedy is quite technically savvy for a politician and was the first-ever Senator to have a website (see Figure 1-4). Not only does he support Net Neutrality, but he uses Textpattern and YouTube[8] to get his message across.

Figure 1-4. www.tedkennedy.com

5. www.textdrive.com

6. www.joyent.com

7. www.alistapart.com

8. www.youtube.com

While it is easy to see that Textpattern has already enjoyed quite a bit of popularity, the best is yet to come, as the saying goes. Some exciting additions are planned for future releases, as well as commercial support being carried out by the core development team. There is also a Textpattern Pro version in development for customers who want features beyond the basic setup.[9] This means that we will continue to see more uses of TXP for business and commercial purposes as it pushes forward beyond the role of a simple blog engine into the arena of enterprise CMSs.

How does Textpattern work?

This section discusses what makes Textpattern tick, including the technology behind it and how a Textpattern site works in terms of the architecture. We will also get into a bit of legalese and figure out why there have been a few licensing changes, resulting in more power being given to the end user and developers alike. Additionally, we will cover the geeky details about how Textpattern works. Then we will start getting into the concepts around what makes Textpattern so versatile.

LAMP platform

Textpattern runs on the freely available dynamic duo of PHP[10] and MySQL.[11] PHP is one of the most widely used server-side scripting languages, and has typically been paired with MySQL, which is the world's most popular open-source database. PHP originally stood for Personal Home Page, but has since changed to a recursive acronym meaning "PHP: Hypertext Preprocessor." MySQL stands for My Structured Query Language. Typically, these two run on an Apache web server[12] installed on the Linux operating system. Together Linux, Apache, MySQL, and PHP comprise what is commonly referred to as the LAMP platform. Zero licensing fees and proven stability have made its usage quite prevalent.

The LAMP platform is used by numerous companies worldwide, such as Amazon, Google, Yahoo!, and Zend. The most notable of these companies is Yahoo!, which created quite a stir upon announcing in 2002 the big switch from its own proprietary language called yScript to the open-source solution of PHP. It also hired the creator of PHP, Rasumus Lerdorf, as its head of Infrastructure Architecture.[13] Yahoo! is quite community-minded and has made many of its code tutorials available for free, so if you are looking for a good place to get articles aside from the official PHP site, be sure to check out the Yahoo! developer center.[14]

---

9. http://team.textpattern.com
10. www.php.net
11. www.mysql.com
12. http://httpd.apache.org
13. www.lerdorf.com/resume
14. http://developer.yahoo.com/php

You do not necessarily need to memorize all that information to make use of TXP, but such tidbits of trivia are good to know. Should you ever want to tinker beneath the hood, these building blocks will be your starting point. Chapter 2 will show you how to get TXP running in a Windows, Mac, or Linux environment for local testing, but when you start using it to power live sites on the Internet, chances are your host will be running the LAMP combination. Regardless of what type of PC setup you have, the practice you do on your local computer will translate more or less seamlessly to developing real production sites.

Licensing

Following in the power-to-the-people spirit of the open-source foundation upon which it is built, TXP is free of charge and flexible with its licensing restrictions. All versions of Textpattern up to 4.0.x are released under the GNU General Public License (GPL), but releases as of TXP version 4.1 will be released under the Berkeley Software Distribution (BSD) license, popularized by the University of California, Berkeley. Without going into all the detailed legal jargon, this basically means that no matter what, TXP will always remain free to use. Believe it or not, the latest change in licensing actually makes TXP even *freer*.

The main difference between the GPL and the BSD license is how they handle derivative works. Both enable anyone to take the source code and reuse it however they see fit. With the GPL, if you make changes or additions to the original work, anything you release based on the original must be licensed under the terms and conditions of the GPL. The BSD license, however, is a little more permissive. While it also ensures that anyone can take the original source and modify it, such derivative works do not necessarily have to be released under the BSD model. The BSD is generally thought to be a bit closer to the completely unrestricted notion of public domain, for which no copyrights exist.

This open-source ideology allows for proprietary commercial works to be built upon technology that originated under a BSD license. This model makes it easier on developers because it does not limit the conditions in which they can deploy their subsequent creations. Even large companies such as Microsoft and Apple have benefited from using open-source technologies as a springboard for developing their own specific corporate software. So what does all this mean for you? Good question. Essentially, it ensures that if you make money by running sites with TXP, say doing development for your clients or by selling products via ecommerce, you do not have to pay any royalties to the originators of the software.

If you do find that it becomes an integral part of your work on the Web, you might consider showing your appreciation by donating financially to those who have worked laboriously to produce it. Likewise, if you have an idea for changing the way things work, you are free to do so under the corresponding licensing. However, if you are savvy enough at PHP programming to do that, you might as well contribute to the core development or write your own plugins. In Chapter 15 you will learn in more detail how to write custom plugins, extending the system to fulfill a specific purpose.

Practically speaking

With those geeky details out of the way, it is time to move on to the fundamentals of Textpattern. The beauty of this system is the way it separates actual content from purely presentational markup. This is one of the key tenets of what have come to be affectionately referred to as **Web Standards**.[15] No longer are we mixing our presentational elements directly in the markup that contains our content. Eye candy is just that and should not clutter up the context of the information being conveyed. Therefore, many purely visual enhancements are relegated to background images—all controlled by a set of external Cascading Style Sheets (CSS) files.

Web Standards can be thought of as the Web emerging from its infancy and heading toward an age of maturity. In the past, different browser makers were fighting each other by offering widely varying implementations of HTML and mixing in their own proprietary syntax. This led to a polarization of the way websites were built, with JavaScript browser detection turning away would-be visitors. The whole Internet was mired by a mess of sites that were inconsistent and incompatible with more than a handful of browsers.

Suppose that every brand of automobile required unique gasoline. Fuel stations would be a pain to find because only a select few would work with your car. Thankfully, those dark days are behind us, and a new dawn has given way to the philosophy that agreement on the basics is best for everyone. Browser manufacturers now compete over who can offer better features and the closest adherence to the standards.

When a visitor arrives at your site, instead of loading a series of static XHTML and CSS files, PHP retrieves the corresponding section or article entry based on the requested URL, merges it with the accompanying page template, and changes it into XHTML before it reaches the browser. Additionally, Textpattern pulls in your CSS, which is also stored within the same MySQL database. The only truly static files you will be dealing with are the images and supporting files that you upload through the TXP content interface, and even they are conveniently administered through the CMS.

From a maintenance standpoint, it is easier than attempting to juggle multiple static files, which means more time spent in the actual CMS and far less usage of FTP to send and retrieve files. Figure 1-5 shows the essence of how Textpattern works from a visitor and an author perspective, storing and retrieving data.

If this all still seems like a dizzying amount of terminology and acronyms being thrown about, not to worry. All will be explained through the course of later chapters. What is important now is that you get a general feel for the concepts behind how Textpattern works since we will cover each aspect at an increasingly granular level as the book progresses.

---

15. www.webstandards.org

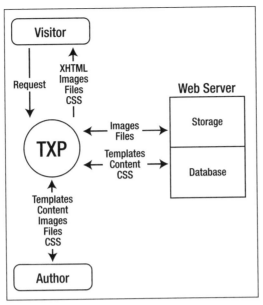

Figure 1-5. TXP functionality

An active community

In addition to this book, several online sources can help you hammer out any trouble-shooting in your understanding of Textpattern. There is quite an active community on the official forum and throughout the rest of the blogosphere. One might even go so far as to say that the Textpattern community is hyperactive. If you want to get involved, by all means—jump in with both feet!

Textpattern FAQs

Like most computer-related questions, you can be sure that whatever topics might come up, someone else somewhere has probably wondered the exact same thing. This is, of course, the purpose for the series of frequently asked questions (FAQs) on the Textpattern website. Here you will find an ever-growing list of recurring inquiries, as shown in Figure 1-6. Even if a predicament is quite off the wall, you would be surprised how many seemingly odd situations have already been tackled. When you are not sure whether you should ask a question on the forum, try searching the FAQs first to see whether the answer has already been addressed.

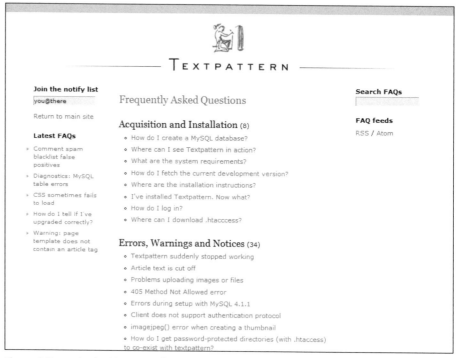

Figure 1-6. www.textpattern.com/faq

Textpattern forum

The next place to turn is the official TXP forum. Here there are a multitude of other TXP users who are very enthusiastic about the system and are always happy to help each other out, as shown in Figure 1-7. While some people consider the lack of paid tech support a drawback of open-source software, others view it as one of its strongest points. Typically, it fosters a community climate of good will. You can think of it like the take-a-penny/ leave-a-penny tray at most restaurants. Sometimes you will find yourself in need of assistance; other times you will be the one offering your expertise. Again, try searching the forum first before asking what might be a redundant question. The forum crowd is friendly enough, but it will save everyone time and effort if you can track down a solution yourself.

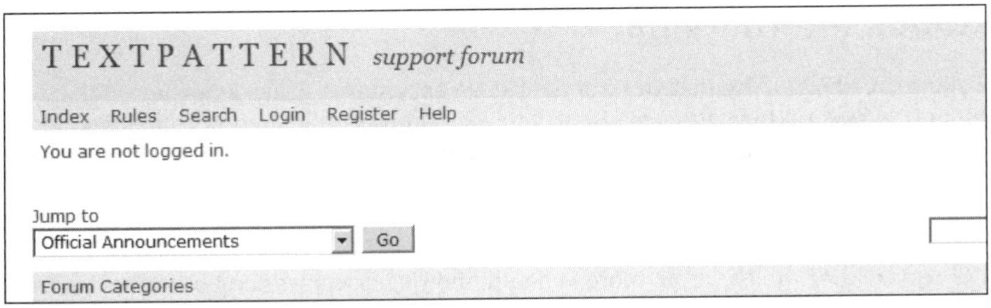

TEXTPATTERN *support forum*

Index Rules Search Login Register Help

You are not logged in.

Jump to
Official Announcements ▼ Go

Forum Categories

Figure 1-7. http://forum.textpattern.com

Textpattern resources

Another site to turn to is Textpattern Resources (see Figure 1-8), located at www.textpattern.org. There are quite a number of plugins, modifications, tips, and tricks documented, many of which originated on the forum and were then archived for easier searching at one central location. This makes an excellent spot to look for additional Textpattern functionality. Whenever an instance arises in which the core functionality of Textpattern does not suit the need of a particular scenario, more often than not someone else has run into a similar limitation and the problem has already been solved via a plugin or creative workaround.

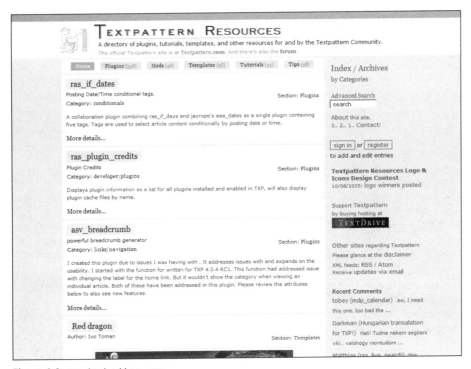

Figure 1-8. www.textpattern.org

TextBook International

If you want a helpful site that works more like an encyclopedia, check out TextBook International at www.textpattern.net. Here, you will find user-submitted documentation in a variety of languages, as shown in Figure 1-9. While most of the common parts of TXP are covered, some areas are still incomplete. Additionally, TextBook International is always in need of good translators to help round out the information and keep it consistent throughout the different languages. In the appendices of this book, you will find a similar TXP syntax listing, which will go more in depth, showing examples and tips for how to best make use of each instance.

Figure 1-9. www.textpattern.net

TXP Magazine

There is even a site dedicated to tracking notable Textpattern sites: TXP Magazine[16] (see Figure 1-10). At the time of this writing, there are nearly 600 sites listed, all of which have to meet a certain level of scrutiny to be accepted into the gallery. One such site is that of Jon Hicks (see Figure 1-11), who is best known for his logo designs of the Mozilla Firefox browser and Thunderbird email program. Another distinctive site is that of award-winning designer Jared Christensen (see Figure 1-12), who is known for his bold use of color and

---

16. www.txpmag.com

outspoken appraisal of various musical genres. There are also several professional sites featured, such as Cobalt Engineering,[17] an acclaimed construction firm based in Vancouver, British Columbia, Canada.

Figure 1-10. www.txpmag.com

Figure 1-11. www.hicksdesign.co.uk

---

17. www.cobaltengineering.com

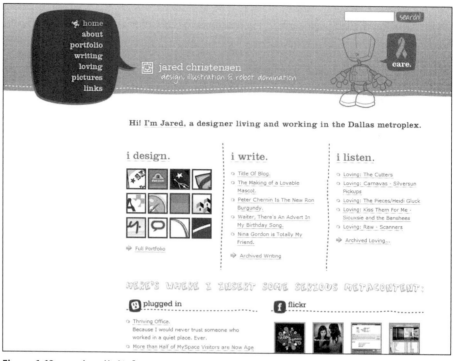

Figure 1-12. www.jaredigital.com

Textgarden

For license-free blog templates that can be used in Textpattern, be sure to check out Textgarden at www.textgarden.org (see Figure 1-13). Here you will find a variety of designs and layouts to choose from. Whether you need something to spruce up an otherwise default-looking blog or want a starting point for learning how to make your own templates, Textgarden should be in your list of essential bookmarks. Many of the templates have been converted because they were popular in other blogging platforms and their authors were kind enough to give TXP users the right to port them over. These templates instantly transform the look and feel of your website, but because they are so commonly used they can make your site seem less unique. You will learn how to do your own templating in later chapters.

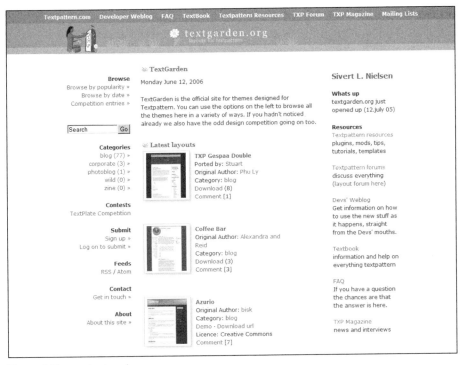

Figure 1-13. www.textgarden.org

Textplates

One of the problems with template repositories is that you cannot always tell at a glance the good from the bad. If you are looking for templates that have been peer reviewed and scrutinized, you will want to visit Textplates at www.textplates.com (see Figure 1-14). It was created by an ambitious young college student at the University of Buffalo named Tom Fadial. He recognized the benefits of Textpattern, but was disappointed by the amount of community support behind creating new templates that others could use. Ironically, one of the rivals of Textpattern—another popular platform called WordPress,[18] which caters specifically to blogs—was the inspiration for starting a contest. This drew many quality contestants, with entries that include photoblog templates, re-skins of the default layout, and even one that boasts streamlined installation as a one-click plugin. After all was said and done, the TXP community had quite a few solid templates to choose from.

---

18. www.wordpress.org

Figure 1-14. www.textplates.com

Key bloggers

Another way to keep up with the Textpattern craze is to follow the blogs of other TXP fanatics. A convenient way to stay abreast of the latest happenings is to subscribe to each site's Rich Site Summary (RSS) or Atom feed with a news aggregator. This way, when new content is posted, you will be alerted from within one central interface instead of having to visit each site daily to check for new updates. If this concept sounds foreign to you, hang in there—RSS and Atom feeds will be covered later in this book.

The authors of this book obviously have their own respective sites from which various CMS serendipities are shared. While it might seem a bit self-serving, we would be remiss if we did not point you to our sites for continued updates on creative implementations of Textpattern:

- Cody Lindley: www.codylindley.com
- Kevin Potts: www.graphicpush.com
- Rob Sable: www.wilshireone.com
- Nathan Smith: www.sonspring.com

Additionally, the aforementioned sites of Jon Hicks and Jared Christensen each contain compilations of helpful material. You should also keep an eye on the blogs of the core TXP development team:

- Dean Allen: www.textism.com
- Mary Fredborg: www.utterplush.com
- Pedro Palazón: www.kusor.com
- Alex Shiels: www.thresholdstate.com
- Sencer Yurdagül: www.sencer.de

At the time of this writing, there is a fairly extensive calendar plugin in development by Team Textpattern. The process was started by Matthew Smith, a Philadelphia-based designer at Artiswork.[19] He sought to fill a perceived gap in many CMSs—the capability to produce a navigable schedule of events for several months, years, or decades. After getting a few other like-minded designers on board, the TXP core developers were commissioned to begin work on the custom plugin.

By the time this book is on store shelves, the plugin will be completed, after which it will be released as open source. Be sure to check for it on the friends of ED code download page corresponding to this book because it will be a power plugin that will be a must-have for both corporate and community organizations. One of the great things about Textpattern is that the development team is not only open to suggestions but is also available for hire to make them into a reality. Often, after the service has been paid for by a few people, everyone benefits from their contributions. This is jokingly known as **ransoming** a plugin, thus setting it free.

Summary

Since Textpattern is not a commercially driven product, the grassroots effort around it is what really keeps the development alive. This is what is commonly referred to as **viral marketing**, in which one person tells another about something that has had a positive impact. In the case of TXP, many users find themselves in a position to give back to the community, so to speak. Due to the exponential impact that word-of-mouth news can have, there are new blogs springing up on a weekly basis. The authors encourage you to jump aboard this bandwagon and learn as you go, helping others as your level of knowledge increases. That is, of course, how this book came to be in the first place. The future holds some exciting possibilities, and we are glad that you are along for the ride.

Now that we have covered some background and fundamentals, the next chapter will delve deeper and explain how to install TXP on your own computer using Windows XP, Mac OS X, or Ubuntu Linux. We will iron out some of the typically rough spots for beginners and give you some tips to simplify the whole process. You will also learn how to get TXP running on a remote Linux web server for actual live site hosting.

---

19. www.artiswork.org

2 INSTALLING TEXTPATTERN

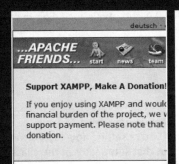

Now that you know the history of Textpattern and you have an understanding of what the software and community is all about, it's time to get down to business. This chapter covers the steps you need to take to download and install Textpattern on your own computer and your hosting account.

The benefit of setting up a local installation is that you can develop and test your site in your own environment. You have full control over your web server and database and don't have to worry about visitors stopping by while you're still building your site. If you're working on upgrading an existing site, you can work on the new version while the existing version is still available on the Internet. And if you're an aspiring plugin developer, you can use a local installation to work out the kinks before using the plugin on a live site. Once you have time to build your site, you have to load it onto a publicly available web server for others to see.

System requirements

Aside from the Textpattern files that you'll learn about downloading and installing in this chapter, there are a few other components that you need to have in place to run Textpattern. If you want to run a local Textpattern installation, you need to install these components locally. At the least, you have to find a web host that uses web servers that meet the following minimum requirements:

- PHP 4.3 and above, including the MySQL and XML extensions
- MySQL 3.23 and above

While the minimum requirements outlined are enough to run Textpattern, the following are the recommended requirements as outlined by the Textpattern development team:

- PHP 4.4.1 and above or 5.0.2 and above, including the MySQL, XML, and mbstring extensions running in mod_php or FastCGI mode
- MySQL 4.1.7 and above
- Apache HTTP Server 1.3 and above or 2.0 and above including the mod_rewrite module
- A web server running a Unix-based operating system including locale support

Clean URL support

To use clean URLs with your Textpattern installation, you need to have the mod_rewrite module installed on your Apache web server. If you're setting up a local install, you'll have no problem using clean URLs (you'll learn about that setup later in the chapter). If you're using a web host, be sure to ask if mod_rewrite is supported.

What are clean URLs?

If you're an experienced Internet surfer, you've undoubtedly seen an ugly URL that looks something like the following:

http://www.example.com/?e=KI7dh&ty=78nduuUD&session=powrIDIN7366

This URL is not only hard for your visitors to read and understand but it also hinders the ability for search engines to crawl and index your site. While you won't see anything quite this bad in Textpattern, here's a simple example. The default First Post article included in the Textpattern install would be accessed using the following URL in ?=messy permanent link mode:

http://www.textpatternsolutions.com/index.php?id=1

While it gets the job done, with clean URL support, you can make that address look much better. Here's the same URL using the /year/month/day/title permanent link mode:

http://www.textpatternsolutions.com/2007/01/25/first-post

While this URL will take a visitor to the same page, the visitor (as well as search engines) can get additional details about the contents of the page just from its address. The use of clean URLs gives your site a boost in terms of both usability and search engine friendliness.

Checking for clean URL support

If you want to confirm whether your host provides mod_rewrite support, create a file named phpinfo.php and add the following code:

```php
<?php
  echo phpinfo();
?>
```

Then upload the file to your hosting account and load it in your browser. Search for the Loaded Modules section of the page and confirm that mod_rewrite is listed, as shown in Figure 2-1.

Loaded Modules	core mod_win32 mpm_winnt http_core mod_so mod_access mod_actions mod_alias mod_asis mod_auth mod_autoindex mod_dav mod_dav_svn mod_dir mod_env mod_imap mod_info mod_isapi mod_log_config mod_mime mod_negotiation mod_rewrite mod_setenvif mod_status mod_userdir mod_cgi sapi_apache2 mod_include

Figure 2-1. Checking loaded apache modules for mod_rewrite

If your host supports mod_rewrite, but you still can't get clean URLs to work, there is still an alternative that you can investigate before resorting to the use of messy URLs. The .htaccess file found at the root of your Textpattern installation contains three lines that are commented out. Try removing the # sign preceding each of the following lines:

```
#DirectoryIndex index.php index.html
#Options +FollowSymLinks
#RewriteBase /relative/web/path/
```

After removing the # sign from the beginning of each line, you have to set the appropriate path to the Textpattern install. Unless you installed Textpattern in a subdirectory, the new line looks as follows:

```
RewriteBase /
```

If you installed Textpattern in a subdirectory, add the name of that directory as follows:

```
RewriteBase /mysubdirectory
```

If after making these changes and uploading your new .htaccess file you still can't get clean URLs working, it's time to contact your host for help or resort to using messy URLs.

If your web host doesn't support mod_rewrite, you can still use Textpattern, but you have to select the messy permanent link mode when setting your site preferences. If you're intent on using clean URLs but don't have mod_rewrite support, you might be able to try an experimental solution such as the one mentioned on the Textpattern weblog in an article titled "Partly messy: Clean urls without mod_rewrite."[1] But keep in mind that the easiest (and officially supported) way to support clean URLs is through use of Apache's mod_rewrite module.

Choosing a host

Using these minimum and recommended requirements, you're now ready to start a search for a web host. There are a multitude of hosting companies that meet or exceed the system requirements for running Textpattern. The specific requirements of the site you're building might lead you to value certain features over others, so be sure to carefully evaluate all your options before purchasing a hosting plan. To get started in your search, check out a listing of web hosts that the Textpattern development team recommends at http://team.textpattern.com/hosts/.

Which version of Textpattern?

Just like many other open-source software applications, the Textpattern developers use the Subversion version control system to manage the Textpattern source code. This means that the latest version of the Textpattern source code is always available for your use. However, unless you want to experiment with the latest Textpattern additions (or you're a plugin developer looking to test out your plugins against the latest source code), it's best to use the stable release versions of Textpattern.

Before being made available for download, release versions of Textpattern are tested by the development team and the Textpattern community. Bug reports made by users are investigated and fixed by the development team to ensure that release versions of Textpattern are as bug-free as possible.

---

1. www.textpattern.com/weblog/135/partly-messy-clean-urls-without-modrewrite-experimental

There are currently two main development branches for the Textpattern source code: the 4.0 branch and the crockery. The 4.0 branch of the source code should be fairly stable, but it's not impossible for bugs to be introduced between official releases. The crockery should be considered experimental and should not be used on live production sites.

Acquiring Textpattern

Once you decide which version of Textpattern you want to use, there are two ways to go about acquiring the files you need to complete the installation. The easiest way is to download the latest installation package. If you consider yourself a more advanced user, you can pull the latest source code from the Subversion repository.

Downloading an official release

To get started with the latest Textpattern release, your first stop is the official download page at www.textpattern.com (see Figure 2-2).

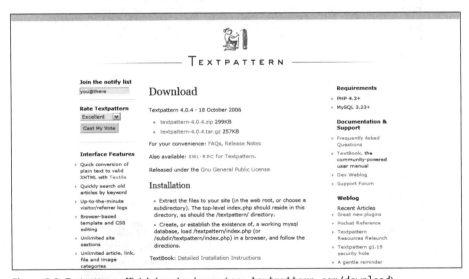

Figure 2-2. Textpattern official download page (www.textpattern.com/download)

You have the choice of downloading either a zip archive or a tarball. Download your archive of choice and you're ready to begin the installation process. Since you'll be walking through the typical install process in this chapter, you'll use the 4.0.4 release version that is the most recent at the time of this writing. And while you might choose to grab the latest source code from the Subversion repository based on the instructions covered later in this chapter, continue with the standard install process using the downloaded release from the Textpattern download page.

Local development on Windows

These instructions are for Windows XP (Home or Professional), but shouldn't deviate much on Windows 2000 or Vista. While it is possible to download and install each of the components—or (as XAMPP calls them) "modules"—of a local server with PHP and a MySQL database, it can be tricky to make them all work well together. You can get a jump start on developing locally with Textpattern by making use of a free and easy-to-use software package called XAMPP.

Installing XAMPP

The first step is to fire up the web browser of your choice and go to www.apachefriends. org/en/xampp-windows.html. Here you see the XAMPP for Windows home page, which should be similar to Figure 2-3. Within the phrase The XAMPP 1.6.0a is available!, click the XAMPP 1.6.0a link to jump to the actual download options. Next, click the Installer link for the [Basic package] to begin downloading XAMPP. Once you finish downloading the installer, you're ready to proceed.

Figure 2-3. XAMPP for Windows home page (www.apachefriends.org/en/ xampp-windows.html)

Double-click `xampp-win32-1.6.0a-installer.exe` to begin the installation process. Choose English from the drop-down menu and click the OK button.

Once the Setup Wizard loads up, click the Next button. You are asked for the location of where to install XAMPP, as shown in Figure 2-4. It's best to leave it at the default value of C:\Program Files (which will install to C:\Program Files\xampp), so click the Next button once more.

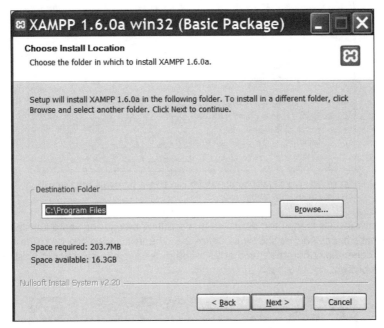

Figure 2-4. The XAMPP Setup Wizard asks where to install XAMPP.

Next, you have a couple of install configuration choices, as shown in Figure 2-5. It is a good idea to have the boxes next to Create a XAMPP desktop icon or Create an Apache Friends XAMPP folder in the start menu checked (or both, if you like). Under SERVICE SECTION, you might install most of the different modules as services, which means that they can (and do by default) launch automatically when you start Windows. If you are not planning to use your local server very often, leave these boxes unchecked. You can easily change this later. Click the Install button.

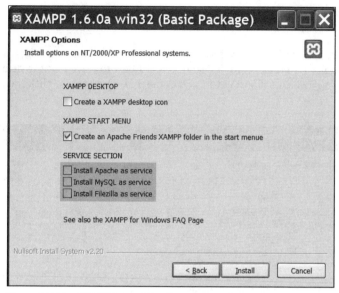

Figure 2-5. The XAMPP Setup Wizard can create shortcuts and setup services for ease of use.

XAMPP now installs many files, displayed in a scrolling box, giving you a constant update about what's happening, as shown in Figure 2-6. The installation can take one to several minutes, depending upon the speed of your computer. Once the install has finished, press the Finish button.

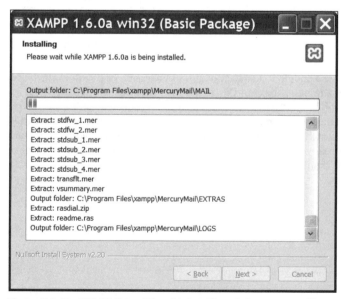

Figure 2-6. The XAMPP Setup Wizard is installing all the necessary files.

Finally, installation is complete and you are asked whether you want to start the XAMPP Control Panel. Click the Yes button, and the XAMPP Control Panel is launched, as shown in Figure 2-7.

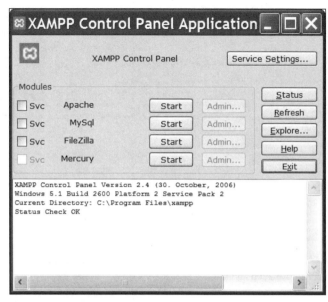

Figure 2-7. XAMPP Control Panel

Using XAMPP

The XAMPP Control Panel (refer to Figure 2-7) enables you to start, stop, check, and refresh the status; and launch the administration sections of each of its modules.

You only need to have Apache (the HTTP server) and MySQL (the database server) running. The other modules, FileZilla (FTP server) and Mercury (email server), can be left turned off; they are not needed for running Textpattern. Click the Start button next to Apache and MySql to load up each.

One program that can interfere with your Apache server is Skype because it uses the same resources to connect to the Internet as a local server. Make sure to shut it down if your Apache server does not start, and try again.

Next to each module is a checkbox labeled Svc. Checking each installs that module as a Windows service. As mentioned during the installation process, services can (and do, by default) launch automatically when you start Windows. If you don't plan to use your local server very often, leave these checkboxes unchecked. Because of XAMPP's handy little Control Panel, running these modules as services doesn't offer any additional benefit. You might also install the Control Panel itself as a service by configuring the Service Settings area (found by clicking the button labeled such).

Click the Admin button of the Apache component to launch your browser and show the XAMPP for Windows page (see Figure 2-8). It contains all the information about your installation, as well as a few helpful utilities.

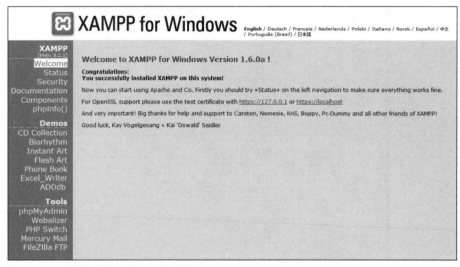

Figure 2-8. XAMPP information and utilities

MySQL setup

With XAMPP installed and running, you can now create a MySQL database and user for Textpattern to use. From the XAMPP for Windows page, click the phpMyAdmin link to launch an easy-to-use database management utility (see Figure 2-9).

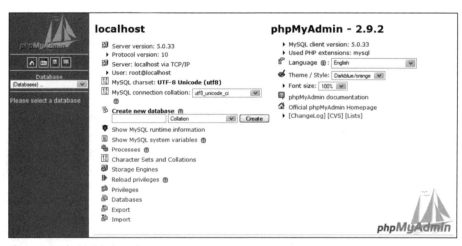

Figure 2-9. phpMyAdmin main page

Creating a User

Click the Privileges link; then click Add new User on the following page.

In an effort to make your local server mirror a remote hosting environment as closely as possible, create a username and password that will reflect that. For the sake of simplicity, I am using an easy-to-remember username of maryfredborg with the password password4textpattern. Needless to say, you should pick something more secure for any live site. In the area labeled Global privileges, click the Check All link. Look things over to make sure they look similar to Figure 2-10 and then scroll to the bottom and click Go. You see this confirmation screen: You have added a new user.

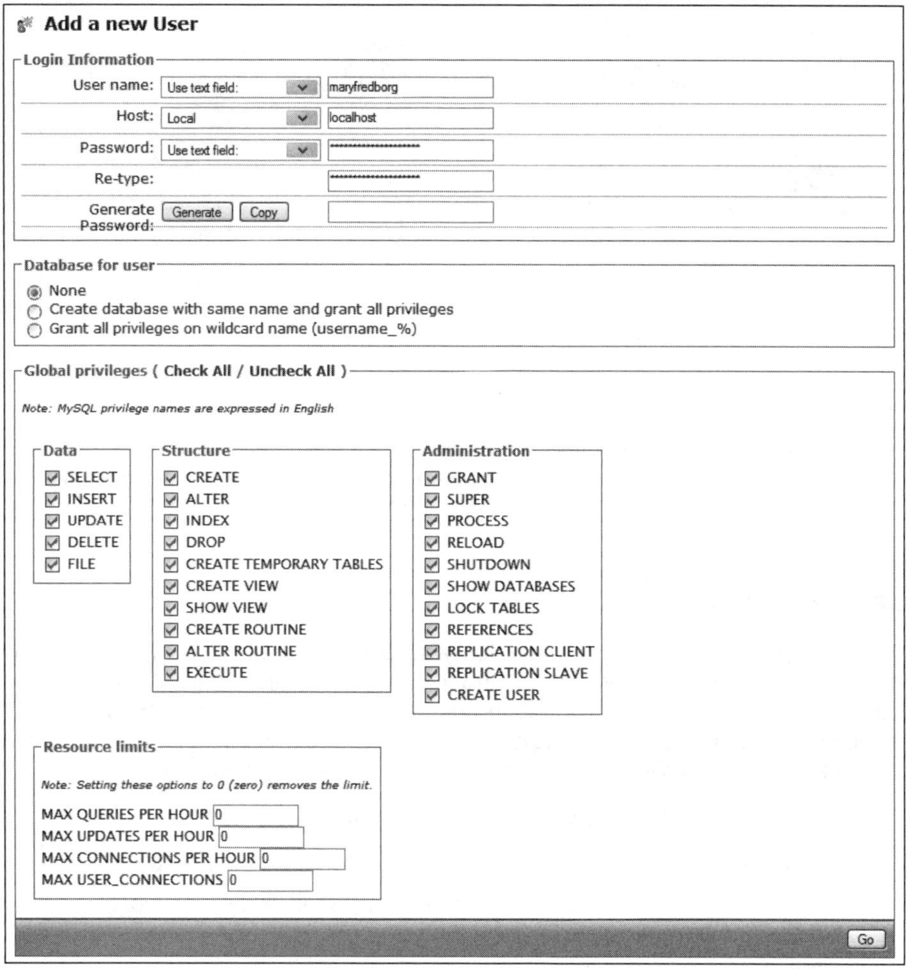

Figure 2-10. Creating a new user in phpMyAdmin

Creating a Database

Click the tab at the top of the screen labeled Databases. On the Databases screen (see Figure 2-11), type in the name of your new database, textpattern, and then click Create. On the following page, you see this confirmation message: Database textpattern has been created.

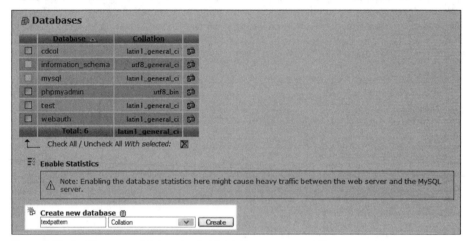

Figure 2-11. Creating a new database in phpMyAdmin

Initial preparations

So far, you have laid the groundwork for a nice local testing environment: you have installed XAMPP, and created a username and database for Textpattern to use. You have only a few more preparations before you install Textpattern.

Show File Extensions

By default, Windows hides the file extension of several types of file, displaying only the file name; for extension-only files such as .htaccess, Windows hides them completely. This can cause great confusion and frustration when attempting to develop for the Web, so it's a good idea to turn this particular feature off. It's easy to do, doesn't harm anything, and can be easily switched back on if you find you don't like having it off.

1. Open up My Computer (it's on the desktop by default).
2. From the Tools menu, select Folder Options, as shown in Figure 2-12.
3. The Folder Options window opens (see Figure 2-13). Click the View tab.
4. Find and *uncheck* the checkbox labeled Hide extensions for known file types. Click OK.

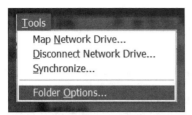

Figure 2-12. Selecting Folder Options from the Tools menu

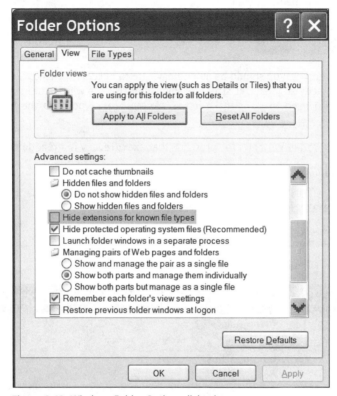

Figure 2-13. Windows Folder Options dialog box

Prepare the Files

If you have not yet downloaded Textpattern, go to www.textpattern.com/download and grab the Zip file of the latest version. (At the time of this writing, it is version 4.0.4.)

1. Extract textpattern-4.0.4.zip by using either the Windows XP built-in "compressed folders" feature, or file archive software such as 7Zip.[2] The result is a folder of the same name that contains several files and folders. Feel free to read through and/or delete the HISTORY.txt and README.txt files because they are not pertinent to the Textpattern installation process.

---

2. www.7-zip.org

2. Rename the `textpattern-4.0.4` folder to `example.dev` and move it to your `C:\Program Files\xampp\htdocs` directory. This directory will be the location that houses your local Textpattern site.

I like to name the directory the same as the public-facing site, except instead of a domain extension such as *.com, I put *.dev at the end. This indicates that the site is in development and helps to differentiate it from the real domain name in the address bar. You can, of course, name your directory something different from `example.dev` to more accurately reflect the domain name of your site.

Update Your HOSTS File

With XAMPP running, you should be able to navigate to http://localhost/example.dev/, but it is not exactly an ideal URL structure since your real site will live at http://example.com/. What you need to do is make http://example.dev/ point to the local install of Textpattern.

First, you need to tell Windows to "pretend" that `example.dev` is a real domain:

1. Open the text editor of your choice and go to File ➤ Open.

2. The Open dialog box is launched. In the File name: textbox, type in `C:\WINDOWS\SYSTEM32\DRIVERS\ETC\HOSTS`. Click Open.

3. You should see one simple line of text, `127.0.0.1 localhost`. You might have more lines than that, but this is the important one. As shown in Figure 2-14, after `localhost`, type a space and then enter `example.dev`. Save the file.

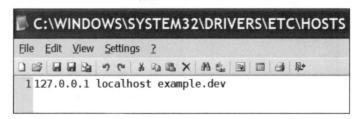

Figure 2-14. Edited Windows HOSTS file

Update httpd-vhosts.conf

Now that Windows recognizes `example.dev`, all that's left is to tell Apache how to handle the request for it:

1. With your text editor open, go to File ➤ Open.

2. The Open dialog box is launched. In the File name: textbox, enter `C:\Program Files\xampp\apache\conf\extra\httpd-vhosts.conf`. Click Open.

3. Replace lines 19–42 with the following and then save the file:

```
NameVirtualHost localhost:80
```

```
<VirtualHost localhost>
  ServerName localhost
  DocumentRoot "C:/Program Files/xampp/htdocs"
</VirtualHost>

<VirtualHost example.dev>
  ServerName example.dev
  DocumentRoot "C:/Program Files/xampp/htdocs/example.dev"
</VirtualHost>
```

You might now be asking this question: Why does this example.dev *type of thing matter? Quite simply, most professional web developers prefer to work with root-relative URL schemes. This means you can write* /files/filename. zip *instead of trying to figure out how many levels deep a page is in the site structure and then having to type* ../../../files/filename.zip. *To an Apache web server, the dot-dot-slash syntax* ../ *means "go up one level." Without root-relative URLs, it is extremely tedious going up and down through directories to reference files within your own site. This way, you can more easily port a local site to a live server. This little extra work is worth it in the long run.*

Update httpd.conf

Only one thing remains: enabling the Apache mod_rewrite module, so that you can enable clean URLS later on.

1. With the text editor open, go to File ➤ Open.
2. The Open dialog box is launched. In the File name: textbox, type C:\Program Files\xampp\apache\conf\httpd.conf. Click Open.
3. Scroll to line 118 to find the line #LoadModule rewrite_module modules/ mod_rewrite.so (see Figure 2-15).
4. Remove the pound symbol (#) from the start of the line and save the file.

```
116 #LoadModule proxy_http_module modules/mod_proxy_http.so
117 #LoadModule proxy_ftp_module modules/mod_proxy_ftp.so
118 LoadModule rewrite_module modules/mod_rewrite.so
119 LoadModule setenvif_module modules/mod_setenvif.so
120 #LoadModule speling_module modules/mod_speling.so
```

Figure 2-15. Enabling the mod_rewrite Apache module

Restart Apache

Finally, stop and then start the Apache module from the XAMPP Control Panel for the changes to take effect.

You should now be able to type http://example.dev/ in your browser and receive this message: config.php is missing or corrupt. To install Textpattern, visit textpattern/setup/. This just means that you have not yet officially installed Textpattern.

Load the following address in your browser: http://example.dev/textpattern/. It begins the installation process.

Installing Textpattern

The first thing you need to do is choose your language. It defaults to English (GB), which is the style of English used in Great Britain. You can change it to English (US) or any number of other languages. For the purposes of this chapter, I assume you chose one of the two variants of English. After clicking the Submit button, you should be on the page shown in Figure 2-16.

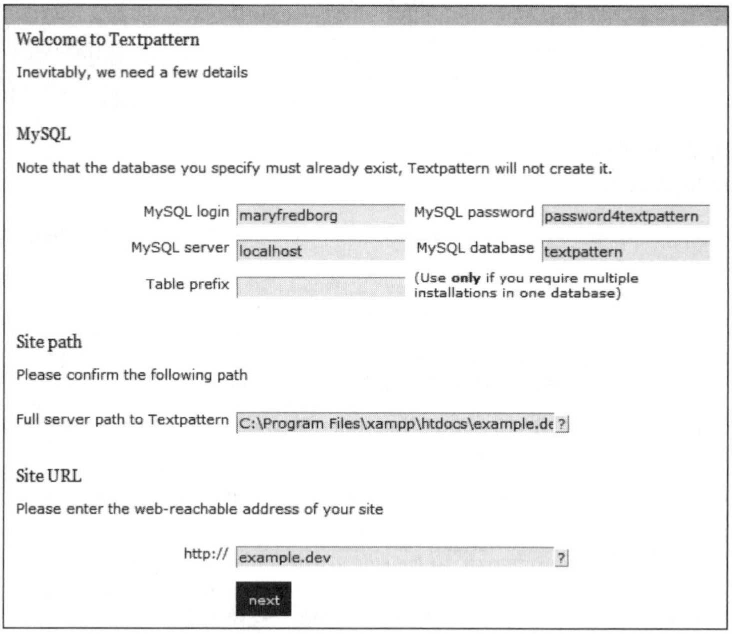

Welcome to Textpattern

Inevitably, we need a few details

MySQL

Note that the database you specify must already exist, Textpattern will not create it.

MySQL login `maryfredborg`	MySQL password `password4textpattern`
MySQL server `localhost`	MySQL database `textpattern`
Table prefix ` `	(Use **only** if you require multiple installations in one database)

Site path

Please confirm the following path

Full server path to Textpattern `C:\Program Files\xampp\htdocs\example.de` ?

Site URL

Please enter the web-reachable address of your site

http:// `example.dev` ?

next

Figure 2-16. Textpattern install details input

Enter the information according to the MySQL database that you set up in the previous steps. As you see, some of the information is prepopulated. You just need to specify your MySQL login, password, and database name. The rest you can leave untouched. Click next.

The next page should look like Figure 2-17. Follow the instructions on the screen and copy the text in the box. Paste this text into a new file, and save it as config.php in this directory: C:\Program Files\xampp\htdocs\example.dev\textpattern\. Feel free to delete the config-dist.php file, which is just an example placeholder. After you make those changes, go back to your browser and click I did it. On the next page (see Figure 2-18), you are prompted to create an administrative account. Enter your name, desired username, password, and email address; then click next.

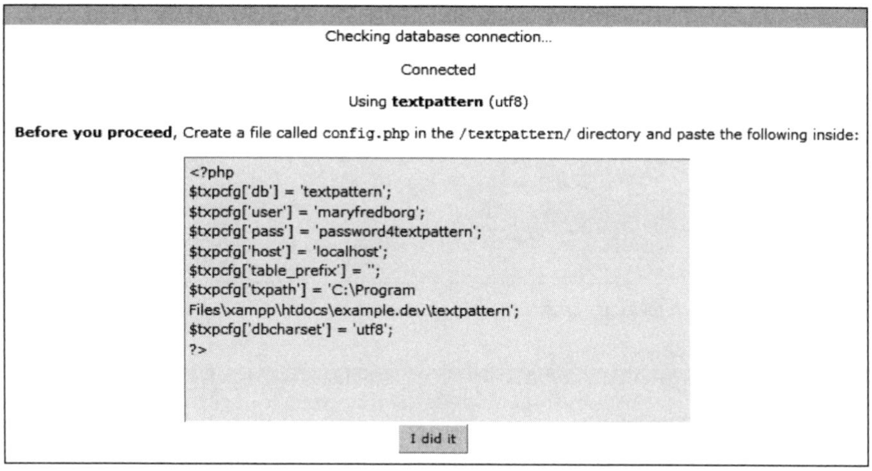

Checking database connection...

Connected

Using **textpattern** (utf8)

Before you proceed, Create a file called config.php in the /textpattern/ directory and paste the following inside:

```
<?php
$txpcfg['db'] = 'textpattern';
$txpcfg['user'] = 'maryfredborg';
$txpcfg['pass'] = 'password4textpattern';
$txpcfg['host'] = 'localhost';
$txpcfg['table_prefix'] = '';
$txpcfg['txpath'] = 'C:\Program
Files\xampp\htdocs\example.dev\textpattern';
$txpcfg['dbcharset'] = 'utf8';
?>
```

I did it

Figure 2-17. Textpattern install config.php contents

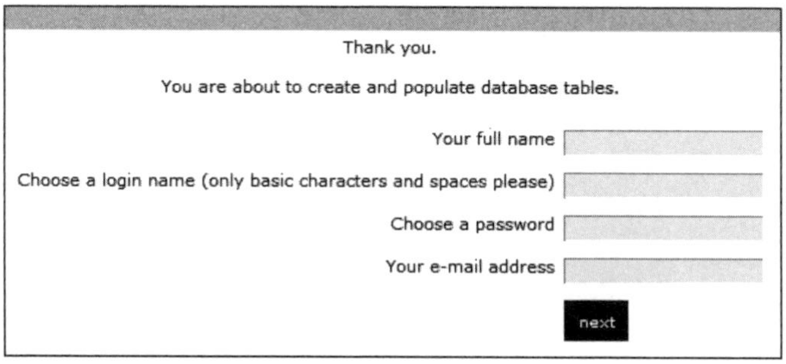

Thank you.

You are about to create and populate database tables.

Your full name

Choose a login name (only basic characters and spaces please)

Choose a password

Your e-mail address

next

Figure 2-18. Textpattern install user account creation

On the next page, you see this confirmation message that Textpattern has been installed: That went well. Database tables were created and populated. You should be able to access the main interface with the login and password you chose. Thank you for your interest in Textpattern. Click the link text main interface and you are taken to the login screen.

Enter the username and password you specified. You then see a page like Figure 2-19, with a large list of possible languages. This page simply shows you that the language you chose has been set as the default, and that you can install further languages if desired. Click the Diagnostics tab at the top of the page, and the screen shown in Figure 2-20 is displayed.

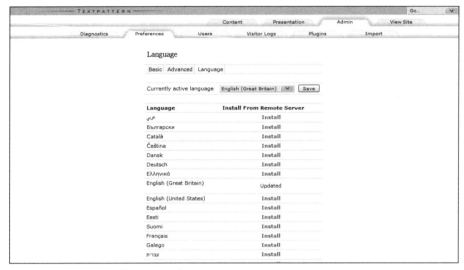

Figure 2-19. Textpattern language preferences

Figure 2-20. Textpattern diagnostics after installation

You should see one error in red, reminding you to delete the setup directory. Do so now and refresh your browser. You should now see the message: All checks passed! Congratulations, you have Textpattern running on your own local server.

Local development on Mac OS X

If you are reading this section of the chapter, you probably march to the tune of a different drummer and are not among the majority of consumers who use a Windows PC. Not to worry—you haven't been left high and dry. This section looks at how to create a local testing environment on OS X. For this installation, you use the free program called MAMP, which stands for Mac, Apache, MySQL, and PHP. This program not only makes things a little easier than compiling Apache and PHP installations from the respective source code but it also enables you to do things with a little more style. If you are the adventurous type, you can even use Subversion (SVN) to get the latest builds of Textpattern for testing.

Installing MAMP

You first need to fire up the web browser of your choice and go to www.mamp.info. Here, you see the MAMP home page, which looks something like Figure 2-21. There is probably a prominent link for MAMP Pro, the retail version of MAMP. However, for your needs, you can simply grab the freely available version. The basic version has all the horsepower of its professional counterpart, just without some of the graphical interface aspects. If you take a liking to MAMP, you might consider purchasing the Pro version because it helps to automate a lot of the grunt work for you. For the purposes of this chapter, you use the basic version.

To get the basic version of MAMP, click the link labeled Download now under the grey elephant icon, which should take you to a download page at Living-E, the parent company that produces MAMP. The URL should be something like this: www.living-e.com/products/ MAMP-PRO/download.php. The page should look something like Figure 2-21.

Figure 2-21. MAMP download page

This chapter does not cover the MAMP Pro installation because it is pretty self-explanatory (not to mention the fact that it costs money). The download you use is simply labeled MAMP. As of this writing, the current stable version is 1.4.1, which is the one used here. Obviously, if there is a newer stable version available by the time you read this, go ahead and use it. There are three possible download types available for MAMP: Universal Binary, PPC, and Intel—because Apple recently switched from Power PC (PPC) processors to Intel-based processors. If you know which of these two processor types powers your Mac, choose accordingly. If you are uncertain, just get the Universal Binary installation file. The Universal Binary takes both types of processor into account and is thus a slightly larger download.

Once you click the Download link, you are taken to a page in which you can enter your personal information, and can opt to receive the Living-E newsletter. If you want to do so, enter your information. Otherwise, just click the Next button to skip that process altogether. A page is displayed, in which you are prompted to begin the download automatically. Once the file has finished downloading, it should be on your desktop (or wherever you store downloaded files). Depending on which file you chose to download based on your processor type, double-click `MAMP_1.4.1_intel.dmg.zip`, `MAMP_1.4.1_ppc.dmg.zip`, or `MAMP_1.4.1_universal.dmg.zip`. The `*.dmg` file by the same name uncompresses. Double-click this file and you see a window that looks like Figure 2-22.

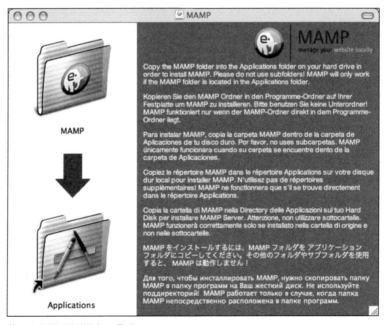

Figure 2-22. MAMP installation

One of the nice things about the MAMP installation process is that it is so intuitive. Simply drag the folder icon with the MAMP logo on it to the Applications folder, just as the arrow indicates. The files begin copying over, which might take a few seconds or minutes depending on your computer's hardware. When it is complete, you can safely eject the MAMP installer file by dragging it to the trash. You can also discard the *.dmg and *.zip files.

If you navigate to the /Applications/MAMP/ directory, you see a file named MAMP Control.wdgt. If you like, you can double-click this file to install an OS X Dashboard widget that enables you to easily start and stop the MAMP servers (MAMP then runs in the background and doesn't clutter up your dock). Dashboard asks you if want to install the MAMP Control widget, which looks something like Figure 2-23. If you want to install it, simply click Keep; it is then added to your assortment of widgets.

Figure 2-23. MAMP Control widget installer

Before you make use of the widget, however, you first need to run MAMP once (by using the actual application file) to change a few things about the default configuration. In the /Applications/MAMP/ directory, double-click the main MAMP.app file. You should see a window that looks like Figure 2-24.

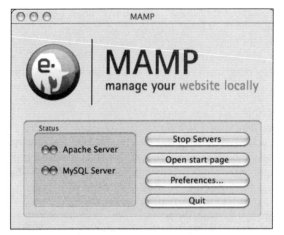

Figure 2-24. MAMP main window

On the main MAMP window, click the button labeled Preferences and then click the sub-menu button labeled Ports. By default, the Apache Port is 8888, and the MySQL Port is 8889. You should change the Apache port to 80, which is the default port for all web servers. This will save having to type :8888 at the end of every web address you want to use locally. To do this, simply click the button labeled Set to default Apache and MySQL ports. Note that the MySQL port changes to 3306. Make sure that the ports have changed to reflect the screen depicted in Figure 2-25.

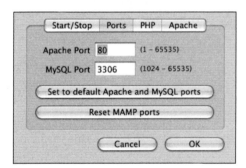

Figure 2-25. MAMP Preferences—Ports

Next, you need to return to the Preferences area and change one more thing. This time, go to the Apache subtab and change the Document Root from the default /Applications/ MAMP/htdocs to reflect your particular username: /Users/username/Sites (note that there is no trailing slash at the end). The reason for this change is twofold. First, it keeps your sites stored separately from the /Applications/MAMP/ directory, so that if you upgrade MAMP, none of your actual web development files is overwritten. Second, this is the native directory for OS X Personal Web Sharing. While you will not actually be making use of Personal Web Sharing in this chapter, it is helpful to keep things consolidated, so that all your locally hosted sites are in the same root directory.

Creating a MySQL database

Now that you have everything squared away with the MAMP install, you can create a MySQL database to house your Textpattern information. With MAMP running, open a web browser and enter http://localhost/MAMP/. (Note the importance of the uppercase letters. If you type lowercase /mamp/, you probably see a Not Found error, which is not what you are shooting for.) You should now see a page that looks like Figure 2-26.

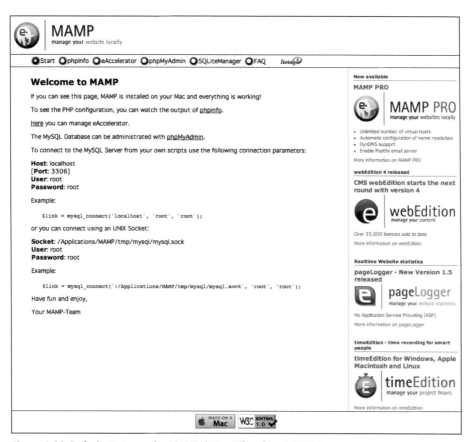

Figure 2-26. Default start page for MAMP (http://localhost/MAMP/)

From here, click the link in the menu named phpMyAdmin. Here, you should see a page that has a sailboat on it, with the word phpMyAdmin written in purple and orange. Click the link named Privileges and on the next page, click Add new User. You could use the default MAMP username and password (root/root) with your Textpattern installation, but that is typically thought of as bad practice. Plus, most hosting companies do not allow you to create a password that is the same as your username.

In an effort to make your localhost mirror a remote hosting environment as closely as possible, create a username and password to reflect it. For the sake of simplicity, I am making my username the same as my Mac login, with my super-secret password: password4textpattern. (Needless to say, you should pick something a bit more secure for your live site.) In the Global privileges area, click the Check All link. Look things over to make sure they look like Figure 2-27 and then scroll to the bottom and click Go. You then see a confirmation screen that says this: You have added a new user.

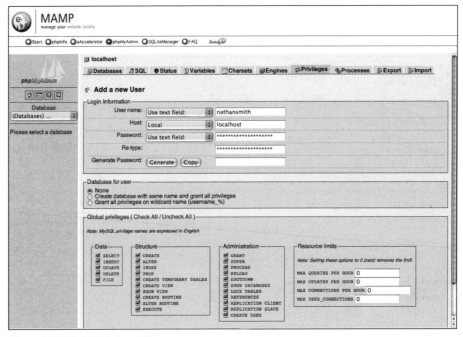

Figure 2-27. phpMyAdmin, adding a user

Now that you have created a username and password, let's make an actual database. Click the Databases tab at the top of the screen. On the Databases screen that displays (see Figure 2-28), enter the name of the new database, in this case textpattern, and then click Create. On the next page, you see a confirmation message: Database textpattern has been created.

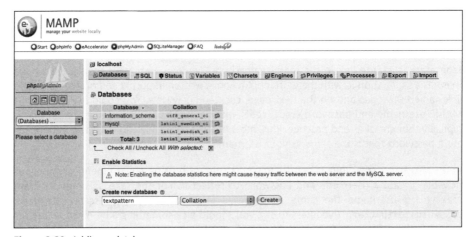

Figure 2-28. Adding a database

Installing Textpattern

So far, you have laid the groundwork for a nice local testing environment. You have installed and configured MAMP, and have a username and database created. If you have not yet downloaded Textpattern, go to www.textpattern.com/download/ and get the latest version. (At the time of this writing, it is version 4.0.4.) Download the Zip file named textpattern-4.0.4.zip, and then find it on your desktop and double-click it. This extracts a folder by the same name. Inside that folder, you see several files and directories. Feel free to read through and/or delete the HISTORY.txt and README.txt files, as they are not pertinent to the Textpattern installation process. Rename the textpattern-4.0.4 folder to example.dev and move it to your /Users/username/Sites/ directory, which is the location that will house your local Textpattern site.

I like to name the directory the same as the public-facing site, except instead of a domain extension such as *.com, I put *.dev at the end. This indicates that the site is in development and helps to differentiate it from the real domain name in the address bar. You can, of course, name your directory something different from example.dev to more accurately reflect the domain name of your site.

With MAMP running, you should be able to navigate to http://localhost/example.dev/, but this is not exactly an ideal URL structure, since your real site will live at example.com. What you need to do is make http://example.dev point to the local install of Textpattern. To do that, you need a text editor that can read hidden files, such as the retail program TextMate (www.macromates.com). Alternatively, you can download the free program TextWrangler (www.barebones.com/products/textwrangler/), which can also edit hidden files.

With the text editor of your choice, go to File ➤ Open or File ➤ Open Hidden, depending on which program you are using. In the window that opens, click Macintosh HD, go to the directory named etc, and open the file named hosts. You should see a pretty small amount of text (see Figure 2-29). On line 7, you see 127.0.0.1 localhost. After localhost, enter example.dev and then save the file. You will probably be prompted for your OS X login password. This is a normal security feature, so don't be alarmed. Enter your password and then click OK.

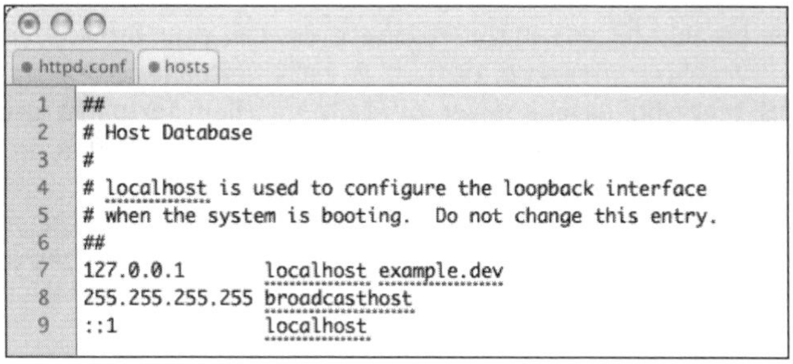

Figure 2-29. hosts file

You need to edit just one more file to make things work properly. With your text-editing program, browse to the /Applications/MAMP/conf/apache/ directory and open the httpd.conf file. Scroll all the way to the end of the file. At around line number 1133, there is this text: # NameVirtualHost 127.0.0.1. The pound sign is an Apache comment, keeping that line of code from doing anything. Remove the #, leaving NameVirtualHost 127.0.0.1; then add this bit of code on the next few lines and save the file (you then need to restart MAMP for the changes to take effect):

```
<VirtualHost localhost>
  ServerName localhost
  DocumentRoot "/Users/username/Sites"
</VirtualHost>

<VirtualHost example.dev>
  ServerName example.dev
  DocumentRoot "/Users/username/Sites/example.dev"
</VirtualHost>
```

By specifically adding the location for localhost, you ensure that no other sites stored within the typical Personal Web Sharing folder are affected. Essentially, this keeps http://localhost/ pointing to the correct location. The next line concerns the new site you are creating locally, which catches http://example.dev/ and makes it point to the new directory that you have created. (Note that it does not work with www.example.dev, so be sure to just type the faux domain name with no www prefix.)

> You might now be asking this question: Why does this example.dev type of thing matter? Quite simply, most professional web developers prefer to work with root-relative URL schemes. This means you can write /files/filename. zip instead of trying to figure out how many levels deep a page is in the site structure and then having to type ../../../files/filename.zip. To an Apache web server, the dot-dot-slash syntax ../ means "go up one level." Without root-relative URLs, it is extremely tedious going up and down through directories to reference files within your own site. This way, you can more easily port a local site to a live server. This little extra work is worth it in the long run.

You should now be able to type http://example.dev/ in your browser and you receive this message: config.php is missing or corrupt. To install Textpattern, visit textpattern/setup/. This just means that you have not yet officially installed Textpattern. Enter http://example.dev/textpattern/ into your browser to begin the installation process. The first thing you need to do is choose your language. It defaults to English (GB), which is the style of English used in Great Britain. You can change this to English (US) or any number of other languages. For the purposes of this chapter, I assume you chose one of the two variants of English. After clicking Submit, you should be at the page shown in Figure 2-30.

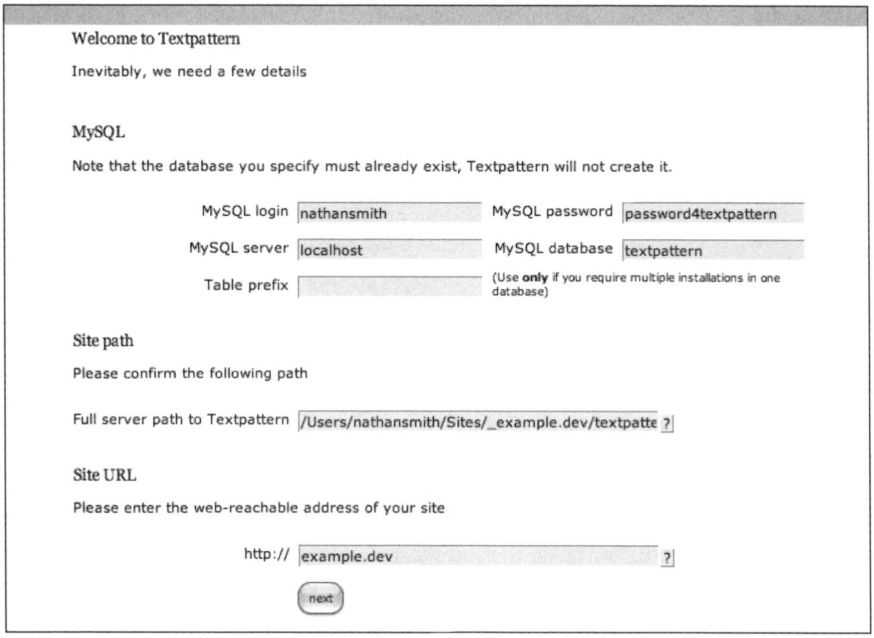

Welcome to Textpattern

Inevitably, we need a few details

MySQL

Note that the database you specify must already exist, Textpattern will not create it.

MySQL login `nathansmith`   MySQL password `password4textpattern`

MySQL server `localhost`   MySQL database `textpattern`

Table prefix ` `   (Use **only** if you require multiple installations in one database)

Site path

Please confirm the following path

Full server path to Textpattern `/Users/nathansmith/Sites/_example.dev/textpatte` ?

Site URL

Please enter the web-reachable address of your site

http:// `example.dev` ?

(next)

Figure 2-30. Textpattern install, database info

Enter the information according to the MySQL database that you set up in the previous steps. As you see, some of the information is prepopulated. You just need to specify your MySQL login, password, and database name. The rest you can leave untouched. Click next. The following page should look like Figure 2-31. Follow the instructions on the screen and copy the text in the box. Paste this text into a new file and save it as config.php in this directory: /Users/username/Sites/example.dev/textpattern/. You can also feel free to delete the config-dist.php file, which is just an example placeholder. Once you have made those changes, go back to your browser and click I did it.

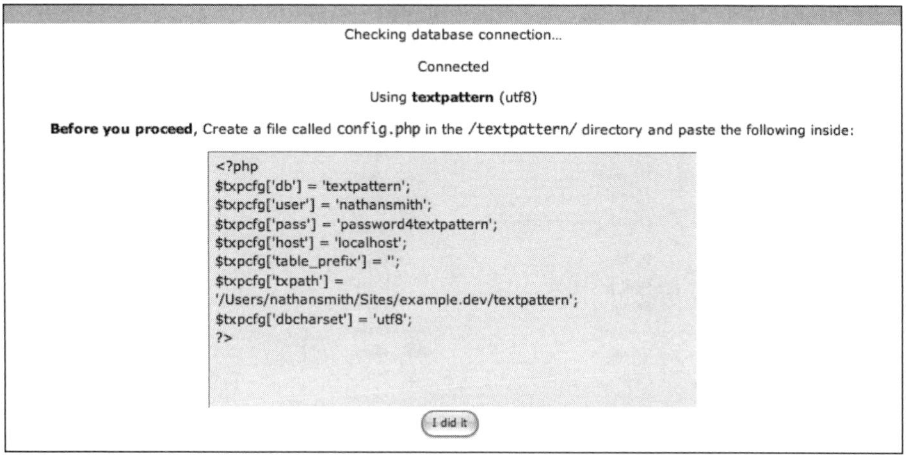

Checking database connection...

Connected

Using **textpattern** (utf8)

Before you proceed, Create a file called config.php in the /textpattern/ directory and paste the following inside:

```php
<?php
$txpcfg['db'] = 'textpattern';
$txpcfg['user'] = 'nathansmith';
$txpcfg['pass'] = 'password4textpattern';
$txpcfg['host'] = 'localhost';
$txpcfg['table_prefix'] = '';
$txpcfg['txpath'] =
'/Users/nathansmith/Sites/example.dev/textpattern';
$txpcfg['dbcharset'] = 'utf8';
?>
```

(I did it)

Figure 2-31. Textpattern install, configuration

On the next page (see Figure 2-32), you are prompted to create an administrative account. Enter your full name, username, password, email address, and then click next.

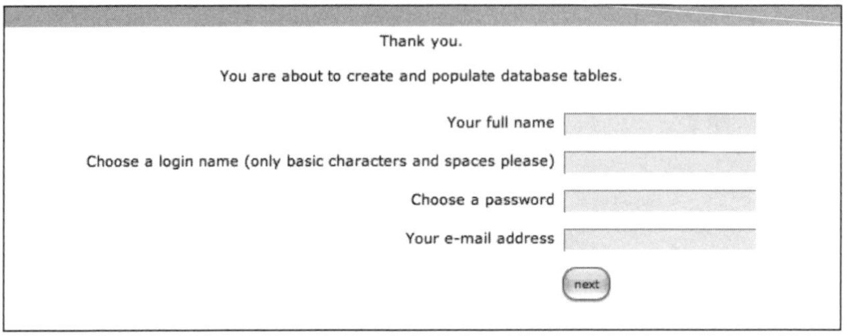

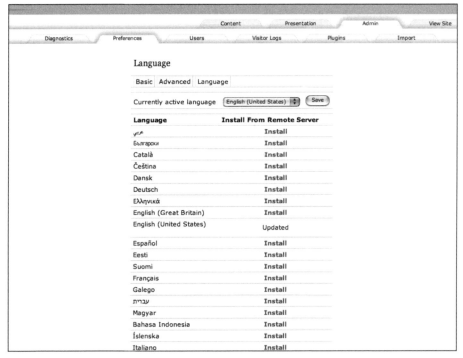

Figure 2-32. Textpattern install, create account

On the next page, you see this confirmation message that Textpattern has been installed: That went well. Database tables were created and populated. You should be able to access the main interface with the login and password you chose. Thank you for your interest in Textpattern. Click the link text main interface and you are taken to the login screen. Enter the username and password you specified. You then see a page that looks like Figure 2-33, with a large list of possible languages. It simply shows you that the language you chose has been set as the default. You can leave things untouched. Click the Diagnostics tab at the top of the page, and you are taken to the screen shown in Figure 2-34.

Figure 2-33. Textpattern install, languages

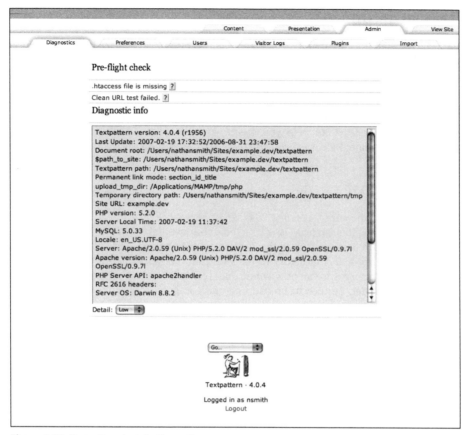

Figure 2-34. Textpattern install, diagnostics

If you see errors in red about the .htaccess file being missing and the Clean URL test failing, it means that you did not copy over the .htaccess file from the Textpattern download to your example.dev folder. The easiest way to do this is to re-extract the downloaded textpattern-4.0.4.zip file, open your text-editing program, browse to the textpattern-4.0.4 folder on your desktop, open the .htaccess file, and then save it again in the /Users/username/Sites/example.dev/ directory. If you receive an error saying that the setup directory still exists, go to /Users/username/Sites/example.dev/ textpattern/ and delete the folder named setup. Click Refresh in the browser and you should now see the confirmation message All checks passed!

Hosted environment setup

If you're ready to install Textpattern on your hosting account, you need to have a File Transfer Protocol (FTP) client to upload the source code to your server.

Database setup

Before beginning the Textpattern installation, you need to have your MySQL database and user setup completed. You have to know the database name, database username and password, and database server name. Make sure that your database is set up and that you have all this information before you proceed with the Textpattern install.

Most web hosts offer the use of web-based database administration tools such as phpMyAdmin[3] or cPanel[4] to help you create your database. Check with your hosting provider to determine the easiest way to create your MySQL database.

FTP files to host

Start by unzipping the textpattern-4.0.4.zip or textpattern-4.0.4.tar.gz file to your local drive. When the archive is extracted, you are left with a directory called textpattern-4.0.4 that contains all the Textpattern files. You have to upload the contents of that textpattern-4.0.4 directory to the web root directory of your hosting account. The web root directory is frequently named public_html, but that ultimately depends on your hosting provider. Be sure to upload only the contents of the folder, not the folder itself.

A multitude of FTP programs are available. If you don't already have a favorite, try one of the following:

- CoreFTP[5] (Windows)
- FileZilla[6] (Windows)
- Transmit[7] (Mac)
- CyberDuck[8] (Mac)

Once your files are uploaded, make sure that the /files, /images, and /textpattern/tmp directories are writeable to support Textpattern's file- and image-upload capabilities.

Install process

Now that the local or hosted environment setup is completed by creating the MySQL database and copying the Textpattern files to the web server, it's time to begin the Textpattern installation process.

---

3. www.phpmyadmin.net
4. www.cpanel.net
5. www.coreftp.com
6. http://filezilla.sourceforge.net
7. www.panic.com/transmit
8. www.cyberduck.ch

Installing Textpattern

1. Once all the Textpattern files are unzipped and uploaded to the web server, you have to determine the URL of the /textpattern/ directory of your Textpattern install. For this example, you install Textpattern at the root of www.textpatternsolutions.com. Therefore, you need to navigate to www.textpatternsolutions.com/textpattern.

2. As the page is loaded, the Textpattern installation process automatically begins. The first step in the install process is to configure the base language for the install, as shown in Figure 2-35. Select your language of choice and click Submit to proceed.

Figure 2-35. Textpattern language selection

3. After you select your language, you are asked to enter information about the database and the path to your Textpattern files (see Figure 2-36). Textpattern intelligently suggests values for the Site path and Site URL based on the location of the installation scripts. In most cases, you shouldn't have to change these values. Simply confirm that they are correct and click next after you enter the database connection information.

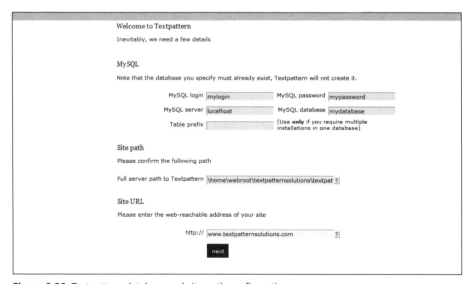

Figure 2-36. Textpattern database and site path configuration

4. Based on the information you entered, Textpattern confirms that it can connect to your database. If successful, a confirmation screen is displayed, as shown in Figure 2-37. As noted on this screen, you need to paste the contents of the textarea into a file called config.php in the /textpattern/ directory of your installation. Take a look in that directory; you see a placeholder file called config-dist.php that comes with the Textpattern download. You can either rename that file to config.php or delete it altogether before you create your new file. Once you have created your config.php file containing the information shown in Figure 2-37, click I did it to continue.

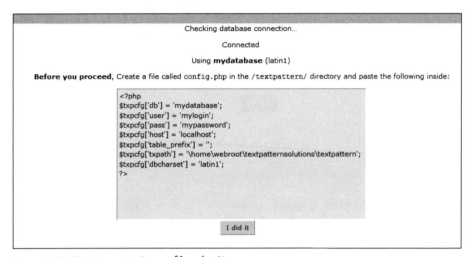

Figure 2-37. Time to create the config.php file

5. You're now asked to create the first administrative user for your Textpattern install. Fill out all fields in the form shown in Figure 2-38, including your full name, login name, password, and email address.

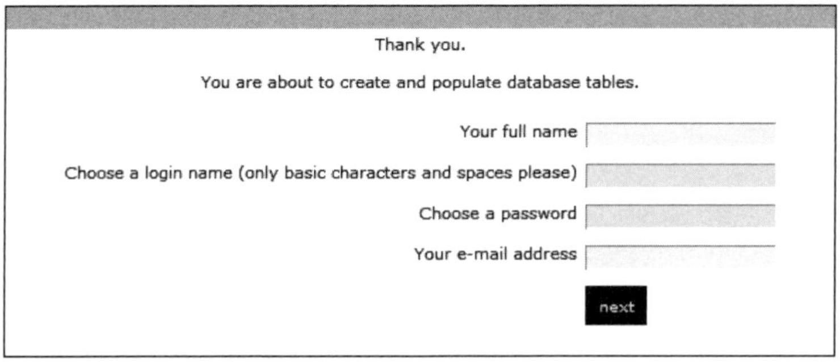

Figure 2-38. Setting up your first Textpattern user

6. At this point, Textpattern creates the necessary database tables and populates them with your first Textpattern user and some minimal test data to verify that your installation is functioning properly. If all goes well, you receive a final confirmation message, as shown in Figure 2-39, and you're ready to log in to the Textpattern admin interface for the first time. Just click the link labeled main interface to continue.

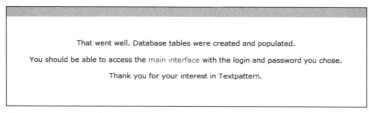

Figure 2-39. Successful completion of the Textpattern installation process

7. You're now ready to log in to Textpattern using the login prompt shown in Figure 2-40. By default, Remain logged in with this browser is checked. When this box is checked, a browser cookie is created so that you're not required to enter your login credentials each time you try to access the Textpattern admin interface. If you're working on a shared computer, it's best to leave this option unchecked.

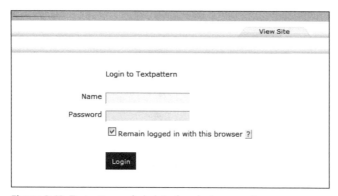

Figure 2-40. Textpattern admin interface login prompt

Checking site preferences

1. After logging in for the first time, you are taken directly to the Admin ➤ Preferences ➤ Language tab to confirm your language preferences (see Figure 2-41).

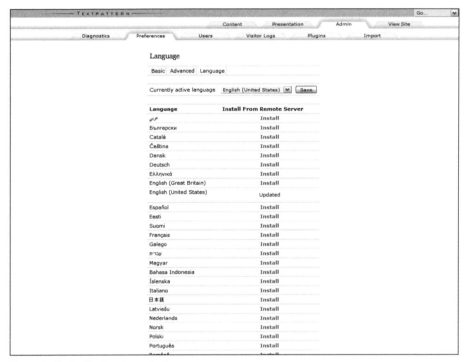

Figure 2-41. Confirming the active language

2. Once you confirm the Currently active language, you can always return to this tab to update your installed language or install new languages. The Admin ➤ Preferences ➤ Language tab always shows the most recent updates available for all languages supported by Textpattern, as shown in Figure 2-42.

3. After confirming your language preferences, click Basic at the top of the page to verify preferences for article publishing and commenting on your site. The default preferences are shown in Figure 2-43.

4. Start customizing your install by setting your site name, URL, and slogan; and confirming the time and date settings. You should also set your desired permanent link mode based on your ability to support clean URLs. Finally, if your site accepts comments, you can customize the rules for posting and presenting them on your articles. (The use of site preferences is covered in more detail later in Chapter 5.)

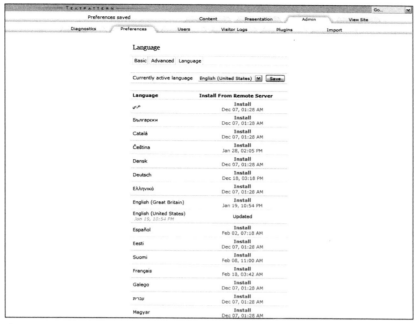

Figure 2-42. The Language tab shows the most recent update time for all language files.

Figure 2-43. The Basic tab shows preferences for article publishing and commenting on your site.

Checking site diagnostics

After you do an initial check of your site preferences, it's time to do a quick diagnostic check of your Textpattern install. The details of the Admin ➤ Diagnostics tab is covered in full in Chapter 5, but before you proceed any further, make sure that there aren't any problems with the install.

The only problem noted with the install as shown in Figure 2-44 is that you haven't removed the /textpattern/setup directory, which contains the scripts used to run Textpattern's install. While this doesn't prevent Textpattern from running, it's always recommended that this directory be removed after the installation process is completed (for security reasons). The scripts in this directory could be used by unauthorized users to connect to your database, so it's best to delete the setup directory as soon as the install process is complete.

Figure 2-44. The Diagnostics tab with preflight check warnings

Once you delete this directory and refresh the Diagnostics tab, your install should pass all diagnostic tests (see Figure 2-45).

Figure 2-45. The Diagnostics tab with all checks passed

Preflight checks

Aside from the setup directory warning shown in Figure 2-44, there are several other pre-flight warnings you might see after installing Textpattern. The following list contains other preflight warnings that you might see on the Diagnostics tab:

- PHP version 4.3 is required. You are running a version of PHP that is lower than 4.3.0.
- The $path_to_site variable is not set. Try updating index.php.
- The directory set in the $path_to_site variable cannot be reached. Try updating index.php.
- A DNS lookup on your web domain failed.
- Your site URL has a trailing slash. Remove the trailing slash.
- The index.php file cannot be found.
- Textpattern cannot write to the images directory. Make the directory writeable.
- Textpattern cannot write to the files directory. Make the directory writeable.
- Textpattern cannot write to the temp directory. Make the directory writeable.
- Clean URLs are only supported on the Apache HTTP server. Use at your own risk.

- The .htaccess file cannot be found.

- The mod_rewrite module cannot be found. Change your permanent link mode to ?=messy.

- File uploads are disabled.

- The /textpattern/setup directory still exists. Remove the directory.

- Your PHP installation is missing the mail() function which means that Textpattern will not be able to send out emails, limiting some functionality.

- Your version of PHP has security related risks. Turn register_globals off or update to a newer version of PHP.

- Old placeholder files exist from earlier versions of Textpattern. Remove the files.

- Certain Textpattern files are missing. Add the missing files.

- Certain Textpattern files are old. Replace the old files with the most recent version.

- Certain Textpattern files have been modified.

- You are running a development version of Textpattern under the Live production status.

- Certain PHP functions are disabled which might limit some functionality.

- Your Site URL preference doesn't match your actual site URL.

- The clean URL test failed. Change your permanent link mode to ?=messy.

- You have MySQL table errors. Try repairing your MySQL database.

Keep in mind that not all preflight warnings prevent your site from functioning properly; they are meant to notify you of potential problems and configuration issues. It's always best to resolve as many warnings as possible, but you might not have total control over them in a hosted environment. For any persistent problems, take the following steps to troubleshoot:

1. Check the Textpattern FAQ.[9] More often than not, you'll find the solution to your problem there.

2. Search the Textpattern Forum[10] to talk to others having the same problems.

3. Post a new topic in the Troubleshooting forum.[11]

Messy URLs for testing

Now that the install process is complete and you verified your site preferences and diagnostics, its time to delve into the process of developing your site. While you already know the benefits of using a clean URL scheme for your live site, clean URLs also add an additional level of complexity to the debugging process as you build your site.

---

9. http://textpattern.com/faq
10. http://forum.textpattern.com
11. http://forum.textpattern.com/viewforum.php?id=3

To simplify the process of building your first Textpattern sites and avoid potential problems that might be brought about by the use of clean URLs, you might find it helpful to use the ?=messy permanent link mode to start out. Waiting until you're nearing completion of your site development helps to isolate potential problems and might save you hours of frustration. If you do choose to use clean URLs from the start, remember to switch to messy URLs when problems crop up to verify that the problems you see aren't related to your permanent link mode.

Advanced topics

Now that the initial setup process is done, you can turn your attention to some of the peripheral accompaniments of Textpattern. One of the important aspects to keep official development on track is Trac (no pun intended). Without further ado, here is what it's all about.

Textpattern development site

The Textpattern development site, shown in Figure 2-46, provides a web-based interface into the Subversion repository that contains the Textpattern source code. The site, powered by Trac,[12] offers a way for you to browse the Textpattern source code without having to download a Subversion client.

Figure 2-46. Textpattern development site

12. http://trac.edgewall.org/

The timeline feature of the development site, shown in Figure 2-47, enables you to search for source code changes based on the date they were checked in to the Subversion repository.

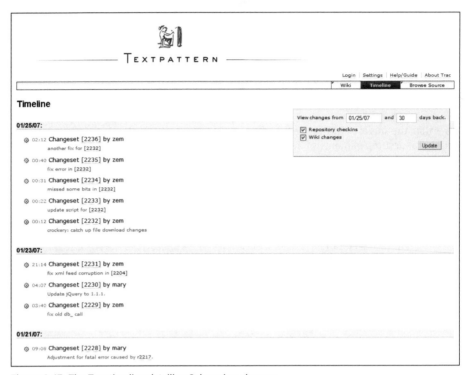

Figure 2-47. The Trac timeline detailing Subversion changes

Clicking a specific revision number displays a color-coded view of the changes introduced by that revision, as shown in Figure 2-48.

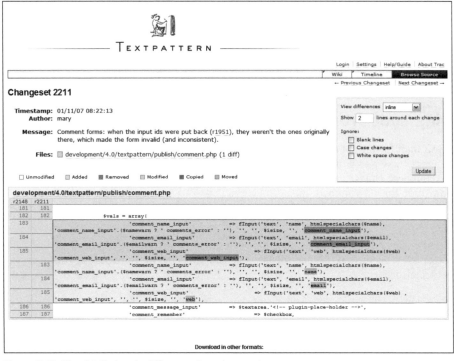

Figure 2-48. The detailed code differences in a changeset

The source browser on the site enables you to view the full source code of all Textpattern files. You start out at the top level of the Subversion repository, shown in Figure 2-49, and then have the ability to drill down through the various releases and development branches used by the Textpattern development team.

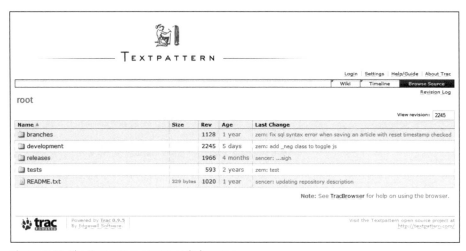

Figure 2-49. The Textpattern source code browser

Finally, if you want to keep up to date with changes to the Textpattern source code without having to constantly check back for changes, you can subscribe to the Textpattern Timeline Rich Site Summary (RSS) feed located at http://dev.textpattern.com/timeline. Each time a code change is checked into the Subversion repository, you're notified in your feed reader. This feed is a great way for plugin developers to stay on top of the latest bug fixes and features that are added to the Textpattern core.

Pulling code from Subversion

If you want to stay in the loop with all the latest changes made to Textpattern, you should definitely take a look at Subversion, which enables you to sync up with the cutting-edge development changes as they are submitted by the core developers. First take a look at how to do this on Windows; then on the Mac.

On a PC

If you're a Windows user, the easiest way to grab code from Subversion is by using the TortoiseSVN client. You can find the latest version available for download at tortoisesvn.net/downloads.

Once you install the TortoiseSVN client, you can easily check out all Textpattern source code—including the 4.0 development branch, crockery branch, and all releases. The following steps guide you through the process of checking out all Textpattern source code:

1. Create a new directory on your local drive. For this example, I created a directory called c:\textpattern.

2. Right-click the directory name in Windows Explorer and select the SVN Checkout option from the menu, as shown in Figure 2-50.

Figure 2-50. Windows context menu with Subversion options

3. When presented with the Checkout dialog box, enter the URL of the Textpattern Subversion repository, http://svn.textpattern.com, and click OK (see Figure 2-51).

Figure 2-51. TortoiseSVN Checkout dialog box

4. Once all the files are downloaded, you're left with a directory structure as shown in Figure 2-52.

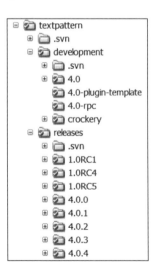

Figure 2-52. Textpattern source code checked out from the Subversion repository

You can now use the SVN export command to copy the files for the version you want to use into a new directory. Check the TortoiseSVN instructions for more detailed instructions on using the client.

Subversion on OS X

If you are the pioneering type or if you just want to know what is coming around the bend, you can grab the latest nightly builds of Textpattern to keep abreast of any changes being made to the system. While official releases might not be done every week, the core development team is always hard at work making incremental improvements to Textpattern. Conveniently, they store all their collective updates to Textpattern in one central location (http://svn.textpattern.com/) and use a system called Subversion (SVN) to sort out all the changes. This allows the developers to check in code, without fear of overwriting each other's work.

To keep tabs on Textpattern development code as it evolves, you'll use a localized Mac installation of Subversion. While in-depth explanation of SVN is beyond the scope of this book, more information can be found at its official site (http://subversion.tigris. org/). Additionally, there is a book dedicated entirely to SVN: *Version Control with Subversion* (O'Reilly, 2004), which can be read in its entirety in online or PDF form (http://svnbook.red-bean.com/). For the purposes of this chapter, I paraphrase Wikipedia:[13]

The Subversion file system is described as "three dimensional." Most representations of a directory tree are two dimensional, but SVN adds a third dimension: revisions. Each revision in Subversion has its own root, which is used to access contents at that revision. Files are stored as links to the most recent change, thus a Subversion repository is quite compact. The storage space used is equivalent to the changes made, not the number of revisions.

Installing Subversion

The first thing you need to do is install Subversion. At the time of this writing, the current version is 1.4.3, and the best place to get a streamlined installer is from Martin Ott's website, in which he graciously provides binary OS X builds free to the community. Go to www.codingmonkeys.de/mbo/ and look for the link to download the Zip file named Subversion-1.4.3.pkg.zip or the latest stable version if a newer one is available. Once it is downloaded, double-click the *.dmg file and it extracts the *.pkg file. Double-click that file and it begins the installation process. Follow the instructions and allow it to install SVN in the default location: /usr/bin/local/. That does it—now Subversion is installed on your computer.

Installing svnX

Now that Subversion is installed, you need to install a graphical user interface (GUI) to help you accomplish your tasks. While some geeks swear by the command line, which is all well and good, you can save some time and effort by using the open-source program called svnX, which is provided free by the French web agency La Chose Interactive. Type this address in your browser: www.lachoseinteractive.net/en/community/subversion/ svnx/download/. Click the blue icon, and the svnX_0.9.9.dmg file (or newer version) begins downloading. Once it finishes, double-click the file on your desktop to initiate the installation process.

---

13. http://en.wikipedia.org/wiki/Subversion_(software)

Now, run svnX by going to /Applications/ and double-clicking the blue svnX icon, which opens two windows: Repositories and Working Copies. For the purposes of retrieving the latest Textpattern builds, you use only the Repositories window; feel free to close the other window. In the Repositories window, click the plus icon (+) and enter this in the text field for Path: http://svn.textpattern.com/. Type something like TXP DEV—Remote for Name. It really doesn't matter. Leave the User and Pass blank. You should now see the newly created repository listed under Name/URL. Double-click the entry and you see a screen that looks like Figure 2-53.

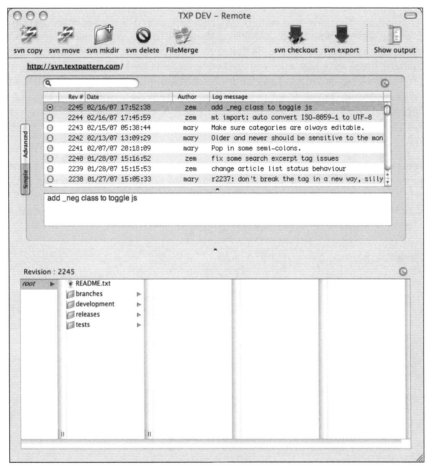

Figure 2-53. Subversion GUI on OS X

Several blue folders display on the bottom half of this screen. Click the development folder and you see the current versions that are undergoing changes. You can poke around here and find the latest builds. Once you find something that interests you, click the green arrow at the top of the screen labeled svn export. It prompts you to choose a location to which you want to download the files. I recommend creating a separate folder in the /User/username/Sites/ directory to house the latest TXP builds, which keeps you from overwriting any local files. Additionally, I highly recommend backing up your localized installation of Textpattern before overwriting it with any of the SVN builds. Further instruction will be added on SVN in later chapters of this book as you dive into creating your own TXP plugins. For now, move on to becoming familiar with the intricacies of the Textpattern admin interface.

Summary

Congratulations! You have successfully installed Textpattern. As a Windows user, in this chapter you learned how to use XAMPP on Windows to set up a localhost environment and you also learned how to use TortoiseSVN to get the latest development builds of Textpattern. If you are a Mac user, you learned how to use MAMP for local hosting and are now familiar with using svnX to retrieve the latest builds of Textpattern via the SVN server. The experience you gained using phpMyAdmin has translated directly into creating and managing databases on a live site because this tool is widely installed on many hosting platforms. Using that knowledge, you successfully created and configured your remote site as well.

The next chapter takes a closer look at using the Admin section of Textpattern, and you'll begin to customize the system to meet your needs. Now that the grunt work of installing everything is complete, you can begin to go deeper into actually using Textpattern. If you need to, take a little break and then come back quickly for Chapter 3. Don't touch that dial, folks, because you're just getting started!

PART TWO THE TEXTPATTERN INTERFACE

3 SITE ADMINISTRATION

ain Time (US & Canada)	
ust clock for daylight saving changes	

Use plugins?	○ No ◉ Yes
ttach titles to permalinks?	◉ No ○ Yes
Allow form override?	◉ No ○ Yes
Articles use excerpts?	◉ No ○ Yes
ire after how many days?	0
r display e-mail address?	○ No ◉ Yes
nent means site updated?	◉ No ○ Yes
ıde e-mail in Atom feeds?	◉ No ○ Yes
t (default is article body)?	◉ No ○ Yes
ved words in article titles?	◉ No ○ Yes

Import from ?	WordPress
Section to import into ?	article ▾
Default article status ?	Draft ▾
efault comments invite ?	Comments

Database Data

Database name ?	wordpress
Mysql user ?	nathansmith
Mysql password ?	password4wordpress
Mysql host ?	localhost

Now that you have completed Chapter 2, you should have a working installation of Textpattern set up on either your local computer or a live server. This chapter looks at all aspects of the Administration area of Textpattern, briefly covering what each part does so that you will have a reference point for later chapters that will go into further detail. In particular, you will find that enhancing functionality with plugins will become an essential part of building out any Textpattern site.

Logging in

Notice that when you are not logged in, there really is not much to the Textpattern interface—not even the version number. There is only one tab, labeled View Site, with a Login to Textpattern area below, as shown in Figure 3-1. This is for good reason because you certainly would not want nonapproved users to see more of the content management capabilities than they are entitled to. Go ahead and enter the username and password that you specified during the setup process. If you are using your own private computer, you might want to click the checkbox labeled Remain logged in with this browser, which will save you from having to retype your details every time you want to use Textpattern. If you are logging in from a public setting such as an Internet cafe, it is wise to leave the checkbox empty so that those using the computer after you do not have full administrative access to your website.

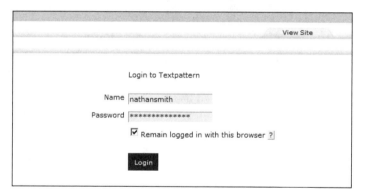

Figure 3-1. Textpattern login screen

Pre-flight check

After logging in, the first thing you should do is check the Diagnostics tab in the Admin area to make sure that there were not any hiccups in the installation process. When all is as it should be, there will be a message displayed in green text that reads All checks passed!

Assuming that everything went according to plan, you should see a screen that looks like Figure 3-2. This Diagnostics section lists all the information about your hosting configuration. You can choose the level of detail that is reported—either High or Low—by using the drop-down menu below the text area. If you are having difficulties or making errors aside from those covered here, please post a detailed description of the problem on the Textpattern forum.

Figure 3-2. Pre-flight check passed

If you see the message as depicted in Figure 3-3 (. . . \textpattern\setup\ still exists), you need to make sure that you delete this directory. If someone knew that you were running Textpattern, they could type in the address www.example.com/textpattern/setup/. While this is not necessarily a huge security hole, it is something that can be easily avoided, so you should make sure to take the necessary precautions and delete this directory after your setup is complete.

Two other errors you might see are Apache module mod_rewrite is not installed and Clean URL test failed. The combination of these two errors probably means that your host does not have mod_rewrite enabled on the Apache servers. If you are running Textpattern in a local testing environment, refer to Chapter 2 for instructions on how to enable this setting. If you are seeing this warning on a live host, you might want to check with your server's administrator to see whether this is something that they can accommodate. Don't worry if this is not available with your hosting package because you can still run Textpattern; you just have to use "messy" URLs instead (this is covered a bit later in this chapter).

Figure 3-3. Pre-flight check warnings

Preferences

What would life be without options? You can have regular or decaf coffee, with or without cream and sugar, or with or without artificial creamer and sweetener. There are full-service or self-service gas stations, each offering different types of gasoline in a variety of octane ratings. Shopping for toothpaste can be a chore because after you pick your brand, you have to narrow down the field of options: original flavor, cool mint, cinnamon, tartar control, or extra whitening? Even orange juice comes with pulp or no pulp, hand-squeezed or processed, and with or without added calcium! You get the picture. I could go on and on, but the point is that people like to have choices, and everyone has preferences. So it is only logical that the next thing you need to do is specify your preferences. Use the Preferences tab, which is located right next to the Diagnostics tab. Basic preferences, shown in Figure 3-4, enable you to control a number of aspects that relate to your site.

Figure 3-4. Basic preferences

When you click the Preferences tab, you should see three buttons labeled Basic, Advanced, and Language with the Basic button selected, indicating that you are in that part of the Preferences area. Resist the urge to click either of the other two buttons (you will visit them in a few minutes). For now, focus your attention on the list of choices underneath the heading labeled Publish.

Publish

Following is a listing of each choice in the Publish section and what exactly each one does:

- **Site name:** This setting is just what it says—the name of your site. By default, it appears in the title area of your browser. It also goes out via Atom and Rich Site Summary (RSS) feeds and is visible to your subscribers, so it should be set accurately. Within your pages, the site name can be displayed in one of two ways. By using the TXP tag `<txp:sitename />`, only the site name will be displayed. By using `<txp:page_title />`, though, you can output the name of your site, along with the current article title. Further use of these tags will be covered in later chapters, as well as in the tag manual.

- **Site URL:** This setting is also pretty straightforward; it needs to be set to the area from which you want to run Textpattern. The fact that you are using Textpattern means that it is set up correctly. Just make sure that you leave it as is, so that the links within your site all work well together. If you are developing your site on a localhost with the intent of porting it over to a live server, you will need to change this setting when you make the switch.

- **Site slogan:** For whatever reason, this setting is something that people often forget to change (perhaps because they do not want to have a witty one-liner describing their site). Like Site name, Site slogan is also broadcast via the Atom and RSS feeds, and it doubles as a description of your site for feed aggregator services. I cannot help but chuckle when I subscribe to the Atom or RSS feed of a respected site that uses Textpattern, only to see it labeled My pithy slogan in my feed reader. Be sure not to make that mistake. Also, note that it can be quite a bit longer than the actual text field might indicate. Personally, I use it solely as a description for syndicated content and do not actually make use of it anywhere on my site. By default, it is displayed using the TXP tag <txp:site_slogan />.

- **Time Zone:** Set the time zone according to the region of the world in which you live. GMT refers to Greenwich Mean Time, which is the time zone for Greenwich, England, and is the location from which all other time zones are measured. If you are unsure how far an offset your time zone is from GMT, you can just check it on your local computer. If you are using Windows, double-click the time in the lower-right corner of your screen, which displays the Date and Time Properties window (Time Zone is the second tab). You should see something that looks like Figure 3-5. If you are on a Mac, click the time in the upper-right corner of your screen and choose Open Date & Time from the drop-down menu. Click the Time Zone button, and you should see a window like Figure 3-6.

- **DST enabled:** This setting enables you to specify whether or not daylight savings is in effect for your area. Not all time zones observe daylight savings time, so it might not be relevant for your particular location.

- **Date format:** This setting is the date format used when you are not on an individual article's page. As a general rule of thumb, it can be thought of as being used when there is more than one article displayed. I tend to keep this option the same as Archive date format for consistency, but that is just a matter of personal preference.

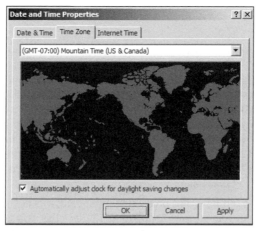

Figure 3-5. Time Zone on Windows

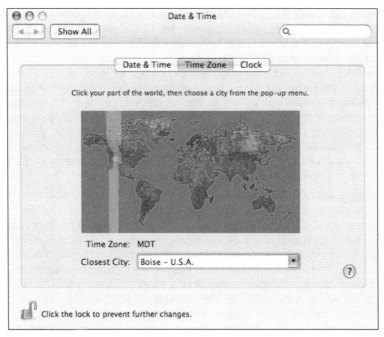

Figure 3-6. Time Zone on Mac OS X

- **Archive date format:** This setting enables you to choose how you want the date displayed on your individual articles. It defaults to the number of hours or days it has been since an article was posted. Personally, I do not care for this format because it is not very informative. The person reading the date cannot easily ascertain at a glance when the article was published. Not only that, but the more time that goes by, the longer the string of digits grows. If your layout is designed to support a certain amount of numbers in a pseudo-calendar of sorts, this can be problematic. It is really just a matter of personal preference, though—you can pick whichever format you like.

- **Permanent link mode:** By default, this setting is set to ?=messy since that is the universally compatible mode. In this mode, your articles will look like this: www.example.com/index.php?id=101, and your sections will look like this: www.example.com/index.php?s=article. As you can see, it is not the prettiest solution—hence the name *messy*. However, the URL is still quite manageable and is still fairly short, even in this mode.

  Settings other than messy require Apache's mod_rewrite module to be enabled. If you see a green All checks passed message on the Diagnostics tab, you can choose any of the other methods available. I tend to use the /section/title format because it most closely resembles a real directory structure (meaning that if someone were to cut off /title in the URL, there would still be a /section available because of the way Textpattern handles sections and articles). The other URL schemes are simply for readability and to keep people from writing similarly titled articles that conflict with each other.

For instance, with the /id/title structure someone could write an article entitled "My Summer Vacation" and then a year later write another article with the same title. The ID of the article would keep each entry unique, like so: www.example.com/101/my-summer-vacation and www.example.com/201/my-summer-vacation. If this were done with /section/title, both URLs would be identical: www.example.com/article/my-summer-vacation. The /year/month/day/title format is helpful for showing the user exactly when the article was written (for example, www.example.com/2006/12/25/merry-christmas). The drawback of using this type of format is that it does not resemble a true directory structure. So if users were to navigate to www.example.com/2006/, they would not find all the articles for 2006; they would be redirected to a 404 page. If this is something your site requires, plugins are available that can emulate this structure.

- **Logging**: No, this setting does not have to do with deforestation. By default, it is set to All hits, but this can have a detrimental effect on your site's performance because it will write visitor info to the MySQL database for each person who comes to your site. While it might be interesting to see what ISP people are using, such data is not entirely relevant or applicable and quickly gets boring. The most logical choice is Referrers only because it lets you know which sites are linking to you and which of those links people are clicking to get to your site. This still involves actively writing information to the database, though, and the referrer logs are somewhat limiting in the amount of data they present. One popular alternative is to set logging to None and instead use something like Google Analytics, which is not only far more robust but also free. This is a more feasible solution because Google deals with tracking the hits instead of your database. For high-traffic sites, overhead can be reduced significantly by just leaving logging off altogether.

- **Use Textile**: Textile (text-style, get it?) is part of what makes Textpattern so great. It is the text formatting minilanguage/syntax that converts pseudocode into usable XHTML. For instance, if you want to make something bold, all you need to type is *this text is bold*; likewise, to make something italicized, you can type _this text is italicized_ (which generates the XHTML output this text is bold and this text is italicized, respectively). Note that even when using Textile, real XHTML can still be intermixed. Any single line breaks add <br /> to break the line, and double line breaks create paragraphs using the <p>...</p> code structure. This line break handling is included in the Use Textile and Convert linebreaks modes. If you choose Convert linebreaks, it will do just that, while not responding to other text formatting syntax; whereas if you choose Leave text untouched, no autoformatting is applied. This can be helpful for articles in which you want to feature snippets of code and you need the code to remain unaltered. This can be handled on a per-article basis, though, so it is best to just leave Use Textile enabled by default. A more in-depth look at full Textile formatting will come later in Chapter 4.

- **Accept Comments?** This setting is pretty self-explanatory. It simply enables you to choose whether or not you want to accept feedback from users in the form of comments on your articles. If your Textpattern-driven site will not have any blogging element to it, feel free to pick No for this option. This choice will cause the bottom portion of the preferences page under Comments to be hidden, as those options are not relevant without comments enabled.

- **Production Status**: This setting has three modes: Debugging, Testing, and Live. By default, the production status is set to Testing, but you will want to change it to Live before making your site public. Debugging is a great way to help you as a developer to identify problems in templates, plugins, and raw PHP code. Testing is used primarily for setting up a site in preparation for making it live. In both modes, the **runtime** is displayed in the code, which is the amount of time taken to build the page. They also show the number of MySQL queries executed and the estimated memory usage. In Debugging mode, all TXP tags encountered while building the page are also visible in the XHTML source code. While this is all very fascinating, it is not at all relevant to your site's users, so be sure to flip the switch to Live before showing it off to the world.

## 3

Comments

Assuming that you left the Accept comments? option set to Yes, you can now move on to the next set of criteria. Most of these settings are pretty easy to figure out, but some are a little more cryptic. Here is the list of the options that are available:

- **Moderate comments?** This option changes whether or not comments appear on your site immediately after they are submitted, or if they will be held in a queue for you to approve (or disapprove) of manually. By default, it is set to Yes, although most users will expect instant feedback when entering a comment, so you might consider setting it to No. You do not forfeit your right to moderate comments by doing so. As the site owner, you have veto power and can always go back through and prune comments you do not want.

- **On by default?** You might have this question: "Wait, this is just the same option as Accept Comments, is it not?" If so, you are right to wonder. The settings are very similar, but here is the difference: with Accept Comments set to No there are no comments, ever; with Accept Comments set to Yes, but On by default? set to No, you still have the option of enabling comments on a per-article basis (which can be helpful in some situations). For instance, if you are writing an editorial column for a newspaper site, you are usually simply expressing your opinion and are not solic- iting feedback. However, from time to time you might want to request write-in responses from your readers, in which case you could enable comments for that one article.

- **Present comments as a numbered list?** By default, all your comments will be contained within an ordered list. Semantically speaking, this is probably the most accurate way to display comments because the list items are enumerated sequentially. If this option is set to No, each comment will be wrapped in a `<div>...</div>` instead of a list item. While this is not quite as semantically rich, it can make for easier styling if for some reason you do not want to style `<ol class="comments">...</ol>`. By using the wraptag and breaktag attributes, you can, of course, present your comments with any tags you want. These types of attributes will be covered later in Chapter 5.

- **Mail comments to author?** With this option enabled, the author of the article receives an email every time someone makes a new comment on your site. This process can be a great way to keep on top of things, but can be quite tedious to keep up with. Another way to handle new comments is to simply set one of your browser's home page tabs to your Comments area in Textpattern. This still lets you see the most recent comments and keeps your inbox comparatively less crowded: www.example.com/textpattern/index.php?event=discuss.

- **Disallow user images?** By default, this option enables user images because the answer to the question Disallow user images? is No. Once you get past the fact that it is a double negative, it actually is quite a handy feature. If it is set to Yes, all user images will be stripped out, and those leaving comments can only add text, not graphics.

- **Default invite**: This is the default phrasing used on your site, which lets people know that commenting is enabled. You can specify this invitational wording globally here and can override it later on a per-article basis.

- **Comments date format**: This option is just like the aforementioned Date format and Archive date format options, except that it applies to the date on which people leave comments. This information can be output along with names and feedback, letting others know how current the discussion is.

- **Comments mode**: This setting has only two choices: popup or nopopup. By default, it is set to nopopup, which is probably for the best. The other option is dependent on JavaScript to create a new miniwindow. Some users have popup blocking enabled in their browsers, whereas others might be viewing your site on a mobile device or using some other technology that does not support JavaScript. It is recommended that you leave this option set at nopopup.

- **Disabled after**: This option enables you to specify a preset amount of time for which comments will be accepted after you post your article. If set to never, people can comment indefinitely. Alternatively, you can have the commenting period autoexpire in increments of one week up until six weeks after the article was first posted. This setting can be overridden on a per-article basis if you need to disable comments sooner. You might override a particular article in which commenting gets out of hand or if you are simply making a short announcement that does not require any user feedback.

- **Automatically append comments to articles?** The default is Yes, which causes the comment form and any comments to appear after the body of your article. If it is set to No, you can still make use of comments, but will have to hard-code the comment form to appear in your template using the `<txp:comments />` tag. This can be useful for instances in which you want the comment form somewhere other than immediately following your article in the source code (it could be used to make the form appear on the other side of the page, for instance). This topic will be covered later when we look at templating.

Advanced Preferences

Now you will visit the buttons that we skipped over before. When you click the first button, Advanced, you are taken to the Advanced Preferences page. That button is replaced by a link labeled Basic, which leads back to the screen you were just looking at. What you should now see resembles Figure 3-7. When I think of preferences, I tend to visualize simple choices such as regular or decaf. When I hear "advanced" preferences, I think of more miniscule nuances such as espresso or French roast. However, the Advanced Preferences in Textpattern are quite essential for the functioning of your site and should not be overlooked or considered to be something that only connoisseurs care about. So, let's run down the list and see what these Advanced Preferences are all about.

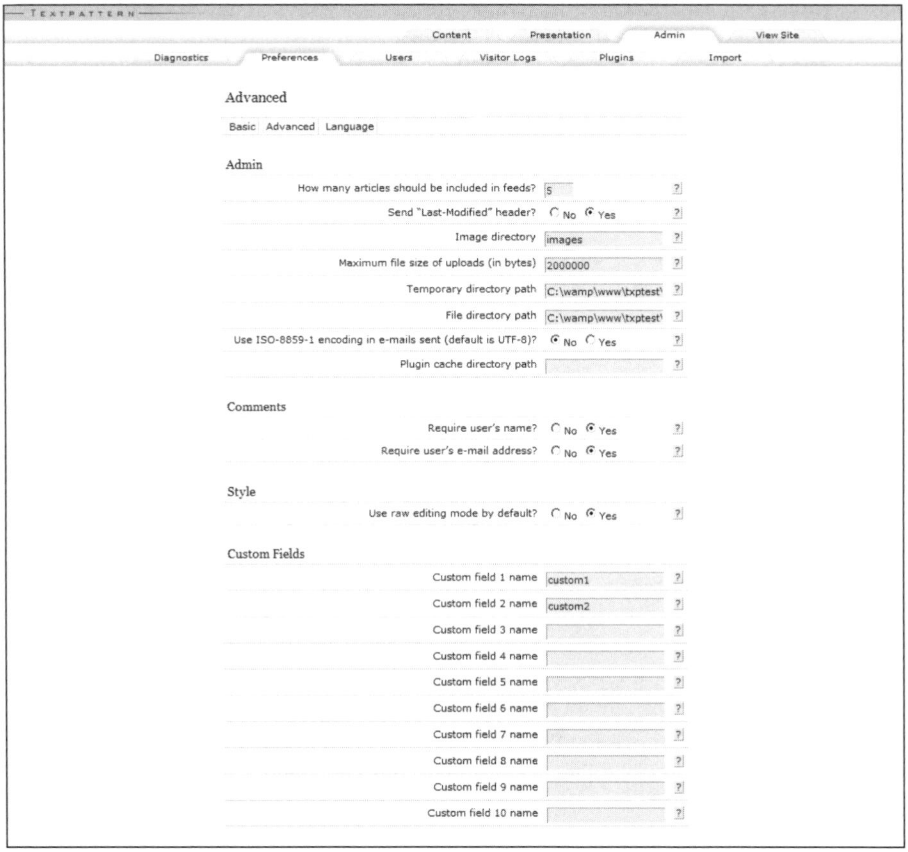

Figure 3-7. Advanced Preferences

Admin

In this portion of Advanced Preferences, you can change the details of your site to match your server configuration. For the most part, you need to change these settings only if you are switching between hosting providers, and the absolute path to your site is different on the server. Even so, have a look at what each of the criteria does.

- **How many articles should be included in feeds?** This option controls how many recent articles go out as XML to your Atom and RSS subscribers. The default is five, but you can set it to whatever you like—it really depends on the frequency with which you post.

- **Send "Last-Modified" header?** If this setting is set to Yes, when someone visits your site, Textpattern asks the visitor's browser if your site has already been visited by reading its HTTP If-Modified-Since header. It then compares this with the date when your site was last modified. If the visitor has been to your site fairly recently, and nothing has changed since then, Textpattern tells the browser to use the version of the site that is in its cache by sending the Last-Modified header response. This saves having to load your site from the database every time and cuts down on bandwidth and server overhead.

- **Image directory**: This is the directory to which images will be uploaded from the Images area (under the Content tab) of Textpattern. The default is images, which refers to www.example.com/images/, but you can change it to whatever you like. Unless you have a specific reason for the change, it can be left as the default. Be sure to have full read and write permissions set by browsing your site structure via FTP, right-clicking the directory, and typing in the number 777 in the text field. It should be labeled something like Numerical value or Octal, depending on your FTP program.

- **Maximum file size of uploads (in bytes)**: This option enables you to set a limit on the file size that authors are allowed to upload. The default is 2000000 bytes, which is approximately 2 megabytes. If that size is too small for the type of files you anticipate uploading, feel free to change it to whatever suits your needs. Be aware that the server's PHP configuration setting has the final authority for maximum file size on uploads. If you need capacity greater than what your server allows, you might need to contact your hosting company. Alternatively, you can simply FTP the file to the server, and "claim" it via Textpattern in the Files area by choosing an Existing file from the drop-down menu and then clicking Create.

- **Temporary directory path**: The Temporary directory is where files, images, and plug-ins are written to while they are waiting to be sorted into the correct place. If you view this directory via FTP at www.example.com/textpattern/tmp/, it is empty because nothing is stored there permanently. Still, it is an important part of how TXP functions, so be sure to have full read and write permissions set to 777, just as with the images directory.

- **File directory path**: As with the images directory, the file directory exists as a place to store files uploaded via the Textpattern interface. It should also be set to full read and write permissions 777, just like the tmp directory and images directory.

- **Use ISO-8859-1 encoding in e-mails sent (default is UTF-8)?** This option has to do with the type of character encoding with which emails are sent. The Latin-1 (ISO-8859-1) encoding used to be the standard, but has since been retired because it pertained mainly to a Western context. Unicode Transformation Format (UTF-8), on the other hand, has encoding for many more characters and thus can handle more languages. It has all the capabilities of ISO-8859-1 and then some. So unless you have a specific need to use ISO-8859-1, leave this option set to No so that you are using the newer UTF-8 standard.

- **Plugin cache directory path**: This directory is used for holding plugins while they are still in development. Unless you are writing a plugin that specifically requires a plugin cache directory to be created, you can just leave this field blank. If you do need to create a directory, log in via FTP, make a directory, and then point to it here in the Admin area.

Comments

Following is a listing of each choice in the Comments section and what exactly each one does:

- **Require user's name?** This option enables you to control whether or not the Name field is required when leaving a comment. For the most part, you should always have at least a name and a message so that there is someone to attribute the comment to. Unless you are building a site with some sort of anonymous commenting system, it is best to leave this set as a requirement for posting.

- **Require user's e-mail address?** There seems to be some debate among bloggers whether a user's email address should be required to post comments. Some feel that it helps lend more accountability because people have to give you their address before they can post anything. However, it has been my experience that if they do not want to divulge their email addresses, users will just use a fake one. For my own site, I have it available as an optional field because people will often post web-related questions and might want an email response from me. For those who do not wish to divulge their personal information, it affords them the luxury of a little more anonymity.

Style

Unless you are one of the few people on the planet who is a fan of black, size 16, Times New Roman font, you will probably be interested in adding a little style to your website. Depending on your preference of how you like to edit Cascading Style Sheets (CSS), this is where you make that choice.

- **Use raw editing mode by default?** When this option is set to Yes, you simply see a full view of your CSS files by default, enabling you to scroll through and edit them as you would in any HTML textarea. If it is set to No, you see your CSS in Textpattern's unique editor, which provides a tabular layout view of your style selectors and values. It is quite an interesting approach to managing CSS, one that is not seen in very many coding programs. As such, feelings tend to be polarized. Some people love it, while others opt to use their trusty hand-coding program—cutting and pasting between there and the TXP interface. Alternatively, you can just upload your static CSS files via FTP and skip the style manager altogether.

Custom fields

Custom fields are a powerful and versatile part of Textpattern and are what make it so easy to repurpose for different uses or add additional functionality to what already exists. Custom fields will be covered at length in later chapters. For now, all you need to know is that they will open up many doors of opportunity as you learn to develop more robust and fully featured websites.

Figure 3-8 shows the Links and Publish options available.

Links

Textile link descriptions by default?	○ No ● Yes ?

Publish

Permalink title-like-this (default is TitleLikeThis)?	○ No ● Yes ?
Use DNS?	● No ○ Yes ?
Use admin-side plugins?	○ No ● Yes ?
Apply rel="nofollow" to commenters' website URL?	○ No ● Yes ?
Use e-mail address to construct feed ids (default is site URL)?	● No ○ Yes ?
Maximum URL length (in characters)	200 ?
Spam blacklists (comma-separated)	sbl.spamhaus.org ?
Allow PHP in articles?	● No ○ Yes ?
Allow PHP in pages?	○ No ● Yes ?
Allow raw php?	● No ○ Yes ?
Ping textpattern.com?	○ No ● Yes ?
Ping ping-o-matic.com?	○ No ● Yes ?
Show comment count in feeds?	● No ○ Yes ?
Use plugins?	○ No ● Yes ?
Attach titles to permalinks?	● No ○ Yes ?
Allow form override?	● No ○ Yes ?
Articles use excerpts?	● No ○ Yes ?
Logs expire after how many days?	0 ?
Never display e-mail address?	○ No ● Yes ?
New comment means site updated?	● No ○ Yes ?
Include e-mail in Atom feeds?	● No ○ Yes ?
Syndicate article excerpt (default is article body)?	● No ○ Yes ?
Prevent widowed words in article titles?	● No ○ Yes ?

Save

Go... ▼

Figure 3-8. Links and Publish settings

Links

- **Textile link descriptions by default?** If you want your Links section to be run through a lightweight version of Textile, choose Yes here. Straight quotation marks and apostrophes will be changed into their curly counterparts for better readability and typographical appeal. Also, freestanding single dashes (-) will be turned into the HTML encoded equivalent –, which is a slightly longer variant used in typesetting. It is up to you, but I recommend turning Textile on for as much as possible, as it really helps spruce up otherwise standard-looking text and properly encodes HTML character entities such as &.

Publish

- **Permalink title-like-this (default is TitleLikeThis)?** This setting applies only if clean URLs are enabled. Along the same lines as the previous setting, this option automatically grabs the text in your article title and converts it to a URL. By changing this setting, the aforementioned article would have this URL as its address: www.example.com/article/WhatIDidLastSummer. As you can see, it is not as easily readable.

- **Use DNS?** If you are making use of visitor logs and want Textpattern to make an attempt to convert IP addresses into human-readable addresses such as my-isp.example.com, switch this setting to Yes. Note that this option takes slightly more processing overhead, so if you notice that it starts to slow things down, you might want to switch it off. If that is a factor, though, you will probably save more system resources on your server if you just turn off logging altogether.

- **Use admin-side plugins?** Like the previous plugins option, this setting can just be left on unless you find that you are experiencing problems using the Textpattern admin interface, in which case it might help you troubleshoot. One excellent admin plugin is the database manager by Rob Sable, one of this book's authors. It enables you to make one-click backups of your entire site and also enables advanced users to run SQL queries against the database directly. For such plugins, this option must be enabled.

- **Apply rel="nofollow" to commentators' website URL?** A favorite method of spammers is to go on unsuspecting blogs and leave comments littered with links to other sites. They do this for two reasons. First, it is a desperate attempt to get people to click these links, find their products or services, and purchase them. Second, these links unfortunately serve as silent leeches on your site, using your site's search engine ranking to boost the relevancy ranking of their own sites. While search engines vary, one constant is that they all attribute more importance to sites with more incoming links. The rel="nofollow" attribute / value essentially tells search engines to ignore those links. Enabling this setting can help curb unwanted spam.

- **Use e-mail address to construct feed ids (default is site URL)?** Much like the Include e-mail in Atom feeds option, this setting gives people another way to gather information about you. Since your site is already publicly known, anyway, leave this option set to No. The Atom and RSS feeds will then use your domain name to uniquely identify your website.

- **Maximum URL length (in characters)**: This option is a security feature to help protect your site against buffer overflow attacks, by which someone can submit an exceedingly long URL to your site and cause a memory access exception. The object of such an attack is an attempt to crash your site. The default is set at 200 characters, after which Textpattern ignores the rest of the text in the URL.

- **Spam blacklists (comma-separated)**: To help prevent comment spam, there are sites devoted to compiling the Internet Protocol (IP) address of offenders. You can think of this option as a "neighborhood watch" of sorts, reporting the digital license plate numbers of known offenders. When your website receives a spam comment and you mark it as such, the IP address is sent to the blacklists you specify. When someone else receives a comment originating from this address, it is flagged as spam, saving the next person the hassle. This also works reflexively, so the diligent spam reporting of others can serve to benefit you. By default, the only address entered is sbl.spamhaus.org. You can find a longer list of maintained blacklists at DMOZ, which is short for DirectoryMOZilla, since the Mozilla Foundation originally maintained this list (www.directory.mozilla.org). This list now lives on at http://dmoz.org/Computers/Internet/Abuse/Spam/Blacklists/.

- **Allow PHP in articles?** If you want to use PHP from within your actual articles, this option enables you to do it. It is not recommended, however, because most of the programming logic should be kept at a higher level and probably should not make its way down into individual articles. That said, if you have a specific need for it, go right ahead, but it is usually safe to leave this setting off.

- **Allow PHP in pages?** If this option is enabled, you can make use of raw PHP in your page templates and forms by typing it within the <txp:php>...</txp:php> tags. By restricting the usage to the TXP tags, it helps keep things more secure. That being said, if you know PHP already, you can do just about anything you want. Simply use Textpattern's opening and closing PHP tags instead.

> As of Textpattern version 4.0.4, the <?php ... ?> tags should no longer be used because of security vulnerabilities in which lesser-privileged site contributors could potentially compromise the Textpattern installation.

- **Allow raw PHP?** This option is available only to enable older sites that still make use of raw <?php ... ?> tags to continue to function properly. As mentioned before, there is nothing to be gained by using these tags instead of the ones that TXP provides. So unless you are upgrading from an older version of Textpattern and have already made use of raw PHP, start by doing things the right way and leave this setting off.

- **Ping textpattern.com?** If you want to phone home to the mother ship and let Textpattern.com know that your site is up and running, you can set this option to send a ping every time your site is updated. This pinging helps to let the Textpattern development team know that you appreciate and are using their software. Additionally, it allows for updates to be displayed in real time à la Blogger.com if the TXP team decides to do so.

- **Ping ping-o-matic.com?** If you want to alert search engines and subscription services that your site has been updated, make sure to set this option to Yes. If you want your site to gather attention, go ahead and flip the switch to broadcast mode here. On the other hand, if you want to keep your site relatively private, simply choose the other option.

- **Show comment count in feeds?** If this setting is on, the number of comments will be displayed in your Atom and RSS feeds as part of the title: Article name here [17].

- **Use plugins?** For the most part, you can leave this setting on all the time. The only instance in which you might want to switch it off is if you are having unfamiliar errors or problems with your site. By setting this option to No you might be able to determine whether indeed it was a plugin causing the problem or whether there is something wrong with Textpattern itself.

- **Attach titles to permalinks?** This option is a handy way to let Textpattern create URLs for you based on your article title. It applies only if clean URLs are enabled, and you have chosen a Permanent link mode of /section/id/title, /id/title, or /year/month/day/title. If you choose /title or /section/title, titles are *always* attached to permalinks. For instance, an article entitled "What I did last summer" would have a URL that looks like this: www.example.com/article/what-i-did-last-summer.

- **Allow form override?** If this option is enabled, you can choose a custom format on a per-article basis. Say you have a hybrid photo blog along with a regular one and want to be able to switch things up without actually putting blog articles into a different site section. This option provides the perfect way to do that because you can have it default to one format, but then can use form override for days when you are feeling particularly contrary or just want to post some sort of unique content.

- **Articles use excerpts?** If this setting is used, there is a box for an excerpt below the main article field when writing articles from the Content area. This option is intended to be used for a summary paragraph about your article, but it can really be used for just about anything. I have seen sites use it for pull quotes or for different portions of a page, such as an image spread. If you are lazy like me, there are a few plugins out there that autogenerate pseudoexcerpts based on the first number of words you choose. In that case, you can turn excerpts off and that textarea will not take up space in your article writing area.

- **Logs expire after how many days?** This option sets the number of days that your referrer logs remain in the Textpattern database. Note that if you do not check your logs regularly, they will continue to back up and add to the database size, albeit at a very gradual pace. This setting pertains to how many days the logs remain saved before they are expunged. If you do not plan to check your logs very often, you should adjust this setting accordingly.

- **Never display e-mail address?** If you do make user email a required field to post or even if you simply provide it as an option, it is common courtesy to hide users' addresses from public view. Unless you are running a site called Spam "Я" Us, which enables poor schmucks to sign up in order to see who can get the most misspellings of Viagra emailed to them per day, be a gracious host and do not display user email addresses. Oddly enough, this setting is a double negative, so answering No actually means you *will* display them. So, make sure it is set to Yes, or else people might just stop commenting on your site altogether.

- **New comment means site updated?** If you have the Send "Last-Modified" header enabled, this option causes the cache to be rebuilt each time there is a comment added, ensuring that as users leave comments, they see them appear on the site (assuming that they are not moderated first). Also, this setting updates your recent comments if you are outputting a list somewhere on your site—in your sidebar for instance.

- **Include e-mail in Atom feeds?** This has always seemed like a pointless option because broadcasting your email address seems like a great way to get spammed. However, since Atom feeds are capable of including an author's email address, this setting lets you dig your own grave in that regard. I recommend that you leave your email out of the Atom feed and simply provide a contact page from your actual site. If you like getting messages about herbal remedies and bogus stock IPOs, be my guest and leave it set to Yes.

- **Syndicate article excerpt (default is article body)?** This option enables you to choose between sending out excerpts of your articles or sending the full text via Atom and RSS. It is up to you which one you want to use. There seems to be an ongoing debate about whether excerpts help to get people interested enough in an article to visit the actual site. Really, this is a factor only if you are displaying paying advertisements on your site and fear that providing full articles will somehow hinder your efforts to generate revenue. While I will not take sides on this issue, I will say that you should write about what interests you, not only to make money.

- **Prevent widowed words in article titles?** Basically, this option keeps article titles from line-breaking with only a single word occupying the second line. Textpattern checks for the last word in a title; if there is more than one word in the title, it adds a nonbreaking space between the last and second-to-last words. When a web browser sees the nonbreaking space character encoding , it treats the two adjacent words as a single chunk, thus causing the text to break to the next line with two words instead of one. A single lonely word is called a **widow** in typesetting for print (and is a faux pas when creating a page). Textpattern can prevent widows for sites that operate as web magazines, or the feature can just be left off.

Manage languages

The other subsection of the Preferences area is Language, as pictured in Figure 3-9, which closely resembles the language choices you were given when first installing Textpattern. If you need to add additional language support for a possibly multilingual site, this area is where you do that. The left column lists all your language choices, while the right column lists the installation links for the corresponding languages. Also of note is the date below each link, letting you know when each language file was last updated. You can compare this date with the date listed for the version of the language file you are currently using. If you so desire, you can then install the newer version to keep up to date. For the most part, though, if you are using English, these files do not change very often.

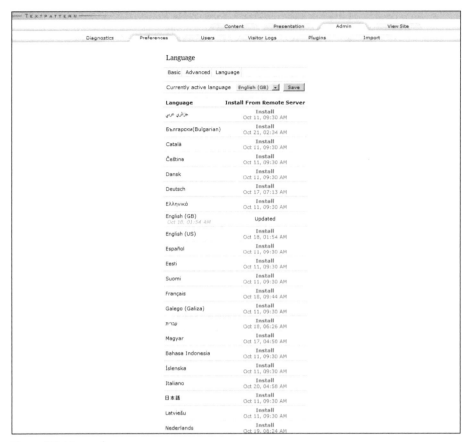

Figure 3-9. Manage languages

At the bottom of the page is a link that says Install From File (experts only), which enables you to upload your own language file via FTP and overwrite the existing settings in the database with your newly uploaded version. While this might seem a little intimidating, if you download one of the language files from rpc.textpattern.com/lang/ and open it in a text editor, you will see that it is pretty straightforward. I like to edit my language file to change the error messages for my comment form, as well as change the button phrasing from Submit to Publish. This is really just a matter of preference and pickiness, however. The standard language file should be just fine for most users.

Users

Now that we have covered the myriad of preferences that Textpattern caters to, let us move on to the Users tab, which is shown in Figure 3-10. This area is comparatively simple, offering a few basic choices. It enables you to change your password and email yourself a copy. Also, it enables you to create new users and assign them various privileges: Publisher, Managing Editor, Copy Editor, Staff Writer, Freelancer, Designer, and None. I am not sure in which instance you would want to actually create a new user and yet assign no privileges. None is available in case you need to revoke user privileges while not entirely disabling the account. Hopefully, this will not be necessary, but in the case of a news magazine site, if someone makes an off-the-cuff-remark in an editorial, it might need to be dealt with.

Figure 3-10. User administration

At any rate, here are the levels of privileges for each potential role:

- Publisher: A Publisher can create, edit, or remove articles, as well as manage links and user comments. A Publisher can take an article out of live circulation by changing its status, enabling it to be edited before being republished. A Publisher can edit site preferences and has access to the entirety of the site design, as well as all sections and categories. A Publisher can also create and delete users, as well as change any user's privileges, including those of other Publishers.

- Managing Editor: A Managing Editor can do everything a Publisher can do except create, delete, or edit privileges for other users.

- Copy Editor: A Copy Editor can make changes to any article, link, or user-submitted comment, and can also make changes to page templates and TXP forms.

- Staff Writer: Staff Writers can create, edit, publish, and delete only articles that they have created; have the ability to upload accompanying images; but cannot affect the work of other authors.

- Freelancer: Freelancers can create and edit articles for which they are the author, and can change those articles from draft to pending status. These articles do not appear live on the site until approved by someone with Managing Editor or Publisher status.
- Designer: A Designer has access to the site's XHTML page templates, TXP forms, as well as CSS. However, a Designer does not have the ability to contribute to site content, so the Designer role is restricted to editing the appearance of the site.

The user account names mimic the structure of a newspaper or magazine editorial office. If your site requires different nomenclature, a bit of Textpattern hacking enables you to change both the user account names (for instance, Publisher to Overlord) and their permission levels. However, this is fairly technical, and requires editing the txp_admin.php and admin_config.php files, so it is beyond the scope of this book. For full details, consult the TextBook article entitled "Modifying User Account Roles and Privileges." [1]

Visitor Logs

Now that you learned how to create and manage new users, it is time to move on to Visitor Logs, which should look something like Figure 3-11. This area is pretty self-explanatory. In the far-left column is the date and time of the visit, followed by the name of the ISP/host, and then the URL of the page hit by the visitor. This, along with the Referrer, will probably be of most interest to you, because it shows which pages people are visiting, and, almost more importantly, who is linking to your website.

At the top center is a search box that enables you to filter through your logs to find something in particular. You can search by IP, host, page, referrer, method, and status. At the bottom left of the page is a checkbox that enables you to see more detail about your visitors, such as their IP addresses. In the far right column and at the bottom right, you can select entries to delete. This is helpful when cleaning up logs you have already viewed instead of waiting for them to expire after the preset number of days specified in Advanced Preferences.

---

1. http://textpattern.net/wiki/index.php?title=Modifying_User_Account_Roles_and_Privileges

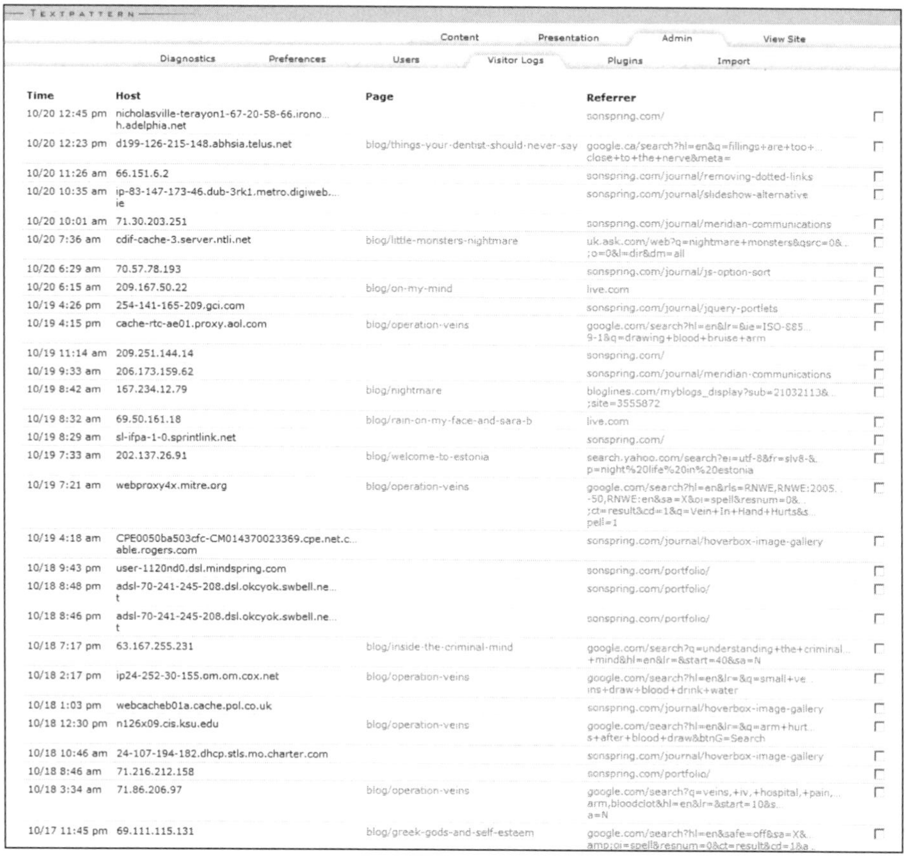

Time	Host	Page	Referrer
10/20 12:45 pm	nicholasville-terayon1-67-20-58-66.irono... h.adelphia.net		sonspring.com/
10/20 12:23 pm	d199-126-215-148.abhsia.telus.net	blog/things-your-dentist-should-never-say	google.ca/search?hl=en&q=fillings+are+too+... close+to+the+nerve&meta=
10/20 11:26 am	66.151.6.2		sonspring.com/journal/removing-dotted-links
10/20 10:35 am	ip-83-147-173-46.dub-3rk1.metro.digiweb... ie		sonspring.com/journal/slideshow-alternative
10/20 10:01 am	71.30.203.251		sonspring.com/journal/meridian-communications
10/20 7:36 am	cdif-cache-3.server.ntli.net	blog/little-monsters-nightmare	uk.ask.com/web?q=nightmare+monsters&qsrc=0&... ;o=0&l=dir&dm=all
10/20 6:29 am	70.57.78.193		sonspring.com/journal/js-option-sort
10/20 6:15 am	209.167.50.22	blog/on-my-mind	live.com
10/19 4:26 pm	254-141-165-209.gci.com		sonspring.com/journal/jquery-portlets
10/19 4:15 pm	cache-rtc-ae01.proxy.aol.com	blog/operation-veins	google.com/search?hl=en&lr=&ie=ISO-885... 9-1&q=drawing+blood+bruise+arm
10/19 11:14 am	209.251.144.14		sonspring.com/
10/19 9:33 am	206.173.159.62		sonspring.com/journal/meridian-communications
10/19 8:42 am	167.234.12.79	blog/nightmare	bloglines.com/myblogs_display?sub=21032113&... ;site=3555872
10/19 8:32 am	69.50.161.18	blog/rain-on-my-face-and-sara-b	live.com
10/19 8:29 am	sl-ifpa-1-0.sprintlink.net		sonspring.com/
10/19 7:33 am	202.137.26.91	blog/welcome-to-estonia	search.yahoo.com/search?ei=utf-8&fr=slv8-&... p=night%20life%20in%20estonia
10/19 7:21 am	webproxy4x.mitre.org	blog/operation-veins	google.com/search?hl=en&rls=RNWE,RNWE:2005... -50,RNWE:en&sa=X&oi=spell&resnum=0&... ;ct=result&cd=1&q=Vein+In+Hand+Hurts&s... pell=1
10/19 4:18 am	CPE0050ba503cfc-CM014370023369.cpe.net.c... able.rogers.com		sonspring.com/journal/hoverbox-image-gallery
10/18 9:43 pm	user-1120nd0.dsl.mindspring.com		sonspring.com/portfolio/
10/18 8:48 pm	adsl-70-241-245-208.dsl.okcyok.swbell.ne... t		sonspring.com/portfolio/
10/18 8:46 pm	adsl-70-241-245-208.dsl.okcyok.swbell.ne... t		sonspring.com/portfolio/
10/18 7:17 pm	63.167.255.231	blog/inside-the-criminal-mind	google.com/search?q=understanding+the+criminal... +mind&hl=en&lr=&start=40&sa=N
10/18 2:17 pm	ip24-252-30-155.om.om.cox.net	blog/operation-veins	google.com/search?hl=en&lr=&q=small+ve... ins+draw+blood+drink+water
10/18 1:03 pm	webcacheb01a.cache.pol.co.uk		sonspring.com/journal/hoverbox-image-gallery
10/18 12:30 pm	n126x09.cis.ksu.edu	blog/operation-veins	google.com/search?hl=en&lr=&q=arm+hurt... s+after+blood+draw&btnG=Search
10/18 10:46 am	24-107-194-182.dhcp.stls.mo.charter.com		sonspring.com/journal/hoverbox-image-gallery
10/18 8:46 am	71.216.212.158		sonspring.com/portfolio/
10/18 3:34 am	71.86.206.97	blog/operation-veins	google.com/search?q=veins,+iv,+hospital,+pain,... arm,bloodclot&hl=en&lr=&start=10&s... a=N
10/17 11:45 pm	69.111.115.131	blog/greek-gods-and-self-esteem	google.com/search?hl=en&safe=off&sa=X&... amp;oi=spell&resnum=0&ct=result&cd=1&a...

Figure 3-11. Referral logs

Plugins

When you first go to this section of the Admin interface, it looks quite sparse (see Figure 3-12) simply because Textpattern does not come with any plugins preinstalled. As your site develops, however, this area will probably grow with the plugins you choose to give additional functionality to your website. To install a plugin, copy the text from within the plugin file that you have downloaded, paste it into the Install plugin textarea, and then click Upload.

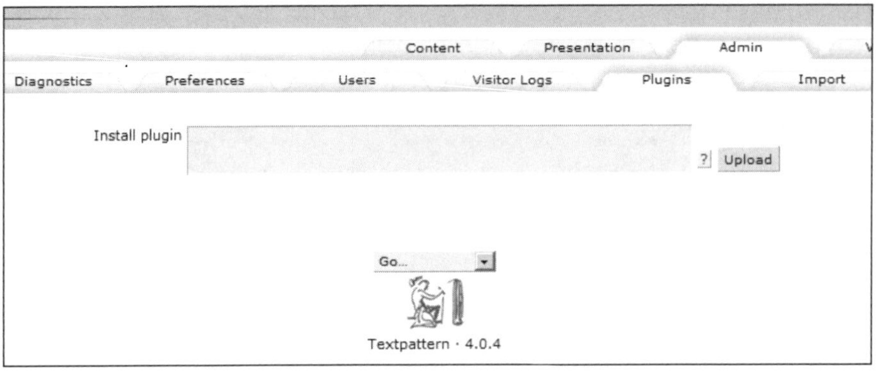

Figure 3-12. Plugins area

You now see a screen with a preview of that plugin's PHP code, as well as the accompanying help file and usage instructions, as shown in Figure 3-13. After you look things over, scroll down to the bottom of the page and click Install.

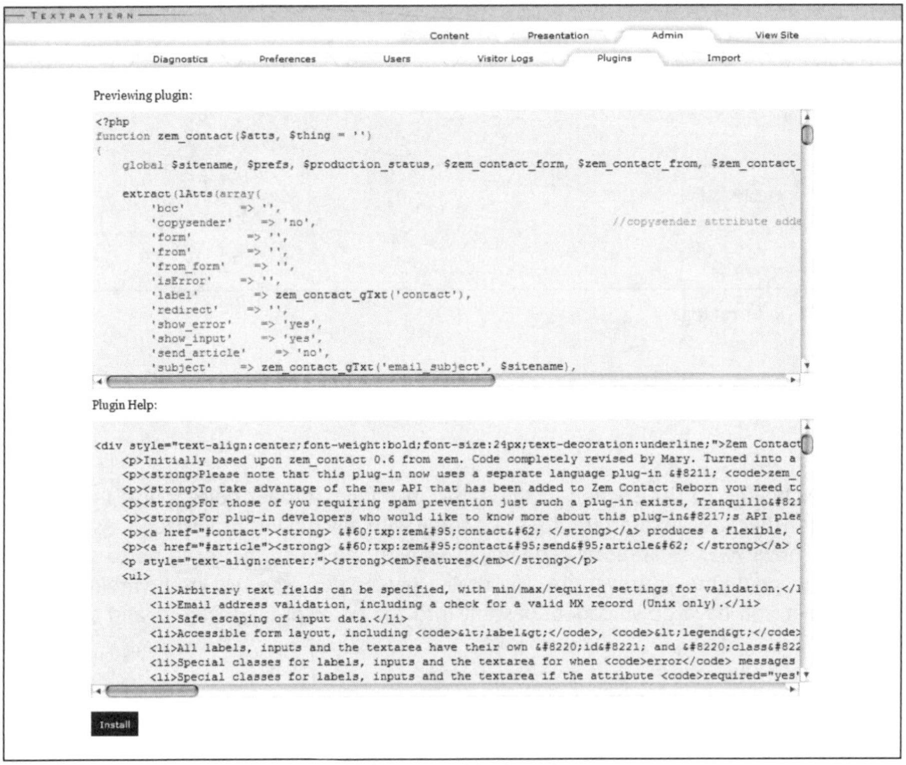

Figure 3-13. Plugin preview

After you install your plugin (or perhaps several plugins), this section of the Admin area starts to look like Figure 3-14. You see that there are typically four links pertaining to each plugin. The first is the author's name with a link to the website. This can be a good way to check on updates to plugins by periodically visiting the author's site, or perhaps subscribing to the Atom or RSS feeds. The next link is in the column labeled Active. You need to actually make each plugin officially active after installation, so make sure that you click on all the No words to change them to Yes. Likewise, when uninstalling a plugin, make sure to deactivate it before just jettisoning it into the void.

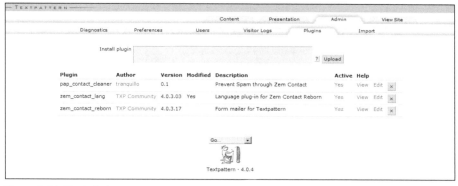

Figure 3-14. Plugin listing

We won't go into more detail here because Chapter 13 covers plugins in much more depth.

Import

This section does just what it says and not a whole lot more, as you can see in Figure 3-15. If you already have a site running using a different content management system (CMS), and it shares the same database host, all you need to do is enter the relevant info. There is a drop-down menu labeled Import from with a few selections: Movable Type (file), Movable Type (SQL DB), Blogger, B2, and WordPress. For the sake of this example, I have set up WordPress on localhost alongside my Textpattern installation. If you are migrating from another system, check with the corresponding vendor about how to export your database.

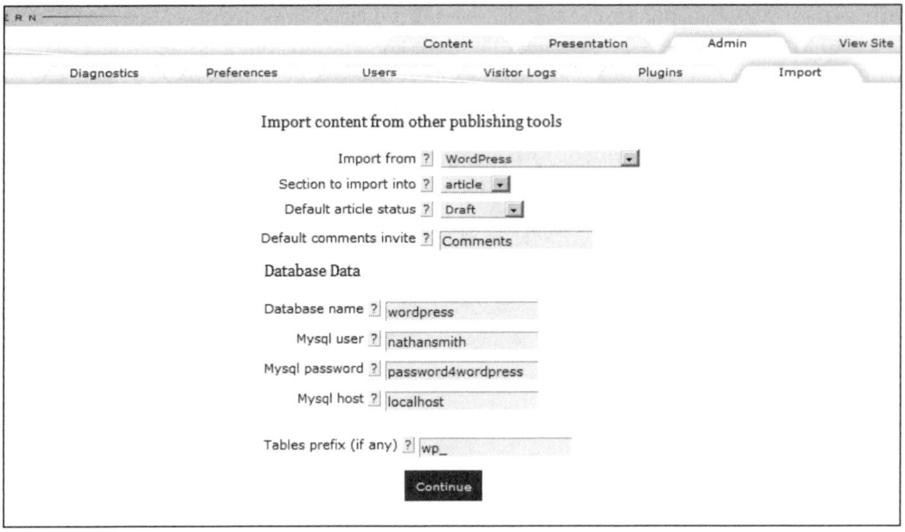

Figure 3-15. Importing from WordPress

The second drop-down menu enables you to pick the Section to import into. This is somewhat limiting, considering that you could be importing from a multisectioned CMS. However, you can always go back through and reassign each article to the correct TXP section. The third drop-down menu enables you to set the Default article status. If you are doing this on a live server, you should probably have it set to Draft, so your new articles don't go out to the world until you have looked them over. If you are doing this on a localhost, it really does not matter. You can also set the Default comments invite in the text field provided.

Finally, make sure to fill out the database details for your other CMS. It is easy to make the mistake of filling in your Textpattern database data, in which case you are telling Textpattern to import itself. After you finish, fill in any applicable table prefixes if you are importing from WordPress or the Weblog ID if you are importing from a Movable Type database. Then hold your breath and click Continue. If everything went according to plan, you should see something like Figure 3-16. Note that if you have a large amount of articles stored in the other CMS, the database import can take awhile. For my example, I just imported a brand new WordPress installation on my own computer, so it was instantaneous.

Figure 3-16. Import is complete

Summary

Well, that about covers it for the Admin area of Textpattern. Hopefully, you have not yet started using this book as a doorstop because the upcoming chapters will be much more interesting. Configuration is the least glamorous part of any web development–related topic, but it is a necessary part of the process. Now that you have solidified the groundwork for Textpattern, it is time to move on to the Content area and start putting virtual pen to paper to share your thoughts with the world. It will then be time to delve into the Presentation area, in which you learn the tools that will transform this default and nondescript website into a thing of unique elegance and beauty. Okay, so maybe we cannot promise beauty, but at the very least you will be more comfortable changing the way your site looks, and it will be a reflection of your creativity.

4 BASIC CONTENT MANIPULATION

PATTERN

Categories   Write

Article Categories ?

[   ] Create

☐ Hope for the Future (0)

☐ Meaningful Labor (0)

Content

Articles   Images

9rules Netwo
Welcome to The 9rules Ne
9rules members are grouped into Comr

Replace image ? [   ] Br

Content

Articles   Images

Title [10 Things Suck About Django]

ort Value [10 Things Suck Al]

URL ? [http://www2.jeffcroft.com/2006/]

tegory ? [Web-Dev ▾] [Edit]

:ription ? [Jeff Croft speaks openly about t]

Now that you have made it through the arduous process of setting up Textpattern (TXP), and have fully tweaked and customized the Admin preferences, it is high time to introduce you to the section in which you will find yourself spending the bulk of your time. This is, of course, the Content area. This chapter covers the basics: creating article categories, making subcategories, and learning the fundamentals of writing in Textile. This chapter also introduces aspects of the authoring interface: form override, custom fields, keywords, article image, and URL title customization. (Form override and custom fields will be covered in depth later in Chapter 13 because these two topics open up further doors to extended functionality.)

Write

When you first log in or whenever you navigate to www.example.com/textpattern/, if the Remain logged in with this browser checkbox has been selected, you arrive at a page with a blank text input field and two textareas. It will look something like the screen shown in Figure 4-1. This area is where you will probably spend the most time managing and creating new content. It is aptly named Write, denoted by the selected tab in the secondary row of navigation. Note that on the left there are three links that, when clicked, expand to show more options: Textile Help, Advanced Options, and Recent Articles.

Figure 4-1. Write tab

Textile Help

The first link, Textile Help, gives you a cheat sheet with many of the common instances for which you might need to use it. There is also a link labeled More, which takes you to a more robust demo[1] that looks like the screen depicted in Figure 4-2. Textile was initially created by the original author of Textpattern (Dean Allen), but is now hosted and maintained by Alex Sheils, who is one of the developers on the core TXP team. The syntax that is listed within the Write interface will be referred to as **Basic Textile** for the purposes of this chapter, and the syntax that is featured exclusively at the Textile demo site will be referred to as **Advanced Textile**. Note that throughout this list you might see (class) included in the syntax, whereas it might or might not be present in the Textpattern interface. This is simply to make you aware of the fact that a class name can be added at these points. Also be aware that whenever you see (class), that element can also accept (#id), {style}, or [language] (see the section later in this chapter titled "Advanced Textile").

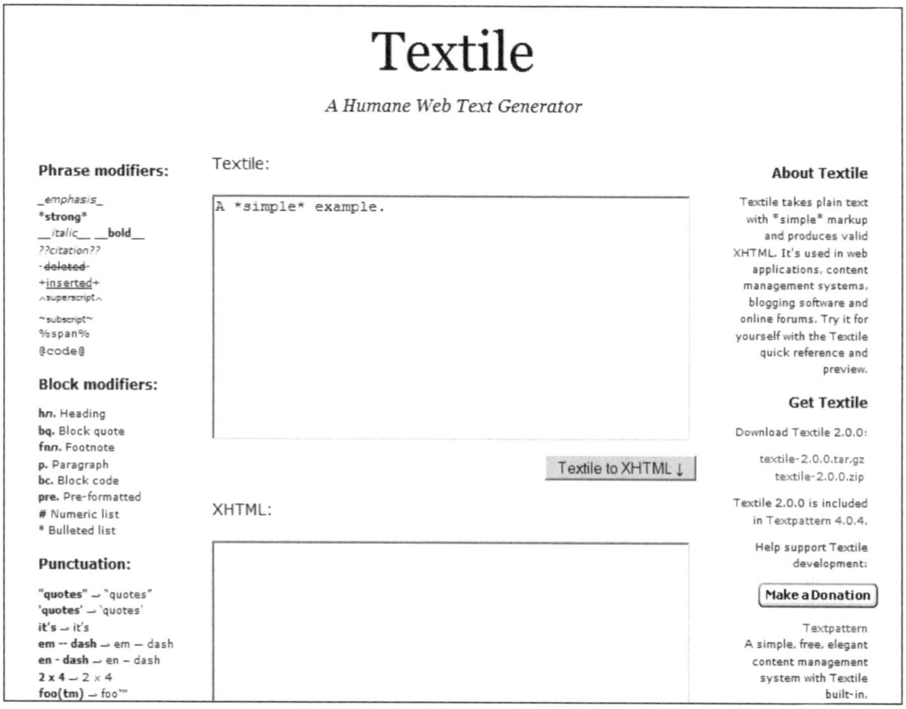

Figure 4-2. Textile generator demo

---

1. http://textile.thresholdstate.com

Basic Textile

According to Dean Allen, the creator of Textpattern, Textile is "a simple syntax for nudging plain text into structurally sound and stylistically rich web content." It is basically a short-hand method of turning regular thoughts and ideas into valid XHTML without having to type angular brackets all the time. In this section, we will examine what makes this possible and hopefully demystify the art of self-publishing on the Web.

header: h*n*(class): This option refers to XHTML headers, which number 1 through 6 and are used to denote semantic structure and importance within a document. For instance, the main heading on a page might be a level 1 heading written like this: `<h1>This is a level 1 heading</h1>`, with subsequent instances of `<h2>...</h2>`, `<h3>...</h3>`, and so on. The italicized *n* in the Textpattern interface simply refers to the number that you need to type to invoke the corresponding header. The nice thing about Textile is that you simply write h*n*. at the beginning of the line, and Textile closes it for you automatically when there is a double line break. Doing so enables you to write headers with single line breaks in them, which are converted to `<br />` automatically. For instance, if you want to write a level 3 heading, you simply type this:

Textile input:

```
h3(class_name). This is my level 3 heading
```

XHTML output:

```
<h3 class="class_name">This is my level 3 heading</h3>
```

Note that you must begin writing your string of text flush against the side of the textarea for it to take effect. If there is a space before the h, your literal XHTML output is simply h3. This is my level 3 heading. That is, of course, not what you are shooting for.

---

*Sometimes you might want to write raw XHTML, which you can do with Textile. Let's say you want to place a horizontal rule, often referred to as a **horizontal line**. In XHTML, it is simply written as `<hr />` (note the self-closing trailing slash; without it, your code is valid HTML but invalid XHTML). Since there is no Textile equivalent, you can just write it as is. However, be aware that if you write it flush against the left side of the textarea, the following is sent to the browser: `<p><hr /></p>`. Oops—that is not what you intended! Do you see what happened there? Textile was expecting regular text and since it did not see any of the predefined syntax such as h3, it just wrapped the `<hr />` in paragraph tags `<p>...</p>` as if it were regular written copy.*

You need not disable Textile entirely for such simple things; just add a space before-hand, and the horizontal rule will be output as expected without any containing tags. Alternatively, you can also write notextile. before text that you want to remain un-affected, which can help to more visibly mark the spot where you disabled Textile. Doing so causes it to kick in at the next double line break. If you use notextile., you have to manually restart Textile using the p. syntax.

Blockquote: bq(class): This option should be used only when you are actually quoting a source. It is not meant to be used as a pull quote, as is often seen in print media. (A **pull quote** is a chunk of text that has been visually emphasized to help capture the essence of an article.) A blockquote is used when quoting an external source that spans several lines. Often, blockquote HTML tags have been abused in the past, being misappropriated simply to indent chunks of text with no regard to the underlying semantic meaning. This negligent usage has even been propagated by expensive web development software such as Dreamweaver, regarded by many to be one of the industry standards for coding. Similar to headings, to make use of a blockquote simply type bq. with no preceding spaces, and the text after it will be enclosed within <blockquote>...</blockquote> tags. What is nice about the way Textile handles blockquotes is that it automatically adds <p>...</p> tags round the text as well, which is required for valid XHTML 1.0 Strict and higher. Some content management system (CMS) choices, such as ExpressionEngine, lack this by default. Following is an example of a blockquote being created in Textile, followed by the XHTML output it generates:

Textile input:

```
bq(class_name). Four score and seven years ago, our fathers brought ➥
forth
on this continent a new nation, conceived in liberty, and
dedicated to the proposition that all men are created equal.
```

XHTML output:

```
<blockquote class="class_name">
  <p>
    Four score and seven years ago, our fathers brought forth<br />
    on this continent a new nation, conceived in liberty, and<br />
    dedicated to the proposition that all men are created equal.
  </p>
<blockquote>
```

> *If you write your blockquote Textile syntax with two periods instead of one (bq..), your blockquote can span several paragraphs. You just need to make sure that you toggle this behavior off by manually adding p. to indicate the paragraph at which you want the blockquoting to stop.*

Numeric list: #(class): This option is pretty self-explanatory. To create a numbered list, or more specifically an **ordered list**, just put a number sign (sometimes referred to as a **pound sign**) at the beginning of each new line. Doing this creates an ordered numerical list. The following is an example of the text that is created. Note that doing single line breaks to make a <br /> within a list tends not to work too well with Textile. So if that is your desired effect, amid other standard writing that you want to be affected by Textile simply put a space before your <ol> and type out an ordered list as you would in normal XHTML.

Textile input:

```
#(class_name) Ordered list item one
# Ordered list item two
# Ordered list item three
```

XHTML output:

```
<ol class="class_name">
  <li>Ordered list item one</li>
  <li>Ordered list item two</li>
  <li>Ordered list item three</li>
</ol>
```

Bulleted list: *: To create a bulleted list, more commonly referred to as an **unordered list**, you simply put an asterisk at the beginning of each new line (Ctrl+8 on Windows/ Command+8 on Mac). This works exactly like ordered lists, except instead of a number there will simply be a generic bullet point. You can, of course, style these bullets differently with Cascading Style Sheets (CSS) or get rid of them entirely and substitute a background image instead. Such tricks are beyond the scope of this chapter, however. For a good book on CSS, check out *CSS Mastery* by Andy Budd (ISBN: 1590596145).[2] Following is an example of the syntax for unordered lists in Textile:

Textile input:

```
*(class_name) Unordered list item one
* Unordered list item two
* Unordered list item three
```

XHTML output:

```
<ul class="class_name">
  <li>Unordered list item one</li>
  <li>Unordered list item two</li>
  <li>Unordered list item three</li>
</ul>
```

(class)*emphasis*: Emphasis is an element of XHTML that is often confused and interchanged with italics. Emphasis is officially written with <em>...</em> tags, whereas italics are written with <i>...</i> tags. While there are some isolated instances in which italics might be preferable, the majority of the web community treats them as being deprecated (although they are still technically allowable in Strict document types). The reason why emphasis is preferred over italics is that it better supports multilingual applicability as well as having more semantic meaning to assistive screen reader technology. For instance, consider a font with Japanese characters. Unlike our westernized Latin character set used in a language such as English, there might not actually be an italicized subset for this particular font. Therefore, adding italics is a moot point. Visually, adding <em> tags might not have any effect, either, but that is not the point. Italics tags exist for one

---

2. www.cssmastery.com

purpose only: to make things italicized. By adding emphasis, we can style the Japanese writing in a different color, larger size, and so on. Screen readers give more audible emphasis to the characters as well; italics typically receive no such distinction. That being said, writing _(class_name)emphasized word here_ will yield `<em class="class_name">emphasized word here</em>`.

(class)strong: Much like emphasis, `<strong>...</strong>` grew out of a departure from purely visual HTML markup. Strong can be thought of as the XHTML version of the outmoded, but not altogether deprecated, bold tag. Just like italics, the bold tag `<b>...</b>` existed for one reason only: to make text bold. Strong, on the other hand carries with it a certain element of semantic value as well as not being restricted to a certain font weight. Granted, many browsers render strong the same as bold and emphasis the same as italics, but it is the subtle nuance that makes all the difference. In Textile, *(class_name)strong text here* yields `<strong class="class_name">strong text here</strong>` when it is output to the browser as XHTML.

??(class)_citation_??: Citation is a little-used XHTML tag (probably because of being misunderstood or perhaps visually mistaken for emphasis or italics). It is a great way to show a citation of a particular source. For instance, in a list of works cited using a particular format, as required by the Modern Language Association[3] or the American Psychological Association,[4] you might want to semantically indicate a source citation. In such cases, `<cite>...</cite>` could be wrapped around the name of a book or semiregular publication. The fact that it tends to be rendered in italics by most browsers is irrelevant because unlike the italics tag it has semantic meaning. Its similarity in default visual style is entirely coincidental. That being said, you can always style away the italics with CSS and instead apply whatever visual standard is necessary for a particular genre of bibliography. In Textile, you can write ??(class_name)Really Good Book??, and it outputs `<cite class="class_name">Really Good Book</cite>` to the browser.

-deleted text- and **+inserted text+**: I mention these two together since they are often seen used in tandem. Deleted text appears ~~with a line through it~~ in the browser by default. It is the XHTML replacement for the now outdated and deprecated `<strike>...</strike>` strikethrough tags. Just as is the case with strong versus bold and emphasis versus italics, the `<del>...</del>` tags are now the preferred method for showing text that has been deleted. This begs the following question: Why would I want to show text that is deleted? I am glad you asked. It is handy in situations in which there was an item for sale, but it is now out of stock. Instead of having the text mysteriously disappear and risk alienating and confusing returning shoppers, it is more helpful to show them the option that was previously up for grabs. Insertion is shown in XHTML by `<ins>...</ins>` and because of its default visual styling in most browsers, it is thought of as having replaced the `<u>...</u>` tags, which was purely for the purpose of underlining text. Because of the prevalence of underlining to denote a hyperlink, however, `<ins>` should not be used unless the accompanying CSS of `text-decoration: none;` is also applied, lest the inserted text look like a link and confuse the user. One possible semantic use of insertion is within `<noscript>...</noscript>` tags, the contents of which are displayed only when JavaScript is unavailable. In this case, the text really is inserted into the document under extenuating

---

3. www.mla.org
4. www.apa.org

circumstances. Another use is to correct something that has been crossed-out via use of the deletion tags. A store that is in the process of lowering its prices might use such a combo.

^superscript^ and **~subscript~**: These two do exactly what their names imply. Superscript elevates text, whereas subscript pushes it down. Superscript ^{...} would be necessary to write Einstein's Theory of Relativity ($E = mc^2$) in XHTML, for which the exponent of 2 is raised above the baseline and also appears in a smaller font size. Likewise, the chemical representation of sulfuric acid, H_2SO_4, is an example of subscript _{...}, in which the numbers hang slightly below the baseline and are written in a smaller font size. By and large, these tags are not used very often, but can help to add clarification to text when they are used correctly, not just for ASCII art. The preceding examples would be written like this: E = mc ^2^ and H ~2~ SO ~4~. It was for the purpose of scientific learning that the Internet was created in the first place, so although these tags are purely presentational, they are so for a reason: to convey mathematical and chemical principles. Therefore, use them as such, or not at all.

"linktext":url: This is the syntax for adding hyperlinks to your writing, something that I anticipate you will want to do quite frequently. linktext is the text that you want to be visible and clickable. The URL portion is then written after the colon. It is important to realize that just writing a link beginning with www does not suffice. If that were the case, your link would point to www.yourwebsite.com/www.example.com/. Therefore, be sure to structure your text like this: "Click Here":http://www.example.com/ and it will yield <a href="http://www.example.com/">Click Here</a>. You should, of course, provide more meaningful and informative text than simply Click Here, but I think you understand what I mean.

!(class)imageurl(alt text)!:linkurl: This works in much the same way as the previous example, in that the URL that follows the colon is a link. The imageurl is simply the path to the image you want to display. Note that if you want this image to also show up in your RSS/Atom feed, you should probably provide the full path, also called an **absolute path**, instead of just the localized path, or **relative path**, to the image. However, if you forget to use absolute paths, Textpattern automatically attempts to fix the URL in the feed. Also, note that if you enclose a word within parentheses *before* the image URL, it is used as a class name, whereas text within parentheses *after* the URL is used as alternate text. For instance, this is how you link directly to an image on your server to ensure that it appears to your subscribers and your site visitors:

```
!(class_name)http://www.yourwebsite.com/images/34.gif ➟
  (Alternate Text Here)!:http://www.example.com/
```

That yields this XHTML on the client side:

```
<a href="http://www.example.com"> ➟
  <img src="http://www.yourwebsite.com/images/34.gif" class= ➟
"class_name" alt="Alternate Text Here" />
</a>
```

Some feed reading services automatically correct relative URLs to images, so if you are relying on it to keep people visiting your site to see your imagery, you might be wasting your time. As a general rule of thumb, if you do not want people accessing information, do not put it online. You, of course, do not *have* to specify an external link every time, but *should* specify alt text for accessibility purposes. To simply display an image but not have a link around it, just write your Textile code like this: !http://www.yourwebsite.com/images/ 34.gif(Alternate Text Here)!.

Advanced Textile

Beyond what is listed in the collapsible area in the Write interface, Textile also supports a variety of other text commands. Since some of them are quite robust and are not likely to be used on a regular basis, as well as the fact that Textile is constantly being improved upon with each release, many of the more-advanced features can be found by clicking More beneath the Textile Help area. This will take you to a demonstration area that you can use to see how the syntax translates into XHTML. Much of the basic syntax covered in the Textpattern interface is repeated there, so we will now focus on advanced syntax.

%(class)span%: Occasionally you might want to visually distinguish some snippet of text within the flow of regular text, yet not necessarily add any implicit semantic meaning to it. For such instances, authors sometimes add a valueless wrapper around their text, which is called a **span**. By default, span tags have no visual distinction or special styling, so they can be styled however the designer prefers. In Textile, writing text like this %(class_name)Text enclosed by a span% yields this XHTML output: <span class="class_name">Text enclosed by a span</span>.

@code@: This syntax is great for adding snippets of code inline with your body text to denote something that the user should take note of, such as a snippet of XHTML, CSS, or JavaScript. It should be noted that it does not create a block of code as seen on some websites. Wrapping text in code brackets also keeps XHTML within them from being parsed and instead converts it into the character-encoded equivalents. Writing @<p>Paragraph Code</p>@ in Textile yields this XHTML output: <code><p>Paragraph Code</ p></code>. Onscreen, it appears to the user like this: <p>Paragraph Code</p>.

fnn. Footnote and **See foo[1]**: This pair can be used together to create a numbered indicator that corresponds with a numbered footnote. The footnote itself needn't be at the bottom of your document, but it is recommended that you place it there so it will function as intended. It is nice that Textile has the intuition to keep the numerical pairing between the indicator and the footnote, as seen here. The lengthy alphanumeric link and the matching ID name might look a bit perplexing. The reason for this is that they adhered to the principle of globally unique identifier (GUID). If there were several articles on a page, each with corresponding footnotes, id="fn1" would quickly be duplicated. In order to function, there most only ever be one single ID name per page. By having a random alphanumeric pairing, they are always unique.

Textile input:

    See foo[1].

    fn1. Foo.

XHTML output:

```
<p>See foo<sup class="footnote"> ➥
  <a href="#fn198522619454032998635b">1</a></sup>.</p>

<p id="fn198522619454032998635b" class="footnote"><sup>1</sup> Foo.</p>
```

p(class). Paragraph: You might be wondering why it is possible to specify a paragraph when Textile converts all double line breaks to paragraphs anyway. But sometimes you might want to add a particular class to a paragraph. For instance, say you want to have a paragraph that contains a notice to the user that you want them to pay attention to. For that, you simply write p(class_name). Notice this paragraph, and it then outputs this XHTML: `<p class="class_name">Notice this paragraph</p>`. Additionally, you need to manually specify a paragraph if you are resuming regular formatting following any of the `..` Textile modifiers, such as the `notextile..` syntax mentioned previously.

bc. Block code: This option works much the same way as a blockquote, but also partially as @code@ does because it creates a block of code by using the preformatted tags of `<pre>...</pre>` with code tags contained immediately inside to add the monospace aspects and to keep the code from being parsed. With only `<pre>`, the contained is still parsed, and you can basically just format things the way you do when writing poetry. With both sets of tags, you can write lengthy chunks of code for highly technical examples. Check out the following example:

Textile input:

```
bc(html). <ul id="navigation">
  <li>
    <a href="home.html">Home</a>
  </li>
  <li>
    <a href="about.html">About Us</a>
  </li>
  <li>
    <a href="services.html">Our Services</a>
  </li>
  <li>
    <a href="history.html">Company History</a>
  </li>
  <li>
    <a href="contact.html">Contact Us</a>
  </li>
</ul>
```

XHTML output:

```
<pre class="html"><code>&lt;ul id="navigation"&gt;
  &lt;li&gt;
    &lt;a href="home.html"&gt;Home&lt;/a&gt;
  &lt;/li&gt;
```

```
        &lt;li&gt;
          &lt;a href="about.html"&gt;About Us&lt;/a&gt;
        &lt;/li&gt;
        &lt;li&gt;
          &lt;a href="services.html"&gt;Our Services&lt;/a&gt;
        &lt;/li&gt;
        &lt;li&gt;
          &lt;a href="history.html"&gt;Company History&lt;/a&gt;
        &lt;/li&gt;
        &lt;li&gt;
          &lt;a href="contact.html"&gt;Contact Us&lt;/a&gt;
        &lt;/li&gt;
      &lt;ul&gt;</code></pre>
```

Visible to user:

```
      <ul id="navigation">
        <li>
          <a href="home.html">Home</a>
        </li>
        <li>
          <a href="about.html">About Us</a>
        </li>
        <li>
          <a href="services.html">Our Services</a>
        </li>
        <li>
          <a href="history.html">Company History</a>
        </li>
        <li>
          <a href="contact.html">Contact Us</a>
        </li>
      <ul>
```

> Just like blockquote, block code also can span several paragraphs. Simply type **bc..** with two periods instead of one, and you can keep your code continuing as long as you need to. Likewise, to toggle this behavior off and return to normal text, simply type **p.** to manually create a paragraph.

pre(class). Pre-formatted: As mentioned in the previous example, using <pre>...</pre> without code tags can help format text for which the spacing and indentation is important. Without it, extra spaces and tabs are simply dropped, and text is formatted as a standard paragraph. For instance, check out the following example: a snippet of a poem by Rudyard Kipling, simply titled "If." Note the lack of converted line breaks. Since this text is contained within a preformatted block, the actual line breaks are retained instead of being converted into their XHTML equivalent of <br />. One nice feature is that Textile still finds straight quotation marks and converts them to their curly XHTML encoded counterparts for easier reading. This differs from the bc. usage because they would stay regular straight quotes for code purposes.

Textile input:

```
pre(poetry). If you can talk with crowds and keep your virtue,
    Or walk with kings - nor lose the common touch,
If neither foes nor loving friends can hurt you;
    If all men count with you, but none too much,
If you can fill the unforgiving minute
    With sixty seconds' worth of distance run,
Yours is the Earth and everything that's in it,
    And - which is more - you'll be a Man, my son!
```

XHTML output:

```
<pre class="poetry">If you can talk with crowds and keep your virtue,
    Or walk with kings - nor lose the common touch,
If neither foes nor loving friends can hurt you;
    If all men count with you, but none too much,
If you can fill the unforgiving minute
    With sixty seconds&#39; worth of distance run,
Yours is the Earth and everything that&#39;s in it,
    And - which is more - you&#39;ll be a Man, my son!
</pre>
```

Visible to user:

If you can talk with crowds and keep your virtue,
    Or walk with kings - nor lose the common touch,
If neither foes nor loving friends can hurt you;
    If all men count with you, but none too much,
If you can fill the unforgiving minute
    With sixty seconds' worth of distance run,
Yours is the Earth and everything that's in it,
    And – which is more – you'll be a Man, my son!

Attributes: These four aspects of Textile can be used to modify the tags with which you pair them. In many of the preceding examples, you saw (class) added to some of the code examples. Likewise, (#id) can be added in the same way. For instance, h2(#welcome). Welcome to my website! outputs this XHTML: <h2 id="welcome">Welcome to my website!</h2>. The language attribute in Textile works much the same way: simply substitute [language] for (class) in any of the previous examples. For instance, the Textile code %[Spanish]¿Hablas Español?% converts to <span lang="Spanish">¿Hablas Español?</span>. The fourth attribute, {style}, requires that you have working knowledge of CSS. If you want to override one particular aspect of your text, you can do so. Note that all of these attributes can be used together. It should be noted that using inline styles is discouraged because it mixes presentation with content.

Textile input:

```
%{font-family: serif;}(hymnal)[Spanish]Tú eres luz, tú eres mi sol%
```

XHTML output:

```
<span style="font-family: serif;" class="hymnal" lang="Spanish"> ➥
   Tú eres luz, tú eres mi sol</span>
```

Alignment: By using these aspects of Textile, you can change the alignment of text. However, they use inline styles, which should probably be avoided anyway. For the sake of completeness, they are covered here, but I really recommend that you not use them at all in actual practice because they mix presentation with the actual content of your writing. Instead, use predefined class names. That being said, here is the corresponding Textile and XHTML:

Textile input:

```
p>. This text is aligned to the right

p<. This text is aligned to the left

p=. This text is centered

p<>. This text is justified at either end
```

XHTML output:

```
<p style="text-align:right;">This text is aligned to the right</p>

<p style="text-align:left;">This text is aligned to the left</p>

<p style="text-align:center;">This text is centered</p>

<p style="text-align:justify;">This text is justified at either end</p>
```

Tables: Much like the alignment syntax, I do not recommend that you actually build your tables using Textile. While it is possible to do so, the input lacks the capability to do fully semantic markup and does not take accessibility for screen readers into account. That being said, here is an example for completeness, as well as a contrasting full XHTML table that can be written without Textile:

Textile input:

```
|_. Name|_. Age|
|Jane Doe|26|
|John Doe|27|
```

XHTML output:

```
<table>
  <tr>
    <th>Name</th>
    <th>Age</th>
  </tr>
  <tr>
    <td>Jane Doe</td>
    <td>26</td>
  </tr>
  <tr>
    <td>John Doe</td>
    <td>27</td>
  </tr>
</table>
```

Better XHTML table (note that tfoot precedes tbody per the World Wide Web Consortium (W3C) recommendation[5]):

```
<table cellspacing="0" class="data">
  <caption>Names and Ages</caption>
  <colgroup>
    <col class="name" />
    <col class="age" />
  </colgroup>
  <thead>
    <tr>
      <th scope="col">
        Name
      </th>
      <th scope="col">
        Age
      </th>
    </tr>
  </thead>
  <tfoot>
    <tr>
      <td colspan="2">
        This would be a summary of the table.
      </td>
    </tr>
  </tfoot>
  <tbody>
    <tr>
      <td>
```

---

5. www.w3.org/TR/html4/struct/tables.html#edef-TFOOT

```
      Jane Doe
    </td>
    <td>
      26
    </td>
  </tr>
  <tr>
    <td>
      John Doe
    </td>
    <td>
      27
    </td>
  </tr>
  </tbody>
</table>
```

Acronyms: When writing, you often use using lingo that is commonly known to you but perhaps new to your readers. Likewise, after first explaining what something means, you might have an abbreviation or acronym for it to avoid having to type it out each time. For instance, instead of the words *United States of America* or *U.S.A.*, we often simply write USA. For accessibility purposes, as well as just to add text clarification, this can be written in Textile as USA(United States of America). In so doing, only the letters USA are visible, but there is a hidden title attribute contained within acronym tags, like so: <acronym title="United States of America">USA</acronym>. In most major browsers, when hovering over an acronym the title attribute displays as a tooltip.

The <acronym>...</acronym> *tags will supposedly be replaced by* <abbr>...</abbr> *sometime in the future, since they enable broader application. All acronyms are abbreviations, but not all abbreviations are acronyms. For instance, the word* etcetera *can be abbreviated as* etc. *but not* ETC. *However, Internet Explorer 6 for Windows fails to properly display the title attribute of* abbr, *so the acronym is still widely used instead because of better support in older browsers.*

Raw XHTML: From time to time, you will include snippets of XHTML that you want to be unaffected by Textile. Such situations differ from usages of <pre> or <code> because you still want the XHTML to have its normal parsing by the browser, but without being first rerouted through Textile. Such instances might include a data table to show statistics in an article, while still desiring Textile for the actual written copy. Such a table might require a certain level of robustness that Textile table formatting cannot provide. If you were to hand-code your own table, you would of course want the XHTML code to be unaffected, lest Textile add in <br /> and <p>...</p> where it was not appropriate. To do that, you can denote where Textile will be disabled using this syntax:

Disable Textile inline:

```
==no This text is unaffected ==
```

Disable Textile for a block of text:

```
notextile. Textile will be disabled until a double linebreak
```

Disable Textile until restarted manually (via p., h*n*., etc.):

```
notextile.. Textile will be disabled until restarted manually
```

Advanced Options

Here I will run through the advanced options available under the Advanced Options link.

Article/Excerpt Markup

This collapsible portion enables you to specify how you will handle article markup on a per-article basis. There are three main choices: Use Textile, Convert linebreaks, and Leave text untouched. If you left things set as the default in the Admin area, Use Textile is the default choice selected. This means that all the syntax in the Textile Help cheat sheet, as well as the more robust capabilities of Alex's demo, are applicable as you write your article. If you choose Convert linebreaks, each new line creates either a new paragraph or an XHTML break tag, depending on whether there are double or single line breaks. The rest of the text is untouched. If you do not want any modification to be done and want to type raw XHTML code instead, simply choose Leave text untouched. This can be helpful for articles that pertain to code, which should not be parsed by Textile, and in which line breaks need to be handled manually.

Keywords

This option can be used to uniquely identify an article instead of relying on a generic set of overarching keywords for an entire site. In the days of yesteryear, keywords were used by search engines to determine the relevance of a site to a set of search terms. However, because keywords are so easy to fake by entering irrelevant words to return false positives for search results, many search engine companies are now relegating them to unimportant status. Still, using keywords can be a good way to give your articles useful descriptors, and some plugins might make use of keywords to retrieve similar articles. Just do not expect miraculous results if you are attempting to do Search Engine Optimization (SEO). Keywords can also be used in conjunction with the `<txp:article_custom />` tag, as will be seen in Chapter 13.

Article image

This field enables you to directly associate one particular image with each article. This is not to say that you cannot also insert other images via the previously covered Textile syntax or simply raw XHTML, but this option enables you to output the image apart from the article text itself, if need be, by using the `<txp:article_image />` tag. If you were running a photo blog or a gallery website in which you did a writeup about each image, this would be an ideal way to do it. Use of this tag will be covered more in the next chapter.

URL-only title

By default, this article derives from the title of your article and typically reflects the title by making all the words lowercase and inserting dashes between them (unless you changed this default setting in the Advanced Preferences in the Admin area, in which case the title would be camelCased). Either way, if you for some reason want to change the URL on a per-article basis, this is the field that you use to do so.

Recent Articles

This link does just what it says: it expands and shows a list of recently modified articles. Note that this does not necessarily mean they were the most recently written. For instance, if you wrote an article a year ago, but have just updated it within the past week, it shows up in this list, yet remains chronologically on your site as it was originally. This option can be good for posting updates to an article without necessarily wanting to draw attention to the fact that it has been updated. It can also be handy for fixing typos.

Categories

In the Categories area you can keep track of the various pieces of content by arranging them into categories. The four main category designations are Article Categories, Link Categories, Image Categories, and File Categories. By default, the Categories area looks like the screen in Figure 4-3. By using the text fields above each list, you can add additional categories. You can also click categories that already exist and make modifications to them. Either way, you will find yourself on a screen that resembles Figure 4-4. Note the drop-down list labeled Parent, which enables you to choose an article category from which the currently selected one will be a descendant. While this does not have any direct impact in the current version of Textpattern, 4.0.4, it might be incorporated as a fuller feature in later versions. Some plugins make use of the parent/child relationship between categories in order to provide means of user "tagging" or slitting up items for sale into related areas for ecommerce.

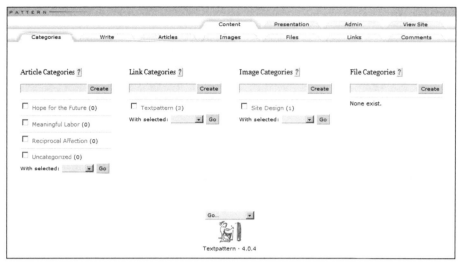

Figure 4-3. Categories tab

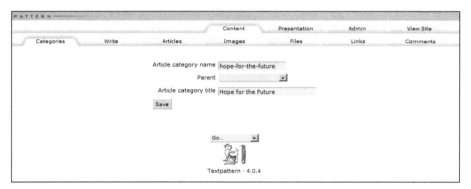

Figure 4-4. Add/edit category

Articles

As you write your articles, they are automatically built into a sortable list that can be accessed from the Articles tab. Since the default installation of Textpattern includes only one article, I have taken a screenshot of the Articles tab from my own site. As you can see in Figure 4-5, the layout is conducive to sorting and editing your articles. If you click the column headers, you can sort articles by any of the following criteria: ID#, Posted (date), Title, Section, Status, or Author. Likewise, if the article you are looking for is not visible on that page, you can search by these same criteria using the text input at the top center of the page.

You can also modify aspects of the article by clicking a checkbox or multiple checkboxes, and then choosing one of the following options from the drop-down menu in the lower-right corner: Change section, Change Category1, Change Category2, Change status, Change comments, Change author, or Delete. You can click the article's ID# or title; you will be taken to the Write tab with that article open, in which you can make updates or changes. Note that if you do so, there is a link labeled View next to the title's text input field. This is a convenient way to go directly to that article's URL to see the article in the context of your site. The < Prev and Next > buttons enable you to browse through in forward or reverse chronological order, without having to return to the Articles overview each time.

Figure 4-5. Articles tab

Images

When you click the Images tab, by default you see a screen listing only one image: the horizontal divider graphic that is included out of the box. Feel free to delete it unless you have some purpose planned for it. As your site grows, the Images listings will become more numerous, just as your Articles listings will. Figure 4-6 shows my own site's Images listing. You can probably tell that this is not a photo-driven website because of the relative sparseness with which I have chosen to use my images. I have not opted to upload or create a thumbnail, nor have I bothered to categorize them. That being said, there's nothing to stop you from treating your graphics with more care and attention.

In the Images section you can browse for images to upload, which enables you to navigate the contents of your hard drive to find what you need. You can also search the images that are already uploaded by these criteria: ID#, Name, Category, and Author. In the Tags category, if you click Textile, Textpattern, or XHTML a pop-up window appears to help you build the appropriate tag or TXP syntax to display the image. If you click any of the image names, you are taken to that image's details page (see Figure 4-7 for an example).

On this page, you can replace the image, which enables you to keep the image's ID the same so that articles that reference it do not need to be changed. You can also upload a thumbnail or have Textpattern create a thumbnail for you by specifying the width and height. If you leave the Crop checkbox unchecked, the thumbnail is scaled to fit; if you check it, the image is trimmed accordingly. In case you are bad at mental math (like me), you can enter only a width or height; the other is automagically calculated to match proportionally. You can also categorize the image, add specific alternate text that you want associated with it, or type in a caption that provides a lengthier description.

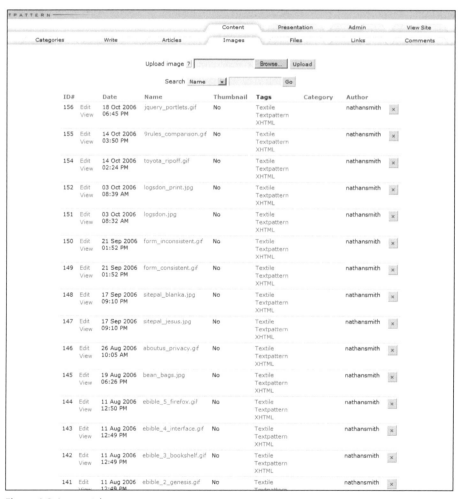

Figure 4-6. Images tab

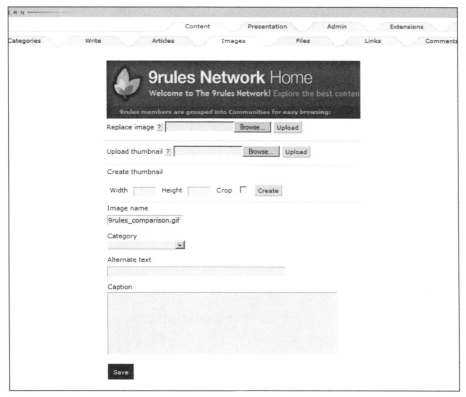

Figure 4-7. Image view/edit info

Files

The next tab over is the Files tab. Since there are no files uploaded for a default installation of Textpattern, Figure 4-8 shows my own site's Files listings. Similar to Images, you can browse your computer for files to upload and search the list of uploaded files by a variety of criteria. Unlike Images, however, your file is not renamed to a sequential number when you upload the file. Also, there are fewer options on an individual file page simply by the nature of a document or archive file versus that of a graphic (as is evident in Figure 4-9). You can categorize the file and add a brief description.

One nice thing about the Files area is that it tells you how many times each file has been downloaded if you are using the specific syntax that the Tag Builder can help you create. However, I prefer to just link directly to my files so that users can see the actual path in the status bar of their browser. Also, I use Shaun Inman's stat-tracking program Mint,[6] which includes a download counter plugin that was written by Steve Smith.[7] It enables me to view my site's traffic as well as file downloads—all from the same user-friendly interface.

---

6. www.haveamint.com
7. www.orderedlist.com/articles/pepper-download-counter

Figure 4-8. Files tab

Figure 4-9. File view/edit info

Links

In the Links section you can add links to external websites that you find interesting. You might be wondering why this section exists when you can just as easily dump links into an article. This is true, but sometimes you might find something of interest that you want to link to, but either due to laziness or lack of time do not want to write up a full article or blog post about it. This is where the Textpattern Links tab comes in handy. Some people choose to use links on the site as the default installation does: with only a few semistatic outgoing references. Others, myself included, tend to update the Links area more often than actually writing articles. The Internet is made up of linkers and thinkers, as they say—and we are all members of both categories.

I often find good articles on design or web development. Although I do not really have anything insightful to add to the article, I still want to bring it to others' attention. So, to my Links area it goes, which has two benefits. First, the links go out via RSS over their own feed, so people can subscribe to them separately from my own articles; second, it enables for easy browsing of a links archive. I find myself referring to my own Links list from time to time when I cannot remember where a helpful article is that someone else wrote.

So, similar to the rest of the subsections in the Content area, you can search links via a variety of criteria and can go back in and edit any links. You can also click the column headers to sort by ascending or descending order. When you click an individual link, you are not actually taken to a separate page, as with Files or Images; instead, the text input fields, the category drop-down menu, and the textarea with that link's information are populated, as shown in Figure 4-10. Note that the Sort Value is identical to the Title. By default, if you do not specify a Sort Value, it simply inherits from the Title field. I suppose that if you wanted to specify an output order you could number every link, but that would be ridiculously tedious. Besides, the way I display links on my site is always with the latest link posted at the top anyway, so sort order is a moot point for the way I use them.

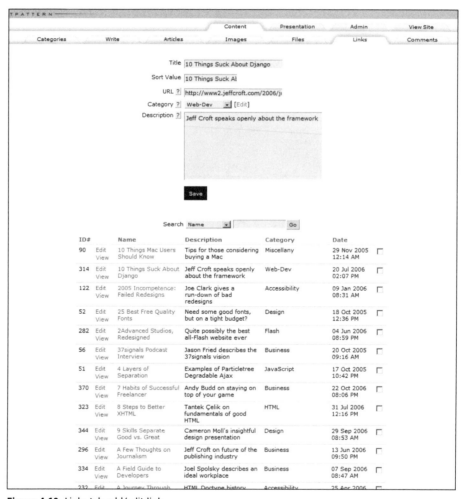

Figure 4-10. Links tab add/edit link

Comments

The last—but certainly not least—aspect of the Content interface is the Comments tab, as shown in Figure 4-11. As your blog is read more often and increases in the number of visitors, two things happen. First, you meet people who are like-minded (or at least share an interest in the topics of your writing). Second, you occasionally find people who really do not think before they speak (or type, in this case). One thing you probably will not have to worry about a whole lot is automated comment spam. The way that Textpattern is set up by default, in order for a comment to be posted, the user must first click a button labeled Preview before the Submit button even appears. This process tends to befuddle automated scripts that might otherwise bombard your site with poorly written advertisements for miscellaneous products. Customization and protection of your Comments form will be covered further in Chapter 5. For now, let us look at how the Comments admin area works.

Like everything else in Textpattern, you can search in just about any manner you choose: via: ID#, parent article, commenter's name, message contents, email address, website URL, or even IP address. The columns are fully sortable in ascending or descending order, per the typical TXP functionality. If you click the name of the parent article, you are taken to the Write tab, in which you can peruse the article to help refresh your memory about the context of the post and the ensuing conversation. If you click the ID# of the comment itself, you are taken to a page that looks like Figure 4-12, in which you can change anything you want. As a common courtesy, though, avoid the temptation of putting words into people's mouths. If they are being offensive, simply delete their comment and/or ban their IP address.

Figure 4-11. Comments tab

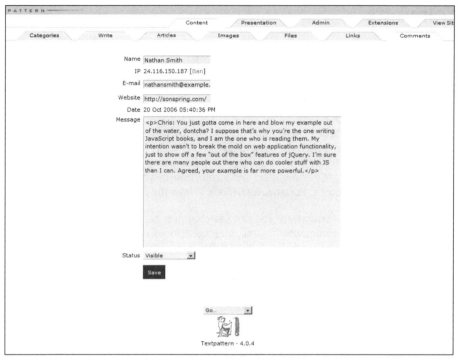

Figure 4-12. Comment view/edit

Summary

If you have fully absorbed all that was contained in this chapter, you now have everything you need in order to be a savvy and even dangerous content creator. You have learned to use Textile with precision to format your writing in ways that would astound mere mortals—but you are not a Jedi yet! You must face the third trial: the infamous Presentation area of the Textpattern interface. In the next chapter, you will learn to wield the power of TXP tags to create a lean, mean content management machine! Okay, so maybe it will not actually be so mean, but it will surely be lean and efficient because that is what Textpattern is all about.

5 PRESENTATION

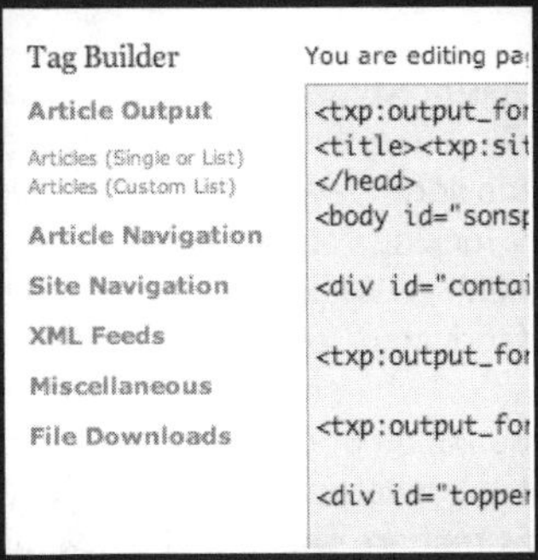

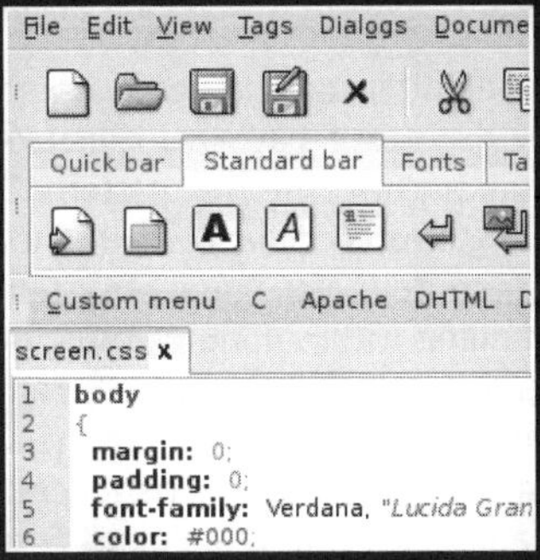

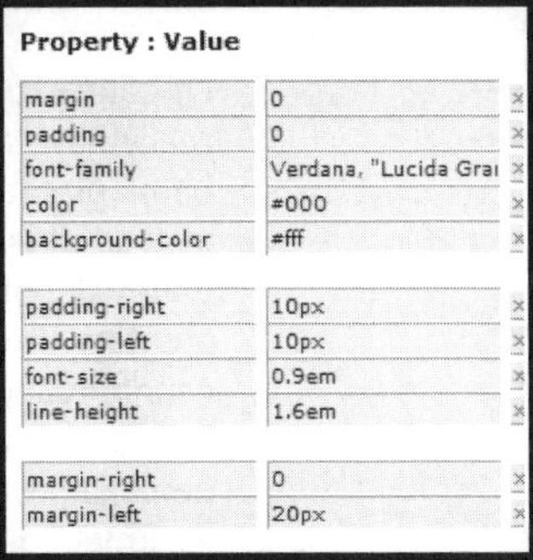

In this chapter you will really start to get into what makes Textpattern so versatile and enjoyable to use when creating websites. While the learning curve for the new syntax might seem quite steep, the close resemblance to XHTML should help to make you familiar with the process rather quickly. While the Presentation area of the Textpattern Admin interface consists of only four tabs, it is by far the most complex part of the entire system. These four portions are: Pages, Sections, Forms, and Style. I have tried to show how they are interrelated, even though they appear differently from left to right as actual tabs. Some of the terminology might be a bit misleading, so it is best to think of *pages* as *templates* and *forms* as *snippets of code*. For the sake of consistency, I will address them by what they are labeled in Textpattern, but just be aware that the term *pages* does not refer to an *.html page, nor does the term *forms* relate to the <form> element.

Overview

In Textpattern, a page is a template containing structural markup that has dynamic tags from which content flows into your site via what you have entered in the Write area of the Content tab. You can think of it as a static XHTML page with openings left for frequently updated portions to be included. If you are familiar with Apache's SSI (Server Side Includes) capability[1] or if you use raw PHP to include files,[2] you probably already have some experience in how this works. If Apache and PHP are not your cups of tea, do not head for the door just yet because we will cover the concept of includes momentarily.

Assuming that you have installed Textpattern at the root of your site and have chosen /section/title for your permanent link mode, sections can be thought of as everything after your domain name but before the title of your article. Figure 5-1 shows the typical hierarchy of Textpattern, as it appears by default after the initial setup process is completed. It consists of three page templates: default, archive, and error_default. The default page template is shared by the default and about sections, while the article section uses the archive page template. The error_default page template is interesting in that it does not actually need to have a section associated with it because it is a catch-all for errors typically caused by someone attempting to reach part of your site that does not exist. That being said, you can create a section to associate with it for testing or type in a gibberish URL to make sure it is caught properly.

Of course, the default installation of Textpattern is pretty vanilla, meaning that it does not really have any distinctive flavor to it. Personally, I like the fact that more emphasis has been placed on making the Textpattern framework developer- and designer-friendly instead of wasting efforts on needless themes or locking you into nested table–based templates like other content management systems (CMSs). While it might be fun to get a rudimentary site running within minutes using prefabricated settings, this momentary elation cannot really compare with the sense of gratification when completing an entirely custom-built site solution. Textpattern tailors to the artisan in all of us, providing a venue to create personal instead of generic user experiences. This is what makes the difference between a gourmet chef and a fast-food employee. Entrées that are cheap and quick might be good in a pinch, but when was the last time you read a restaurant review praising the Big Mac?

---

1. http://httpd.apache.org/docs/1.3/howto/ssi.html
2. www.php.net/include

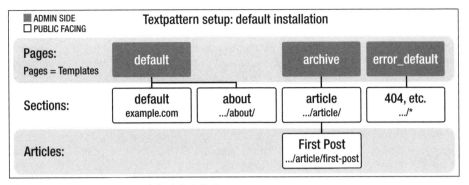

Figure 5-1. Textpattern setup: default installation

In that regard, Textpattern presupposes a bit of design skill and familiarity with CSS. With a little talent and some persistence, you can create sites that are far more complex than what Textpattern appears to be at first glance. Figure 5-2 depicts the information architecture hierarchy for the Godbit Project website, which will be covered at length in Chapter 15. For now, just peruse the diagram to get a general feel for what can be done beyond the initial setup phase. If the default installation is the tip of the iceberg, Godbit.com could be considered as being located somewhere near the waterline because Textpattern can be used to construct and manage sites with even greater depth.

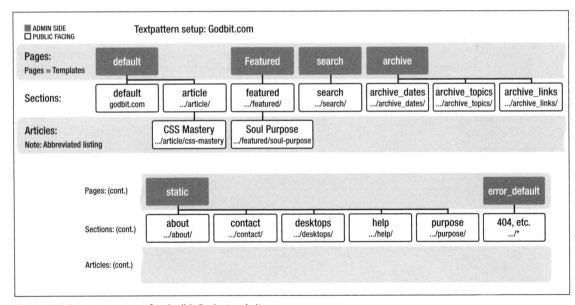

Figure 5-2. Textpattern setup for Godbit Project website

Pages

Now that we have covered some of the overarching concepts behind the structural aspects of Textpattern, it is high time we looked at the actual components that comprise this area. When you initially click the Presentation tab, the first visible subtab is Pages (see Figure 5-3). You notice that the default DOCTYPE being served is XHTML 1.0 Transitional, but you can, of course, change it to whatever you like. Personally, I prefer XHTML 1.0 Strict because it encourages further separation of content and presentation by doing away with attributes such as align.[3] Additionally, it is the highest document type that can be effectively served as content-type="text/html"; whereas XHTML 1.1 is supposed to be served as application/xhtml+xml, which unfortunately cannot be interpreted correctly by the decrepit Internet Explorer (IE) 6 or the new IE 7. Since these two browsers comprise a large market share, it is my recommendation that people use XHTML 1.0 Strict.[4] Additionally, some JavaScript compatibility issues can arise when serving a document as application/xhtml+xml, so it is best to stick to the text/html MIME type.

> *Please be aware that although HTML 4.01 Strict is preferred by some web development code experts such as Roger Johansson[5] and Robert Nyman,[6] Textpattern outputs XHTML by default. It does so for tags that are self-closing (also called self-terminating) in XHTML, but are not in HTML. Such tags include image <img /> and break <br />, which occur regularly in your articles if you use Textile for formatting, not to mention that the actual TXP syntax such as <txp:article /> resembles XHTML. It is therefore best that you stick with either XHTML 1.0 Transitional or move up to XHTML 1.0 Strict.*

Oddly enough, in the Pages area there is not a way to simply create a new, blank template. Instead, you have to use the text field toward the bottom labeled ...or, copy page as, which enables you to create a new page template and edit it further from there. With that peculiar snafu aside, the rest of the interface is pretty intuitive and easy to learn.

---

3. www.24ways.org/advent/transitional-vs-strict-markup
4. www.sonspring.com/journal/xhtml-10-rollback
5. www.456bereastreet.com/archive/200512/beginners_should_start_with_html_not_xhtml
6. www.robertnyman.com/2005/11/02/html-or-xhtml

Figure 5-3. Pages/template area

Tag Builder

Down the left side of the Pages area you see a series of links, each of which expands to reveal a set of helpful tools that can help you build the necessary <txp:... /> tags to power your site. The main categories of tags include Article Output, Article Navigation, Site Navigation, XML Feeds, Miscellaneous, and File Downloads. As you build your site, the tags that you probably will use most frequently are those that control Article Output, as well as miscellaneous tags such as Page Title, CSS Link, and Output Form. There are also a slew of other tags that are not included in the cheat sheet, but their usage will be covered in later chapters and in the comprehensive tag manual at the end of this book. For now, you can get started by learning the essentials and then build from there. When you click any of the Tag Builder links, a pop-up window appears that resembles the one depicted in Figure 5-4. It is recommended that you use Tag Builder to start out, but gradually learn to write TXP tags by hand because it will save you time in the long run as well as keep you from adding unnecessary attributes via the wizard approach.

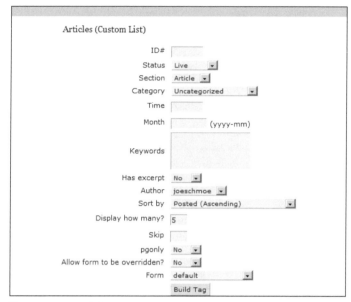

Figure 5-4. Tag Builder pop-up window

Article Output

Articles (Single or List)—<txp:article />: For this tag, there are a variety of options from which you can choose, all of which are not necessary depending on what you are trying to do. I will just run down the list of choices as they appear in the Tag Builder pop-up window.

- **Status**: This field can be Live, Sticky, Pending, Draft, or Hidden. These choices correspond to the top-right fieldset when you have clicked the Write tab. When creating a new article or editing an older one, you can set these options. Likewise, the Tag Builder pop-up window helps you construct a TXP article tag that outputs only these specific types. If you do not specify any restrictions, it displays articles of live status.

- **Time**: This field accepts three values: Past, Future, or All. Past is the default, which causes articles to appear as they are posted, keeping future articles from appearing at all until their specified dates arrive. If you enter Future for this setting, only articles with dates in the future will be visible, whereas all past articles will not be displayed. This could be good for instances in which you are using Textpattern in an event planning setting, in which past events are no longer relevant. If you choose All, both past and future articles will be visible. There is no setting for *Present* because the instant you post an article, from a logical standpoint it is considered to be in the Past. The present, as far as a computer is concerned, is literally only the current moment in time, which is always passing by. Heavy philosophy, huh?

128

- **Search all sections**: This attribute, which can be either Yes or No, is used only when the TXP article tag is being used for search results. If you do not enter anything for this attribute, the search results default to the settings specified in the Sections tab of the Admin interface. For the most part, you probably want to handle it from there, but this attribute enables you to override the global setting in specific instances.

- **Search sticky article**s: Much like the previous attribute, this option enables you to specify whether or not articles that have been deemed sticky are included in search results. The default is No and there is no way to set this globally. You probably will not want to usually include sticky articles in your search results because they are meant to have a place of more permanence and prominence on your site (for instance, a company announcement that needs to stay on the front page for an indefinite amount of time).

> *Sticky articles are simply articles that have a more permanent place on a page. They stick in place, unaffected by other articles being added; hence the term **sticky**.*

5

- **Display how many?** This attribute does exactly what it says. If you want a listing of 5 articles, type 5 in the text field. If you want only a single article, just type 1. If you do not specify anything at all, the default of 10 articles will display.

- **Skip**: This option corresponds to the offset attribute, and I have suggested that it be changed to reflect that. At the time of this writing, though, Skip is how it is worded. Anyway, it enables you to specify the number of articles that will not appear. If you are attempting to build a listing of article titles, but have 2 full articles shown on the same page and do not want to be redundant, you might enter 2 in this field. Doing so would build a list, but skip/offset the latest two articles by the number you have specified.

- **Page by**: This option is used in conjunction with the <txp:older>...</txp:older> and <txp:newer>...</txp:newer> tags. These tags navigate through pages containing a listing of articles, and the pageby attribute of the <txp:article /> tag tells Textpattern how many articles to skip with each click of Older and Newer. More on this topic will be covered in Chapter 15.

- **Sort by**: This attribute can accept a number of values in either ascending or descending order: Title, Date posted, Last modification, Section, Category 1, or Category 2. It can also sort via random criteria, which will force the list to be regenerated each time the page loads.

- **pgonly**: Setting this attribute causes a counter to be incremented on the server side, but never displayed in the actual XHTML. It is useful for situations in which you want to use the pageby attribute because it enables Textpattern to keep track of which sequence in a series of articles is currently being displayed. Thus, it knows how far to jump forward or backward, based on the user's navigational choice. It is recommended that unless you are actually making use of it, you should leave the attribute out entirely.

- **Allow form to be overridden?** This attribute defaults to Yes and can safely be left out unless you specifically want to restrict an article from being overridden. It can be controlled on a global basis via the Advanced portion of the Preferences area. Likewise, it can be done on a per-article basis from the Write interface. Note that previously overridden articles will remain as is, regardless of whether you disallow future instances.

- **Form**: This is an attribute you will be using quite frequently to control the form/snippet via which the article info will be formatted. For instance, you might want to have the full body of the article displayed in some instances, yet show only a listing of headlines in others. By using this selection, you can create different <txp:article /> tags for each specific need.

- **List form**: This tag is meant for outputting a list of articles when you are not on an individual article's page (it takes effect when you are on a /section/ of the site).

Articles (Custom List)—<txp:article_custom />: This tag is similar to the typical article tag, but in my opinion is far more versatile and powerful. While you can output articles only from the current section with the other tag, with article_custom you can pull in articles as lists or in their entirety from completely different sections. Therefore, this tag makes up the backbone of a multisectional news or community site. Following are options you can use in the Tag Builder pop-up window, although all of them need not be used.

- **ID#**: This option enables you to build a custom article that outputs only a specific article, which is beneficial if you want the benefits of Textile formatting on an otherwise static part of your site. You can then go back in, edit this same article, and treat it as an actual HTML file instead of a dynamic portion of a blog that gets replaced when new articles are written. You can see the unique ID of each article in the left column of the Articles portion of the Content area.

- **Status**, **Section**, **Category**, **Time**, **Sort by**, **Display how many?**, **Skip**, **pgonly**, **Allow form to be overridden?**, and **Form** all work exactly the same as they do for the <txp:article /> tag, so I will not repeat their purposes here. Refer to the previous discussion for information.

- **Month**: This aspect works much like the Time aspect. You simply type in the year and month in a four-digit and two-digit format, respectively. A list of articles from that particular month is then output, which comes in handy for constructing hand-coded archive functionality.

- **Keywords**: This option enables you to use the Keywords portion of the Write interface of the Content area to group articles that have similar properties or characteristics. For instance, if you want to output all articles with the keyword of important, you can do so. Likewise, you can also specify multiple keywords, separated by commas.

- **Has excerpt**: This option can be used to display only articles that have an excerpt saved. Those without are not shown. The default is No and it can safely be omitted unless this functionality is specifically required for your particular needs.

- **Author**: This attribute enables you to output an article or list of articles by a particular author. This is helpful if you are setting up individual profile pages for each site author and want to provide a list of recent works by each person alongside basic biographical information.

Article Navigation

Previous Article Title—`<txp:prev_title />`: This option simply outputs the title of the previous article if one exists.

Next Article Title—`<txp:next_title />`: This option outputs the title of the next article if one exists.

Previous Article Link—`<txp:link_to_prev>...</txp:link_to_prev>`: This tag creates a link to the previous article, if one exists. It can accept one attribute, showalways="y", which causes it to remain on the screen as plain text, even if no previous article exists.

Next Article Link—`<txp:link_to_next>...</txp:link_to_next>`: This tag creates a link to the next article if one exists. It can accept one attribute, showalways="y", which causes it to remain on the screen as plain text even if no previous article exists.

Older Articles Link—`<txp:older>...</txp:older>`: This link paginates in reverse chronological order through a listing of articles and skips in increments set via the pageby attribute of the `<txp:article />` tag. It can accept one attribute, showalways, which keeps the text present on the screen even when there are no older articles.

Newer Articles Link—`<txp:newer>...</txp:newer>`: This link paginates in forward chronological order through a listing of articles and skips in increments set via the pageby attribute of the `<txp:article />` tag. It can accept one attribute, showalways, which keeps the text present on the screen, even when there are no newer articles.

Site Navigation

Homepage Link—`<txp:link_to_home />`: This tag creates a link back to the home directory of your Textpattern installation. It can take one attribute of class, which is converted to the equivalent XHTML attribute and value. Assuming that you installed it at the root of your domain, it takes you back to www.example.com. If you are developing your site in a temporary location, it behooves you to use `<txp:link_to_home />` to avoid future conflicts when you change URLs.

Section List—`<txp:section_list />`: This tag can take a variety of attributes and is used to create navigation for your site based on the sections that are available. Like the Homepage Link tag, I tend not to make use of this tag, but I list it here in case you find a need for it. Here are the possible attributes and their values:

- **Include default section**: This attribute enables you to either include or exclude the default section from your list. Sometimes you might not want a link to home to appear among the other links because you might want to put it elsewhere, such as on your site's logo.

- **Text to use for default section link**: Assuming that you do include the default section, this is the text used for that link. The default section is peculiar in that you do not have control over what it is named, as you do with all other sections. So instead of having a link labeled default, it enables you to put something more appropriate, such as home.

Sections: This attribute accepts a comma-separated list of sections that you want to be displayed. If it is left blank, all sections display. This attribute is of higher importance than Exclude, so if you specify anything here, leave that one blank.

- **Exclude**: If (and only if) you left Sections blank, enter the sections that you do not want to appear here. If it is blank, no sections are excluded and all are visible.

- **Label**: This tag is unnecessary, but if you enter a value, it serves as the first item in the list. If you specify a wrap tag of ol or ul, the label appears as the first list item.

- **Label tag**: If specified, the label can have a unique wrap tag. For instance, you might want to have a definition list <dl> as your wrap tag, in which the label for the entire listing is a <dt>, but the sections are contained within <dd>. If left blank, the label simply inherits the break tag specified for the entire list.

- **Wraptag**: If entered, this value specifies the container for the list. If you want an unordered list, simply type ul; likewise, if you want an ordered list, type ol. Note that you do not need to specify a closing tag because Textpattern handles it for you. Also, be aware that if you choose either of those two for wraptag, your List break tag is automatically li. You can just as easily use div or some other block level element if you so desire.

- **CSS class**: This is the class name applied to the wraptag element. If you do not specify a class, the default is class="section_list".

- **CSS class for active list item**: This is the class attribute and value associated with the section that a visitor is currently on. For instance, if a visitor is browsing your archive section, and you have specified active for this attribute, the tag and class value might look like this: <li class="active"><a href="/archive/">archive </a></li>.

- **List break tag**: Typically used in conjunction with wraptag, break places the tag of your choice around each section name. When using ordered or unordered lists, the break tag does not need to be specified because it is automatically li. If you are not using a dependent pairing such as that one, br can be used. Textpattern is intuitive enough to know that <br /> is a self-closing tag.

Category List—<txp:category_list />: Like Section List, this tag can accept a number of different attributes, so I do not repeat the ones that are shared between the two, such as wraptag or break. Note that if no class is specified, the default is class="category_list". Here are attributes unique to Category List:

- **Type**: This attribute accepts one of four possible values because Categories apply to multiple aspects of your content: article, links, image, or file.

- **Parent**: This attribute enables you to specify the parent category, if one exists, for the listing of categories you want to output.

- **Categories**: Much like the way Sections work in the Sections List tag, this attribute enables you to specify which categories are displayed and takes a higher precedence than Exclude.

- **Section**: This attribute enables you to specify which section the category listing will be restricted to. It can coexist with the Categories attribute and displays the categories you choose.
  - **Link to specific section**: If this attribute is set to Yes, the links for all categories are applicable only to the currently active section. If you enable it, do not specify a Section because it will be overridden and apply only to the current one, anyway.

Popup List—`<txp:popup />`: This tag is not really titled correctly because it just creates a drop-down `<select>...</select>` list of `<option>...</option>`, which are essentially being used as links to the various categories or sections within your site. Due to accessibility reasons, and because this is not really a proper use of a drop-down element, it is not recommended that you use it. All other attributes, such as `label` and `wraptag`, work the same way as previously mentioned TXP tags.

Recent Articles—`<txp:recent_articles />`: This tag outputs a listing of recently written articles or it can be used to generate a listing of posts that range from older to newer. It accepts all the criteria that were covered already, so simply refer to them. The same functionality can be achieved by using `<txp:article_custom>`, so it is a matter of preference if you actually use this tag.

Recent Comments—`<txp:recent_comments />`: Unlike its counterpart pertaining to articles, this tag is actually essential to display a list of comments that have been made on your site. It outputs a link with the name of the person, followed by the article on which they commented: John Doe (Article Name). The attributes that the tag accepts have been covered already.

Related Articles—`<txp:related_articles />`: This tag outputs a list of related articles, based on the criteria of your choosing. It can accept a myriad of attribute choices, all of which should be quite familiar to you by now. The one unique aspect is that it enables you to choose how they are related: by Category 1, Category 2, or both.

Search Input Form—`<txp:search_input />`: This tag outputs a search form that scours your site for the relevant search term. It is not incredibly robust, but is quite good at finding text strings, regardless of their surroundings. For instance, a search for dog returns both dog and dogmatic. If you do not specify a section, it defaults to what you chose in the Sections tab, depending on which ones you have opted to be searchable. You can also choose what text will appear on the button, as well as the width of the search field (Input size). The rest of the attributes are pretty standard.

XML Feeds

Articles Feed Link—`<txp:feed_link />`: This tag outputs an XML feed in either an RSS 2.0 or Atom 1.0 format. Of course, there's nothing keeping you from constructing two different feeds and providing links to both. You can also specify whether it is an in-body feed or one called from the `<head>...</head>` of the document in the format drop-down menu. The `<a href...` refers to a feed you would make as a normal clickable link; and the `<link rel...` choice is the type that should be added in the head.

Links Feed Link—<txp:link_feed_link />: This tag enables you to provide either an RSS 2.0– or Atom 1.0–formatted XML feed for entries to your Links via the Content portion of the Textpattern Admin area, which enables people to subscribe to your articles and links separately. Of course, if you want them in the same feed, you can use a /section/ of your site specifically for outgoing links and have that merged with your normal XML because they would both essentially be articles, albeit used in different ways.

Miscellaneous

Page Title—<txp:page_title />: This tag outputs the name of the site, coupled with the title of the article, which can be separated by whatever you choose. If you want to add a vertical bar to format your page title like Site Name | Title of Article, you need to enter | for the separator, which ensures that the necessary whitespace appears after the site name and before the article title.

CSS Link (Head)—<txp:css />: This tag simply outputs a reference to an external CSS file. Like the XML feeds, there can be one of two formats, <link rel... or css.php..., which are both for use within the <head>...</head> of a document. If you use the link method, it outputs the full reference to the file. Though css.php accepts multiple attributes, the only one it actually uses is Name. If you use the css.php format, it outputs only the raw URL for the CSS file, but does not actually use it to affect presentation. You can use this format if you need to import multiple CSS files from a single style tag, like so:

```
<style type="text/css" media="all">
@import "<txp:css format="url" n="default">";
@import "<txp:css format="url" n="company">";
@import "<txp:css format="url" n="products">";
@import "<txp:css format="url" n="contact">";
</style>
```

Code such as this yields the following:

```
<style type="text/css" media="all">
@import "http://example.com/textpattern/css.php?n=default";
@import "http://example.com/textpattern/css.php?n=company";
@import "http://example.com/textpattern/css.php?n=products";
@import "http://example.com/textpattern/css.php?n=contact";
</style>
```

Site Name—<txp:sitename />: This tag outputs the string of text that is stored in the Site name text input field in the Preferences portion of the Admin area.

Site Slogan—<txp:site_slogan />: This tag outputs the string of text that is stored in the Site slogan text input field in the Preferences portion of the Admin area.

Breadcrumb—<txp:breadcrumb />: This tag outputs a series of indicators pertaining to a page's location in the site hierarchy. (It might look like this: Home ➤ Section ➤ Article.) The tag accepts several attributes. The separator works much as it does in <txp:page_title />—by adding a visual break between words in the breadcrumb. Link breadcrumbs enables you to specify whether the words contain links or are plain text. You can also add a CSS class for links as well as the containing wrap tag via CSS class. If no wrap tag is specified, the default is a paragraph: <p>...</p>. If label is left blank, the site's name is used instead. The title attribute controls whether sections are displayed by their raw titles or whether their names are used instead (either y or n).

E-mail Link (Spam-Proof)—<txp:email />: This tag does just what it says: it produces a "spam-proof" email link on your site that will (hopefully) protect you from email spam, or at least the automated type. It should be fairly self-explanatory. Link text refers to the text within the opening and closing anchor tags. Link tooltip refers to the title attribute, which is given to the link itself. Supposing that the email address you wanted to encode is john.doe@example.com, the following would be the corresponding TXP and XHTML code. As you can see, it is impossible to discern the contents of the original address, though it appears as a mailto: link on the page.

Textpattern code:

```
<txp:email email="john.doe@example.com" linktext=➡
"Email - John Doe" title="Click to Email!" />
```

Encoded XHTML:

```
<a
href="&#109;&#97;&#105;&#108;&#116;&#111;&#58;&#106;&#111;&#104;&#11➡
0;&#46;&#100;&#111;&#101;&#64;&#101;&#120;&#97;&#109;&#112;&#108;&#101;➡
&#46;&#99;&#111;&#109;" title="Click to Email!">Email - John Doe</a>
```

Links List—<txp:linklist />: This tag outputs one or many links that you have entered in the Links area of the Content tab of Textpattern. You should already be familiar with all the attributes and their input fields.

Password Protection—<txp:password_protect />: This tag creates a prompt for a username and password for the page template on which it is used. If users do not enter the correct password, they are taken to your error_default page template. Note that you can also create a template named error_403, which handles all errors that occur due to HTTP Error 403 Forbidden"—a result of a failed user/password/login attempt.

Output Form—<txp:output_form />: This tag is one of the staple ingredients of building a Textpattern site. It can be used to output any form (snippet) of code that you have created. It is incredibly simple, taking only one attribute: the name of the form to be produced. Typically, it is used to output forms that are of the misc (miscellaneous) type in the Forms portion of the Presentation area, although it can be used for just about anything.

Language—<txp:lang />: This single tag requires no attributes. It is simply meant to be used within the <head>...</head> of a document, like so:

```
<html xmlns="http://www.w3.org/1999/xhtml" xml:lang="<txp:lang />"➡
 lang="<txp:lang />">
```

On a site that uses English of the United States variety, such as www.w3.org, it looks like this:

```
<html xmlns="http://www.w3.org/1999/xhtml" xml:lang="en-us" lang=➡
"en-us">
```

File downloads

File Download List—`<txp:file_download_list />`: This tag builds a list of file downloads, based on criteria that you specify. You are no doubt familiar with all these attribute choices already. The files that it pertains to are uploaded via the Files portion of the Content area in the Textpattern Admin interface.

File Download—`<txp:file_download />`: This tag builds the link for a single file download, based on criteria that you specify. If no form is specified, it defaults to the files form. In some instances, it might not be the format you would prefer, which is why there is the next option.

File Download Link—`<txp:file_download_link><txp:file_download_name />`</txp:file_download_link>: This tag enables for greater control in formatting the text/code around the File Download link. You are no doubt familiar with all these attribute choices already. As far as I can tell, neither the Name nor Description inputs for this Tag Builder actually have any bearing on the output. Aside from that, it is pretty straightforward.

All Pages

The column on the far right side of the Pages area has a listing of all page templates. By clicking the name of any of them, you can edit the contents. Likewise, by clicking the x on the right of each one, you will be presented with the option to delete it—a confirmation box appears, asking Really Delete? Clicking OK deletes the section, whereas clicking Cancel leaves things unchanged.

Sections

Now that you know how to construct page templates, it is time to create some site sections to associate with said templates. When you click the Sections tab, you will see a screen that looks like Figure 5-5. You will notice that the Default section does not contain as many options as the subsequent sections, mainly because it is the very first page that is loaded when people type in your domain name. As such, you cannot delete or change the Default, aside from specifying between Uses page and Uses style.

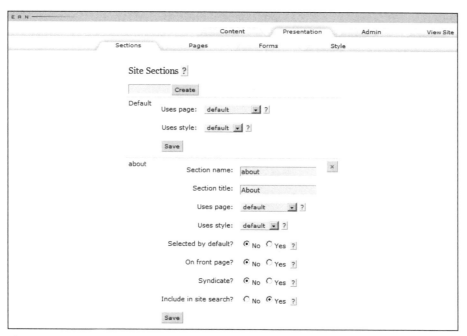

Figure 5-5. Site Sections area

For the rest of the sections, however, you can tweak quite a few things. After creating a section (or with an existing section), you can change the name/title and specify which page/style each one uses. There are also a series of choices possible via radio buttons: Selected by default?, On front page?, Syndicate?, and Include in site search?. Selected by default? can be Yes for only one section because it pertains to which section is selected in the Write portion of the Content area. On front page? refers to whether articles in this section will be listed in a listing produced by the <txp:article /> tag on the index page or whether these articles will appear only when the user is on the corresponding /section/ of the website. Syndicate? controls whether an Atom or RSS feed is produced for new articles posted to this section. Include in site search? controls whether a section is used in search results.

Forms

In the Forms area (which might be more appropriately named *Code Snippets*), you build all chunks of code that control the dynamic aspects of your site. When you click the Forms tab, you see a screen that looks like Figure 5-6. The column on the right side of the page is a listing of all the available forms, both the defaults and those that have been user-created. Unlike the Pages area, multiple Forms can be deleted by checking the corresponding checkbox, choosing Delete from the drop-down menu, and then pressing Go.

Figure 5-6. Forms/snippets area

Tag Builder

You see the familiar Tag Builder links on the left side of the page, which are divided into the following tag types: Articles, Links, Comments, Comment Details, Comment Form, Search Results, and File Downloads. As was mentioned in the previous description of the Tag Builder, this is not a comprehensive list of Textpattern tags; they are simply some of the most commonly used tags. (For a full listing, refer to the tag reference appendix in the back of this book.) For now, we will look at the tags that are listed and briefly cover how to use them. Since most of the attributes are similar to those in the Tag Builder for Pages, I will not repeat them here.

Articles

Permanent Link—`<txp:permlink>...</txp:permlink>`: This is the typical format for a permanent link, with `<txp:title />` as the text inside the link. However, I do not recommend using this format because it places the title attribute and value `title="Permanent link to this article"` on every single link. This is bad for several reasons. First, in terms of accessibility, a person using screen reading software will have this phrase spoken repeatedly to them if they have the title attribute enabled. Second, it creates a needless tooltip in nearly every browser when the user hovers the mouse over a link. Third, the popular blog ranking and search engine site Technorati gets tripped up on title attributes, saving them as the title of your posts instead of the text within the link. Therefore, I recommend the following format instead (using permlink as a self-closing tag):

```
<a href="<txp:permlink />"><txp:title /></a>
```

This outputs the following XHTML:

```
<a href="http://example.com/section/title-of-article">➥
Title of Article</a>.
```

> *The* Permanent Link *tag also allows for an inline style attribute to be assigned. It is recommended that you not use it because inline styles are the modern-day equivalent of using the antiquated* <font>...</font> *tag, mixing presentation with content. If you are not sure what this means, just trust me—do not use inline styles with the* permlink *tag or in any other XHTML element.*

Posted—<txp:posted />: This tag outputs the date on which an article was created. You probably do not need to add any attributes because the defaults simply inherit from the settings in the Preferences portion of the Admin area. If you need to override it, you can do so by entering a Time format string such as: %b %d, %Y, which would result in something similar to May 10, 2007. Likewise, by entering a Locale, it corresponds to the language to be used. Unless you have a specific reason to change this, it will default to the Preferences portion of the Admin area.

Title—<txp:title />: This tag simply outputs the title of the article, based on what you entered in the Write portion of the Content area.

Body—<txp:body />: This tag displays everything within the large text area that you wrote in the Write portion of the Content area.

Excerpt—<txp:excerpt />: This tag displays everything within the large text area that you wrote in the Write portion of the Content area. Note that the two are not necessarily mutually exclusive. If you have need for two separate chunks of content, it is possible to mix the <txp:excerpt /> and <txp:body /> tags together on the same article page. Depending on how you have the Atom/RSS syndicated, it might not be the best idea.

Section—<txp:section />: This tag simply outputs the name of the current section. If you choose Yes for Link to a list of other articles in this section?, it simply makes the word a link that goes to www.example.com/section. If not, the word is plain text.

Category 1—<txp:category1 />: This tag creates a list of links to articles that share the same first category. For instance, if you had a category named Travels, it would present you with all articles that have Travels set as Category 1, but would exclude those that have Travels set as Category 2.

Category 2—<txp:category2 />: This tag creates a list of links to articles that share the same second category. For instance, if you had a category named Fishing, it would present you with all articles that have Travels set as Category 2, but would exclude those that have Fishing set as Category 1.

Article Image—`<txp:article_image />`: This tag presents the article image that has been specified in the Article image text field under Advanced Options in the Write portion of the Content area. Escape refers to whether (X)HTML characters are escaped in the `title="..."` and `alt="..."` attributes, such as <, >, &, and so on. You can also assign a specific ID, which is helpful to provide an anchor link to the image for reference. Additionally, you can specify a CSS class. It is recommended that you do not use inline style or alignment; instead, set these stylistic changes by using the hook(s) of ID, class, or descendent selectors from the parent element.

Comments Invite—`<txp:comments_invite />`: This tag presents the user with an invitation to comment on the article, based on the phrase specified in the Preferences portion of the Admin area, unless it has been overridden on a per-article basis in the Write portion of the Content area. By default, it also shows the number of comments that have been made, although it can be disabled via the Tag Builder. You can also choose Text only to output only the invite phrase and the number of comments. This is useful if you merely want to provide it for informational purposes or if you want to wrap your own hand-coded link instead of using the default.

Author—`<txp:author />`: This tag enables you to output the "real name" of the author, as specified in the Users portion of the Admin area. You can make it into a link to other articles by the same author by entering either 1 for Yes or 0 for No. You can restrict the listing to a particular section, but if you do not it applies to all sections for which the author has written articles. If you do not specify a single section, you can choose whether the list of articles pertain to the section the user is currently viewing. This can help avoid redundancy.

Links

Link—`<txp:link />`: This tag outputs a link with default formatting. You specify one addition, the `rel="..."` attribute, which is meant to show relationship. This is not a commonly used attribute, but one that is used for the XFN. The XHTML Friends Network was pioneered by the Global Multimedia Protocols Group in an effort to help links be more semantic in showing the relationship between linkers. More information can be found at the XFN website.[7]

Link, title=Description—`<txp:linkdesctitle />`: This tag does nearly the same thing as `<txp:link />`, except it uses the description provided with the link in the `title="..."` attribute.

Link Name—`<txp:link_name />`: This tag provides only the name of the link and gives the option to escape (X)HTML code, which is helpful for situations in which you wanted to show the name of the link, but not necessarily make it the clickable text. For instance, you might want to have the URL be the link, but have the name be nearby as plain text to add further information.

Link Description—`<txp:link_description />`: Similar to the Link Name tag, this tag outputs only the text stored in the link description. It accepts a variety of attributes, which should be old hat for you at this point.

---

7. www.gmpg.org/xfn/

Link Category—`<txp:link_category />`: This tag outputs the category of the link as plain text. It accepts some fairly typical attributes.

Link Date—`<txp:link_date />`: This tag outputs the date when the link was posted and defaults to what was chosen in the Preferences portion of the Admin area, unless specifically overridden.

Comments

Comments—`<txp:comments />`: This tag outputs a list of comments according to the criteria specified.

Comments Form—`<txp:comments_form />`: This tag enables you to specify some aspects of the comment form. Aside from the already thoroughly covered attributes, you can specify the following: Input size, Message textarea columns, and Message textarea rows. Input size and Message textarea columns both refer roughly to the width of the text input fields and textarea, whereas Message textarea rows pertains to how tall the textarea will be. You could size things this way, but I recommend leaving them as the default and instead target dimensions via CSS.

Comments Preview—`<txp:comments_preview />`: This tag enables you to place a Comments Preview area at a specific location in your template. It is helpful to use this tag and also provide a blurb informing users that they are looking at only a preview of their comment, lest they think it is the real thing (and never hit Submit).

Comment Details

Comment Permanent Link—`<txp:comment_permlink>...</txp:comment_permlink>`: This tag is meant to be wrapped around the text of your choosing, so that if users want to link directly to that comment's anchor, they can do so. It assigns each comment a unique ID in the link, so that it can be easily referenced from external sources. The default is a pound sign (#), but via the `ajw_comment_num` plugin you can output the actual number of that comment within the article, which makes it a little more descriptive.

Comment Name—`<txp:comment_name />`: This tag outputs the name of the person leaving the comment. You can also disable the link to the person's website by choosing No to Link to commenter's email address/website?. I recommend that you leave it set to Yes (or just use the tag without `link="..."` at all because it defaults to Yes). You should, of course, disable the email portion of this under the Advanced Preferences portion of the Admin area by choosing Yes for the choice labeled Never display e-mail address?.

Comment E-mail—`<txp:comment_email />`: Unless you want people to absolutely hate you and/or never leave comments on your site, then—for the love of all that is good—please do not use this TXP tag! It is basically like calling open season for all spammers to bombard your poor visitors with junk mail. It potentially overrides the setting specified in the Advanced Preferences portion of the Admin area, so just leave it alone.

Comment Website—`<txp:comment_web />`: This tag outputs the URL to commenters' websites. Assuming that you have the `<txp:comment_name />` also producing a link to their sites, you probably won't need to use this tag unless you want it to be specifically readable. If so, go right ahead.

5

Comment Time—<txp:comment_time />: This tag outputs the date on which the comment was posted using the time format specified in the Preferences portion of the Admin area. You can override it if you want by setting specific attributes, but it makes more sense to just set it once: "Fixodent and forget it."[8]

Comment Message—<txp:comment_message />: This tag works much like the <txp:body /> tag does—by simply outputting the contents of the person's comment. Textile, of course, strips out potentially harmful tags before saving them to the database as raw XHTML.

Comment form

Comment Name Input—<txp:comment_name_input />: This tag generates the input text field for where users can enter their names. For accessibility purposes, it is also recommended that you include the necessary <label> tag to ensure that people using assistive technologies such as screen readers can properly use your comment form. The same goes for the E-mail, Web, and Message fields as well. Here is an example of what part of an accessible comment form might look like in XHTML code:

```
<p>
  <label for="comment_name_input">Name</label>
  <br />
  <txp:comment_name_input />
</p>
<p>
  <label for="comment_email_input">Email</label>
  <br />
  <txp:comment_email_input />
</p>
<p>
  <label for="comment_web_input">Website</label>
  <br />
  <txp:comment_web_input />
</p>
<p>
  <label for="message">Message</label>
  <br />
  <txp:comment_message_input />
</p>
```

Comment E-mail Input—<txp:comment_email_input />: See Comment Name Input.

Web Input—<txp:comment_web_input />: See Comment Name Input.

Comment Message Input—<txp:comment_message_input />: See Comment Name Input.

---

8. Obscure reference to a pointless advertisement for denture adhesive.

Remember Details Checkbox—`<txp:comment_remember />`: This tag creates a checkbox that either writes or deletes a cookie enabling your website to identify repeat visitors. The cookie is given to the users' browsers when they leave a comment, so when they return they need not reenter all their information.

Comment Preview Button—`<txp:comment_preview />`: This is the only button that is visible initially when users enter their comments. After pressing it, a preview of their comment is produced on the screen, and only then does the actual Submit button appear. The reason for this is twofold. First, it enables users to look over their potential contribution to the discussion, affording the opportunity for proofreading. Second, it cuts down on automated comment spam, in which people write scripts to brute-force unwanted comments, which usually contain junk advertisements, or links to sites in an attempt to boost search engine page rankings.

Comment Submit Button—`<txp:comment_submit />`: This button does just what it says: it submits the comment to the database. The comment then appears on the site or is held in queue until you have a chance to moderate and approve the comment—at which point it then appears on the site.

Search results

Search Result Title—`<txp:search_result_title />`: This tag outputs the name of the article that is found via a search of your site. In terms of functionality, it is identical to `<txp:title />`.

Search Result Excerpt—`<txp:search_result_excerpt />`: Unlike the other search_result_ tags, this one is actually necessary. It is generated dynamically because the concentration of the relevant search terms is rendered on the fly and presented on the Search Results page. So, place this tag where you want the snippet of contextual information to be displayed for each search result.

Search Result Date—`<txp:search_result_date />`: This tags works the same way as the `<txp:posted />` tag: it outputs the date format specified in the Preferences portion of the Admin area.

Search Result URL—`<txp:search_result_url />`: This tag is equivalent to `<txp:permlink />` when used in a self-closing fashion. It outputs the full URL of the article that contains the corresponding search result.

File downloads

File Download Link—`<txp:file_download_link>...</txp:file_download_link>`: This tag works exactly as it does in the Tag Builder for Sections.

File Name—`<txp:file_download_name />`: This tag works just as it does in Sections, outputting the name of the file that was given when the file was uploaded via Textpattern's Files interface.

File Description—`<txp:file_download_description />`: This tag outputs the description that was given in the Files interface. It accepts some normal criteria and can be set to strip out XHTML code before rendering. Additionally, you can specify a wrap tag. If none is provided, it defaults to plain text with no wrapper.

143

File Category—`<txp:file_download_category />`: This tag outputs the category that was given in the Files interface. It accepts some normal criteria and can be set to strip out XHTML code before rendering. Additionally, you can specify a wrap tag. If none is provided, it defaults to plain text with no wrapper.

File Created Time—`<txp:file_download_created />`: This tag outputs the timestamp for the date/time when the file was created, according to the format you specify. If none is given, it defaults to the settings from the Preferences portion of the Admin area. (See the tag reference appendix for more advanced date formatting options.)

File Modified Time—`<txp:file_download_modified />`: This tag outputs the timestamp for the date/time when the file was last modified, according to the format you specify. If none is given, it defaults to the settings from the Preferences area of the Admin tab.

File Size—`<txp:file_download_size />`: This tag outputs the size of the file according to the applicable measurement that you choose, such as kilobytes (KB) or megabytes (MB). You can also specify how many digits after the decimal point are deemed significant figures. If neither of these criteria is set, it defaults to KB and two digits after the decimal point.

File Download Count—`<txp:file_download_downloads />`: This tag needs no attributes and simply outputs the number of times each file has been downloaded, assuming that you use the TXP tags/XHTML syntax and do not link directly to the file itself. I must admit that I do not use Textpattern to track my download count; instead, I opt for third-party stat tracking via Mint. It is really just a matter of preference.

Style

Now that we have covered some of the basics behind the TXP tag syntax, it is time to take a brief look at how the style management is handled in Textpattern. This portion of the chapter is not an in-depth look at the language or syntax of CSS; instead it covers how CSS is handled in Textpattern. There are basically two ways to edit your CSS in the Textpattern interface. The first is no doubt most familiar to you because it is essentially the same process as using any text editor, albeit more rudimentary. The second way of editing styles can be done with the CSS editor, which is unique to Textpattern.

To be honest, I am not a big fan of using Textpattern to edit CSS at all; I prefer to edit static CSS files by hand and upload them using FTP. There are two reasons to do it this way. First, code highlighting and ease of indentation in programs such as Notepad++ on Windows,[9] TextMate on Mac OS X,[10] or Bluefish on Linux[11] makes variations in code syntax far easier to read. For an example of the default Textpattern CSS in each of these programs, see

---

9. http://notepad-plus.sourceforge.net

10. www.macromates.com

11. http://bluefish.openoffice.nl

Figure 5-7. When using Textpattern to manage CSS, I habitually find myself pressing the Tab key, only to have it move between form elements in the browser. If this is a problem for you as well, there is a plugin available that allows for Tab to be used for text formatting instead of the normal behavior of switching focus.[12]

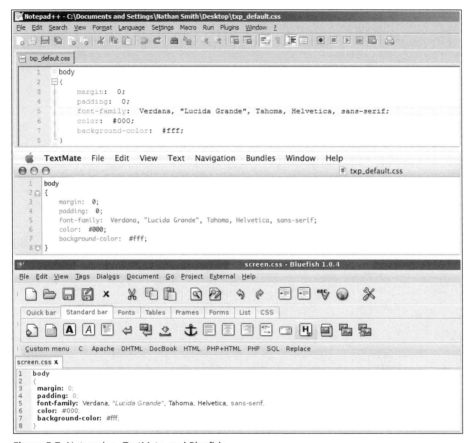

Figure 5-7. Notepad++, TextMate, and Bluefish

5

---

12. www.utterplush.com/txp-plugins/upm-insert-tab

Raw CSS

Sometimes you might be working on a project that requires using the Textpattern interface for CSS or you might just prefer keeping everything in one browser-accessible location. At any rate, when using the Raw CSS area, you see an interface that looks like Figure 5-8. There's really not much to it—just a simple textarea into which you can type your code. Assuming that you already know CSS, there is not much else to say. As you create new styles, simply change the name you're referencing in your templates like so:

TXP code:

```
<txp:css format="link" media="all" n="company" />
```

XHTML output:

```
<link rel="stylesheet" type="text/css" media="all"➨
href="http://example.com/textpattern/css.php?n=default" />
```

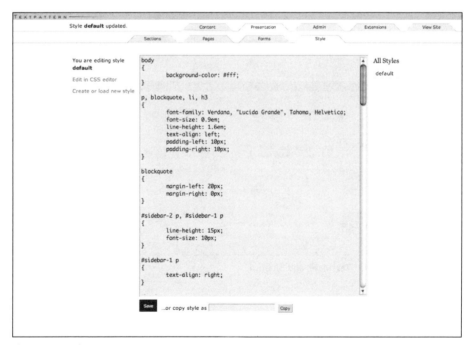

Figure 5-8. Style area/Raw CSS

CSS editor

When you are in the Raw CSS area, if you click Edit in CSS editor, the stylesheet is loaded into the interface depicted in Figure 5-9. If you want this to be the default when you start out in the Style area, you can change this setting in the Advanced Preferences portion of the Admin area. Next to Use raw editing mode by default?, click No.

Figure 5-9. Style area/CSS editor

In the style editor, there are several things that can be done. First, you can add a new **selector**, which is what comes before the set of curly brackets, indicating what is being affected by the properties and values contained therein. By adding a new selector and pressing Submit, that selector is appended to the bottom of the CSS file with an empty set of property/value. If you click the blue plus sign (+) next to any of the selectors, it adds another property/value pair.

Likewise, if you press the red delete (x) icon next to any of the values, that value and its property will be removed. If there is only one pair of property/value for a selector, the entire selector will be removed when you click the delete icon. Likewise, you cannot save an empty selector. Make sure that you press Save after you make all your changes, or else they will be lost.

If you want to create a new stylesheet based on one that already exists, you can use the ...or copy style as text input field to specify the name of your new stylesheet. If you just want to start with a blank slate, you can click Create or load new style at the top of the left column. If there are new styles aside from the default, there will also be a delete icon next to their names under the heading All Styles.

Summary

Congratulations! You have made it through Textpattern boot camp, having covered the three major aspects of the Textpattern interface: Admin, Content, and now Presentation. Next up, we will kick it into high gear as you are challenged to think outside of the box and push the sites you develop in new and creative ways. In Chapter 6, you will learn more about how the Textpattern model works by using good semantics and advanced templates. You will also follow the fictional band Buzzbomb and watch its site evolve with TXP.

PART THREE **CUSTOMIZING TEXTPATTERN**

6 THE TEXTPATTERN MODEL

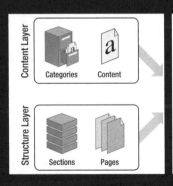 

The layered complexity of Textpattern makes it very appealing to both novice and experienced developers. It is easy to construct a simple website—a blog, a corporate site, or a photography portfolio—and build both horizontally and vertically. Sections can be added on like rooms to a house, and functionality can be built deeper into existing pages.

That flexibility and extensibility are not accidental. Dean Allen and his band of developers have created an amazingly modular architecture that enables both out-of-the-box publishing and heavy-duty customization. This architectural model is a marked advantage of Textpattern. Chapter 6 covers the theory and basics behind that model, and how that foundation influences everything you create in Textpattern.

The semantic ideal

Since the late 1990s, the use of Web Standards in web development has increased exponentially. Jeffrey Zeldman's famous cascading style sheets (CSS) redesign of A List Apart and subsequent book, *Designing with Web Standards*, kick-started a movement that has resulted in a thriving community of standards-conscious developers. Their influence has led to the widely publicized redesigns of `Wired.com`, `ESPN.com`, and other major sites, plus countless number of smaller destinations.

The idea of a standards-based Web, in which all browsers and development tools play by the same rules, holds deep appeal to those who architect the online world for a living. Not only does it make your life easier but it also leads to faster-loading, more accessible content for your sites' visitors.

The fact that using Web Standards enables developers to move away from table-based layouts and crude presentational markup is not the only reason why the movement has sprung from a few seeds into a full-blown garden. In fact, the benefits are many. Stripping the noise from HTML leads to smaller file size, easier maintenance, and more future-proof technology. But the single greatest benefit—and one of the core battle cries of Web Standards—is the slow but steady creation of a more semantic Web.

Data about data, page hierarchy, and layers

The word **semantic** gets paired with Web Standards quite a bit. It's worth taking the time to define this explicitly. The Webster definition is short: "Of or relating to meaning, especially meaning in language." In web development, it means creating documents whose structure reflects the content—and it all starts with metadata.

Metadata is "data about data" and provides a high-level summary of the document. The end goal of metadata is to better describe how a document relates to other documents on the site and ultimately the rest of the Web. At a minimum, it includes the title, description, and keywords, but it can also extend into authorship, copyright, search engine information, and more.

But even if the metadata is explicit, it means little if the structure of the page does not reflect its content. In a nutshell, a **semantic structure** means using tags as they were designed—to describe what the content means. Paragraphs are wrapped in the <p> tag; ordered and unordered lists use <ol> and <ul>, respectively; and headings are marked up with <h1> through <h6> to cluster content into a logical hierarchy. These tags transform otherwise meaningless text into a well-formed, detailed document with a clear flow of information.

"Old school" development techniques muddied this water with heavy-handed and obsolete HTML. For instance, this 1990s-era code is still common:

```
<table bgcolor="#000">
  <tr>
    <td width="200px">
      <font size="3"><bold>Shopping List</bold></font><br>
      <font size="2">milk<br>
      organic baby carrots<br>
      cheese<br>
      chicken fajita Hot Pockets</font>
    </td>
  </tr>
</table>
```

Using a more semantic model, the tables and presentational markup (<font> and <bold>) are stripped out to distill the markup down to its most fundamental level:

```
<h3>Shopping List</h3>
<ul>
  <li>milk</li>
  <li>organic baby carrots</li>
  <li>cheese</li>
  <li>chicken fajita Hot Pockets</li>
</ul>
```

The current semantic Web has three components, or layers. The **structural layer** is defined by the HTML and provides structure to the document's information (in the preceding example, it orders the food items into a sensible grocery list). The **presentational layer** is controlled via CSS and is responsible for the visual aspect of the HTML, or how things appear in a browser. Finally, the **behavioral layer** resides in JavaScript and provides a foundation for interactivity and functionality standard HTML and CSS cannot provide. Like peanut butter, jelly, and bread, they work in perfect tandem. This model is the commonly accepted "three-dimensional" model you can read about on hundreds of sites and in dozens of web development books.

The fourth dimension

The three-layer model lives comfortably in three separate files, with the HTML providing the anchor for the stylesheet and JavaScript. This succinct package can run with or without a web connection, can be accessed by anyone with a browser, and can be edited by anyone with a passing knowledge of HTML.

For thousands of years, scientists thought people were composed of bones, muscles, and organs. Then, in 1953, James Watson and Francis Crick opened the world's eyes to DNA, the final microscopic element that ties everything together. Looking at the grand semantic Web picture more closely, you also find a less-obvious inner layer as well. Folded into the structural HTML is the **content layer** that quietly ties the other layers together—the "DNA" of the web pages.

The current Web model, as packaged and promoted by the World Wide Web Consortium (W3C), does not allow—and never has allowed—a means to fundamentally separate content from structure, which is why the concept might seem alien at first. Since HTML 1.0, text and markup have been intrinsically woven together into one file. The primary content is tangled up with all kinds of markup—from the navigation, to the copyright in the footer, to the metadata that isn't even visible in a browser window.

What's the point?

At the end of the day, the goal of separating content from structure is easier site maintenance. Years ago, if you wanted to make the body text blue instead of black, you had to manually edit, save, and reupload every page. Today, editing a single line in a CSS file can change 100,000 pages in one-half second because that visual information—the presentation layer—has been outsourced to a style sheet. The process is now a hundredfold more efficient.

If you want to make a major *structural* change to your layout (for example, adding a third column to the body or a new button to the navigation), you still have to edit, save, and reupload every page, just like before. The solution is to remove the content and leave only the HTML skeleton. When those bones can be outsourced into HTML templates, just as the visual information is outsourced to a CSS file, those structural changes become as easy and fast as presentational changes.

Unfortunately, separating content and structure requires third-party intervention. Content management software is used to administer raw content separately from HTML templates and then assemble these elements into a single HTML page for the end user's browser to render.

The Textpattern semantic model

Textpattern is a content management system (CMS) that enables the web developer to control the melding of content and structure on a very granular, tightly controlled, and completely customizable level. To accomplish this, Textpattern adheres to its own semantic architecture. As you can see in Figure 6-1, everything revolves around the explicit management of content and structure and then weaving them back together for the visitor's browser.

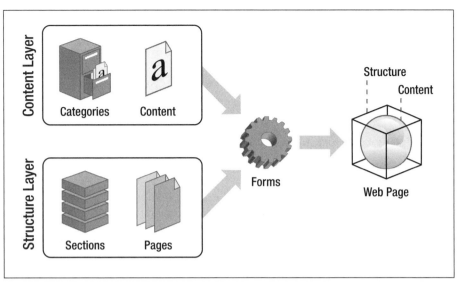

Figure 6-1. Textpattern's semantic model separates the content and structure of a page and then weaves them together with forms.

The content is accessed through the Content tab in the Admin interface. All text articles, images, files, and other content are housed in this area and are organized by categories, which are metadata-like in their capability to organize content. You'll learn more about content in Chapter 7.

The structure layer, controlled in the Presentation tab, is a bit more complex because sections (which are the broad site dividers) work with pages (which act as the actual templates) in a symbiotic relationship. Pages use forms—which are snippets of code—to pull content from the content layer before the template is output as a web page. (This is covered in detail in Chapters 8 and 9.)

The building blocks

Most Textpattern development is done in the Content and Presentation tabs. These tabs and their technical functionality are described in depth in Part 2 of this book, but let's review the critical building blocks from Figure 6-1.

Categories

Categories help group content meaningfully. Figure 6-2 shows how Textpattern employs categories for articles, links, images, and files, which are critical to the organization of a site, no matter what size. For instance, if you set up a blog about food courts in malls, your categories might include "pretzel stands," "national fast-food chains," "pizza," and "ice cream shops." Subsequent posts would be linked to one or more categories. After the content is attributed to these semantic buckets, that information can be used in a myriad of ways, such as providing a list of relevant articles or creating a sitemap organized by category (or even designing category-specific landing pages).

Figure 6-2. Textpattern enables you to organize articles, links, images, and files with categories.

Articles

Articles are where the bulk of the content resides. An article can be thought of as a singular, complete page of content, such as a blog post, corporate "about us" page, catalog entry, or any other unique block of content that can exist on a single page. Every article has a multitude of data attached to it: categories and section attributions, custom data fields, timestamps, URL information, and more. There are hundreds of tags and plugins designed to parse, display, and organize an article's data.

Sections

Whereas categories are the semantic cataloging of content, sections serve as the broad structural site divisions. Sections mimic traditional directories on a server. In the blog about mall food courts, there might be one section called blog, in which all the posts are stored, and another called contact, in which visitors can contact the author. These sections would be represented by their own URLs: www.mallfoodcourt.com/blog and www.mallfoodcourt.com/contact, respectively.

Pages

Pages are the ground floor of your structural templates and the foundation for forms to interact with content. Pages are essentially blank canvases and are amazingly flexible. A single page can simultaneously determine the output of a landing page, an individual article page, or even search results. Textpattern requires every section be linked to a page; this allows it to know what to display when the user lands on a web page located within a section. As an example, you might have a section called contact and link it to a page called contact_foodcourt; when the user lands on the contact web page, they see the template defined in contact_foodcourt.

Forms

If articles are the building blocks of the site, and pages act as the foundation on which a template is built, forms act as the cement that binds everything together—the decisive ingredient that seamlessly weaves together the content and structure layers. Forms are the most complex and most powerful components of Textpattern. They house the majority of the markup and are largely responsible for the system's extensible, flexible architecture.

The tag language

The Textpattern tag system mimics the structure and rules of well-formed XML, the most widely employed Web Standard. This has several advantages. Perhaps most importantly, it makes the code easy to understand. Once developers learn a few house rules, they can jump in and create, tweak, and delete segments of Textpattern code with confidence. Many CMSs require the author to learn a complete programming language such as PHP or Perl to make even the most rudimentary alterations. Textpattern is nowhere near as complex.

By following an XML-like structure, all tags must close or be self-closing, and tags—just like the HTML—must follow a properly nested order. This ensures that there is little room for questionable code, and Textpattern takes advantage of the consistent logic to render pages as intended.

Textpattern's tags are also written in plain, readable syntax. For instance, you might see this on any given Textpattern site:

```
<txp:if_individual_article>
  <txp:article form="article_full" />
</txp:if_individual_article>
```

In this example, you tell Textpattern the following: If the web page is rendering an individual article such as a blog entry, render that article using the form `article_full`. It is difficult to imagine writing easier code; tags are given human-readable names, and their variables are enclosed in natural-language attributes inside the tag. Notice that the `<txp:if_individual_article>` and `<txp:article />` tags are both properly closed. Like XML, not adhering to this rule prevents a file from working.

Knowledge portability

A key advantage of TXP is "knowledge portability." Because the language is simple and the architecture open to almost any configuration, the concepts in Part 3, even those illustrated by the following test site, can be easily applied to your own web project. In fact, once a fundamental understanding of the Textpattern semantic model is achieved, the ideas and principles can be applied to a host of development hurdles.

The testing ground: Buzzbomb

The beauty of Textpattern is that it supports just about any kind of site you want to build—a simple blog, a website for a sports team, a church site, a company's corporate site, or anything else you can think of. The architecture was designed to accommodate almost any idea. Other contemporary (and more well-known) development platforms are designed to be blogging software first and CMSs second; in this case, blogging is just an easy application of a greater system.

6

Now that you know about the semantic model and how Textpattern separates the content and structure layers for easier development, you can confidently move forward in building a site. Part 3 of *Textpattern Design and Development Solutions* covers everything you need to build a basic website using TXP. In fact, you will develop a site for the fictional punk band Buzzbomb to help work through the concepts and code. (You can see a preview of the Buzzbomb home page in Figure 6-3.)

Figure 6-3. The band's home page

The installation will be a testing ground for all the major building blocks of a simple Textpattern site. You'll learn the following:

- How categories affect the organization of content, how to create them, and how to exploit their power for your site.
- How to create, modify, and use articles for everything from blog posts to landing pages to customized metadata.
- How to create and edit sections and how to link them to pages.

- How to turn blank pages into powerful, extensible templates using the Textpattern tag language, including conditional statements.
- How to use forms for building fast-loading, easily managed sites.

You'll set up a blog (the "BuzzBlog") with comments and an archive of past posts, a basic contact page, a terms of use page, a photo gallery, customized error pages, and more. You'll use categories, sections, forms, custom fields, conditional arguments, and plugins to help illustrate the grand Textpattern architecture, and how the four layers of the semantic Web interact with the software's structure. In short, you'll learn how Textpattern works by example.

Summary

The four-layer model of the Web can be truly achieved only with a CMS because there is no easy way to natively separate content and structure without the assistance of server-side software. Textpattern's specialty is the elegant and extensible division, management, and assemblage of content and structure, from a user-friendly interface for adding content to a functionally deep back end for building templates. This will become evident as the rest of the book unfolds and as you go through the development process of a band website.

6

7 CREATING THE CONTENT: CATEGORIES AND ARTICLES

The Content tab in Textpattern is where all content generation gets done. When web administrators dole out access to the TXP interface, it's common for writers to have access only to this section because any significant content updates or additions can be accomplished within a few screens, as seen in Figures 7-1 and 7-2. In the four-layer model of the semantic Web discussed in Chapter 6, everything related to the generation of the Content layer is controlled here.

Figure 7-1. The Content tab as it appears to a Textpattern admin

Figure 7-2. The Content tab as it appears to people with Staff Writer status (they cannot access the other tabs to make template changes)

The Content tab has seven subsidiary tabs: Categories, Write, Articles, Images, Files, Links, and Comments. The Write, Images, Files, and Links tabs are for generating content. You can add, edit, or delete any piece of a site's content from one of these pages. Categories administers the categories for the four previous tabs, Articles simply presents a list of all articles generated from the Write tab, and Comments displays all visitor comments left on your site.

Although this chapter will also touch on Images and Links, it will concentrate on the Categories and Write tabs. They provide the deepest levels of functionality and represent the bulk of content generation and organization on most Textpattern sites.

Categories

A **category** is the Textpattern way of organizing content from a semantic point of view. The Categories tab enables you to control the categories of all the Textpattern content types (articles, links, images, and files). These categories can be named whatever you want as long as they provide organizational value to your site's bucket of content.

Creating a category

Creating a category is very simple. After navigating to the Categories tab, you see an overview of all your categories in the site for articles, links, images, and files, as seen in Figure 7-3. To create a new category, simply enter the name into the field at the top of the appropriate column; then click Create. That's it. The page will refresh and you'll see your new category appear in the list.

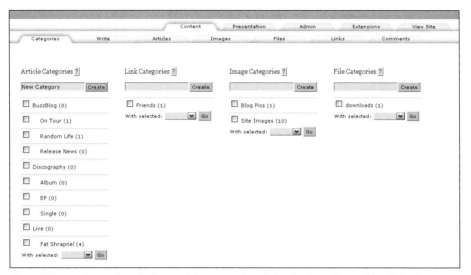

Figure 7-3. The Categories tab shows all the categories of the site, including articles, links, images, and files.

Categories vs. sections

The difference between categories and sections in Textpattern can be confusing at first. Think of sections as broad site dividers like physical folders on the server that break apart the site's architecture. Every article must be attributed a section. By contrast, categories are not required; they exist purely for content organization that might or might not relate to the physical structure of the site.

For instance, in the Buzzbomb site we created three categories for the band's releases: Album, EP, and Single. Any article for the discography has one of those three *categories* attached to it, but *all* of them fall into the Discography *section*. BuzzBlog, which has its own section, also has a collection of categories such as Random Life, On Tour, and Release News.

A single category can also describe a single article type that appears in multiple sections. Consider a news site: the sections might be World News, Money, and Lifestyle. In Textpattern, you might create a category called feature article that can be applied to full-length articles appearing in any one of those larger areas.

It is worth repeating that a section attribution is *required* for every article, and an article can be associated with *only one* section at a time. By contrast, an article can be linked with up to two categories (or none if not needed). A section containing only one "sticky" article, such as your site's disclaimer or the home page's static text, might not need a category.

Multiple categories vs. tagging

Different content management systems (CMSs) and blogging software have conflicting nomenclature when it comes to the back end. In Wordpress, for instance, an article can have unlimited categories; a review of a restaurant might fall into these categories: reviews, restaurants, New York City, Asian Fusion, and more. This type of taxonomy—in which a piece of text is referenced by a host of keywords instead of falling neatly into a single category—is often called **tagging**. Bloggers like having lots of categories at their disposal because posts' topics can be all over the map, making traditional organization structures inadequate.

Textpattern has caught some flack for allowing only two category associations per article because people want to tag their content. There are two easy ways around this:

- **Use a plugin for multiple categories**: Rob Sable has developed a plugin called rss_unlimited_categories[1] that enables unlimited category associations for articles. It replaces the dual drop-down menus with a multiselectable list, offering the same functionality as Wordpress. This plugin also enables the output of the categories as a list or tag cloud.

- **Use Textpattern keywords**: True tagging and multiple categories are not the same. Tagging content is associating any word and phrase that fits the piece, not picking from a predetermined list of possible categories. Textpattern enables traditional tagging functionality out of the box through the Keywords field on the Write tab. A list of articles with similar keyword values can be output via a standard <txp:article_custom /> tag. In this case, any articles containing the keyword "reviews" will appear in the list:

  <txp:article_custom form="yourform" keywords="reviews" />

Nesting

For organizational efficiency, Textpattern supports category **nesting**. Although TXP offers unlimited nesting, it shows only eight levels of nested categories: the top-level category and then seven hierarchical levels beneath it. This provides no production-level value, only visual reference for the author. For instance, say you operate a music news site. You might have the following categories:

- reviews
  - albums
    - originals
    - re-releases

If you called a list of articles with the category reviews, Textpattern would return only a list of articles explicitly linked to the category reviews. Any articles with a category of albums, originals, or re-releases would be ignored, even if they fall within the parent reviews

---

1. www.wilshireone.com/textpattern-plugins/rss-unlimited-categories

category. However, nested categories are recorded in the database as such, so the concept provides an interesting programming hook for plugin developers. (In fact, one plugin was written to generate a site navigation based solely on hierarchical categories.)

For the Buzzbomb site, you can see nested categories in action in Figure 7-3. Nesting them like this provides no production value when developing the site, but helps to visually organize the categories in Textpattern.

Category names vs. titles

From the Categories tab, clicking a category name brings up a subsidiary screen like the one in Figure 7-4 with three fields: Article category name, Parent (drop-down menu for nesting categories; see the previous discussion), and Article category title. The Article category name field is used for database queries and URLs, and thus has hyphens; whereas the Article category title is the human-readable version that would actually appear on a web page if called by Textpattern.

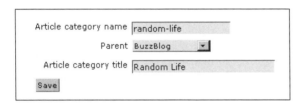

Figure 7-4. The category options enable you to define a category name and a category title.

Using the example in Figure 7-4, you might see Textpattern use the Article category name to generate a URL such as buzzbomb.textpatternsolutions.com/buzzblog/?c=random-life.

In an article form, calling the category **name** is simple:

```
<txp:category />
```

But that code renders random-life. We have to explicitly instruct Textpattern to produce the clean **title**:

```
<txp:category title="1" />
```

And that code produces Random Life. Keep in mind that the name and title are not bound by the same words; the name could be random-life, while the title could be Random Thoughts on Life, Death and Rock 'n' Roll.

Categories in URLs

Category names do not appear in any URL combination because they are for organizing content, not dictating the site's structure. This is a fine distinction. It is easy to think of categories as "subsections," so a URL such as yoursite.com/section/category/title is

7

obvious. But this is not the way Textpattern is built. Categories serve the same role as meta keywords: data for semantic organization.

Sections can be in a URL string because every article *must* have *only one* section, leaving only one possible URL combination: yoursite.com/section/title. Think about articles with more than one category: both yoursite.com/section/**category1**/title and yoursite.com/section/**category2**/title would go to the same article, diluting the value of permanent URLs. Take that idea for more than two categories—or worse, articles that have been tagged with 20 keywords—and you immediately see the problem.

All this being said, the entire argument has one significant caveat: you can have category *landing pages*. These URLs come in two forms, and neither is pretty.

Option 1: Database query string

Example: www.site.com/destinations/?c=hawaii. As you can see, even in clean URL mode, TXP still requires a database query. In this case, the section is destinations and the category is hawaii. (If you were running Textpattern in "messy URL" mode, the URL would be: www.site.com/index.php?c=hawaii.)

You're asking this, "Why the heck does the dumb 'c' and question mark thing have to be in the URL? Why can't I just have a nice clean URL with the category name?" Good question. Because Textpattern uses the format of www.site.com/section/title, it can't use the format of www.site.com/section/category because if an article title and category name were the same, the URL would try to resolve to two different places. Remember what you learned in high school physics: a single object cannot occupy two places at the same time or the whole space-time continuum will implode, ending existence as we know it.

Option 2: The painfully obvious URL

Example: www.site.com/category/hawaii/. Here, Textpattern inserts the word category into the URL before actually referencing the category title hawaii. The section name is left out completely.

Articles

An article in Textpattern is any piece of text that is dynamically displayed on the site. Except for rare exceptions, one article equals one web page, regardless of length. The CMS provides a myriad of options and fields for each article, which allows for a fairly wide array of customization and applications. For instance, one article in your site might be a single paragraph to introduce a section; another might be a 1,000-word essay buried under a tangle of submenus; another might comprise your privacy policy page. Any piece of text can be controlled with an article. Using Figure 7-5 as the launch pad, let's explore the interface.

Figure 7-5. An entry in the Buzzbomb blog uses many of the fields available on the Write tab.

Article title

This first field on the article page is the most important field for an article. In fact, it's the only field that is required. An article can have nothing else—not even content in the body—but it must have a title because the title drives the URL and provides the unique "hook" for the Textpattern system to locate, organize, and display an article in a web page.

When Textpattern generates a URL from the title field, it strips out all characters that are not lowercase alphanumeric (0–9 or a–z), so the URL for the article Viva La Baltimore looks like this: buzzbomb.textpatternsolutions.com/buzzblog/viva-la-baltimore.

Customizing the URL

One of Textpattern's most useful (and lesser-known) features is its capability to customize an article's URL string. While the URL of the article is initially generated from the title field when you click Publish for the first time, simply opening Advanced Options on the left reveals a field called URL-only title on the bottom. Similar to a category name and title, these two fields do not have to contain the same content—Textpattern has already tied them together. This field accepts any characters legal in a URL string. For instance, the previous article's URL could be one of any of the following:

- viva-la-baltimore
- vivalabaltimore
- viva_la_baltimore
- baltimore

Generally, it's best to keep the URL as close to the article's title as possible and to use hyphens, not underscores. Hyphens are not only more legible in human scanning, but search engines also recognize them as spaces, whereas underscores are interpreted as full stops.

In addition, Textpattern forbids any two articles from sharing the same URL. You might have two articles titled Site Update, but their URL values must be different—for instance, site-update-oct-2006 and site-update-apr-2007. As you can see from the error message shown in Figure 7-6, Textpattern tells you when you've infringed on another article.

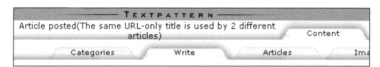

Figure 7-6. Textpattern will warn you when two articles share the same URL.

Body and Excerpt

The main content of your articles lives in the Body and Excerpt fields. While Textpattern offers additional places to store data (keywords, custom fields, and so on), the Body and Excerpt fields are designed to hold the long guts of your pages. Functionally, they are the same. You could write a 1,000-word blog entry in the excerpt and a 100-word summary in the body; from Textpattern's point of view, the fields are identical twins separated only by their labels.

The Body and Excerpt fields are very versatile in the type of content they can hold:

- Entering plain text makes it easy for technically less-savvy authors to write, since Textile parses the plain text into HTML. This is probably the most common content in Textpattern sites. As you can see in Figure 7-7, TXP even provides a means of previewing both the HTML and final output for quality control. Chapter 4 covers Textile in depth.

- For those requiring more finite control, Textile can be turned off for authors wanting to write their own HTML. This can be especially valuable if the content of an article becomes laden with complex tables, code examples, or other tag-heavy applications beyond the scope of Textile.

- For even more flexibility, you can write both plain text *and* HTML into the same article; Textile will leave your HTML alone, but still work its magic on the plain text.

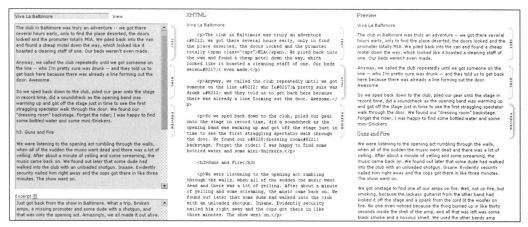

Figure 7-7. Textpattern provides three different modes of viewing your content: the editable fields, the HTML markup, and a preview of the final output.

- Certain nonarticle Textpattern tags can be parsed directly from an article field. For instance, Rob Sable's rss_google_map plugin[2] generates a Google map based on values entered into the plugin, and the actual tag sits right inside an article's Body or Excerpt field. You could also use standard TXP tags such as <txp:output_form /> to pull external material right into your passage of text.

- Finally, you can execute PHP code right from an article, which allows for the ultimate in flexibility because several advanced applications—such as a shopping cart, forum, or complementary CMS—might require advanced custom programming to integrate with Textpattern. Since running server-side code might present a security risk in a multiauthor environment, the site admin can disable this capability in the Advanced Preferences area of the Admin tab.

Status

One of the more unique features of Textpattern is the capability to give articles different status levels. It might seem obvious to have two different states—on and off—but Textpattern offers a deeper level of control by providing additional options in how articles are handled.

Draft, Pending, and Live

Conceptually, these different status levels try to approximate the traditional workflow of a printed publication such as a newspaper or magazine. In those environments, there are many writers, editors, and administrators; and pieces fly from one desk to another, getting reviewed and edited before finally going to press. During that workflow, the article's status level also changes—starting at Draft and then moving to Pending before an editor gives the final okay and the article goes Live.

---

2. www.wilshireone.com/textpattern-plugins/rss-google-map

By default, every new article is set to Live, but there are many times when you won't finish the article in one sitting, so you mark it as Draft. This keeps the article from appearing on the website, but saves the content for later editing. Draft acts as its name would indicate: as a testing ground for reviewing and revising before pushing the content to the rest of the world.

Realistically, few Textpattern-driven sites will have a workflow as complex as a newspaper, and a status level such as Pending might never be used. It is best employed when multiple writers need to version a piece of text, and appropriate user accounts and their corresponding permissions are used to control what content goes online.

Finally, an article set to Live is exactly that—live on the website. It can still be edited and its status can always be demoted to Draft or something similar.

> In a multiauthor site, as in any networked environment, it is often necessary to control the level of access a user or group of users retains in the production situation. Each author is given a level of access based on job responsibility. By default, Textpattern offers these titles—Publisher, Manager, Copy Editor, Staff Writer, Freelancer, Designer, and None—each with different levels of editorial power. For more information, refer to "Users" in Chapter 3.

Hidden

An article with the status of Hidden becomes exactly that—invisible. Other user accounts (even freelancers) can see Hidden articles from other authors, but all traces of the content are taken offline. Functionally, it is identical to Draft. The value comes when multiple articles are in the editorial queue, and the Draft status actually means something different from Hidden in the site's workflow.

Sticky

Sometimes, you need to have text on your site that deviates from the normal article flow. For instance, in a blog, you might have a short blurb introducing the archive page; in a corporate site divided by sections, you might need sectional landing pages. In other words, a piece of content anchored in place that won't expire or fall behind newer articles. The Sticky status enables you to "stick" a piece of content to whatever you want. For instance, take a look at Figure 7-8.

As you can see, the sticky article appears on the sectional landing page *outside* the list of normal articles with a Live status. Articles with a Sticky status become their own rogue content that has to be called deliberately and specifically from an article tag using the status attribute. The example might use the following slice of Textpattern code:

```
<txp:article status="sticky" form="sticky_article" />
<txp:article form="list_of_articles" />
```

The logic is simple: show the sticky text attributed to that section followed by the list of normal articles. Again, you must tell Textpattern to pull the sticky article with the status attribute.

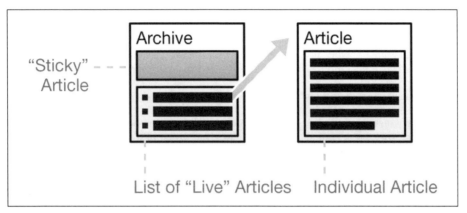

Figure 7-8. In a blog environment, a sticky article might be used to introduce the archive page.

Sections and categories

You attach the section and categories to the article on the Write tab. We'll cover sections in depth in the next chapter, but for now, remember that every article requires a section for Textpattern to properly triangulate it with the rest of the content. In Figure 7-9, the post "Viva la Baltimore" appears in the buzzblog section, but falls into both the On Tour and BuzzBlog categories.

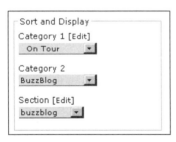

Figure 7-9. Every article must have one section applied with the option of additional categories.

Categories, which we covered at the beginning of this chapter, are optional. They provide a second, purely semantic organizational level that you might or might not need. A small site with only a few pages could very well do without categories, but any large-scale content, especially content divided up into many small pieces, could benefit strongly from the additional management that categories offer.

Keywords

In Textpattern, keywords were initially conceived to tie relevant articles together, almost like a crude tagging system. As the product matured, the content was opened up to more practical uses, and the field is now a completely open value whose subject matter can be used to accomplish all sorts of tasks.

The first and most obvious use is to employ keywords for metadata use. Since the value is pulled in a single tag (and has no attributes), the code is very simple:

```
<meta name="keywords" content="<txp:keywords />" />
```

We'll cover creating a full array of custom metadata later in the book, but this is one of the first steps. The TXP development crew has given us another tag called <txp:meta_keywords /> that creates the exact output as the previous example, but in one succinct bit of markup:

```
<txp:meta_keywords />
```

Fortunately for developers using Textpattern, an article's keywords are not limited to metadata use. Like custom fields, the value of the Keywords field can be used as article triggers and filters. For example, suppose that you ran a blog about your local music scene. Every time you posted an entry, you threw in a couple of keywords: any bands mentioned in the post, the name of the venue, and any local celebrities who might have been involved. Some time later, you write a feature-length story about Buzzbomb, the rising star in the local scene. You know it will be linked to by a lot of other sites and you want to take advantage of that traffic by pointing readers to past articles you've written about Buzzbomb. At the end the article, you might plug this into your article body:

```
<ul class="relatedarticles">
<txp:article_custom form="quicklinks" keywords="Buzzbomb" limit="5" />
</ul>
```

The quicklinks form (set to be an article type) might look like this:

```
<li><txp:permlink><txp:title /></txp:permlink> (<txp:posted />)</li>
```

And the resulting output would pull the five most recent articles with the keyword Buzzbomb into an unordered list at the end of your feature article. The final HTML output would be the following:

```
<ul class="relatedarticles">
  <li><a href="...">Buzzbomb Rocks the Casbah</a> (8 October 2006)</li>
  <li><a href="...">Too Good to Name Influences?</a> ➥
(21 September 2006)</li>
  <li><a href="...">The Man Behind the Buzzbomb Magic</a> ➥
(9 July 2006)</li>
  <li><a href="...">Buzzbomb Announces New Album: Monkey Funk</a> ➥
 (1 July 2006)</li>
  <li><a href="...">Are We Ever Going to Get a New Album? ➥
</a> (28 June 2006)</li>
</ul>
```

This saves you the trouble of manually hunting down the last five articles you wrote about the band and provides you with a snippet of code you can reuse over and over—just change the keyword and you have an instant list of related material. Coke Harrington, a prolific Textpattern plugin writer, created the plugin chh_related_articles[3] to automate this process. It searches all articles for related keywords (or custom fields) and outputs a list of related material.

Images, Files, and Links

Our trip through the Content tab would not be complete without exploring the three other tabs that supply Textpattern with content: Images, Files, and Links. In theory, this is where all nonarticle content resides.

Images

The Images tab is used to upload any type of image file related to the site, including supporting graphics for articles as well as images used in the design of the site. Since Textpattern gives you three different ways to call the image—Textile, Textpattern, and plain HTML—the tool is a powerful repository. Let's walk through the process.

The first thing to do is set your image categories from the Categories tab. TXP gives you only one predetermined category: Site Design, which you might or might not wish to change or even keep. Once that is settled, return to the Images tab and use the Upload file field to find your image. For the Buzzbomb site, we wrote a blog post on a show in Baltimore and want to upload a picture to support the story. We use the Upload image field to find the picture and then click Upload. This brings up the second screen, in which we can edit the image's details, as seen in Figure 7-10.

---

3. www.cokesque.com/code/117/chhrelatedarticles

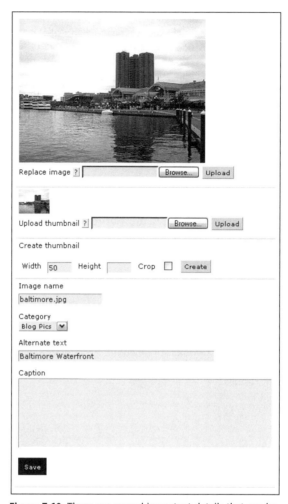

Figure 7-10. There are several important details that can be fleshed out after uploading an image.

In this second screen, several key details need to be fleshed out. First (and most important), write some short alternate text for the image if it's any kind of photo, logo, or other primary graphic. This is the text that appears in the alt attribute of an HTML image tag. If it's any type of image whose loss will not affect a reader's understanding of the site (such as a minor background image or a spacer pixel), leave the field blank.

Second, pick a category for the image. While this is more important for photo blogs or other image-heavy sites when you need to organize using categories, it never hurts to have that metadata attached to your files.

Textpattern also enables you to create a thumbnail of the image on the fly. Although you could upload your own thumbnail, simply entering a height or width and clicking Create will do it for you.

After all changes are made, press Save, and Textpattern returns to the index of uploaded images, as shown in Figure 7-11.

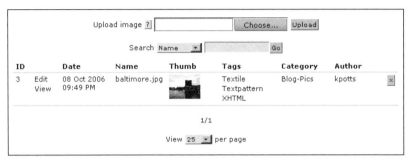

Figure 7-11. Textpattern shows you the thumbnail of the image and different tags for using the image.

This screen provides three ways to call the image on your site: Textile code, a Textpattern tag, or a normal HTML image tag. It's important to remember that TXP renames your graphics on the server, so although you uploaded baltimore.jpg, the name on the server is actually 3.jpg, which corresponds to the ID number of the image. Textpattern ensures that no two images ever have the same name.

Up to version 4.0.3 of Textpattern, clicking a selection under Tags would launch a pop-up window with code. Version 4.0.4 improved this system. Now, clicking any selection under Tags brings up a new browser window with a richer menu of options, as seen in Figure 7-12.

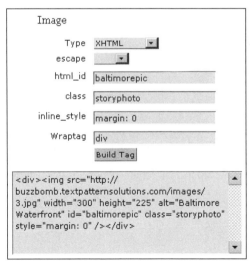

Figure 7-12. When a selection is clicked in version 4.0.4, Textpattern launches a new page with a tag-building menu for images.

7

Textile

Choosing Textile from the Type drop-down menu produces the following code:

```
!http://www.textpatternsolutions.com/Buzzbomb/images/3.jpg ➡
(Baltimore Waterfront)!
```

Because Textile tags do not allow any advanced attributes, they are best left for quick image calls in an article's body. In fact, they can be used only where Textile is parsed—the article body, excerpt, or a comment—so their usefulness is limited.

Textpattern

When Textpattern is picked from the Type drop-down menu, the following code appears:

```
<txp:image class="storyphoto" html_id="baltimorepic" id="3" ➡
style="margin: 0" wraptag="div" />
```

As you can see, a Textpattern tag allows for all of the attributes available from the tag generation menu. A Textpattern tag can be called from pages, forms, articles, and more. The versatility and brevity of the tag makes it a popular development choice.

XHTML

Finally, choosing XHTML from the drop-down menu renders the following:

```
<div><img src="http://www.textpatternsolutions.com/Buzzbomb/ ➡
images/3.jpg" width="300" height="225" alt="Baltimore Waterfront" ➡
 id="baltimorepic" class="storyphoto" style="margin: 0" /></div>
```

This is the full-blown HTML call that can be manually tweaked to the finest nuance. For instance, you might need to apply a class to the wrap tag or adjust the alt attribute text in one instance—options simply not available from a Textile or Textpattern tag. In addition, you can use the image path to call images in the Textpattern repository from your CSS files:

```
.header { background: url(/Buzzbomb/images/3.jpg) 0 0 no repeat; }
```

Files

The Files tab is intended for downloadable files. Just about anything is accepted: music files, big image files, PDFs, Word documents, and so on. The functionality is similar to the Images tab; there is an index page of available files and a place to upload new ones. Uploading a new file brings up a small screen of options (see Figure 7-13).

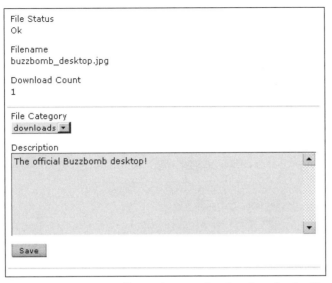

Figure 7-13. Textpattern offers a minor set of options for uploading files.

Even though the options might seem limited, Textpattern provides no fewer than *eleven* unique tags for organizing and rendering downloadable files (compared with just three for images). It is important to accurately fill in this information because all of it can be parsed onscreen, from the file category (<txp:file_download_category />) and description (<txp:file_download_description />), to the date it was created (<txp:file_download_created />), to the number of downloads since its release (<txp:file_download_downloads />).

Similar to images, Textpattern gives each file a unique ID number. The difference is that the CMS does not actually rename the file as it does with images, but instead creates a unique redirect based on the ID. For instance, if we build a Textile, Textpattern, or XHTML tag based on the previous Buzzbomb desktop background, the parsed HTML would produce a URL like this:

http://www.textpatternsolutions.com/Buzzbomb/file_download/2

When loaded, it would prompt the browser to download the file Buzzbomb_desktop.jpg. The integrity of the file name remains.

7

Links

The idea behind links comes from the popular sidebar construct of blogs, in which authors can create a list of links (or blogrolls) to their favorite sites. While the construct does not present a tremendous amount of flexibility or creative room beyond its intended use, it is excellent for what it sets out to accomplish and can be stretched—in a pinch—for other uses. The interface is simple enough, as shown in Figure 7-14.

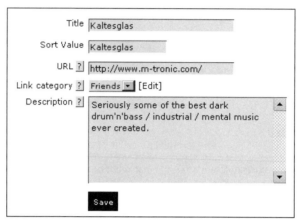

Figure 7-14. The interface for the Links tab

The Sort Value enables you to control the order in which the links appear by using alphanumeric values. TextBook[4] provides the best example: 1, 10, 100, 101, 11, 1B, 2, A, B. If nothing is entered, the field adopts the value of the title after you press Save, but this can be edited afterward if you want to sort articles by a certain value.

Title, URL, Link category, and Description are all self-explanatory and can be called with a host of Textpattern tags, including <txp:linklist />, <txp:link />, <txp:linkdesctitle />, <txp:link_name />, <txp:link_url />, and more. As a simple example, in the right column of the Buzzbomb site, we added a small list of our favorite bands. Here is the small bit of code to output the links:

```
<txp:linklist category="Friends" sort="linkname desc" ➥
wraptag="ul" form="plainlinks" />
```

Textpattern is pulling all links from the Friends category and then sorting them alphabetically. The list is being wrapped in a <ul> tag, which means that the form plainlinks wraps each link in an <li> tag, like this:

```
<li><txp:linkdesctitle /></li>
```

---

4. www.textpattern.net/wiki/index.php?title=Links_Subtab

The `<txp:linkdesctitle />` title is an efficient choice because it's a single tag that not only generates the `<a>` tag but also the anchor text (using the link's title) and the content for the `title` attribute (using the link's description). In the end, the final output would be the following:

```
<ul>
  <li><a href="http://www.m-tronic.com/" title="Seriously some of the ➥
  best dark drum'n'bass / industrial / mental music ever created."> ➥
  Kaltesglas</a></li>
</ul>
```

Summary

This chapter covered the elements of creating content for your Textpattern site. You will spend most of your time on the Write tab, plugging away at content, but the Images, Files, and Links tabs also provide an avenue of supplementary content that can be called into your site in a variety of ways. The next chapter will cover the foundational elements of structure, from templates to stylesheets, and then tie them together onto a single page.

7

8 CUSTOMIZING THE PRESENTATION: SECTIONS, PAGES, FORMS, AND STYLE

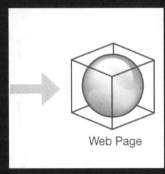

The Presentation tab of the Textpattern interface (see Figure 8-1) is the central brain of the system, in which the threads of content are sewn into the fabric of structure. After building the broad sections of a site, you use forms to weave a web between articles and pages, crafting the output with an extensive library of tags and plugins.

Figure 8-1. The Presentation tab has four main tabs for creating templates and stylesheets.

In a multiauthor environment, staff writers and freelancers have no access to the Presentation tab, and those attributed with Designer status have access to *only* the Presentation tab because any design-related changes, from template changes to Cascading Style Sheet (CSS) edits, happen within this screen.

The Textpattern developer is given three building blocks in which to craft HTML templates—Sections, Pages, and Forms—with another tab (Style) for stylesheets to control the cosmetic presentation. The process of building an HTML page out of Textpattern involves all four pieces.

Since each article must be attributed to only one section, Textpattern must first identify an article's section to render the content correctly. Each section is tied to a single chosen page. A page is a blank canvas that can have just about any type of code, but at the very minimum, a page possesses numerous calls to forms whose job is to actually pull the requested content from the article into the template. Finally, Textpattern compiles the page—pulling in all the content referenced by forms and plugins—and generates the HTML (see Figure 8-2) that is sent to the browser.

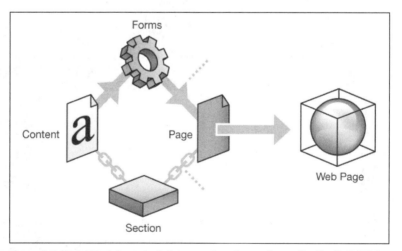

Figure 8-2. Textpattern figures out the correct section and compiles the final HTML for output by using that section's attributed page.

When creating your site's templates, there are several key steps in working with these components. You will learn about each step in more detail throughout the chapter by doing the following:

1. Build the HTML/CSS design outside of Textpattern before building the functional templates inside the CMS.

2. Decide on the site's major sections and create them within the Sections tab. The sections usually (but not always) map to the main navigation.

3. Convert raw HTML into a Textpattern template using pages and forms. This step includes using article-type forms to pull in some text you entered in the Content tab.

4. Tie the page to the proper section.

5. Duplicate the page as needed and customize the code to fit other sections after finalizing the first template.

Build the HTML and CSS first

It's much easier to simply build the design and corresponding HTML and CSS outside of Textpattern and then convert the static markup over to TXP templates. While the CMS's interface is elegant and fast, it's much slower than crafting a plain HTML and CSS mockup right on your hard drive and testing locally.

Traditionally, web designers create their designs in Photoshop and Illustrator, and then "slice" the designs into HTML. The Buzzbomb site is no different. The home page design was created in Photoshop, and was chopped up into web-ready files, including a plain HTML file and corresponding stylesheet. Figure 8-3 shows a snippet of the HTML for the Buzzbomb home page before it was moved into Textpattern. You'll examine this code in its entirety throughout the rest of the chapter.

It is critical to plan and build as many HTML prototypes as you can *before* editing templates inside Textpattern. Think about all the different web pages you'll need and the visual widgets appearing on each. The more planning you do *before* mucking about the CMS, the smoother the development process will unfold. In any given Textpattern site, you might have the following:

- Article display
- Comment display
- Comment submission form
- Article archive
- Photo galleries
- Search results
- File downloads
- Sectional landing pages

8

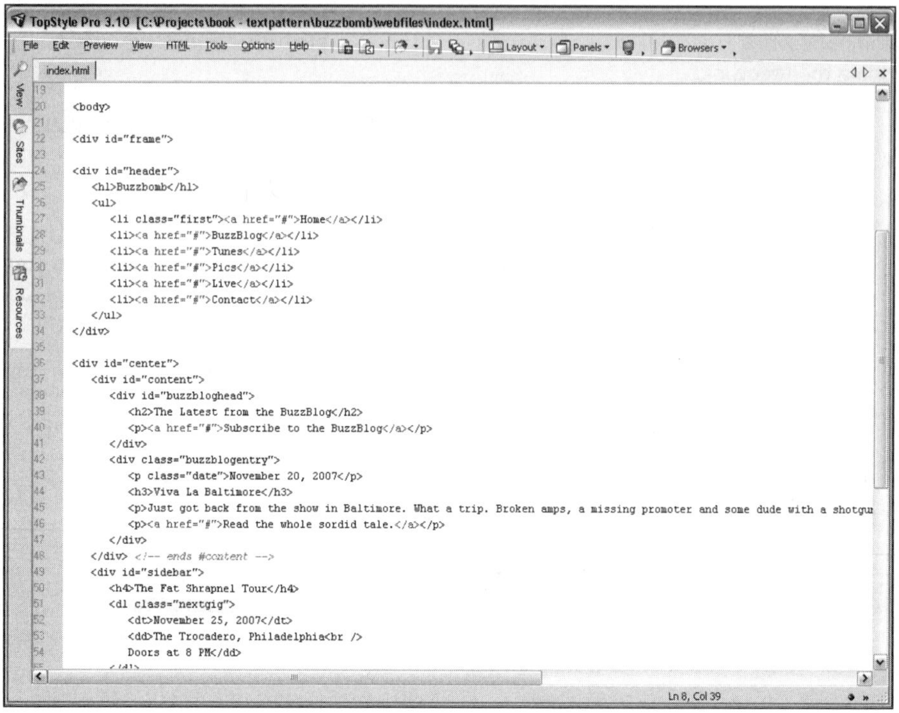

Figure 8-3. Before even opening Textpattern, the Buzzbomb home page was fully realized in plain HTML and CSS outside the content management system (CMS).

Create your sections

Chapter 7 covered the major differences between sections and categories. To recap, think of **sections** as file folders on a web server holding different buckets of content—physical partitions segregating stacks of articles. **Categories**, by contrast, are semantic values placed on articles to help give the content meta-like meaning. As discussed previously, an article *must* be attributed a section, whereas categorization is purely optional, in the same way a traditional HTML page must sit somewhere on the server, but might or might not have any meta information in its markup.

It's important to consider the architecture of your site from the beginning. While sections are easily created, edited, and deleted, it makes development much easier when you have a final product mapped out and can start building toward that goal instead of trying to generate a site's structure while knee-deep in TXP details. It would be like trying to determine the carpet color of a skyscraper before deciding how many floors it will have.

Sections commonly align with a site's main navigation. In the case of the Buzzbomb site, the sections reflect the primary links in the header: Home, BuzzBlog, Tunes, Pics, Live, and Contact. This is not always the case, and is certainly not required by any means, but it can make development easier when there is a clear correlation.

Chapter 6 discussed Textpattern's capability to support many different site architectures. Following are a few examples of sections that might exist in different types of websites.

Basic blog:

- Home (default)
- Post Archive
- Contact

Corporate website:

- Home (default)
- About Us
- News and Press Releases
- Products and Solutions
- Contact Us

Photography portfolio:

- Home (default)
- Latest Photos
- Portfolio
- Contact Us

Newspaper:

- Home (default)
- Local
- Sports
- Weather
- Entertainment

For the sample site for Buzzbomb, we'll go with the following sections:

- Home (default)
- BuzzBlog (the band's blog)
- Tunes (the discography)
- Pics (a few pictures of the band)
- Live (some tour dates)
- Contact

Let's review the Sections tab. Although the options are few, they wield tremendous control over your templates.

Creating a new section

To create a new section, simply enter a name in the topmost field and click the Create button. The section and its options are generated and placed in alphabetical order, so you
might need to scroll down a bit. For example, say you want to create a section for the
Buzzbomb site called Pics, in which you anticipate having a collection of the most recent
photos. After clicking Create, you see the options shown in Figure 8-4.

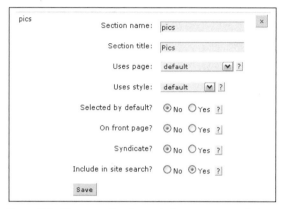

Figure 8-4. When a section is created, you are presented
with the default options.

The concept behind section names and titles is the same as categories, covered in Chapter
7. The name is referenced by the Textpattern system and is used for database queries and
generating URLs. The title, by contrast, is the human-readable version intended for screen
display. When using the `<txp:section />` tag, Textpattern uses the name by default and
must be instructed to use the title. For instance, suppose the following code was in this form:

You have navigated to the **`<txp:section />`** section.

The code produces the following:

You have navigated to the pics section.

Instead, you need to tell Textpattern to use the title instead:

You have navigated to the **`<txp:section title="1" />`** section.

That produces the following, which is more natural:

You have navigated to the Pics section.

Almost every native and plugin-based tag in Textpattern has attributes that control its output. Many of these attributes are binary, meaning they are positive or negative, either on or off. Traditionally, binary information is rendered as 1/0, in which the number 1 indicates that the value is true, and the zero indicates that the value is not true. Unfortunately, a few Textpattern tags are inconsistent in the way they determine a positive or negative value. Most use the 1/0 technique (as with the previous `<txp:section />` tag), but a few still use on/off or yes/no terminology. Functionally, all three mean the same thing, but it can be confusing to someone who hasn't spent a lot of time in the CMS.

Filling in the options

Below the Section name and Section title in the section options, you'll see two important drop-down menus: Uses page and Uses style. After producing a template with a page and forms, that page must be linked to the section in the first drop-down menu. *This link is critical to building a Textpattern site.* In the preceding discussion, this linking process fulfills step 2 of how a called article ends up in HTML:

1. Textpattern looks to see what section is attributed to the article.

2. Textpattern then looks to see what page is linked to the section.

3. From that page, Textpattern builds the final HTML output.

When you create a new page under the Pages tab, this drop-down menu is automatically updated. Sometimes you have only one page whose template works for every section. However, you're just as likely (probably more so for complex sites) to have a different page for every section so every section can have its own unique design or structure.

The concept for attributing a style—that is, a CSS file—is not much different. You might have one stylesheet that works wonderfully across every section, just as you might have a different stylesheet for every section, depending on the design of the site. When you create a new style under the Style tab, this drop-down menu is updated to reflect the new options. Of course, this drop-down menu's value is contingent upon whether you choose to use Textpattern's CSS editor. If you're working with an external stylesheet, this option does nothing.

8

Choices, choices

The final options for each section are wrapped up in four radio buttons that define how a section interacts with the rest of the site:

- **Selected by default?** This option is simple enough. When checked, it becomes the default choice when creating a new article. Only one section can have Yes checked at any given time.

- **On front page?** This option dictates whether content attributed to that section should appear on the default landing page of the site. This might be confusing at first, but consider a simple blog. You have a section called Blog that houses all your daily posts, but you also have a section called Photo Album that is designed to showcase your photography. You want your blog content to appear on the home page, so you click Yes for that section. On the other hand, you want to keep your photos regulated to a subsidiary section off the site's landing page, so you click No for the Photo Album section.

- **Syndicate?** This option controls whether that section's content is syndicated through Textpattern's generated RSS or Atom feed. Using the preceding example, you might choose to syndicate both the Blog content and the Photo Album content, or just the Blog content.

- **Include in site search?** This option is fairly self-explanatory. If there's a section whose content you do not want to appear in Textpattern's search results, simply click No.

> Note that this does not affect how external search engines crawl your site. If you want to hide content from Google, MSN, Yahoo!, and other commercial spiders, you need a robots.txt[1] file.

Creating templates with pages

A page is the foundation of HTML templates—it is the place where the HTML and the text meet before being output to a browser, the final merge of the content and structure separation discussed in Chapter 6. In Textpattern terms, it is the place where forms call the articles' content. It's also where the CMS decides whether to render an article's individual web page, a section landing page, a 404 error page, or a search results page, all of which can be controlled via tags in a single page. (For more information on building these multiple templates into a single page, see Chapter 11.)

While the default Textpattern template leaves some clues as to how to start building your template, it's best to just start from scratch. Figure 8-5 shows what a clean TXP page looks like.

---

1. Learn more about robots.txt files at SearchTools.com: www.searchtools.com/robots/robots-txt.html

Figure 8-5. A page in Textpattern is a completely blank canvas for creating HTML templates.

The middle field is just a big blank area for writing the HTML template, but you will rarely see a blank page like this. In fact, the only way to create a new page is to *duplicate* an existing one. (Since the page default is permanent, there will always be something to duplicate.) This is done at the bottom of the browser window in the field to the right of the Save button.

The right column is just a list of your pages, with a delete button to the right of each. There is no limit to how many pages you can have. Different setups require a different number of templates—simple Textpattern sites might only need one page; more-complex sites might need dozens.

The left column is the developer's toolbox. The main headers expand to reveal a variety of Textpattern tags, from XML feeds and article tags to file downloads and meta information (refer to Chapter 5 for more information).

The big copy and paste

Okay, so you have developed HTML and CSS outside the CMS and created your sections to define the overall architecture. Life is good. The next step is to start creating the templates to house the site's content. This is not that hard—you're not doing much more than replacing dummy text in the HTML prototype with database queries to pull in dynamic content.

First, you need to move the stylesheet and images over to the server. For simplicity and speed, it's usually more efficient to work through an FTP program for managing these pieces of the site, especially during the rapid back-and-forth, tweak-and-check of early site development. While you could build your site using Textpattern's CSS editor and image upload facility, it's simply more effective to work with these files natively independent of the back end.

At this point, you need to decide whether to create a test environment in TXP or make changes right to the live site. If you have a local installation, this isn't an issue. (See Chapter 2 for detailed instructions on creating a local installation.) But if you're working on a live server—especially on a site that relies on a current design—you need to create a testing ground for development. In the case of Buzzbomb, you're creating the template for the home page, so you'll create a page called homepage_test. Since the home page is pulling content from the buzzblog section, you can link that section to the new test page, as shown in Figure 8-6.

Figure 8-6. After creating a test page called homepage_test, you link it to the buzzblog section.

After uploading the supporting image and stylesheet files and creating a test page, let's move on to the big copy and paste. You can take the entire prototype HTML file and copy it right into the homepage_test Textpattern page (see Figure 8-7). After ensuring that the paths to the CSS file and image directory are correct, click Save and conduct a quick test of the page by loading the section's URL (for instance, www.example.com/sectionname if you're using clean URLs; www.example.com/index.php?s=sectionname if you're using messy URLs) and see whether your new template is there. If all goes well, it will look exactly like your original prototype.

Figure 8-7. The prototype HTML gets pasted directly into a page for testing.

Forms

You now have a functioning page and section working in tandem to produce some HTML from Textpattern. The next step is to take advantage of the rich tag language in TXP and convert static markup into flexible, dynamic templates by using forms. Textpattern forms, as mentioned in Chapter 5, can rightfully be called "code snippets." They are sections of code and markup referenced by pages when needed. Think about your music library—when you want to make a mixed CD, you're pulling from only a dozen or so albums, even though you might have 100 on the shelf. In Textpattern, you might have 100 forms ready, but a page might use only 3 or 4.

Breaking it down

One of the primary goals of a Textpattern page is to minimize the amount of hard-coded content on the page by moving any piece of content, HTML, PHP, or TXP tag over to forms that can be called at any time by the CMS. Any code *not* outsourced is subsequently changeable only by editing the page itself and this is a grossly ineffective use of the CMS's inherent efficiency. You should be able to change the structure of the site by changing only a form or two, not combing through your pages and editing them individually.

With this in mind, you need to carefully disassemble the HTML and identify the following elements:

- **Sections of dynamic content**: This is the stuff that is pulled from the Content tab into your template by using `<txp:article />`, `<txp:article_custom />`, and other tags for articles, links, images, and files. They are easy to spot; generally any actual text inside the HTML file becomes a dynamic field.

- **Pieces of static code that can be reused by other templates**: A site footer is a common example: the HTML can be moved into a form and treated as an include, referenced by all templates but updated from one piece of source markup.

- **Any page-specific content that will never appear on another template**: For example, a contact page might have some special markup for a contact form that will never see the light of day anywhere else.

The first two elements live in forms *outside* the page, and the last can exist either *inside* a page as hard-coded markup or reside in a form like the others.

Let's examine the five different types of forms at our disposal, which are selectable in the drop-down menu at the bottom of each form screen. They include Article, Comment, List, File, and Misc. Every form must be attributed to one of the five types, and how a form is categorized carries considerable weight in the CMS. For instance, you might have a form with article-specific tags (such as `<txp:body />` or `<txp:title />`) that is called from an `<txp:article />` tag on your page. However, that form should be filed under the Article type to work. Anything else might cause nothing to display when the final HTML is rendered from your template. Let's discuss the finer points of difference between the form types.

Article forms

Article forms are used in conjunction with the `<txp:article />` and `<txp:article_custom />` tags to pull content from your articles (stored under the Content tab) into your page templates. They are the magic links that render blog posts, landing pages, static content, and any other block of text in your article database. Since articles can hold a variety of content, from text to images to Textpattern plugin tags, the article-type form is a powerful, versatile tool that is mission-critical to building Textpattern-powered sites. In fact, you would be hard-pressed to find a TXP page that is *not* calling an article-type form.

Comment forms

Comment forms are for the display and collection of comments. You'll notice on the primary form-creation page that there are quite a few tags for the handling of your visitor's feedback. There are specific tags for building the feedback form, displaying a list of recent comments and for the display of the actual comments on the article web page. (See Chapter 5 for a descriptive list of each tag and Chapter 10 for getting them to work.) Since comments are a foundational element of content-based sites, Textpattern provides a formidable arsenal of tools for customization.

Link forms

Textpattern's concept of links revolves around the tradition of blogs outputting a blogroll or list of favorite links in the sidebar of the site. While the feature might have been fashionable at the time of TXP's genesis, it's now a bit long in the tooth, stunted by limited set of features and versatility. But it remains in the software, nonetheless, and provides developers with another set of content options. A form with a link type uses link-specific tags such as <txp:linklist /> and <txp:linkdesctitle />, which are designed solely to output content stored within the Links tab.

File forms

Very much like the other categories, forms with the type of file are designed to output a narrow definition of content—in this case, data stored within the Files tab. Textpattern offers more than ten unique tags to handle this information, and this is where they appear.

Misc forms

Forms with a misc type are a bit different from the rest because they are used for just about everything else. The easiest way to think of the misc type is as a traditional server-side include—that is, a piece of code that can be called into any template. Because the Misc type deliberately frees the form from any specific type of content, it becomes a Swiss Army knife tool for pulling a variety of content, including other forms. As an example, although a misc-type form *could not* render a <txp:title /> tag (an article-specific tag that outputs an article's title), it *could* contain a <txp:article /> tag that referenced a proper article form containing the <txp:title /> tag.

Dismantling the prototype

Now that you've examined the form options, it's time to examine the HTML prototype for the Buzzbomb home page and move it into different kinds of forms, converting static code to dynamic, database-driven templates. Let's take a look at the page's HTML. Using the previous guidelines, you need to identify dynamic content, static content that can be reused, and any content that is unique to the page that doesn't need to be outsourced. Figure 8-8 shows a quick breakdown.

8

```html
<!DOCTYPE html PUBLIC "-//W3C//DTD XHTML 1.0 Strict//EN" "http://www.w3.org/TR/xhtml1/DTD/xhtml1-strict.dtd">

<html xmlns="http://www.w3.org/1999/xhtml" xml:lang="en" lang="en">
<head>
        <meta http-equiv="content-type" content="text/html; charset=utf-8" />
        <title></title>
        <meta name="description" content="" />
        <meta name="keywords" content="" />
        <style type="text/css" media="screen,projection">
                @import 'buzzbomb.css';
        </style>
        <link rel="stylesheet" type="text/css" href="#.css" media="print" />
        <link rel="home" title="Home" href="/" />
        <link rel="search" title="Search this site" href="#" />
        <link rel="author" title="Send feedback" href="#" />
        <link rel="contents" title="Site Map" href="#" />
        <link rel="shortcut icon" type="image/ico" href="#" />
</head>

<body>

<div id="frame">

<div id="header">
        <h1>Buzzbomb</h1>
        <ul>
                <li class="first"><a href="#">Home</a></li>
                <li><a href="#">BuzzBlog</a></li>
                <li><a href="#">Tunes</a></li>
                <li><a href="#">Pics</a></li>
                <li><a href="#">Live</a></li>
                <li><a href="#">Contact</a></li>
        </ul>
</div>

<div id="center">
        <div id="content">

                <div id="buzzbloghead">
                        <h2>The Latest from the BuzzBlog</h2>
                        <p><a href="#">Subscribe to the BuzzBlog</a></p>
                </div>
                <div class="buzzblogentry">
                        <p class="date">November 20, 2007</p>
                        <h3>Viva La Baltimore</h3>
                        <p>Just got back from the show in Baltimore. What a trip. Broken amps, a missing promote
                        <p><a href="#">Read the whole sordid tale.</a></p>
                </div>

        </div> <!-- ends #content -->
        <div id="sidebar">

                <h4>The Fat Shrapnel Tour</h4>
                <dl class="nextgig">
                        <dt>November 25, 2007</dt>
                        <dd>The Trocadero, Philadelphia<br />
                        Doors at 8 PM</dd>
                </dl>
                <dl class="upcominggig">
                        <dt>November 28, 2007</dt>
                        <dd>Washington, DC</dd>
                        <dt>Dec 1, 2007</dt>
                        <dd>Boston</dd>
                        <dt>Dec 3, 2007</dt>
                        <dd>NYC</dd>
                </dl>

                <h4>Get "Monkey Funk"</h4>
                <p>Get the <a href="#">latest album</a> from BuzzBomb Monkey Funk, featuring the single "You Dro

                <h4>Friends</h4>
                <ul class="linklist">
                        <li><a href="http://www.m-tronic.com/" title="Seriously some of the best dark drum&#39;n
                </ul>

        </div>
</div> <!-- ends #center -->

<div id="footer">
        <p>BuzzBomb is built with <a href="http://www.textpattern.com">Textpattern</a>. The band is fake, but th
</div>

</div> <!-- ends #frame -->

</body>
</html>
```

Left margin labels (top to bottom): Reusable Static Content, Reusable Static Content, Dynamic Article Content, Dynamic Article Content, Dynamic List Content, Reusable Static Content

Figure 8-8. The prototype HTML can be broken down into dynamic and static content blocks.

Creating forms containing static content

First, let's take care of the easy stuff by moving the header, main navigation, and footer into separate forms with a misc type applied to each. By allocating these blocks of markup to forms, the code can be reused across different templates by simply creating a `<txp:output_form />` Textpattern tag to reference the forms, as shown in the following code. The first form will be called meta and contain the following markup pulled from the top of the document:

```
<!DOCTYPE html PUBLIC "-//W3C//DTD XHTML 1.0 Strict//EN" "http:// ➥
www.w3.org/TR/xhtml1/DTD/xhtml1-strict.dtd">
<html xmlns="http://www.w3.org/1999/xhtml" xml:lang="en" lang="en">
<head>
  <meta http-equiv="content-type" content="text/html; charset=utf-8" />
  <title></title>
  <meta name="description" content="" />
  <meta name="keywords" content="" />
  <style type="text/css" media="screen,projection">
    @import 'buzzbomb.css';
  </style>
  <link rel="stylesheet" type="text/css" href="#.css" media="print" />
  <link rel="home" title="Home" href="/" />
  <link rel="search" title="Search this site" href="#" />
  <link rel="author" title="Send feedback" href="#" />
  <link rel="contents" title="Site Map" href="#" />
  <link rel="shortcut icon" type="image/ico" href="#" />
</head>
```

This form contains mostly static content—things that won't change from web page to web page—but it also contains metadata information that *does* change depending on which page the visitor is viewing. (The metadata is emphasized in the preceding code.) This presents the opportunity to nest dynamic content (article-dependent meta information) within a static form, something we'll explore when we cover creating dynamic meta information in Chapter 11.

The second block of static code is the header logo and the primary navigation. We'll call the form header+nav:

```
<div id="header">
  <h1>Buzzbomb</h1>
  <ul>
    <li class="first"><a href="#">Home</a></li>
    <li><a href="#">BuzzBlog</a></li>
    <li><a href="#">Tunes</a></li>
    <li><a href="#">Pics</a></li>
    <li><a href="#">Live</a></li>
    <li><a href="#">Contact</a></li>
  </ul>
</div>
```

8

The main navigation is fairly simple: it contains no drop-down menus or subsidiary links, and it maps cleanly to the sections you created earlier. There are many plugins designed to dynamically generate menus from sections, categories, or even specific clumps of articles, and they can be used in forms as effectively as vanilla HTML. For the Buzzbomb site, you'll use a simple plugin called cbs_navigation_menu[2] that builds a menu from defined sections. This is what the form header+nav looks like when you use the plugin's syntax instead of pedestrian HTML:

```
<div id="header">
  <h1>Buzzbomb</h1>
  <txp:cbs_navigation_menu
    sections="default,buzzblog,tunes,pics,live,contact"
    titles="Home,BuzzBlog,Tunes,Pics,Live,Contact"
    break="li"
    activeclass="active"
    wraptag="ul"
    ids="first,,,,," />
</div>
```

The final chunk of reusable HTML is the site's footer. You'll create a new form called footer and add the following HTML:

```
<div id="footer">
  <p>BuzzBomb is built with <a href="http://www.textpattern.com"> ➡
Textpattern</a>. The band is fake, but the CMS is real.</p>
</div>
</div> <!-- ends #frame -->
</body>
</html>
```

After creating these three forms, you can replace the HTML on the homepage_test page with <txp:output_form /> tags, which is the standard means of dropping misc-type forms into a page. The code in the page now looks like this:

```
<txp:output_form form="meta" />
<body>
<div id="frame">
<txp:output_form form="header+nav" />
<div id="center">
  <div id="content">
  ... main content ...
  </div> <!-- ends #content -->
  <div id="sidebar">
  ... sidebar content ...
  </div>
</div> <!-- ends #center -->
<txp:output_form form="footer" />
```

---

2. http://textpattern.org/plugins/636/cbsnavigationmenu

Creating forms that contain dynamic article content

The concept behind forms with an article type is not that much different from forms with a misc type. The goal is to remove static HTML from the page template, but instead of simply calling unchanging blocks of HTML like the site footer, you're referencing blocks of code pulling article content from the database.

Article-type forms are a bit more complex than their misc-type brethren. Textpattern provides a menu of article-specific tags designed for article-type forms for the purpose of displaying data related to articles. Article-type forms exist to make your article data appear in a page; they can do little with tags relating to files, comments, or lists.

In fact, if article-specific tags (such as `<txp:title />` and `<txp:body />`) are placed directly onto a page, nothing will happen unless they are wrapped inside a conditional `<txp:if_individual_article>` tag, or they live inside a form with an article attribution.

Section-sensitive article output

When learning Textpattern, it's always easier to see a piece of code in action to better understand the CMS. Let's return to the Buzzbomb site—there are two key areas of the home page prototype requiring article-type forms to pull in content from the TXP database: the latest blog entry in the center and the list of upcoming performances in the right column.

Let's start with the blog post. The goal for the home page is to show the latest entry to the Buzzblog; since the band doesn't post too often, showing any more than the most recent is probably overkill.

Under the Content tab, we wrote an article called "Viva La Baltimore" about the band's exploits at a show in Baltimore. There's nothing particularly unique about the entry itself: it has a title, some content in the body, and some more content in the excerpt field. We placed it within the On Tour category and within the buzzblog section.

Now that there is some real content, you need to transform the HTML you created for the prototype into template-ready code. Normally, you would create a *new* form with an article attribution (and you will in a moment), but because this is the primary content of the home page, it's common practice to use the form default that Textpattern provides for just this purpose. (Please note that using default is *not* required. You could create your own article-type form for the home page's content and it will work just as well.)

So let's take the snippet of the dummy markup currently displaying the blog entry and place it into the form default:

```
<div class="buzzblogentry">
  <p class="date">November 20, 2007</p>
  <h3>Viva La Baltimore</h3>
  <p>Just got back from the show in Baltimore. What a trip. Broken ➡
  amps, a missing promoter and some dude with a shotgun, and that was ➡
  only the opening act. Amazingly, we all made it out alive.</p>
  <p><a href="#">Read the whole sordid tale.</a></p>
</div>
```

8

The next step is to replace the content you used for mockup purposes with Textpattern tags that will call real content from the database. This is a very granular, tangible example of separating content from structure, discussed in Chapter 6. The HTML remains the same, but database hooks pull in content dynamically, so the CMS can use the single clump of HTML over and over with different content. Let's take a look at the revised form:

```
<div class="buzzblogentry">
  <p class="date"><txp:posted /></p>
  <h3><txp:title /></h3>
  <txp:excerpt />
  <p><a href="<txp:permlink />" title="<txp:title />">Read the whole ➥
sordid tale.</a></p>
</div>
```

The Textpattern tags—each designed to pull in a different aspect of an article—are emphasized in the example. Let's briefly examine each of these tags:

- <txp:posted /> pulls in the article's post date and time. The display of this information can be wildly customized and is set in the Preferences area of the Admin tab. (The formatting follows **strftime**,[3] which formats display for local time settings and can be overridden manually inside the tag using the format attribute.)

- <txp:title /> shows the article's title. You use this tag twice in the form—first as the actual title of the blog post (wrapped in the <h3> tag), but also as the permanent link's title text.

- <txp:excerpt /> outputs the content in the excerpt field of an article. Like <txp:title />, it's a straightforward database call that you'll use often to grab a specific piece of an article.

- <txp:permlink /> means "permanent link" and is used to create a link to the article's permanent page. The tag actually has two different formats: a container version and a single version. The single version, which you're using in the previous form, is self-closing and renders the actual URL. (The container tag renders the URL and the <a> tag and wraps around the anchor text: <txp:permlink>anchor text</txp:permlink>.)

Now that you have an article-type form for displaying the Buzzblog post, you need to reference it from the page. As discussed previously, to render an article-type form, you need to use one of two Textpattern tags: <txp:article /> or <txp:article_custom />. The <txp:article /> tag is section-sensitive, meaning that it pulls in only articles attributed to the current section. Because you have instructed Textpattern to display the section buzzblog on the home page (set in the Sections area of the Presentation tab), any content attributed to the buzzblog section (like the article "Viva La Baltimore") will appear on the home page. So, to display the form, you'll use the <txp:article /> tag like so:

---

3. http://us2.php.net/strftime

```
<txp:output_form form="meta" />
<body>
<div id="frame">
<txp:output_form form="header+nav" />
<div id="center">
  <div id="content">
    <div id="buzzbloghead">
      <h2>The Latest from the BuzzBlog</h2>
      <p><a href="#">Subscribe to the BuzzBlog</a></p>
    </div>
    <txp:article limit="1" />
  </div> <!-- ends #content -->
  <div id="sidebar">
  ... sidebar content ...
  </div>
</div> <!-- ends #center -->
<txp:output_form form="footer" />
```

The <txp:article /> tag is emphasized in the preceding code. Notice that the
<txp:article /> tag has a limit attribute, which simply restricts the tag's output to one
article—which, by default, is the most recent entry. (If the limit attribute is left out, TXP
falls back on the default of the ten most recent articles.) Typically, the <txp:article />
tag also has a form attribute, which tells TXP what form to use to render the output.
However, because you're using the form default, a form does not need to be specified in
the <txp:article /> tag.

As you can see, linking article output with a template is straightforward. Create a form
with your template snippet, set it to an article type, and attach it your page with an
<txp:article /> tag.

Multiple templates within a single page

Let's explore some of the deeper power of Textpattern's templates. Now that you've set up
the Buzzblog post on the home page, you need to create the template for the whole blog
entry—the individual page that encases the actual post. In other words, when users click
the permanent link you created previously, they will be transported to this page:
buzzbomb.textpatternsolutions.com/buzzblog/viva-la-baltimore. You need to define
what that web page will look like.

One of the strongest efficiencies of Textpattern is its capability to nest multiple templates
within a single page. Using **conditional tags**, which are simple if statements, you can
place multiple article tags in a page and define which one is activated (depending on
where the user is within the site). The home page for Buzzbomb might have the following
templates built right into the same page:

- The home page Buzzblog excerpt, which was covered previously
- The full Buzzblog entry, which is where users go when they click the permanent link
- The search results

8

In the interest of keeping the example simple, we'll cover only the first two (although we'll tackle the third in Chapter 11). You already created a form for outputting the Buzzblog blog entry summary on the home page, so let's move on to creating the article-type form for rendering the entire article. Figure 8-9 shows what you want it to look like when you're done.

Figure 8-9. An individual blog entry for the Buzzbomb site.

As you can see from Figure 8-9, the overall shell of the site remains the same. You retain the header, footer, and right column. In fact, you're changing only the left column, essentially swapping out the Buzzblog entry summary for the full text of the article. Here is the HTML for rendering the full article you used in the initial mockup:

```
<div id="buzzblogheadarchive">
  <p>Filed Under "On Tour"</p>
</div>
<div class="buzzblogentry">
  <p class="date"> 7 October 2006</p>
  <h3>Viva La Baltimore</h3>
  ... blog entry text ...
</div>
```

You'll follow the same process as you did with the other form. Leaving the actual HTML structure alone, the blocks of text are replaced with Textpattern tags that pull the article's content from the database. You'll create a form called buzzblog_entry, select article in the Type drop-down menu, and add the following code:

```
<div id="buzzblogheadarchive">
  <p>Filed Under "<txp:category1 title="1" />"</p>
</div>
<div class="buzzblogentry">
  <p class="date"><txp:posted /></p>
  <h3><txp:title /></h3>
  <txp:body />
</div>
```

Again, the Textpattern tags are emphasized in the code example. You'll recognize several from the previous article-type form for the home page showing the post summary, including <txp:posted /> and <txp:title />, which are used to display the date and article title again. In addition, there are two important new tags:

- <txp:body /> is a straightforward tag that displays the article's main content. There are no attributes or options; it simply renders whatever you placed in the big window in the Write tab, which could be text, images, plugins, PHP code, or even more TXP tags. (For more information, check out the "Body and Excerpt" section in Chapter 7.)

- <txp:category1 /> outputs the first category to which the article is assigned. You'll remember from Chapter 7 that you need to add the title attribute for Textpattern to render the *title* of the category, not the *name*. (As you might suspect, there is also a <txp:category2 /> tag that functions the same in all respects, except it outputs the second category to which the article is attributed.)

Now that you have the new form to render the whole blog entry, you need to attach it to the page. Like the default form, you'll use the <txp:article /> tag on the page to reference the new form buzzblog_entry. Here is the code:

```
<txp:article form="buzzblog_entry" />
```

You'll notice that you don't use the limit attribute this time. Textpattern automagically recognizes that the form is being rendered for an individual page and only one article should be displayed, so setting a limit of one is redundant. However, because you're not using the form default, you need to specify which form the tag should use to render the article, which is accomplished through the form attribute. You instructed the system to use the buzzblog_entry form for this instance.

But can you just add this tag right to the page? Unfortunately, it's not quite so easy. Here is where the magic of conditional tags comes into play. Let's jump right in with the <txp:if_individual_article> tag and see how it would appear on the page:

```
<txp:output_form form="meta" />
<body>
<div id="frame">
<txp:output_form form="header+nav" />
<div id="center">
  <div id="content">
    <txp:if_individual_article>
      <txp:article form="buzzblog_entry" />
```

8

```
<txp:else />
  <div id="buzzbloghead">
    <h2>The Latest from the BuzzBlog</h2>
    <p><a href="#">Subscribe to the BuzzBlog</a></p>
  </div>
  <txp:article limit="1" />
</txp:if_individual_article>
</div> <!-- ends #content -->
<div id="sidebar">
... sidebar content ...
</div>
</div> <!-- ends #center -->
<txp:output_form form="footer" />
```

The logic is simple. You're telling Textpattern the following: if you're loading an individual article—such as the kind reached via a permanent link—use this article-type form to load the whole article; if you're not hitting an individual article, go ahead and output the landing page using the form default. This way, two unique article templates are driven seamlessly from one page, reducing the amount of extra code that needs managing.

Textpattern offers a host of conditional tags. Some are used in pages and others are used in forms, but it enables developers to write quick and effective if-else rules that deeply extend the potential of templates.

Section-independent article output

On the Buzzblog home page, you need to create one more set of article tags that will output the tour date information in the right column. Because these articles are not inside the buzzblog section—they are attributed to the Live section—you have to pull this information using the <txp:article_custom /> tag, which is designed specifically for rendering article data independent of what section the user is in.

First, let's examine the right column and see whether you can organize the markup more efficiently. There are three distinct sections: the latest tour dates (The Fat Shrapnel Tour), a small promotional piece for the new album (Get "Monkey Funk"), and a few links to other bands. Each of these can be outsourced to separate forms. For simplicity, you'll move the content of each to a misc-type form that can be easily referenced on the site. The new sidebar code looks like this:

```
<txp:output_form form="meta" />
<body>
<div id="frame">
<txp:output_form form="header+nav" />
<div id="center">
  <div id="content">
    ... content ...
  </div> <!-- ends #content -->
  <div id="sidebar">
```

```
      <txp:output_form form="sidebar_tour" />
      <txp:output_form form="sidebar_promo" />
      <txp:output_form form="sidebar_friends" />
   </div>
</div> <!-- ends #center -->
<txp:output_form form="footer" />
```

You'll use these misc-type forms to hold the code for each blurb. This is certainly not required, but when the blocks of HTML are compartmentalized, maintenance becomes much less of a headache.

For the tour dates, you'll focus on the contents of the sidebar_tour form. Looking at the prototype HTML, you find the following bit of code:

```
<h4>The Fat Shrapnel Tour</h4>
<dl class="nextgig">
  <dt>November 25, 2007</dt>
  <dd>The Trocadero, Philadelphia<br />
  Doors at 8 PM</dd>
</dl>
<dl class="upcominggig">
  <dt>November 28, 2007</dt>
  <dd>Washington, DC</dd>
  <dt>Dec 1, 2007</dt>
  <dd>Boston</dd>
  <dt>Dec 3, 2007</dt>
  <dd>NYC</dd>
</dl>
```

The design splits the tour dates to stylize the next tour date differently from the rest, so visitors can easily see where the next gig is being held. To accommodate the design, you need two <txp:article_custom /> tags, each linking to its own article-type form—one for the next gig and the other for the rest of the upcoming gigs.

Before you get started, let's review the article entry for a typical tour date (see Figure 8-10).

There is no large body of content required for a tour date entry. Instead, you focus on some key data pieces such as the venue and start time stored in custom fields, and the category (which in this case is critical to ensuring that the tour date shows up in the sidebar).

Now that you have a good idea of what kind of content is involved, you can create the article-type forms to display the information. You'll create a form called sidebar_tour_next, select Article as the type, and use the following code:

```
<dt><txp:posted /></dt>
<dd><txp:custom_field name="live_venue" />, <txp:title /><br />
Doors at <txp:custom_field name="live_starttime" /></dd>
```

You're using two familiar tags—`<txp:title />` and `<txp:posted />`—along with a couple of `<txp:custom_field />` tags to pull in the bits of content stored in the left column of the Write tab, shown in Figure 8-10. (You'll learn more about custom fields in Chapter 12.) You can create another form called `sidebar_tour_upcoming` and use a similar block of code, sans the custom fields showing the venue and start time:

```
<dt><txp:posted /></dt>
<dd><txp:title /></dd>
```

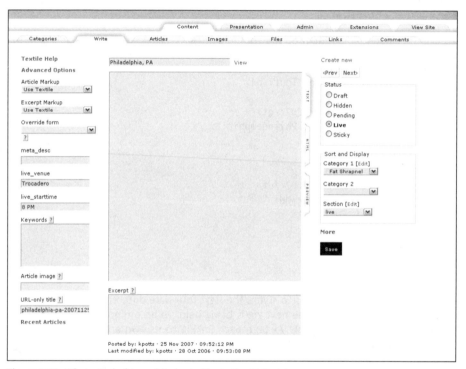

Figure 8-10. What a typical tour date looks like in the Write tab.

This form just shows the date of the show and in what city it's located. It's a fairly simple form, but you'll often find that some forms (especially those of the article variety) contain very little code, sometimes as little as a single Textpattern tag such as `<txp:title />` or `<txp:body />`. There is no obligation to make any form any more complex or bloated with code than what the situation demands.

Next, you create two `<txp:article_custom />` tags to access the new forms:

```
<h4>The Fat Shrapnel Tour</h4>
<dl class="nextgig">
  <txp:article_custom
    form="sidebar_tour_next"
    time="any"
    limit="1"
```

```
      sort="posted asc"
      section="live" />
  </dl>
  <dl class="upcominggig">
    <txp:article_custom
      form="sidebar_tour_upcoming"
      time="any"
      limit="3"
      offset="1"
      sort="posted asc"
      section="live" />
  </dl>
```

Because the <txp:article_custom /> tag is not tied to the section in which it appears, you have to dictate the parameters from where the articles are pulled. First, you'll notice that both tags are pulling from the live section, in which all tour date articles reside. You'll also notice that each has a time attribute set to any. Because these articles are set in the future, you must deliberately tell Textpattern to pull all articles from the live section, no matter what the timestamp is, because the TXP default is to output only articles that have a past date.

You will also notice each tag has a limit attribute, which caps the output to one and three articles, respectively. The second tag also uses an offset attribute, which forces the list of articles to begin after the specified amount. Since the first tag calls the first article, you need to offset the second tag to avoid rendering the forthcoming tour date twice. Finally, each tag is calling its respective form, which you defined previously.

The <txp:article_custom /> tag has a tremendous amount of attribute options that can be mixed and matched to satisfy just about any article criteria, from specific categories and sections to article status and from keyword values to the author of the material. It has great value when it comes to formatting an archive list of articles or in situations that demand extremely narrow output parameters.

Summary

At the end of the day, linking article data to a page template is not too difficult. With a couple of well-written forms and an understanding of a few key Textpattern tags, you'll be hooking up templates left and right before you know it. As you learn the system and conduct trial-and-error experiments, it is highly recommended to keep the Textpattern Wiki's tag listing[4] readily available. It contains almost every tag with corresponding attributes and is an invaluable reference as you learn the nuances of the Textpattern language.

---

4. http://textbook.textpattern.net/wiki/index.php?title=Alphabetical_Tag_Listing

9 TYING CONTENT AND STRUCTURE TOGETHER

Because of the separation of content and structure, the CMS design stresses that all site content resides within the Content tab of the interface. This material is accessible by using different type of forms—usually article-type forms—linked from pages. Chapter 8 explored the relationship between pages, forms, and content, and how the Textpattern architecture uses them as the three key building blocks for the website.

Understanding this trio's inner relationship is crucial to unlocking the full potential of Textpattern. While you started peeling back the layers of functionality and complexity in the BuzzBlog example in the previous chapter, you'll now go farther and start building out different parts of the Buzzbomb site using pages, sections, forms, and different kinds of content. You'll explore lists of articles, landing pages, contact pages, and basic photo galleries.

Building static pages

The definition of a **static page** is a bit nebulous and somewhat dependent on the context of the rest of the site. For example, a common blog is mostly composed of the author's posts, and this section is considered "dynamic" because the content is constantly changing. A static page for a blog might be an about page, a colophon, or a contact page. By contrast, a corporate website is built from static content. There might be some sections that rely on regularly changing content (for instance, press releases, which might be added weekly), but the bulk of the content is stuck in neutral.

Think of a static page as a web page of largely permanent text that stands alone, offset from the regular flow of content. Its URL is usually an indicator as well, and might look like www.yourblog.com/about or www.yourbiz.com/contact. In Textpattern terms, it's usually a section containing only one article.

For Buzzbomb, most of the content is dynamic, meaning that the pages change with regularity. You do, however, have a brief terms of use blurb that the band's record company lawyers required to be appended to the footer of the website. This is a good example of a static page because no one will touch this text anytime soon, and it falls well outside the normal content of the site.

Laying the static page's foundation

Since the static terms of use page is off by itself, it needs its own page and section to define the structure.

First, you need to create the page that the section will link to, which is easily done by navigating to the Pages area of the Presentation tab and copying the default page using the copying function at the bottom of the screen. (Refer to Figure 8-7 in the previous chapter.) Call the new page static_page. Although this is what you'll link to the new section, you don't have to do any customization to the code at this time; you just need a placeholder you can edit later.

After that, you need to establish a unique section for the static page called terms. After navigating to the Sections area of the Presentation tab, you create a new section with a fairly standard options set and link it to the page static_page. Look at Figure 9-1 to see what the final section options look like.

Figure 9-1. By creating the static page for the site's terms of use, you created a new section called terms that links to a page called static_page. This sets the foundation for the web page going forward.

Now that you have the section and corresponding page set, you have a URL to access for testing. If you retain clean URL mode, you can access buzzbomb.textpatternsolutions. com/terms for development. It also sets the stage for the actual content, which you'll create next.

Creating the static page content

Creating the content for a static web page is no different from creating content for any other web page; the difference comes in how it's presented by the templates. For the Terms of Use page, you simply head to the Write area of the Content tab, enter a title (Terms of Use), and fill out the body, supplied by those always-helpful lawyers. The only setting you need to pay attention to is the section attribution, which needs to be terms. There is no need for the excerpt or categories because the text will never be displayed out of context of the Terms of Use web page.

Creating the template for the static page

You now have the section, page, and article for Terms of Use. It's time to bring them all together. To do this, you need to create a new article-type form to display the content, make a few edits to the template static_page, and then tie them together with a Textpattern <txp:article /> tag.

First, you'll create an article-type form called static_text that will be used to display the content of the article you just created. Because this isn't a blog entry with comments or other complex interactive elements, the tag selection is minimal:

```
<div class="staticentry">
  <h3><txp:title /></h3>
  <txp:body />
</div>
```

You created a containing <div> and then simply output the title and body text. Next, you need to link this form into the page with a <txp:article /> tag. The final template is simple:

```
<txp:output_form form="meta" />
<txp:output_form form="header+nav" />
<div id="center">
  <div id="content">
    <txp:article form="static_text" />
  </div> <!-- ends #content -->
  <div id="sidebar">
    <txp:output_form form="sidebar_tour" />
    <txp:output_form form="sidebar_promo" />
    <txp:output_form form="sidebar_friends" />
  </div>
</div> <!-- ends #center -->
<txp:output_form form="footer" />
```

You'll recognize this code from Chapter 8 because the bulk of it was also used for the home page. You're changing only the middle part inside the content <div>, but this time there's no need for conditional tags because the template is designed to handle only a single article, nothing more. Now, when the user visits the Terms of Use page, they'll see a page just like the one in Figure 9-2 that shares the same overall template as the home page, but houses just a single block of text.

This technique works well for just about any type of site needing a stand-alone page that deviates from the rest of the content.

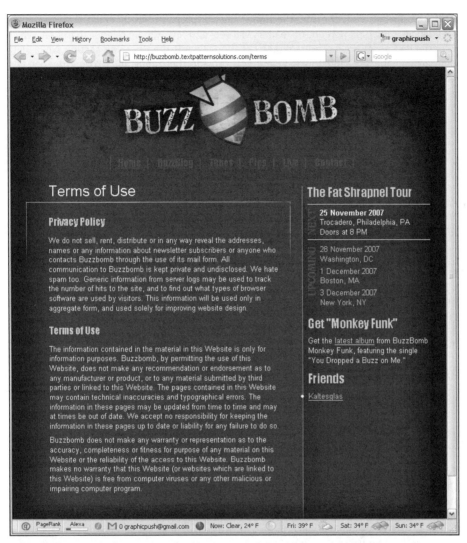

Figure 9-2. The final Terms of Use page blends wonderfully with the rest of the site.

Creating an archive page

For any sites that publish periodical content on a regular basis—whether a blog, news, articles, or other growing collection of work—there should be a way for users to review a list of older material. A common format is a centralized archive page that organizes content categorically, chronologically, or both, depending on what makes sense for your website. An archive page is especially common for blogs. In fact, you'll adapt the concept to the Buzzbomb site.

When a user first visits the site, the home page displays the most recent BuzzBlog entry. This article is what 99 percent of readers will see, and few will dig deeper than that, which is perfectly fine. However, users might occasionally visit the BuzzBlog section while skipping around the site, and this is where you provide the opportunity to dig deeper into older content. In the end, you want three blocks of messaging on the BuzzBlog page:

- A small bit of introductory text to help users orient themselves after arriving.
- The most recent blog entry highlighted, so new visitors immediately recognize the last entry and when it was posted. This is the same entry that appears on the home page.
- A list of older articles, ordered by date.

As shown in the following steps, you use a slightly different technique for each piece. You'll start with the basics and then move step by step through getting those three blocks of text where they belong.

Creating the section and page

Before you start slinging forms and <txp:article /> tags all over the place, you need to create a foundation for the BuzzBlog archive page by setting up a new section and page and then linking them together. The process closely mirrors what you did for the preceding static page.

First, you create a new page called buzzblog. There's no need to change any HTML or code right away—simply copying the default page is a good enough start. Second, you need to create a section. Keeping in mind that the section name appears in the URL, you should pick something obvious and semantic; in this case, buzzblog works perfectly. (Keep in mind that you already created the buzzblog section awhile ago because that's what you used for the "Viva la Baltimore" example; you're just walking through the process again.)

Every time you create a major section of the website, you follow a similar path. Occasionally, two or more sections reference the same page as their template, but the steps generally mimic what you did in the past two examples.

1. Create a new page duplicated from the default page (or whatever template works best for you).
2. Create a new section and make sure that the page you created in the first step is selected in the Uses page drop-down menu so the section and page are linked.
3. Edit the new page to display the correct content.

Editing the archive template

Now that you have the shiny new section and page to work from, you can start building the template for the blog archive. As discussed before, you want to include three distinct pieces of content when a user clicks the BuzzBlog link in the main menu: a small bit of introductory content, the first blog entry emphasized by showing its excerpt, and the remaining blog entries listed chronologically below that. From a Textpattern perspective, there are three different `<txp:article />` tags that accomplish this process.

Placing sticky content

The first task is to create some introductory text. Like creating any other content, you simply open the Write tab and type the opening message. There is nothing too special about this action, except that you need to select two important options. First, you need to choose Sticky as the Article Status and you need to make sure that buzzblog is chosen as the section.

The sticky status was discussed in Chapter 7 and you put it into practice now. When an article is tagged as sticky, it is removed from the normal flow of content. A simple `<txp:article />` tag pulls in articles with only a live status; you must deliberately tell Textpattern to go ahead and grab the sticky articles with the status attribute, like so:

```
<txp:article status="sticky" form="simple" />
```

When the status attribute is set to sticky, only articles with a sticky status are invited to the party. The sticky article status was created for exactly the kind of situation the BuzzBlog archive page presents. You have the normal flow of articles within the section—the blog entries—but you need another article for this landing page that also falls within the BuzzBlog section, but is *not* a blog post. Let's look at some code and see how it all works.

First, here is the template as it stands now for the archive page:

```
<txp:output_form form="meta" />
<txp:output_form form="header+nav" />
<div id="center">
  <div id="content">
    ... content ...
  </div> <!-- ends #content -->
  <div id="sidebar">
    ... sidebar content ...
  </div>
</div> <!-- ends #center -->
<txp:output_form form="footer" />
```

You left the content area blank, which is where you will focus the development efforts. Because this section is pulling the same content as the home page—articles inside the buzzblog section—you can reuse some of the TXP code from the default page:

```
<txp:output_form form="meta" />
<txp:output_form form="header+nav" />
<div id="center">
  <div id="content">
    <txp:if_individual_article>
      <txp:article form="buzzblog_entry" />
    <txp:else />
      ... the landing page content ...
```

9

```
        </txp:if_individual_article>
      </div> <!-- ends #content -->
      <div id="sidebar">
        ... sidebar content ...
      </div>
    </div> <!-- ends #center -->
    <txp:output_form form="footer" />
```

Let's think about this conditional statement for a second. Both the home page and the BuzzBlog archive page are pulling articles attributed to the buzzblog section, but only the template for the section buzzblog needs to contain the <txp:if_individual_article> tag because that is where the article will ultimately appear. (In other words, the URL will be www.site.com/**buzzblog**/article-title, not www.site.com/**default**/article-title.) You'll reuse the form buzzblog_entry that you created in Chapter 8.

Now you need to worry about what users see when they visit the landing page. In reference to the preceding code snippet, it is everything between the <txp:else /> tag and the closing </txp:if_individual_article> tag. You start with the sticky text, which serves as the introduction to the landing page, adding to the previous Textpattern code example:

```
    <txp:output_form form="meta" />
    <txp:output_form form="header+nav" />
    <div id="center">
      <div id="content">
        <txp:if_individual_article>
          <txp:article form="buzzblog_entry" />
        <txp:else />
          <txp:article status="sticky" form="simple" />
          ... the rest of the landing page content ...
        </txp:if_individual_article>
      </div> <!-- ends #content -->
      <div id="sidebar">
        ... sidebar content ...
      </div>
    </div> <!-- ends #center -->
    <txp:output_form form="footer" />
```

So when users are within the buzzblog section—and they are not visiting an individual page—they see the sticky text as an introduction to the rest of the archived content. This text appears above the archived articles, which you'll add next.

Adding the most recent article

Now that you built the template and appended some introductory text, you need to start building the main content of the landing page, which is the list of past blog entries. Before you dive into the big list of past writing, you highlight the most recent blog post, which involves the second <txp:article /> tag. In fact, this new tag is the only thing you add to the template's code:

```
<txp:output_form form="meta" />
<txp:output_form form="header+nav" />
<div id="center">
  <div id="content">
    <txp:if_individual_article>
      <txp:article form="buzzblog_entry" />
    <txp:else />
      <txp:article status="sticky" form="simple" />
      <txp:article limit="1" form="buzzblog_archive_recent" />
      ... the rest of the landing page content ...
    </txp:if_individual_article>
  </div> <!-- ends #content -->
  <div id="sidebar">
    ... sidebar content ...
  </div>
</div> <!-- ends #center -->
<txp:output_form form="footer" />
```

Let's examine the addition. It's a normal <txp:article /> tag, which means it is pulling content from the section in which it's operating—in this case, the buzzblog section. The limit attribute caps the output at only one article, and you're rendering that single article using the form buzzblog_archive_recent, which contains the following code:

```
<h4>The Most Recent Entry</h4>
<div class="buzzblogmostrecent">
  <h5><a href="<txp:permlink />" title="<txp:title />">➥
<txp:title /></a></h5>
  <txp:excerpt />
  <p class="date"><txp:posted /></p>
</div>
```

So the archive page is now set to output some introductory text using a sticky article, followed by highlighting the most recent blog post. Since you can't have every past entry represented by a full excerpt, the remaining list will be simplified.

Adding a list of all past articles

The third and final piece of the puzzle for this archive page is the actual list of all past articles, which sits below the most recent article, but displays a simple list of titles and post dates instead of the full excerpt. The overall execution isn't too much different from the previous example, but because you're dealing with a list of articles instead of just one, you need to build the forms intelligently.

Since you're pulling content from the buzzblog section, you'll be using another <txp:article /> tag, but this time it has some additional markup around it in the page. Here is the new code:

9

```
<txp:output_form form="meta" />
<txp:output_form form="header+nav" />
<div id="center">
  <div id="content">
    <txp:if_individual_article>
      <txp:article form="buzzblog_entry" />
    <txp:else />
      <txp:article status="sticky" form="simple" />
      <txp:article limit="1" form="buzzblog_archive_recent" />
      <h4>Past Buzzblog Entries</h4>
      <dl>
      <txp:article limit="999" offset="1" ➥
form="buzzblog_archive_past" />
      </dl>
    </txp:if_individual_article>
  </div> <!-- ends #content -->
  <div id="sidebar">
    ... sidebar content ...
  </div>
</div> <!-- ends #center -->
<txp:output_form form="footer" />
```

Because this is a list of articles, you had to remove any *non-repeating* HTML outside the form; in this case, the <h4> and <dl> (which stands for "definition list") get displayed only once. If they were inside the form buzzblog_archive_past, a new set of <h4> and <dl> tags would be rendered for every single article.

Because the <txp:article /> tag is designed to show all articles, you raised the limit to "999" to ensure that you don't miss anything. (The default for the limit attribute is ten.) In addition, you also included the offset attribute, which means the list of articles skip the first one in the series so you don't display the most recent article twice. Finally, you instructed the tag to use the article-type form buzzblog_archive_past, which contains the following markup:

```
<dt><a href="<txp:permlink />" title="<txp:title />">➥
<txp:title /></a></dt>
<dd>Posted on <txp:posted /> in <txp:category1 title="1" /></dd>
```

This form repeats over and over until Textpattern reaches the end of the list. As you can see in the final screenshot of the archive page (see Figure 9-3), you have four articles that get displayed. Each is displayed using the preceding code, which is related to the <dl> tag surrounding the <txp:article /> tag in the page, so the final output is a tidy definition list that looks something like this:

```
<dl>
  <dt><a href="http://buzzbomb.textpatternsolutions.com/buzzblog/➥
on-the-road-again"
        title="On the Road Again">On the Road Again</a></dt>
  <dd>Posted on 3 October 2006 in On Tour</dd>
  <dt><a href="http://buzzbomb.textpatternsolutions.com/buzzblog/➥
```

```
a-blog-entry"
        title="A Blog Entry">A Blog Entry</a></dt>
  <dd>Posted on  1 October 2006 in Random Life</dd>
  ... etc ...
</dl>
```

So you successfully created a blog archive page that includes three key elements: some introductory copy, the latest blog entry highlighted, and finally a list of all the remaining entries in chronological order. At the end of the day, the page looks like Figure 9-3.

Figure 9-3. The final blog archive page, complete with introductory text, the most recent blog entry highlighted, and a complete list of all entries.

Creating a contact page

Just about any site, from businesses to blogs to online communities, has a contact page. Sometimes it's an elaborate section full of global office addresses, a list of principals, and complex inquiry submission forms; and sometimes it's just an email address. Whatever you as a designer choose to do, the fact remains that you need a dedicated place on your website for people to contact you.

For the Buzzbomb site, you have ordained that the contact page can be accessed from the main menu by using the Contact link. You build a single page with some introductory copy and a contact form by building on some of the techniques laid out earlier in the chapter (and also learn some new concepts).

Section and page wonder duo

Start where you began with the other examples and create a new page and section. Since this contact page is very similar in structure to the static content page at the beginning of the chapter, you'll follow a near-identical procedure.

First, copy the page static_page from the first example to a new page called contact. You're copying this one because its simplicity most closely matches what you want to accomplish in the new contact page. Like before, you don't need to make any changes to the new page contact just yet.

Next, create a new section called contact. You choose the same options as the first example (refer to Figure 9-1), except that you link to the new page contact in the Uses page drop-down menu. Now that a new landing page for the section is established (visible at buzzbomb.textpatternsolutions.com/contact), you can start filling it with content.

Adding some introductory copy

The next step is to add some introductory content to the page before the web form to encourage people to send you some email. To do this, you simply create a new article in the Write area of the Content tab, give it a title and some content in the large body field, and then attribute it as a sticky article and select contact as the article's section.

To get the content to appear on the contact page, you mimic what you did for the blog archive page. In fact, you steal some code wholesale:

```
<txp:output_form form="meta" />
<txp:output_form form="header+nav" />
<div id="center">
  <div id="content">
    <txp:article status="sticky" form="simple" />
  </div> <!-- ends #content -->
  <div id="sidebar">
```

```
      ... sidebar content ...
    </div>
  </div> <!-- ends #center -->
  <txp:output_form form="footer" />
```

Within the structure you see a familiar line of bold markup, which is the line you used in the blog archive web page to call the introductory copy. Since it worked so well there, and since you haven't introduced any different functionality, it makes sense to simply reuse the markup. The <txp:article /> tag uses the status attribute to pull the only sticky article, which is then processed using the article-type form simple, which looks like this:

```
<h3><txp:title /></h3>
<txp:body />
```

You could realistically use this code and technique to create introductory copy on any landing page of the Buzzbomb site. Employing small reusable forms is a leading contributor to Textpattern's efficiency and flexibility as a website development platform; designers can build a library of small, easy-to-digest bits of code that easily plug into a variety of development equations.

Adding the contact form

The final step of the contact page is to build a form that the visitors can use to submit requests for information, tour dates, merchandise, and more. Textpattern users are fortunate in having the option of using a PHP-based form or a mature plugin called zem_contact_reborn that generates a contact form based on the attribute values you set in the plugin's tag. (You'll learn about both techniques later in the chapter.)

Regardless of the technique you employ, house the contact form in a separate Textpattern form (which will be called contact_form) to keep the root page clean. Since it's not holding any article-specific information, it will be a misc-type form. To reference this from the page, you'll add the following lines of code:

```
<txp:output_form form="meta" />
<txp:output_form form="header+nav" />
<div id="center">
  <div id="content">
    <txp:article status="sticky" form="simple" />
    <txp:output_form form="contact_form" />
  </div> <!-- ends #content -->
  <div id="sidebar">
    ... sidebar content ...
  </div>
</div> <!-- ends #center -->
<txp:output_form form="footer" />
```

You're now all set up to create the contact form. Let's examine the two options.

9

Using a raw PHP-driven solution

For those possessing knowledge of PHP and wanting the ultimate level of customization, Textpattern supports the ability to embed raw PHP scripts inside the content management system (CMS). PHP code can be placed directly on a page, tucked away in a form (as you're doing), or even added to an article. This is valuable not only for contact forms but also for advanced functionality not easily supported by Textpattern, such as forums, rating systems, and ecommerce packages.

There are literally hundreds of contact forms written in PHP. They range from free, simple forms to complex, feature-rich solutions that require a license fee. It's impossible to recommend any specific script, but you should try and use one that supports the following:

- An email-checking function, which is just a short contingency script to ensure that email addresses are well formed (like theguy@theplace.com).

- The capability to dictate required fields.

- Built-in security measures, including the "scrubbing" of content so malicious markup, header injections, and other threats can't be sent through email.

- Some type of visual feedback when a form either goes through successfully or cannot go through because of a specific error. (And the level of detail in error messages is important—you want people to understand *why* the email did not make it.)

> Hotscripts.com *is a listing of thousands upon thousands of free scripts, in PHP and other languages. It has a list of free and for-pay PHP scripts designed just for user inquiries.*

Using Textpattern plugins

In December 2004, a plugin called zem_contact was offered to the Textpattern community. The source code underwent several quick revisions and was then donated to the general TXP community to continue development. That plugin, which is now called zem_contact_reborn, has become one of the most valued and widely employed pieces of software in Textpattern-driven sites.

Essentially, the plugin enables a developer to create a complete functioning inquiry form from simply filling out a few options in the tag itself. No knowledge of PHP or any kind of scripting is necessary. At its most basic, the tag looks like this:

```
<txp:zem_contact to="theguy@theplace.com" />
```

This tag produces a complete contact form with a name, email, and message field that sends the message to the email address specified in the to attribute. While this is pretty handy in and of itself, the plugin's writers have also included a litany of additional tags and options for customizing the output to a very granular level. In addition to being able to redirect to a thank you page, send a copy of the message to the sender, or specify "thank you" text, developers can also build more-complex forms with a variety of elements, including text fields, message areas, checkboxes, radio buttons, drop-down menus, and more.

For the Buzzbomb site, you create a more complex form that takes advantage of the tag's rich pool of options. This is the code that appears in the TXP form called contact_form:

```
<txp:zem_contact to="theguy@theplace.com">
  <txp:zem_contact_text label="Your Name" break="" /><br />
  <txp:zem_contact_email break="" /><br />
  <txp:zem_contact_select
    label="You Are"
    list="A Ravenous Fan,A Forward-Thinking Promoter,➥
A Jealous Record Company Rep,Common Street Trash"
    break="" />
  <br />
  <txp:zem_contact_textarea label="Your Message" break=""➥
cols="30" rows="12" /><br />
  <txp:zem_contact_submit label="Click It" />
  <div class="checkbox">
    <txp:zem_contact_checkbox label="PS, send me free stuff"➥
break="" required="no" />
  </div>
</txp:zem_contact>
```

As you can see, you not only use the standard name and message fields but also provide the opportunity for visitors to identify themselves via the drop-down menu and request some free stuff via the checkbox. (You added a small amount of additional HTML markup to control styling, which is sometimes necessary given that individual tags do not allow the attribution of classes or IDs.) The final contact page looks like Figure 9-4.

This flexibility has made zem_contact_reborn the go-to choice for developers across the community. It's fast, easy, and flexible enough to handle just about any contact form. Visit the Textpattern Forum[1] to read more about the plugin or for general troubleshooting. It is available to download for free from Textpattern Resources.[2] To learn more about installing plugins, see Chapter 13.

---

1. http://forum.textpattern.com/viewtopic.php?id=13416

2. http://textpattern.org/plugins/701/zem_contact_reborn

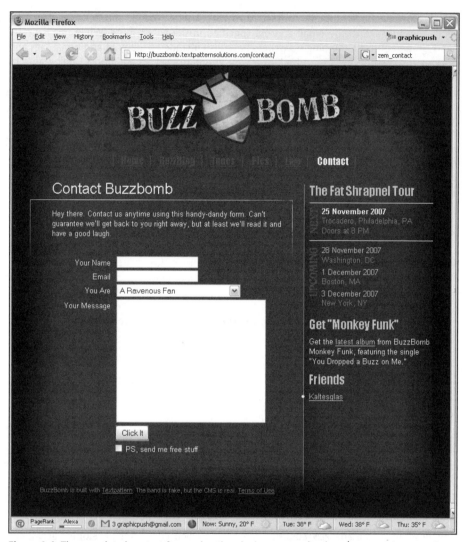

Figure 9-4. The completed contact form using the plugin zem_contact_reborn employs a variety of customized tags.

Creating a basic photo gallery

One of the big sections of the Buzzbomb site is the photo gallery section, in which the band can display photos from the tours, publicity shots, and more. The pictures are drawn from the Images tab in the CMS, which not only categorizes the pictures, but also enables the creation of thumbnails, captions, alternate text, and more. (For more information about the mechanics of the Images tab, see the section "Images, files, and links" in Chapter 7.)

Textpattern is a mixed bag of tricks when it comes to handling images. It is adept at creating just about any type of image-based content, from photoblogs to complex galleries, but relies on plugins to accomplish any significant functionality. Native tags are minimal at best, woefully inadequate at worst. This section discusses the tags that Textpattern provides, but also delves into some common third-party add-ons, including rss_thumbpop, which has become the de facto plugin for generating galleries.

Section and page (again)

If you followed along in this chapter, you realize that when creating big additions to your Textpattern websites, you almost always generate a new section and page as your starting point. The photo gallery is no different.

First, copy the page contact you created earlier in the chapter since its simplicity will come in handy when you start editing the template. Name the new page pics. When choosing which page to duplicate for your new section, always try to copy one that is closest in terms of code to minimize customization. In this case, the page contact contains only one line that needs deleting; the rest of the template is sound.

In addition, create a new section called pics, select all the standard options for a static page (refer to Figure 9-1), and link to the new page pics from the Uses page drop-down menu. (There is no specific reason why the section and page share the same name, but it can be convenient for organizational purposes when everything falls within the same nomenclature.) Once this link is in place, you can move forward and edit the templates.

Adding introductory copy (again)

In staying true to the previous two examples, you add some introductory copy using the same techniques discussed earlier. You copied the page contact because almost every line of code remains intact; in fact, the only line that is removed is the reference to the contact form. Once that's done, you're back to the familiar template:

```
<txp:output_form form="meta" />
<txp:output_form form="header+nav" />
<div id="center">
  <div id="content">
    <txp:article status="sticky" form="simple" />
  </div> <!-- ends #content -->
  <div id="sidebar">
    ... sidebar content ...
  </div>
</div> <!-- ends #center -->
<txp:output_form form="footer" />
```

As you can see, the bolded line is the same. Since the <txp:article /> tag is contextual to its section, you don't need to change a thing. The page contact automatically picks up the sticky article for the contact section, and the page pics automatically pulls the sticky article for the pics section.

9

All you need to do is access the Write tab, enter a title and some introductory copy, and then attribute the section pics to the article. Like before, the article-type form simple outputs this content. Once you have the opening content settled, you can move into creating the photo gallery.

Creating the photo gallery

Chapter 7 discussed the Images tab inside the CMS and how to upload images and create thumbnails. You learned how to create categories for the images and use that meta information to organize the content. For the photo gallery section of the Buzzbomb site, you put those tools into practice.

TXP tags vs. plugins

While Textpattern is capable of complex functionality out of the box, it cannot be everything to everyone and it falls painfully short in some areas. Thankfully, its extensible architecture allows plugin writers tremendous latitude in adding a range of capabilities, from small visual tweaks to large architectural alterations. You saw this in action in the previous example when the powerful plugin zem_contact_reborn created an entire custom contact form with only a few tags.

When it comes to managing images uploaded to the Images tab, Textpattern falls short in providing basic capabilities. Thankfully, several plugin writers have taken the baton and run far, and the Textpattern community now has a library of extremely useful add-ons that enable designers to take full advantage of their images.

One of the most useful plugins is rss_thumbpop. It creates a series of thumbnails from a defined category of images and links each to the full-scale version in a new popup window or in the current window as a new page. Its application is fairly basic, but extremely powerful, and simple enough that it has become one of the most popular TXP plugins to date. You'll use it in the following photo gallery page.

Using rss_thumbpop for the photo gallery

For this example, you don't need any <txp:article /> tags beyond what you already employed for the sticky article. Instead, you'll use the plugin to reference images directly from the database.

You uploaded a bunch of images to two categories: "The Band" (pictures of Buzzbomb members) and "Places" (pictures of tour locations). Each image has a thumbnail 100 pixels wide, and each has appropriate text for the alt attribute. You'll use rss_thumpop to render the thumbnails for each category. Let's take a look at some code:

```
<txp:output_form form="meta" />
<txp:output_form form="header+nav" />
<div id="center">
  <div id="content">
    <txp:article status="sticky" form="simple" />
    <txp:rss_thumbpop
      category="The-Band"
```

```
            mode="float"
            showcaption="0"
            label="Pictures of the Band" />
        <txp:rss_thumbpop
            category="Places"
            mode="float"
            showcaption="0"
            label="Places We've Been" />
    </div> <!-- ends #content -->
    <div id="sidebar">
        ... sidebar content ...
    </div>
  </div> <!-- ends #center -->
  <txp:output_form form="footer" />
```

The tag <txp:rss_thumbpop /> contains many attributes and can accommodate many designs. You're using only a couple of options here, namely the definition of the categories (the first tag renders all images attributed to the category "The Band"; the second tag pulls anything tagged "Places"), setting the mode attribute to float (as opposed to relying on a table-based layout), and then turning off the display of captions. By default, these tags will render HTML similar to this:

```
<div class="rssThumbs">
  <div class="rssThumbLabel">Pictures of the Band</div>
  <div class="rssThumbFloat">
    <a target="_blank"
href="http://buzzbomb.textpatternsolutions.com/images/18.jpg"
      onclick="window.open(this.href, 'popupwindow', 'width=370,➥
height=253,resizable');
              return false;">
      <img class="rssThumb" src="http://buzzbomb.textpattern➥
solutions.com/images/18t.jpg"
          alt="Rockin out at a crazy angle." title="" />
    </a>
  </div>
</div>
```

This code example shows only one image, but you can see how the plugin is creating the wrapper tags around the label, the HTML anchor tags (including the JavaScript that loads a new window), plus the class names for various <div> tags you can use for cascading style sheet (CSS) styling. Since you elected to float the images, you need to add a rule to the CSS file telling any <div> with a class of rssThumbFloat to actually float. For instance:

```
#center .rssThumbFloat {
  float: left;
  width: 120px;
}
```

9

225

The images now float to the left. (For more information on floating in CSS, consult the excellent Floatutorial[3] created by Max Design.) There's really not much else to do except add more images and let the plugin do all the work for you. Figure 9-5 shows the final photo gallery.

Figure 9-5. The photo gallery uses the rss_thumbpop plugin to organize and display pictures you uploaded from the Images tab.

---

3. http://css.maxdesign.com.au/floatutorial/

Summary

By now, you should understand the basics of tying content and structure together using pages, sections, forms, and articles. This can be done from vanilla Textpattern tags and from plugins; and can use normal articles, sticky articles, and even content housed in other tabs, such as Images. The concepts in this chapter reinforce the ideas initially presented in Chapter 8 and represent the fundamental building blocks of TXP-based sites. Once the relationship between sections, pages, forms, and articles is understood, you can accomplish just about anything with Textpattern.

9

Although Textpattern is a versatile content management system (CMS) that can easily handle just about any type of website, it has always been very strong at powering blogs and media sites that are updated constantly. Part of the appeal of those sites is the natural conversation that develops between the author and reader, and the core building block behind that dialogue is the ability to comment on a blog entry.

In fact, the commenting phenomenon has spread beyond traditional blogs and made its way into more mainstream media as well as sites with longer article-like content. TravelWithYourKids,[1] a website powered by Textpattern, is not a blog at all; it is a collection of articles focusing on tips for traveling the world with kids. However, each article provides the opportunity for the reader to comment on the article. More and more sites are adopting this conversational web design.

Thankfully, Textpattern provides a rich development environment for commenting. You can customize the display of comments and the comment submission field. By using a host of plugins, as well as the Textpattern inherent architecture, you can craft a reader participation experience to rival any site.

Activating comments

The reality is that some sites have no need for comments. Longer prose, formal writing, photography galleries, corporate websites, and others simply might not need two-way communication between author and reader. Textpattern provides the means to activate or disable comments on both a global and per-article basis.

Global off switch

The Textpattern CMS provides the ability to globally activate or deactivate comment functionality. By default, it is turned on, but if you're developing content with a static feel not appropriate for reader feedback, simply navigate to the Preferences area of the Admin tab and change Accept comments to no. After doing so and clicking Save, the second set of options on the screen (seen in Figure 10-1) disappear.

> Note that disabling comments from the Admin tab affects the entire site. Any comment forms attached to article forms simply do not appear, and any articles that could previously accept comments have the submission form for new comments disabled.

---

1. www.travelwithyourkids.com

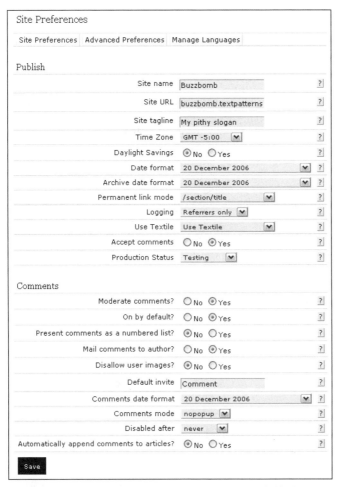

Figure 10-1. After selecting no in the Accept comments field, the bottom options disappear since they relate only to comments.

Comment expiration

Under the Comments header in Figure 10-1, you see a series of options relating specifically to comments and how they operate on your site. One useful option in this menu is the capability to set an expiration date for commenting ability. This is a good way to keep conversations fresh and comment spam at bay since the CMS systematically disables comments article by article depending on the time limit set in this drop-down menu. Unfortunately, the field is not customizable—you can choose only between one and six weeks.

Article-level control

In addition to the global on/off toggle, it is also possible to disable comments on a per-article basis. This would, of course, require comments to already be activated across the site (see the previous section) and the templates to be in place and visible to the end user.

You might want to disable comments for a single article for any number of reasons. Some articles rank higher in search engines and are therefore premium targets for comment spam. Other entries might have discussions that have gone on way too long, and the remarks are getting out of hand. Still other articles become long in the tooth and need to be retired to a noninteractive, read-only stasis.

To turn off a specific article's commenting capability, navigate to the article via the Articles area in the Content tab and click its title to load it into the Write tab. Once in the main editing screen, click the More link in the bottom right (just above the Save button). As you can see in Figure 10-2, more options display, including a small panel with an on/off toggle for that particular article's comments. Simply click Off, click Save, and then you're in business.

Figure 10-2. You can disable commenting for a single article.

Comments and articles

The Textpattern commenting system—and how to integrate comments with articles—are some of the most frequently discussed subjects in forums and blogs. A tremendous amount of the Textpattern code and database real estate is consumed with the collection, management, and output of comments. The result is a feature-rich system that is not always intuitive to less-experienced Textpattern users.

It is helpful to understand that every comment is attached to its parent article, and that association dictates how and where the comment gets displayed (there are very few instances in which a comment can be displayed outside the context of its original article). Also, like an article, each comment has a unique ID (for instance, 000124) that is assigned consecutively as comments are entered into the system.

The display of comments and the submission form is handled in forms, just like articles, except that the forms are given an attribute of comments instead of article. Textpattern has its own library of tags that only work inside comment-type forms. Both types of forms work in tandem, and, as described in the following section, they often find themselves mixed up together.

Comments forms

In its default installation, Textpattern provides several forms ready for customization. In fact, you might find yourself not needing to create any other comment-type forms because of the foundation the system has already laid. Let's explore these forms in depth.

Comments

The Comments form controls the display of individual comments. It's designed to be a small piece of code that is reused over and over—every comment that is displayed with the article is output from this template. This form cannot be deleted or renamed because it is the default form called by the Textpattern tag `<txp:comments />`. The default Textpattern install includes the following inside Comments:

```
<txp:message />
<p class="small">&#8212; <txp:comment_name /> &#183; ➡
 <txp:comment_time /> &#183;
 <txp:comment_permlink>#</txp:comment_permlink></p>
```

Notice the tags specific to outputting comment information. (It is interesting to note that as of Textpattern 4.0.4, the default installation still uses the depreciated `<txp:message />` tag, which has since been upgraded to the more semantic and functionally robust `<txp:comment_message />` tag.) In total, Textpattern contains eight tags designed to render different comment attributes (described in detail in Chapter 5). These tags can be mixed and matched to your choosing. They all can exist in the comment-type form to output a comment's data, even repeating if necessary.

> If you review Figure 10-1, you'll notice that the third option under the Comments header is Present comments as a numbered list?. This choice affects the output of this form as it dictates whether the form is going to be wrapped in an `<li>` element. If you change this option to No, you remove any Textpattern-generated formatting. You can always manually place your comments back in an ordered list.

10

In the site for Buzzbomb, you enabled basic commenting for the BuzzBlog. The Textpattern default tag selection remains largely intact, but the output is customized so the design is more in line with the rest of the site's look and feel. The revised form uses the following markup:

```
<div class="comment">
  <txp:comment_message />
  <p class="details">Posted by <txp:comment_name /> ➡
 on <txp:comment_time />
  <txp:comment_permlink>#</txp:comment_permlink></p>
</div>
```

Some different HTML is added to enable more visual control with the stylesheet, as you can see in Figure 10-3.

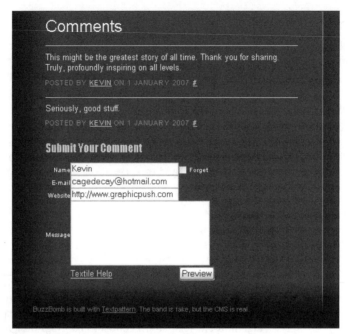

Figure 10-3. The form Comments is customized with its own HTML to better control the output of reader comments.

Comment_Form

The second form you need for operating comments is the code that controls the actual submission form. In the default Textpattern install, this form is called comment_form, and like Comments, it cannot be deleted or renamed because it serves as the default form when the CMS goes looking for the HTML form to place with the article. Unlike the repeating comments-type form that controls the output of the comments, described previously, this form appears only once on the page. Its purpose is to collect comments, not display them, as shown in Figure 10-4.

The content of comment_form in its default state is a jumble of table-based markup and tags. The Textpattern tags that manifest inside this submission form create the actual HTML form elements (usually an <input /> tag), but the corresponding form labels need to be created in addition. For instance, the <txp:comment_name_input /> tag outputs the following:

```
<input type="text" name="name" size="25" class="comment_name_input" ➡
 id="comment_name_input" />
```

In the form, this needs to be complemented with a <label> tag:

```
<label for="name">Name</label>
<txp:comment_name_input />
```

Figure 10-4. The comment submission form in the Textpattern default install is created with tables. This form can be easily customized in the comment_form form.

In the Forms area of the Presentation tab, the left column has a heading called Comment form that contains the tags that can be used for the submission form. Chapter 5 describes these comment-related Textpattern tags in detail and also contains an example of an accessible, well-structured HTML form.

As with the other comment-type form, the tags for creating the HTML input fields can be mixed and matched, depending on your site's design. Some, like <txp:comment_web_input /> and <txp:comment_remember />, are optional, and you might decide to omit them completely from your submission form to simplify the commenting process for your audience. Even the author's name and email address are optional, as long as you correctly set your preferences in the Advanced Preferences tab.

Popup_Comments

Viewing and adding comments in a separate pop-up window is an antiquated technique from the pioneering days of blogging, when reader feedback systems were inconsistent and the scripts that administered them were relegated to their own web page to avoid breaking the page housing the actual blog post. Today, very few blogs remain faithful to this technique. Readers expect comments to exist in context on the same page as the article.

For better or worse, Textpattern still supports this method. The Preferences page with the drop-down menu labeled Comments mode (refer to Figure 10-1) controls whether comments are displayed in the normal browser window or in a pop-up window. The comments-type form popup_comments houses a basic HTML shell for adding the other forms. You can add whatever formatting and styles to this page you want, just like any other page in Textpattern. The popup_comments form can be deleted or renamed; if you are not placing your commenting system inside a pop-up window, you should delete this form.

Adding comment functionality to articles

Now that you know the basics of the various comments-type forms, you need to integrate comments into the site. This can be accomplished several ways, but before you start throwing Textpattern tags into your pages, you need to ensure that the settings are properly set in the Preferences tab.

Important preference settings

The Textpattern CMS offers developers many options from the Preferences tab, and these choices control your entire site and wield tremendous influence on the functionality of Textpattern. Nowhere is this truer than in the commenting system. In the Textpattern administrative interface, navigate to the Basic area of the Preferences tab; as you saw in Figure 10-1, the bottom half of this screen is consumed by options affecting comments. The default installation preselects a number of critical options regarding comments, some of which need to be changed.

In the first group of options, make sure that Accept comments is set to Yes; otherwise, the bottom set of options—the ones controlling comments—do not appear. Chapter 3 covers each of the various comment options in depth, so just a few critical choices are covered here to ensure that your site's development runs as smoothly as possible:

- **On by default?** Choose this option wisely. It controls whether the article-level control, discussed previously, is set to On or Off by default when creating a new article. For simple blogs and other sites actively soliciting reader response, it should probably be set to Yes; for sites that only occasionally allow comments, No might work better. (And if choosing No, make sure that you manually enable comments for each article in which you want the feedback mechanism to appear.)

- **Present comments as a numbered list?** Select No for this option. You want granular control over the HTML, not have Textpattern create the markup for you. (You can always wrap the comments in a numbered list later on.)

- **Comments mode**: This option should be set to nopopup.

- **Automatically append comments to articles?** This option should *always* be set to No. If set to Yes, Textpattern automatically displays an article's comments and comment form after every <txp:article /> tag, which can create huge problems for templates that contain more than one <txp:article /> tag. By selecting No, you elect to manually place the <txp:comments /> and <txp:comment_form /> where you want in your template.

Other Preferences settings—including the ones in Advanced Preferences—largely control the semantics and peripheral output of comments. But the preceding four options determine the fundamental manner in which Textpattern displays and administers comments, so making sure that these switches are correctly flipped can avoid a lot of problems down the road.

Adding comments directly to the <txp:article /> tag

You have now examined forms for both articles and comments, and it's time to merge them together. As discussed in Chapter 8, article information is output via the <txp:article />

tag and is contextual to the section to which the page is linked. The `<txp:article />` tag references a specific article-type form that contains a miniature template dictating how the article information is rendered. In Chapter 8, you laid the foundation of BuzzBlog with the following code on the page:

```
<txp:if_individual_article>
  <txp:article form="buzzblog_entry" />
<txp:else />
  <div id="buzzbloghead">
    <h2>The Latest from the BuzzBlog</h2>
    <p><a href="#">Subscribe to the BuzzBlog</a></p>
  </div>
  <txp:article limit="1" />
</txp:if_individual_article>
```

When an individual entry is output, it uses the form buzzblog_entry. This form contains the following:

```
<div id="buzzblogheadarchive">
  <p>Filed Under "<txp:category1 title="1" />"</p>
</div>
<div class="buzzblogentry">
  <p class="date"><txp:posted gmt="0" /></p>
  <h3><txp:title /></h3>
  <txp:body />
</div>
```

This form renders the blog post in its entirety. Since you want to add commenting functionality after the display of the entire article, you need to append the `<txp:comments />` tag (the one that displays the comments) and the `<txp:comment_form />` tag (the one that displays the actual submission form) to the end of this form. Here is the revised form buzzblog_entry to include commenting:

```
<div id="buzzblogheadarchive">
  <p>Filed Under "<txp:category1 title="1" />"</p>
</div>
<div class="buzzblogentry">
  <p class="date"><txp:posted gmt="0" /></p>
  <h3><txp:title /></h3>
  <txp:body />
  <txp:comments />
  <txp:if_comments_allowed>
    <txp:comments_form />
  </txp:if_comments_allowed>
  <txp:if_comments_disallowed>
    <p>Comments are turned off for this article.</p>
  </txp:if_comments_disallowed>
</div>
```

10

Let's explore this new syntax. The beginning of the code is the same as before: Textpattern renders the body of the blog post inside the <div> buzzblogentry. But before the closing </div> tag, some new markup for displaying the comments was added.

First is the <txp:comments /> tag. As discussed previously, it outputs the existing comments, one after the other, by using the form Comments. (You can use a different form simply by adding a form attribute to the tag.)

After the comments are finished, you tell Textpattern to display the comment submission form. Since you don't know whether comments will be enabled or disabled down the road, a small conditional statement is set up that says if comments are enabled, go ahead and display the submission form using the <txp:comments_form /> tag; if they are disabled, don't show the form but offer a small note saying Comments are turned off for this article.

You can, of course, render the submission form before the display of the comments or place them in different parts of the page. This is simply an example of how most sites structure the functionality. People familiar with blogs or media sites in which commenting is allowed are used to reading the current comments first and then finding a comment submission form at the bottom of the web page. This code represents the most efficient way of doing that.

Rendering comments from their own <txp:article /> tag

Just like the blog post's title, excerpt, or date, comments are intrinsically tied to their parent article. An article-type form referenced from an <txp:article /> tag could hold any value of the original article; for instance, you might have an article-type form displaying just the title, another displaying just the posted date, or another displaying just the contents of a custom field. Similarly, an <txp:article /> tag could link to an article-type form housing just comment-related output.

Get started with the following code on the page to output an article's content:

```
<txp:if_individual_article>
  <txp:article form="buzzblog_entry" />
<txp:else />
  <div id="buzzbloghead">
    <h2>The Latest from the BuzzBlog</h2>
    <p><a href="#">Subscribe to the BuzzBlog</a></p>
  </div>
  <txp:article limit="1" />
</txp:if_individual_article>
```

Instead of adding all the comment-related code to the article-type form buzzblog_entry, you could create another article-type form called buzzblog_entry_comments to house that code. The following might be the contents of the new form buzzblog_entry_comments:

```
<txp:comments />
<txp:if_comments_allowed>
  <txp:comments_form />
</txp:if_comments_allowed>
<txp:if_comments_disallowed>
  <p>Comments are turned off for this article.</p>
</txp:if_comments_disallowed>
```

As you can see, it's the same code as before, but simply outsourced to its own article-type form. To call this form from the page, change the markup to the following:

```
<txp:if_individual_article>
  <txp:article form="buzzblog_entry" />
  <txp:article form="buzzblog_entry_comments" />
<txp:else />
  <div id="buzzbloghead">
    <h2>The Latest from the BuzzBlog</h2>
    <p><a href="#">Subscribe to the BuzzBlog</a></p>
  </div>
  <txp:article limit="1" />
</txp:if_individual_article>
```

This way, Textpattern renders the entire contents of the article and then renders the comments afterward. Functionally, you make the same content manifest—at the end of the day, you'll get the blog post followed by its comments with either technique. In this scenario, you simply split the duty between two article-type forms. Depending on your development style and personal preference, this might or might not work for you.

Comment administration

The rise of reader feedback on blogs and news media sites has fostered a great dialogue between content publishers and content consumers. People can express their reactions, and authors can gain a sense of their audience's taste and limits, to say nothing of the ideas and additional information that contributes deeply to an article's overall value.

But like most two-way communication, there is the good, the bad, and the ugly. You can hope that the good kind of feedback is the norm—that is, commenting used for constructive purposes. The bad kind of feedback usually starts with good intentions, but the dialog becomes increasingly weighed down by personal attacks, flame wars, trolling, and other seedy doings of unscrupulous readers. The ugly cannot even be considered feedback. It arrives on the back of blogging's perennial bugbear: comment spam. The first is encouraged, the second can be moderated, and the last must be stricken immediately and ruthlessly from your site. Textpattern developers can accomplish all three within the TXP platform.

10

Comment moderation

The right to freedom of the press grants people the opportunity to publish scathing, non-sensical rants against their government and neighbors at will in any medium, without reprimand from a governing body. While this works on a macro level for a society of millions, it is less appealing for writers publishing on a more intimate website level.

Some websites are as open as can be, and comments of all quality and tone are accepted; others are run by benevolent dictators who quietly operate from behind the curtain; still others are administered by fanatical editors who delete comments with opposing viewpoints with frighteningly little hesitancy. As a producer of content, it helps to identify where you fall and to maintain that level of control with consistency. Your style of moderation contributes to the tone and value of your site.

You can do several things to moderate comments on your site. Some are subtle, others are drastic, but they all can contribute to better online conversations.

- **Publicly state your site's commenting policy near the comment submission form**: This policy does not have to be a long diatribe of legalese, but it helps to warn readers that if their comments are beyond the tolerance of the site, they will be deleted. State your grounds for deletion, including language concerns for family-oriented sites, linking to adult material, aggressive verbal attacks on other readers, and so on.

- **Moderate comments *after* public submission**: Basically, this means combing through recent comments and manually deleting them after you come across inappropriate reader-submitted content. This is a manual process that is not efficient time-wise, but might be sufficient for low-traffic sites with well-behaved citizens.

- **Moderate comments via email**: On the Preferences tab (refer to Figure 10-1), the first option under Comments is Moderate comments?. By default, this option is set to No, but changing it to Yes means that every comment submitted to your site arrives in your email first. (When users submit the comment, they are presented with a note telling them the site is being moderated.) Implementing this feature means that you must judge every comment on an individual basis and make them visible from the Comments area of the Content tab. This technique should be reserved for sites under fire from a disgruntled readership or a spam onslaught because it can be frustrating from a user perspective and might upset the well-behaved segment of the population.

- **Disable commenting capability on an individual article**: This is very handy when a particular thread gets out of hand. (Similarly, you can always tell Textpattern to turn off commenting for all articles after a certain period of time. This option is also found on the Preferences tab.)

Combating comment spam

The ability to receive reader comments on your site is tainted with the prospect of combating an ever-growing amount of comment spam, an example of which is shown in Figure 10-5. Although spammers used to focus on bringing email servers to their knees, they have now turned to the open market of blogs to carpet bomb sites with advertisements for explicit sex and low-cost pharmaceuticals.

Textpattern used to fly under the radar of spammers, whose efforts were spent on more popular blog software such as Moveable Type and Wordpress. But the release of version 4.0.3 in December 2005 also saw the first Textpattern-focused spam bots hit Textpattern-driven sites, and reports of spam infiltration started popping up in the forums. The development team has since worked (and continues to work) on spam-fighting technologies in the product.

Figure 10-5. Typical comment spam can be nothing more than a bunch of URLs.

Regardless, despite the software's best efforts, some spam does get through. There is, unfortunately, no blanket all-in-one solution, but there are some steps you as the site's admin and designer can take to reduce the amount of incoming spam:

- **Retain the comment preview function**: The Textpattern comment submission form requires readers to click preview before they can actually submit their comment, and many developers try to remove this extra step to not annoy their readers. While it is possible to remove this functionality through some hacking of the source code, the preview-first, then-submit path is a powerful first line of defense against spammers. Removing it is akin to taking away a castle's walls and hoping the moat is enough to stop the invading army.

10

- **Turn on comment expiration**: In the Preferences pane (refer to Figure 10-1), disable comments after a certain period of time. As a site's pages age, they slowly gain incoming links, and thus search engine popularity, making them top-shelf targets for spammers who think hitting an older article won't get noticed. Disabling comments after four or six weeks eliminates this problem and causes minimal fuss for readers, most of whom visit your site for more recent material.

- **Use spam-deterring plugins**: As a last resort, you can employ plugins that can help stem the tide of unwanted spam. Some plugins, such as asy_captcha (which requires readers fill in a captcha code—the distressed, graphic letters spam bots cannot read), are very intrusive to the user experience. Others, such as mrw_ spamkeywords_urlcount (which flags a comment as spam if there are too many URLs in the content), work in the background.

Note that turning on comment moderation does not stop spam at all. While valuable for moderating comments, noted previously, it alerts you only when spam arrives and provides no protection from the stuff in the first place.

Summary

Soliciting reader comments is a powerful tool for building site traffic because it brings your audience into the content-creation fold and provides them a role in your site's growth. Textpattern provides a powerful set of tools for aggregating and moderating reader feedback. An article's ensuing conversations can add tremendous value to the original article, as long as the comments don't devolve into flame wars or become hot spots for spam.

11 BEYOND THE BASICS

404 Not Found

The requested page was not found.

Missing Page! [404 No

Unfortunately the page you are looking fo
never existed in the first place. Please ch
think there is a problem with our site, ple
Otherwise, use our search box below or

Search Results

Viva La Baltimore

Just got back from the show in Baltimore
missing promoter and some dude with a
the opening act. Amazingly, we all made

The previous few chapters explored in some depth how Textpattern pulls the content and structure together when building pages. Sections, categories, forms, and pages have all been covered, and you should feel reasonably confident when building basic templates for displaying your content. However, like most software, 80 percent of what you'll use the system for consumes only 5 percent of the content management system (CMS) functionality. In other words, even with all the work done to this point, you have barely scratched the surface of what you can accomplish with Textpattern.

This chapter builds on the previous material's concepts. Pages, sections, and forms are part of the greater discussion going forward as you delve into the granular customization of your site—tweaking error pages and search results, building dynamic meta information for every page, and optimizing the templates inside pages to output various screens depending on where the user navigates. You'll explore more Textpattern tags and plugins, and learn more about a very powerful aspect of articles that has been largely left alone: custom fields.

Creating error pages

Creating a custom error message in Textpattern is a fairly painless process. It is a very important feature for many content-based sites and commercial businesses because they don't want to lose visitors because of a missing page. Smart web design dictates that you create an error page that is useful—one that tells the user what's wrong, but also guides them in a helpful direction (unlike the Spartan error messages many servers default to, as shown in Figure 11-1).

Figure 11-1. Many servers default to minimal and extremely unhelpful error messages.

Many articles have been written about designing a better error page, most notably "The Perfect 404"[1] on A List Apart. You'll apply some of those principles to the Buzzbomb site and draft a world-class 404 page that contains not only some helpful links but also a search feature to speed visitors on their way.

---

1. www.alistapart.com/articles/perfect404/

Building a default error page

On a perfect Internet, pages would never get moved, links would always be relevant and accurate, and sites would never go down. Unfortunately, the Web is a giant teeming organism that is constantly shedding old material, and the need for contingency pages has never been more important. Designers redesign websites, and content gets shifted; people forget to pay their hosting, and entire domains disappear; servers get updated, and suddenly scripts stop working; search engines reference old links in their cache; and humans (being mistake-prone creatures) do a lot of misspelling when they type URLs.

Because of all this, web servers have several different "HTTP standard response codes" to describe different problems. There are dozens (described in full at Wikipedia[2]), but only a few are ever seen by users. The **4xx Client Error** and **5xx Server Error** series are most prevalent and include these popular hits:

- 400: Bad Request
- 401: Unauthorized
- 403: Forbidden
- 404: Not Found
- 500: Internal Server Error

When a specific page has a problem loading or can't be found, the server returns a 4xx error; when there is a server-side problem—such as Textpattern (which is run on server-side code) failing completely—a 5xx error is returned. Error 404 is, of course, the most well known. To accommodate users, you'll create a Textpattern-driven page that dynamically figures out the error and returns appropriate text to let them know what went wrong.

In the default Textpattern installation, there is a page called error_default. This template displays your error information, so you need to edit the content to match the design of the rest of the site. You'll adopt the code from the page static_page (which was used for the terms of use page in Chapter 9) because it represents the existing site template with the minimal amount of customization:

```
<txp:output_form form="meta" />
<txp:output_form form="header+nav" />
<div id="center">
  <div id="content">
    <txp:article form="static_text" />
  </div> <!-- ends #content -->
  <div id="sidebar">
    <txp:output_form form="sidebar_tour" />
    <txp:output_form form="sidebar_promo" />
    <txp:output_form form="sidebar_friends" />
  </div>
</div> <!-- ends #center -->
<txp:output_form form="footer" />
```

2. http://en.wikipedia.org/wiki/List_of_HTTP_status_codes

11

The only thing you need to change in the template is the `<txp:article />` tag. Since the Textpattern error pages do not look for article-related tags when they are parsed, you have to replace the `<txp:article />` tag with some plain HTML and some tags designed for outputting error messages. The CMS provides three tags for just this purpose:

- `<txp:error_status />` outputs the actual error code with its requisite error message (for example: 404 Not Found).
- `<txp:error_message />` outputs a short description of the error (for instance: The requested page was not found).
- `<txp:if_status>` is a conditional tag that can be used for customizing output based on the actual error code. It employs the attribute status to determine which error code trips the if-else argument.

Use the first two TXP tags in the new version of the page error_default:

```
<txp:output_form form="meta" />
<txp:output_form form="header+nav" />
<div id="center">
  <div id="content">
    <div class="staticentry">
      <h3><txp:error_status /></h3>
      <p><txp:error_message /></p>
    </div>
  </div> <!-- ends #content -->
  <div id="sidebar">
    ... sidebar content ...
  </div>
</div> <!-- ends #center -->
<txp:output_form form="footer" />
```

You replaced the `<txp:article />` tag with some manual HTML and two error-related Textpattern tags. It represents a very basic incarnation of a TXP error page and would render something similar to the Buzzbomb page in Figure 11-2.

The template inside the page error_default could detect whatever error occurred and dynamically display the appropriate text onscreen. While this is better than a generic server-generated message, it's not particularly helpful or user-friendly. The next section discusses how to customize the error page.

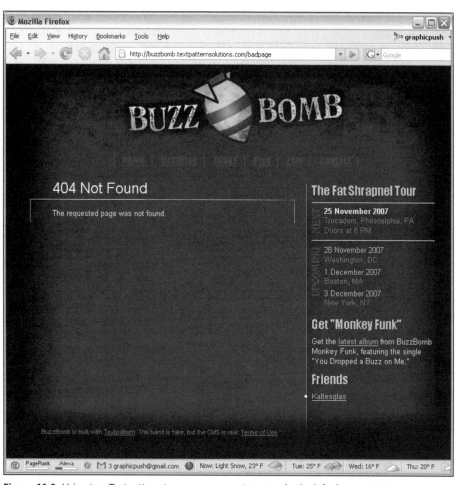

Figure 11-2. Using two Textpattern tags, you can create a very basic default error page.

Customizing error pages

When creating error pages for your website, it's helpful to put yourself in the mindset of your users. While you know your site inside and out, newcomers might get lost and start clicking links and manually entering URLs that (in a lapse of brilliance) you failed to account for. When users get lost, they get frustrated, so it's best to address the problem immediately with a friendly error page that points people in the right direction before they leave your site.

A big part of that user-friendliness is messaging. While the general web populace kind of gets what a 404 is, throw them onto a page with a 403 error and they'll be as lost as a horse jockey in a NASCAR race. Confusing people—intentionally or not—is never a good strategy. You need to explain the meaning of errors, how they got there, and how users can find the content they want. You can start by customizing the Textpattern error pages.

There are two basic ways to customize error page content. The first way is to create a new page for each error variation you want customized, and the second is to use the conditional <txp:if_status> tag on the error_default page to dynamically serve more intelligent messaging. Both techniques are discussed in the following sections.

Option 1: Creating individual error pages

Textpattern recognizes the error_default page as the default template for all HTTP standard response codes. In addition, it also recognizes pages with error_### name formatting as specific templates designed for whatever error number is in the name and uses it *before* falling back on error_default.

For instance, the previous 404 page can be customized to be more user-friendly. For Textpattern to use a different template when displaying only 404 errors, create a new page called error_404. By design, Textpattern will use this page over error_default for just 404s.

The new page will have a similar structure as error_default, except that you can change the messaging liberally. For instance:

```
<txp:output_form form="meta" />
<txp:output_form form="header+nav" />
<div id="center">
  <div id="content">
    <div class="staticentry">
      <h3>Missing page! <em>[<txp:error_status />]</em></h3>
      <p>Unfortunately the page you are looking for has been moved, ➥
deleted or never existed in the first place. Please check your URL, ➥
and if you think there is a problem with our site, please ➥
<a href="/contact" title="Contact the Buzzbomb crew">contact us</a> ➥
immediately. Otherwise, use our search box below or return to our ➥
<a href="/" title="Buzzbomb home">homepage</a>.</p>
    </div>
  </div> <!-- ends #content -->
  <div id="sidebar">
    ... sidebar content ...
  </div>
</div> <!-- ends #center -->
<txp:output_form form="footer" />
```

The new messaging is far more user-friendly than the generic error message from TXP. The design also retains the official HTTP standard response code generated by the <txp:error_status /> tag, which can help webmasters and more technically savvy visitors understand exactly what the server is saying.

Option 2: Using conditional tags on a single error page

While the technique of creating individual error pages using the error_### naming convention works well, Textpattern provides developers with a slightly more efficient way of customizing error messages. By using conditional tags on the single error_default page, you can establish a single template that not only figures out what error has occurred but also dynamically displays the content of your choice.

To accomplish this, use the <txp:if_status> tag, which is a conditional tag that allows for simple if-else statements regarding errors. Its only attribute is status, the value of which dictates whether the if-else argument is tripped. For instance, take a look at the following code:

```
<txp:output_form form="meta" />
<txp:output_form form="header+nav" />
<div id="center">
  <div id="content">
    <div class="staticentry">
    <txp:if_status status="404">
      <h3>Missing page! <em>[<txp:error_status />]</em></h3>
      <p>Unfortunately the page you are looking for has been moved, ➡
deleted or never existed in the first place. Please check your URL, ➡
and if you think there is a problem with our site, please ➡
<a href="/contact" title="Contact the Buzzbomb crew">contact us</a> ➡
immediately. Otherwise, use our search box below or return to our ➡
<a href="/" title="Buzzbomb home">homepage</a>.</p>
      <txp:else />
        <h3><txp:error_status /></h3>
        <p><txp:error_message /></p>
    </txp:if_status>
    </div>
  </div> <!-- ends #content -->
  <div id="sidebar">
    ... sidebar content ...
  </div>
</div> <!-- ends #center -->
<txp:output_form form="footer" />
```

You can see that this version adopts the new friendlier messaging from the previous example, but also uses the colder TXP-generated messages for errors other than 404. Since 404 is by far the most common error people run into, it might be acceptable to customize the message for only this particular problem and let the Textpattern default handle the rest.

At the end of the day, the individual error pages and the single error page with conditional statements produce the same customized result for a 404, as seen in Figure 11-3. The technique you choose to use to create the new content is up to you.

11

Figure 11-3. The customized 404 error page shows friendlier and more helpful text.

In the customized message you see in Figure 11-3, notice the reference to a search box below the text. The next section covers adding search functionality to a site (using this specific error page as the starting point) as well as customizing search results.

Adding search functionality and customizing search results

As you know, one of the biggest advantages of using Textpattern as your CMS is its separation of content and structure. Because it uses a database to store all the content in easily managed chunks, it is relatively simple to add search functionality to the website. By using the Textpattern built-in search construct, you can use the system's speed in producing search results as well as the dedicated tag library to customize those results.

In the previous section, you created a customized page for 404 errors, which is an important aspect of building an accessible and usable site. However, one of the most important things you can do on an error page is to provide users with a quick way to find the content they need—or the closest approximation. Since the Buzzbomb site does not have a site map, you can point them in only two directions: the home page (somewhat helpful) and a search feature (very helpful). The following sections discuss adding that search box as well as setting up a new section and page to customize the template of the results.

Adding the search box

Most sites have a search box in the header that is persistent across the entire domain, but the site for Buzzbomb is small enough that the primary menu is enough to help users get around intuitively. However, because Textpattern uses the same tags and code for the search box—whether it's on a single page or every page of the website—you can always take the code you're about to create and apply it site-wide.

To build the input field and button, Textpattern uses only a single tag: `<txp:search_input />`. This tag has several key attributes: `section`, `label`, `button`, `size`, `wraptag`, and `form`. Add the following to the error template:

```
<txp:search_input label="Search the Buzzbomb Site" ➥
button="Search" size="15" wraptag="p" section="search" />
```

These attributes dictate that the entire construct be wrapped in a `<p>` tag, that the text above the input field say Search the Buzzbomb Site, that the input field have a size of 15, and that the actual button text say Search. The `section` attribute, by contrast, does not control any visual element; instead, it tells Textpattern to go ahead and use the section search as the template for displaying the results. This tag with these attributes produces the following HTML:

```
<form action="http://buzzbomb.textpatternsolutions.com/search/" ➥
method="get">
   <p>Search the Buzzbomb Site<br />
   <input type="text" name="q" value="" size="15" />
   <input type="submit" value="Search" /></p>
</form>
```

Customizing search results

Now that you created a search input using the `<txp:search_input />` tag, it's time to design the template of the actual results. Out of the box, Textpattern handles search results through the page default using the article-type form search_results (which is included in the default installation), so even if you do not change anything else from this point on, the Buzzbomb home page serves double-duty as the template for any searches done from the error page.

If you want, you can use the page default to display custom search results using conditional statements (specifically `<txp:if_search>`), but using that code can quickly junk up

11

253

a template. To avoid these if-else statements in a single page, Textpattern enables designers to choose an alternative section to house the template. You did just that in the preceding tag by using the section attribute to direct search queries to the eponymous section search.

For this to work, obviously you must first set up a section dedicated to this purpose and a page to go along with it. The page search can be duplicated right from static_page, a template that was used in previous tutorials. The customization of that page will be discussed in just a moment, but you'll first create the section. Figure 11-4 shows what it might look like from the back end.

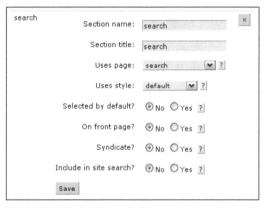

Figure 11-4. Options for a dedicated search section

The new section uses the page search, which you'll customize in just a moment. It's also recommended to select No for all options; this section is largely transparent from a functional content standpoint and exists only for displaying the results.

Once you establish the section, you can customize the page search to which it is linked. You'll recognize the base template from several tutorials in Chapter 9, and true to form, you change only a bit of code in the middle, like this:

```
<txp:output_form form="meta" />
<txp:output_form form="header+nav" />
<div id="center">
  <div id="content">
    <div class="staticentry">
      <h3>Search Results</h3>
      <txp:article searchform="search_results" />
    </div>
  </div> <!-- ends #content -->
  <div id="sidebar">
    ... sidebar content ...
  </div>
</div> <!-- ends #center -->
<txp:output_form form="footer" />
```

Although the bulk of the template stays the same, the <h3> tag is manually included this time since it will never change, and a call to the form search_results was added using a <txp:article /> tag and the searchform attribute. A search results page does not need to be any more complicated than this simple setup. The bulk of the customization comes in the form that displays the results.

Since search_results is an article-type form, you can use all the standard, article-specific Textpattern tags such as <txp:title />, <txp:permalink />, and so on. In addition, the system also provides several search-specific tags, including the following:

- <txp:search_result_date /> returns the date. Functionally, it is the same as the <txp:posted /> tag.

- <txp:search_result_excerpt /> returns an excerpt of the post that shows where the search term occurred in the text. For instance, in bringing up a search query for the word promoter, the article "Viva La Baltimore" displays the following: . . . find the place deserted, the doors locked and the **promoter** totally MIA. We piled . . . is also great. We never did hear from the **promoter**, so getting paid's gonna be fun. Up next: . . . You can control the HTML tag used to highlight the search terms; by default, matching words are emphasized with a <strong> tag.

- <txp:search_result_title /> is a simple tag that returns the title of the article already linked. It is functionally equivalent to <txp:permlink><txp:title /></txp:permlink>.

- <txp:search_result_url /> returns a linked version of the URL. It is the same as explicitly writing out <txp:permlink><txp:permlink /></txp:permlink>.

These tags don't offer any mind-blowing new functionality, but they can make your development efforts slightly easier. In fact, several of them are employed in the new version of the form search_results:

```
<h5><txp:search_result_title /> ➡
[Posted <txp:search_result_date />]</h5>
<p><txp:excerpt /></p>
<div class="resultdetail">
  <p><txp:search_result_excerpt /></p>
  <p><txp:search_result_url /></p>
</div>
```

11

Since Textpattern enables designers to mix and match standard article tags with search-specific tags, the familiar <txp:excerpt /> tag is also included to let people read the article's synopsis as well as see the bits of text that include the search string. In the end, the new form outputs a result like the one in Figure 11-5.

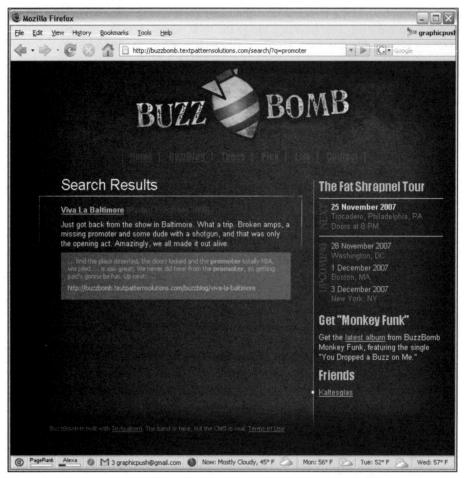

Figure 11-5. The customized version of the search_results form uses standard article tags as well as search-specific article tags.

Customizing metadata information

One of the great strengths of the Web is its "searchability," the capability of search engines to index and almost instantly retrieve a single document from a pool of billions. This technology drives internal search engines (the ones responsible for a single site) and external engines (the ones that crawl the entire Web, such as Google, MSN, and so on).

One of the key ingredients to this magic is metadata. Metadata is information about information; it is a summary of a document's contents that is attached to the document itself. Just about any file type has the capability for some level of summarizing information: Microsoft Office files, audio and video files, images, proprietary documents, and, of course, HTML documents.

Just about every good web developer has some passing understanding of basic web meta-data. In essence, there are three tags that search engines pay attention to: the document title, the document description, and the document's keywords. There are many, many more tags as well (and even alternative metadata systems such as the Dublin Core Metadata Initiative[3]), but this section focuses on the three most common (and most used) tags.

Splitting up the forms

You have probably noticed that all the examples of whole pages start with a single line of code:

```
<txp:output_form form="meta" />
```

This misc-type form was created in Chapter 8 and was designed to hold all the web page's metadata as well as some core information (such as the DOCTYPE). At the time, it was not important to tweak it too heavily because the focus was on developing the body of the pages. The content of the form meta includes several empty metadata tags:

```
<!DOCTYPE html PUBLIC "-//W3C//DTD XHTML 1.0 Strict//EN" ➥
"http://www.w3.org/TR/xhtml1/DTD/xhtml1-strict.dtd">
<html xmlns="http://www.w3.org/1999/xhtml" xml:lang="en" lang="en">
<head>
  <meta http-equiv="content-type" content="text/html; charset=utf-8" />
  <title></title>
  <meta name="description" content="" />
  <meta name="keywords" content="" />
  <txp:css format="link" media="screen" n="buzzbomb" />
  <link rel="stylesheet" type="text/css" href="#.css" media="print" />
  <link rel="home" title="Home" href="/" />
  <link rel="search" title="Search this site" href="#" />
  <link rel="author" title="Send feedback" href="#" />
  <link rel="contents" title="Site Map" href="#" />
  <link rel="shortcut icon" type="image/ico" href="#" />
</head>
```

11

Now that the bulk of the site is built out, you can focus on this information by applying many of the techniques used up to this point. It helps to think of the metadata section as a miniature web page—you have static content and you have dynamic content. You need to treat each differently, so you'll find yourself mimicking some of the development strategies from Chapter 8, in which you looked at a large block of code, identified different types of content, and split the markup into more manageable pieces.

---

3. www.dublincore.org

Moving the static metadata

The meta form contains a lot of information. Between the <head> tags, there is an obvious split between static and dynamic content. You'll start with the easy stuff and move the static content over to its own form, which includes everything from the cascading style sheet (CSS) call down to the shortcut icon:

```
<txp:css format="link" media="screen" n="buzzbomb" />
<link rel="stylesheet" type="text/css" href="#.css" media="print" />
<link rel="home" title="Home" href="/" />
<link rel="search" title="Search this site" href="#" />
<link rel="author" title="Send feedback" href="#" />
<link rel="contents" title="Site Map" href="#" />
<link rel="shortcut icon" type="image/ico" href="#" />
```

Move it into a form called meta_static. Since there is no dynamic data being pulled, you can attribute it as a misc-type form. To pull the data back into the master meta form, use a simple <txp:output_form /> tag, like this:

```
<!DOCTYPE html PUBLIC "-//W3C//DTD XHTML 1.0 Strict//EN" ➥
"http://www.w3.org/TR/xhtml1/DTD/xhtml1-strict.dtd">
<html xmlns="http://www.w3.org/1999/xhtml" xml:lang="en" lang="en">
<head>
  <meta http-equiv="content-type" content="text/html; charset=utf-8" />
  <title></title>
  <meta name="description" content="" />
  <meta name="keywords" content="" />
  <txp:output_form form="meta_static" />
</head>
```

Moving the bulk of the static material out of the way makes the immediate code more manageable. While you could theoretically move the DOCTYPE out as well, it does not offer any performance or code management advantages, so leave it as is. Next, you'll focus on the dynamic content.

Going dynamic

When creating dynamic metadata, it's best to think of everything between the <head> tags in an HTML document as its own web page. You'll create an article-type form that a <txp:article /> tag uses to pull in article-specific content, just as you did with the primary content many times in the past few chapters. In fact, you'll mimic the previously established structure very closely.

Before getting in too deep, let's define what metadata content will be dynamic and where that content is going to come from. Let's examine each piece:

- **The web page title.** This is the content that fits between the `<title>` tag at the very top of the HTML document and is the text that appears in the top chrome of a browser window. Textpattern has a built-in tag for precisely this function: `<txp:page_title />`. It automatically figures out what type of page the user is on (the home page, a section landing page, an individual article page, and so on) and generates the appropriate text in the form of Site Name: Article Title. Your example should output something like this: Buzzbomb: Viva La Baltimore.

- **The web page description.** This is the text that fits inside the HTML string `<meta name="description" content="description goes here" />`. Textpattern provides no native tag for this content, so you use a custom field for storing the content and the Textpattern tag `<txp:custom_field />` for outputting it. Under the tab Admin ➤ Preferences ➤ Advanced Preferences, there is an area for editing custom fields (see Figure 11-6); the Buzzbomb site employed three (the first is meta_desc). (These fields appear in the left column of the Content ➤ Write tab.)

- **The web page keywords.** This is the text that sits inside the keyword's metatag right below the meta description. Like the page title, Textpattern provides a built-in means of collecting and displaying this content using the Keywords field in the Write screen and the tag `<txp:keywords />`. The structure of the keyword's HTML tag will be similar to the description. (Textpattern also offers another tag called `<txp:meta_keywords />` that generates the HTML tag along with the value of the Keywords field, but it works only with individual article pages. You need to manually define the HTML markup around the `<txp:keywords />` tag to ensure that the content is displayed on section landing pages and the home page as well.)

Figure 11-6. The Buzzbomb site uses three custom fields; the first is used for the page's meta description.

Now that you defined what metadata will be dynamic and where the content is going to be pulled from, you can build the form meta_dynamic for outputting this information (remember that because these fields are tied intrinsically to the article itself, the form will be an article-type form):

```
<title><txp:page_title /></title>
<meta name="description" ➡
content="<txp:custom_field name="meta_desc" />" />
<meta name="keywords" content="<txp:keywords />" />
```

The preceding code example is fairly basic and assumes that metadata information (particularly the description and keywords) was entered into every page. If Textpattern runs across a page that does not have this information, the form still outputs the HTML tags, but with nothing in the content attribute. To avoid rendering these empty HTML tags, use the TXP tag <txp:if_custom_field> or a plugin such as chh_if_data[4] to detect whether content actually exists for the description and keywords.

This is an interesting form because the content is tied directly to the article, but is being collected in very different ways. The title is automatically generated without any input from the developer, the description is manually pulled from a custom field, and the keywords are entered into the Keywords field. In the end, the previous code would render the following markup for the article "Viva La Baltimore":

```
<title>Buzzbomb: Viva La Baltimore</title>
<meta name="description" content="We had a crazy show in Baltimore ➥
-- gunshots, fire and a missing promoter were all part of the fun." />
<meta name="keywords" content="baltimore, shotgun, tour, amp fire, ➥
promoter, buzzbomb" />
```

> Regarding the title of the web page tag, there is no explicit need to use the Textpattern <txp:page_title /> tag. Since this is an article-type form, you can pull any aspect of an article, such as its title, its excerpt, the value of a custom field, the section and category names, and more. You could conceivably write a custom string such as <txp:sitename />: <txp:section title="1" />: <txp:title />. There is even a plugin called ob1_title that produces more complex page titles.

Now that you established the article-type form to render the metadata, you need to link it back to the form meta so it appears on every web page.

Bringing the metadata to the people

Throughout the development of the Buzzbomb site, you employed both normal articles (such as "Viva La Baltimore") and sticky articles (which have largely served as content for sectional landing pages). You used conditional tags to make sure that they were output under the proper conditions, but in the end, just about every page developed up to this point has had *some article* attached to it.

The metadata works identically to the normal content. Most web pages have a unique article—normal or sticky—that contains some content. Chapter 9 discussed developing an archive page for blog entries. In Textpattern terms, it is a landing page for a section. You created unique content for the section landing page and applied the template as a sticky article. If you recall, a conditional tag told Textpattern what article to render based on where the user was.

---

4. www.textpattern.org/plugins/530/chh_if_data

```
<txp:if_individual_article>
  <txp:article form="buzzblog_entry" />
<txp:else />
  <txp:article status="sticky" form="simple" />
</txp:if_individual_article>
```

This simple code instructs the system to render any individual article with the form buzzblog_entry and the sticky article for the section landing page with the form simple. More importantly, the conditional tags prevent both the normal and sticky articles from rendering at the same time. *The trick to creating functional dynamic metadata is mimicking the structure used to output the regular content.* In this case, the meta form contains the following code:

```
<!DOCTYPE html PUBLIC "-//W3C//DTD XHTML 1.0 Strict//EN" ➥
"http://www.w3.org/TR/xhtml1/DTD/xhtml1-strict.dtd">
<html xmlns="http://www.w3.org/1999/xhtml" xml:lang="en" lang="en">
<head>
  <txp:if_individual_article>
    <txp:article form="meta_dynamic" />
  <txp:else />
    <txp:article status="sticky" form="meta_dynamic" />
  </txp:if_individual_article>
  <txp:output_form form="meta_static" />
</head>
```

Notice that you retained the same structure in the markup, but referenced the same form meta_dynamic in both cases. That is deliberate. Since the metadata format (title, description, and keywords) does not change whether it's an individual article or a section landing page, you can employ the same template for each. What *is* important is the fact that the conditional tag <txp:if_individual_article> determines what *content* is being plugged into the template.

Section landing pages and sticky articles

Here's where it gets tricky. For section landing pages, you established that the metadata will be housed in a sticky article. However, in some of the sections you created over the past few chapters, you did not use a sticky article for any type of introductory copy in the actual visible content. A prime example is the search results page shown earlier in this chapter; navigating to that page as-is renders no metadata at all.

To get those section landing pages showing metadata, you need to create sticky articles for them even if none of the content appears on the screen. These sticky articles have to include only four things: an article title, content inside the Keywords field, content inside the meta_desc custom field, and a section attribution. Textpattern pulls the sticky article's contents with the meta_dynamic form you established before, even though none of the content may appear in the visible browser window.

Metadata for the home page

To throw another wrench into the system, defining metadata for the home page can be a challenge because there is no tangible section to throw a sticky article at. As you progress

11

through this final piece of the puzzle, keep in mind that there are multiple ways in Textpattern to solve this problem—you can easily accomplish this same task with different article, custom field, form, and section combinations. Simply follow one path that works for this situation.

One of the weirder things about Textpattern is its handling of the default web page. While it is a section in a technical sense (called default), you can't attribute articles—normal, sticky, or otherwise—specifically to the default section. To get around this for the Buzzbomb site, you must manually create a "real" section specifically for the home page, called homepage, as shown in Figure 11-7.

Figure 11-7. Creating a new section for handling metadata on the home page

There are no special requirements for the section except that it must have On front page? selected so articles attributed to the section actually show up on the home page. Once this is created, you can create a new article specifically for the metadata information on the home page: fill in a title, fill in content in the Keywords field, fill in content in the meta_desc custom field, and select homepage as the section. Once you have the section and article created, edit the form meta to ensure that it appears.

```
<!DOCTYPE html PUBLIC "-//W3C//DTD XHTML 1.0 Strict//EN" ➥
"http://www.w3.org/TR/xhtml1/DTD/xhtml1-strict.dtd">
<html xmlns="http://www.w3.org/1999/xhtml" xml:lang="en" lang="en">
<head>
  <txp:if_section name="">
    <txp:article_custom section="homepage" status="sticky" ➥
form="meta_dynamic" />
  <txp:else />
    <txp:if_individual_article>
      <txp:article form="meta_dynamic" />
    <txp:else />
      <txp:article status="sticky" form="meta_dynamic" />
    </txp:if_individual_article>
  </txp:if_section>
  <txp:output_form form="meta_static" />
</head>
```

The previous code is wrapped inside another conditional tag: `<txp:if_section>`. This tag checks to see whether the page that is loaded is the default page (using the name attribute with an empty value[5]), and if so, to output the article you defined with the `<txp:article_custom />` tag. Right now, you're probably shaking your head in bewilderment. In the spirit of long-winded explanation, here are the two most obvious questions answered.

1. **Why do you need to use the `<txp:if_section>` conditional tag?** For the Buzzbomb home page, you have two sections whose content is directed to appear on the default page: buzzblog (which produces the actual blog excerpt visible on the page) and homepage (the section you just created specifically for the metadata). Both of these sections have sticky articles. If you were to leave the form meta alone, using only the `<txp:if_individual_article>` tag, both sticky articles would have their content called by the form meta, and you would end up rendering more than one set of metadata HTML tags. The `<txp:if_section>` tag tells Textpattern, "Look, if this page is the home page, use this fancy `<txp:article_custom />` tag; otherwise, go ahead and use the metadata template you defined for the rest of the site."

2. **Why do you need to use a `<txp:article_custom />` tag?** A plain `<txp:article />` tag would pull the content that is relevant to the current section. Unfortunately, there are *two* relevant sections, buzzblog and homepage, so it would pull both and you'd again end up with two sets of metadata tags on the web page. By using a `<txp:article_custom />` tag, you can use all the filters in the normal `<txp:article />` tag (most importantly, status and form), but define the section using the section attribute as well—a critical differentiator that tells TXP to use *only* the sticky article from the homepage section.

There are multiple ways to get the metadata to show up for the home page, but none of them is completely obvious. Individual site architectures dictate how the overall metadata templating is handled, and a variety of article and form combinations can be used to get the correct content on the correct pages.

Summary

As you can see from this chapter, Textpattern goes deeper than a cursory glance would suggest. Its flexible architecture allows for explicit control over the most granular details of a website, as you learned when designing the error pages, search results, and a dynamic metadata template. There are very few—if any—areas of customization the CMS does not allow you to tackle, which makes it such a powerful and transparent system for site developers.

11

---

5. For more information on the `<txp:if_section>` tag and its name attribute, consult the TXP tag reference: http://textbook.textpattern.net/wiki/index.php?title=Txp:if_section.

PART FOUR **EXTENDING TEXTPATTERN**

12 CUSTOM FIELDS

This chapter covers all aspects of custom fields in Textpattern. You'll learn how to define and customize your custom fields, store content in your custom fields, and use the data stored in your custom fields with both built-in Textpattern tags and Textpattern plugins.

The discography section on the website of your favorite fictional punk band, Buzzbomb, will be used to demonstrate the uses of custom fields. The discography contains a listing of the band's albums, so each article in the section will represent a Buzzbomb album. The title field will be used for the album name, and the article body will be used for a brief description of the album. You will then use several custom fields to hold specific details—including the record label, producer, and year of each album.

What are custom fields?

Since we've already covered the basics of creating a new article in Textpattern, you're familiar with the use of the standard fields in the Admin ➤ Content ➤ Write tab to store data such as your article's title, body, and excerpt. While these three fields are enough to create a typical blog or news post, there are times when you'll want to store additional information. Although this information could be added to the article body, there would be no way to enforce consistency in data entry, formatting, and styling across articles.

Textpattern's answer to this dilemma is custom fields. Textpattern was designed with ten additional unused fields attached to each article. By enabling one of these custom fields, you'll give yourself an extra spot to store data. Each custom field can hold up to 255 characters of text data, and it's up to you to define which of the 10 fields you want to use and what they'll be called.

Setting custom field names

The first step of using a custom field is to enable and name it within the Textpattern administration interface. To configure the custom fields, take the following steps, as shown in Figure 12-1:

1. Navigate to the Admin ➤ Preferences ➤ Advanced Preferences tab.

2. Find the Custom Fields section, which is the fourth section down on the page.

   You'll notice that by default, custom fields 1 and 2 are set up and named custom1 and custom2, respectively. The first three custom fields were used for other areas of the Buzzbomb site, so you start with the fourth field.

3. Add the name RecordLabel in the Custom field 4 name text input.

4. Add the name Producer in the Custom field 5 name text input.

5. Add the name Year in the Custom field 6 name text input.

6. Click the Save button at the bottom of the page to store the new custom field names to the database.

Figure 12-1. Custom field names are set in the Advanced Preferences tab.

Setting values in custom fields

Now that you've set up the three custom fields, you're ready to start using them for content entry:

1. Navigate to the Admin ➤ Content ➤ Write tab.

2. Click the Advanced Options link to expand the menu.

3. For each custom field that was just activated, an additional text field appears under the Advanced Options menu, which enables you to add your additional content to each article that you post (see Figure 12-2).

4. Add the album name and details to the standard article title and body fields.

5. Add values to the three new custom fields RecordLabel, Producer, and Year.

6. Click the Publish button to save the article.

12

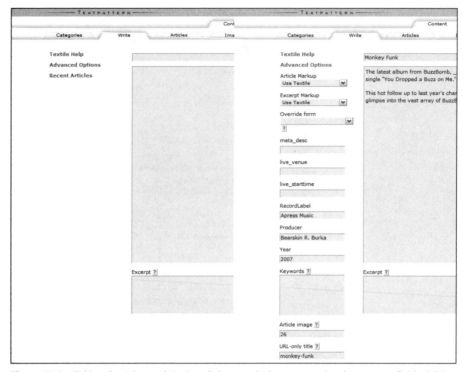

Figure 12-2. Clicking the Advanced Options link expands the menu and makes custom fields visible.

Custom field tags

Now that you've defined your custom fields, you can post your first article to the discography section, including data in your new custom fields. Once your article is posted, it's time to display that data on your article form. There are two tags that enable you to display the custom field data on an article form:

- `<txp:custom_field />` is used to display custom field values.
- `<txp:if_custom_field />` is used to generate conditional output based on custom field values.

Since custom fields are attached to articles, these two custom field tags must be used on an article form or on a page within a `<txp:if_individual_article />` conditional tag.

Using the <txp:custom_field /> tag

Start by using a simple article form that displays the title and body of your article, as shown in Figure 12-3.

1. Navigate to the Admin ➤ Presentation ➤ Forms tab.

2. Click the Create new form link to create a new article form.

3. Use the following code to create the article form:

```
<h4><txp:title /></h4>
<txp:body />
```

4. Assign a name to the form. Call it discography.

5. Select article from the Type drop-down list and click the Save New button to save the new form.

Figure 12-3. Create a new article form to display articles in the discography section.

With a basic article form in place, you can add the <txp:custom_field /> tag to display the values from the three custom fields under the article body.

Declare the name attribute of the <txp:custom_field /> tag so that Textpattern knows which custom field to display. You'll notice that the names you specify in the tags match the names of the fields that were already configured on the Admin ➤ Preferences ➤ Advanced Preferences tab.

1. Add the following code to the bottom of the discography article form (as shown in Figure 12-4):

```
<h4><txp:title /></h4>
<txp:body />
<p><txp:custom_field name="RecordLabel" /></p>
<p><txp:custom_field name="Producer" /></p>
<p><txp:custom_field name="Year" /></p>
```

2. Click the Save button to save your changes.

Figure 12-4. Add custom field tags to the article form.

Using the <txp:if_custom_field /> tag

The <txp:if_custom_field /> tag enables you to generate conditional output based on the value stored in a custom field. In its simplest form, the tag is used as follows:

```
<txp:if_custom_field name="foo">
  <p><txp:custom_field name="foo" /></p>
</txp:if_custom_field>
```

In the preceding example, Textpattern checks the custom field named foo on the current article to see whether it has any content. If it does, the code between the opening and closing <txp:if_custom_field /> tags is included in the form output. If not, nothing is included.

The <txp:if_custom_field /> tag also supports the <txp:else /> tag, which allows for a traditional if/else structure to be built. For example:

```
<txp:if_custom_field name="foo">
  <p><txp:custom_field name="foo" /></p>
<txp:else />
  <p>bar</p>
</txp:if_custom_field>
```

As in the first example, Textpattern checks the field named foo on the current article to see whether it has any content. If it does, the code between the opening <txp:if_custom_field /> tag and the <txp:else /> tag is included in the form output. If not, the code between the `<txp:else />` tag and the closing `<txp:if_custom_field />` tag is included in the form output.

Extending the discography example

After having set up a basic article form to display your custom field data (refer to Figure 12-4), you can enhance that form by using the `<txp:if_custom_field />` tag to conditionally display some additional data. You'll start by demonstrating potential additions to the form and then update the discography form you already created.

You already set up the display of the Producer custom field on the form. Because the `<txp:custom_field />` tag displays only the value of the field, you need to add your own label to the form as follows:

```
<p> Producer: <txp:custom_field name="Producer" /></p>
```

But what if there's no value stored in the Producer field? You'll end up with a label without an associated value. To prevent this from happening, you can use the `<txp:if_custom_field />` tag as follows:

```
<txp:if_custom_field name="Producer">
  <p>Producer: <txp:custom_field name="Producer" /></p>
</txp:if_custom_field>
```

The addition of the `<txp:if_custom_field />` tag to the form prevents the Producer label from appearing on the screen if there is no value stored in that field.

To take this one step further, if the Producer field is empty, you can display another message instead of showing nothing:

```
<txp:if_custom_field name="Producer">
  <p> Producer: <txp:custom_field name="Producer" /></p>
<txp:else />
  <p>Self Produced</p>
</txp:if_custom_field>
```

Now, if there is no value stored in the Producer field, Self Produced displays on the screen instead of showing nothing.

Finally, you can extend your original form by adding a conditional check to the RecordLabel field. This check tests the field for a particular value and generates output accordingly as follows:

```
<txp:if_custom_field name="RecordLabel" val="Apress Music">
  <p>Record Label: <txp:custom_field name="RecordLabel" /> ➡
(current label)</p>
<txp:else />
  <p>Record Label: <txp:custom_field name="RecordLabel" /></p>
</txp:if_custom_field>
```

12

With this check in place, you can designate which record label is the band's current label. In order to load all these changes, you need to edit the discography form that you already created, as shown in Figure 12-5.

1. Navigate to the Admin ➤ Presentation ➤ Forms tab.

2. Click the discography link in the form list to edit the form.

3. Update the form with the following code:

```
<h4><txp:title /><h4>
<txp:body />
<div class="albummeta">
<txp:if_custom_field name="RecordLabel" val="Apress Music">
  <p>Record Label: <txp:custom_field name="RecordLabel" /> ➥
(current label)</p>
<txp:else />
  <p>Record Label: <txp:custom_field name="RecordLabel" /></p>
</txp:if_custom_field>
<txp:if_custom_field name="Producer">
  <p> Producer: <txp:custom_field name="Producer" /></p>
<txp:else />
  <p>Self Produced</p>
</txp:if_custom_field>
<txp:if_custom_field name="Year">
  <p>Year: <txp:custom_field name="Year" /></p>
</txp:if_custom_field>
</div>
```

4. Click the Save button to save your changes.

Figure 12-5. The updated form, including conditional tags

Ordering articles by custom fields

Now that you've added articles to the discography section and built an article form to display each article, it's time to generate an article listing to display your articles on the discography page. You can use either the `<txp:article />` tag or the `<txp:article_custom />` tag to generate the list. Both of these tags enable you to specify a sort attribute to order the article listing by any article field. While an article listing might typically be ordered by posting date or title, you'll order the list by a custom field.

In your discography section, you want to highlight the most popular albums first on the page by ordering the discography listing by album sales. To do that, you can add one more custom field and use that field as the value for the sort attribute on the article listing tag.

There are two key points to remember when ordering by a custom field:

- The sort attribute must be a named column on the textpattern table in your database. Each custom field is named custom_1, custom_2, custom_3, and so on in the database. So, even if you call the seventh custom field Sales, you have to use the database field name, custom_7, for sorting purposes.

- The sorting is done alphabetically, which means that for sales of 50, 200, and 1100, you have to enter 0050, 0200, and 1100 to maintain the proper ordering.

The new custom field and sorting can be set up by taking the following steps:

1. Navigate to the Admin ➤ Preferences ➤ Advanced Preferences tab, enter the name Sales for Custom field 7 name, and save your changes.
2. Add a value to the Sales field for each article in the discography section.
3. Create an article listing tag that specifies the new sort field (`<txp:article sort="custom_7 desc" />`) to order the albums by sales in descending order.

Now that your form code is complete, you can see the final results on the Buzzbomb discography listing in Figure 12-6 and on the individual disc page in Figure 12-7.

12

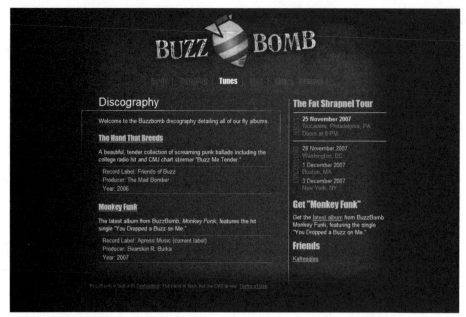

Figure 12-6. Buzzbomb discography listing page

Figure 12-7. An individual disc in the Buzzbomb discography section

Plugins and custom fields

The following plugins might be useful if you are a regular user of custom fields. See Chapter 13 for a detailed explanation of how to install and use Textpattern plugins.

rss_admin_show_adv_opts

The rss_admin_show_adv_opts plugin automatically expands the advanced article options menu on the Admin ➤ Content ➤ Write tab (as shown in Figure 12-2) without you having to manually click the Advanced Options link. If you're a heavy user of custom fields, you should use this plugin because it saves you a click each time you navigate to the Admin ➤ Content ➤ Write tab to edit or create articles.

www.wilshireone.com/textpattern-plugins/rss-admin-show-adv-opts

sed_pcf

The sed_pcf plugin enables you to store multiple values in a single custom field. If you find that you need more than ten custom fields, this plugin is the way to go. There are a variety of options for storing data, which are all outlined in the plugin's documentation.

http://txp-plugins.netcarving.com/plugins/packed-custom-fields

Summary

This chapter introduced you to Textpattern's custom field functionality. It detailed the steps needed to set up and use custom fields within a Textpattern installation. It also covered the <txp:custom_field /> tag and the <txp:if_custom_field /> tag and showed how the tags can be used in Textpattern article forms.

One of the most powerful features of Textpattern, custom fields can be used in a variety of ways to enhance your site's content and layout. While the examples provided in this chapter illustrate some of the most common uses of custom fields, you're certain to come up with creative ways to use custom fields to your advantage.

12

13 USING PLUGINS

```
# ...........................
# This is a plugin for Textpat
# To install: textpattern > ad
# Paste the following text int
# ...........................

H4sIAAAAAAAAA71ae28bNxL/2/4UjE
ZTftd7+ZIbkPPRzbuNZInF1yOPObJ4
ucXxL8etW6GNVBm+nY9bg/4In4AcSN
29/K1KylFioT/YXaxLRoOG4lwiyOzR
3AJ2uRYGZufjocO2Fml+Uyd75caQwc
8rRYyYzxwI2n6T1LpM1Tfm/2WDNxKz
SjOjNiKMGnavClh9K1giljKDdRXXHk
hSD93yBogXhSo5iCENEyEbBEGrYU3E
BTsHHsslvGWWKYogQ/api5bZirQKjJ
```

Article listings by date or by
category/section. Archive menu by m
year with totals

Flexible thumbnail image gallery in tal
float format.

Enable unlimited categories (tags) per
article.

Textpattern · 4.0.4

In this chapter, you'll learn about the use of Textpattern plugins to extend the base functionality of Textpattern. The chapter covers how to install and activate plugins, how to view plugin documentation and source code, and how to uninstall plugins.

What is a plugin?

While Textpattern has a wide array of built-in features and tags, one of its best features is its plugin architecture, which enables any number of additional features and tags to be plugged into your Textpattern installation.

A Textpattern plugin is simply an additional piece of code that can be installed into Textpattern. The plugin code is then loaded along with the base Textpattern code, giving you access to all the tags and features within the plugin, just as if it were included in Textpattern itself.

The benefit of using a plugin is that you have the ability to upgrade the version of Textpattern you're using and still maintain the custom functionality that the plugin provides without modifying the base Textpattern code.

Public-side vs. admin-side plugins

Textpattern provides the ability to load plugins for use either on your public site or within its own admin interface. When building a plugin, the author must designate whether the plugin should be loaded on the public site only, or on both the public site and within the admin interface. In addition to public-side and admin-side plugins, library plugins can be created by plugin authors to store functions used by multiple plugins. Library plugins do not offer any functionality on their own, but can be called by other public-side or admin-side plugins.

Public-side plugins typically define a new tag or set of tags that you can use on your forms and page templates as you build your site. Public-side plugins can also be used to catch page requests or predefined events within Textpattern to introduce alternate behavior. You'll find plugins that cover a wide range of functions such as building date-based article archives, building image galleries, creating contact forms, customizing Rich Site Summary (RSS) feeds, customizing comments, and integrating with third-party statistics programs. And these are just a few representative plugins.

Admin-side plugins are typically created to enable greater customization of the content-entry process, to add site-management features, or to set preferences for more complex plugins. For example, the `glx_admin_image` plugin adds several advanced image-editing features and automatic thumbnail creation to the Content ➤ Images tab, while the `rss_admin_db_manager` plugin adds a fully featured database management system to your Textpattern install.

Finding plugins

The authoritative resource for Textpattern plugins is the Textpattern Resources website located at www.textpattern.org. One section of the site is a compilation of plugins written by dozens of plugin authors. All plugins (just like Textpattern) are free for you to use. You can start by browsing through plugins by category or use the site's advanced search feature to locate a specific type of plugin.

Each plugin has its own page on the site, which typically includes a brief description of the plugin, a link to the plugin author's website for more information on the plugin, and a link to download the plugin (see Figure 13-1).

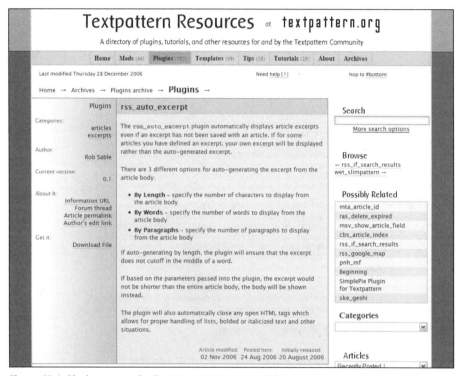

Figure 13-1. Plugin page on the Textpattern Resources website

13

Installing plugins

When following a link to download a plugin, one of two things happens. Many plugins are made available as a forced file download. If a plugin is made available in this format, your browser prompts you to download the file to a local drive. All other plugins display within your browser window, as shown in Figure 13-2.

```
# rss_auto_excerpt v0.2
# Automatic article excerpts
# Rob Sable
# http://www.wilshireone.com/

# .....................................................................
# This is a plugin for Textpattern - http://textpattern.com/
# To install: textpattern > admin > plugins
# Paste the following text into the 'Install plugin' box:
# .....................................................................

H4sIAAAAAAAAA71ae28bNxL/2/4UjE6IV1dZK81x2kiyglx77xYoUheHu5xhUFpKYrNaLkiu
ZTftd7+ZIbkPPRzbuNZInF1yOPObJ4fc8PFwOP5kxq/GrYxvRGtixsPX45Y25oYXVt2Iu4XQ
ucXxL8etW6GNVBm+nY9bg/4In4AcSNdK48ubceu9mrMf+Dx1zAZh9qbQEkdGwGdtbT6O4+12
29/K1KylFioT/YXaxLRoOG4lwiy0zK0XNwIp7wDQhlu5YFzD71Qwj84gBWhg73MQKscDeP1q
3AJ2uRYGZufjocO2Fml+Uyd75caQwcUIhZyeTNfD2XFR0ximT4Eqn12tBZsuVCJmu+aaxjTM
8rRYyYzxwI2n6T1LpMlTfm/2WDNxKzIml4xnYYytuWGZsmwuYMrwW5GwrbRrJPHL+4z9fcmW
SjOjNiKMGnavClh9K1giljKDdRXXHk5qpraVHHBDCkICOCDX3K6FZnYN6+CJlDhbiUzABEz7
hSD93yBogXhSo5iCENEyEbBEGrYU3BZaADLkYwn1QTYMiHm6RatUCI6Yg0zhlepP47zyhkb1
BTsHHss1vGWWKYogQ/api5bZirQKjJdabZya3ilz1dyPA/cincHvVM6mxmqVrWZ/umffimx1
19PYj7CXf/hqNBxOmMnFQi7viV1WbOZgQ7VkizXXfGEhf5hVQcfDUqcxCDo92ZX3L6UT81hx
WyR+rqTvAepK83z9aHF5ueKxMqcx2pQcB9G765n5PUvJvD1a79OIYlRkBiOKwqnuwEQJlykL
4LVcMumidiOTBCQDRk5Gcdky5wbiSzkSBL8R5JqcG5yQmVU1wb2GoK0q0sTnJDNQ2Gw9SyDm
pG5q7JbjU511sAxyT2bGC17FMBSW9wJL7MFq00izwoi6ZQBuSCnQE301Gky040Vv4LmAH2xb
mBD+U7GZmY8yn8bwwG65ljyDQgTmw1nnA8at1XJeWGHAen+BRBJ3fJOnwqeHK4FTKLWz05ep
ndi7fCyXNzJL5K1MCp7eeGu8XNnJKWOBZrdoMgRSRdJla9hi9dc38NNiMXEJPEQKhog/x3iH
acUifhgr6AdK+WIeqgxUKnz3cRBiHc211NrUhKEVqc6GYIB4q8o2S6WhWM/5SvQYmNfPV1hK
UkeCBd0JNQLcDJFUSztUNbcVjGZhJNMyy1eIHT1QEEEgFhjuED08z21nCmXT2PuUYkSR2F3N
ItkX/R5LuV5B8C8VrpA/iy6D4CgrXaBKtMohcnPTrYEK5eZqJ70JWHO/XKQKnMyzeyjmUPn/
dvXdt6RKv6pOjNziGaRqS+U+B7mAAjIzIV3AHWhzA8ZWaYL5r5m0PJULgA5WEHe4QcEw7XtG
2oLT3rG7xS3WCgGBaUA8mFWB69AbJbCq8IVNspbh3zt135U5VUvxYJS0ubVM55rFs9Or524o
fc/gG7HkRWrHLFQIXxr89J99VvuOv/Sz5xeDQLfnvW1jTzqI83E70VMhEteA8AGA+f5WdhD1
Ezawp0KtFR9PMToKF+L0I8bhIbA454IUg5uKv9AbN+p2q2WR1jXjKMp/CpGz97DtQErg0Pnx
MPBgAmxcxL5TWhyFLzLkegg84aY9e7/RDBs5pt6yudWuId+PNGx1i4BpTOHQ92UA/oSyhvus
bxUQgMTmkRjpI1tg/3nETMNJv98/Yhan5GVFRz8PunQL7ofCcMgwoWh44wCheb5v8wc86TEE
3Cbn2YOYFyn0QocQ00TVE4QuqibjyfUmiAvgNhBkOPggwJTPRboL8B2jYX/ayHPBNfocMkZ8
```

Figure 13-2. Compiled plugin displayed in a browser

Whether the plugin is displayed within your browser or downloaded to a local drive, the installation process is the same:

1. If you downloaded a plugin file to a local drive, open the file in a text editor and copy the entire contents of the file to the clipboard.

2. If you're viewing a plugin in the browser window, copy the entire contents of the browser window to the clipboard.

3. Navigate to the Admin ➤ Plugins tab (shown in Figure 13-3).

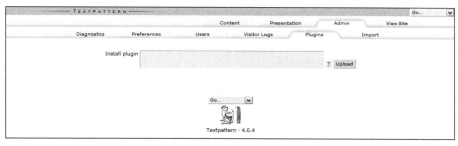

Figure 13-3. You install and manage your plugins on the Plugins tab.

4. Paste the contents of the clipboard into the textarea labeled Install plugin at the top of the page.

5. Click the Upload button to load the plugin into your Textpattern install.

6. Once the plugin has been uploaded, you see a preview of the plugin code and help so that you can verify the contents of the plugin and confirm that you want to continue the installation process, as shown in Figure 13-4.

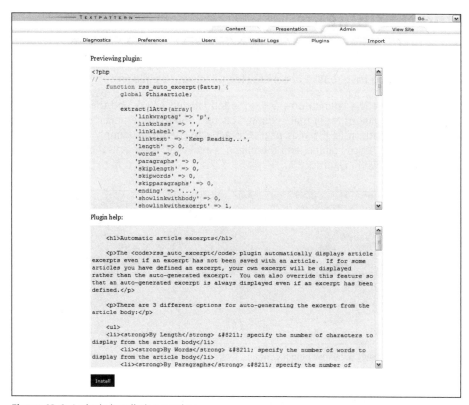

Figure 13-4. A plugin installation preview

7. To complete the installation process, click the Install button at the bottom of the page.

8. Once the plugin is installed, it appears in the plugin listing on the Admin ➤ Plugins tab, as shown in Figure 13-5.

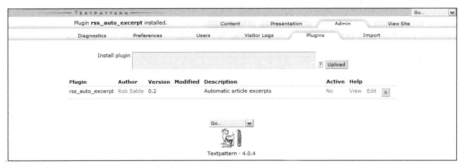

Figure 13-5. The newly installed plugin is now listed on the Plugins tab.

Activating plugins

Once a plugin is installed, its code and help are loaded into the txp_plugin table in your Textpattern database. However, once a plugin is installed, it's still not available for use on your site, and you have to take one more step to activate the plugin.

Notice that there is a column on the Plugins tab labeled Active, and the plugin you just installed has a value of No in that column. This tells you that the plugin code will not be loaded by Textpattern as it builds pages. To activate the plugin, simply click the hyperlinked No in the Active column, and the plugin is activated. After activation, the label displays Yes, as shown in Figure 13-6.

Figure 13-6. The newly activated plugin contains a value of Yes in the Active column.

To deactivate the plugin, just click the Yes link in the Active column. The ability to activate and deactivate plugins within your Textpattern install can be very useful. Instead of having to delete a plugin entirely, leaving a plugin in an inactive state enables you to easily turn it back on without having to go through the installation process again.

Viewing plugin help

Each plugin you install probably contains documentation to help you learn how to use the plugin. If you click the View link in the Help column of the Plugins tab listing, you are taken to a plugin's help page, as shown in Figure 13-7. If the plugin does not contain any help, you see a message letting you know that there is no help for the plugin.

Figure 13-7. A plugin's help page contains documentation about how to use the plugin.

The content of the help page varies depending on the plugin author, but you typically find a brief explanation of the plugin and details on the various options available when calling the plugin.

Viewing and editing plugin code

13

After an encoded plugin file is installed into Textpattern, you have an opportunity to view and edit the plugin code. If you're an aspiring plugin author, this can be a great way to learn. But if you're not an experienced PHP developer, editing plugin code on your live site can be dangerous. Keep in mind that as soon as you make changes to plugin code, the changes immediately take effect on your site. If you're looking to make changes to a plugin, it's safest to make the changes on a test site first. If you want to write your own plugin, see Chapter 14, which covers all the details necessary to get you started.

To view a plugin's source code, click the Edit link next to the Help column of the Plugins tab listing. The source code displays in a large textarea, as shown in Figure 13-8, enabling you to edit and then resave the plugin code.

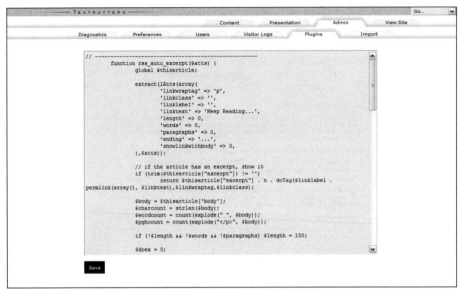

Figure 13-8. The plugin source code editor

If you made any changes, click the Save button at the bottom of the page when you finish. Again, keep in mind that as soon as you save your changes, they immediately go into effect on your site.

Once a plugin has been modified, it is noted on the Plugins tab, as shown in Figure 13-9.

Figure 13-9. If a plugin is resaved, it is marked as modified.

Uninstalling plugins

Once a plugin is installed, you always have the option to remove the plugin from your Textpattern install. Clicking the X button in the rightmost column permanently deletes the plugin from the txp_plugin table in your database, and the plugin will no longer be available for use.

Plugins tab

You have now learned about the functions that can be performed on the Plugins tab, but there are a few more pieces of information on the page. Each plugin is listed by name and includes the plugin's author with a hyperlink to the author's website, the plugin's version, and a brief description of the plugin, as shown in Figure 13-10.

Figure 13-10. The Plugins tab contains details about installed plugins.

Summary

This chapter introduced you to Textpattern plugins, which can be used to extend and enhance the base functions and features provided by Textpattern on your public website and with Textpattern's own admin interface. It detailed the steps needed to locate, install, and manage plugins.

Your first stop to find the latest plugins available for Textpattern is the Textpattern resources website, located at www.textpattern.org. If you can't find what you're looking for, keep reading; Chapter 14 steps you through the process of creating your own Textpattern plugins.

14 WRITING PLUGINS

Content

Preferences

Users

Advanced

Basic Advanced Language

Admin

How many articles should b

Send "Las

Section name: plugin-test

Section title: plugin-test

Uses page: plugin-test

Uses style: default ?

Selected by default? ⦿ No ◯ Yes ?

On front page? ⦿ No ◯ Yes ?

Syndicate? ⦿ No ◯ Yes ?

clude in site search? ⦿ No ◯ Yes ?

```
# A basic Textpattern plugin.
# Rob Sable
# http://www.wilshireone.com/

# ...........................
# This is a plugin for Textpat
# To install: textpattern > ad
# Paste the following text int

H4sIAAAAAAAAA3VRW2vCMBR+bn5FCE
w71+1xNG05SeLV1R0rNOkMLSdE2Jsf
2VLypEr8zMr2hpV8dY+Dkb6yAJzGOU
Kzl+ER9OM+eE6bFuhzfZR34EHLiTB1
/aN3Pv9B9OrPeIuhiWBG718aaTE89r
```

This chapter covers all the steps necessary to write, test, and release your own Textpattern plugins. It starts by walking you through the steps you need to take to set up a local plugin development environment. It then moves you through several plugin examples and references time-saving helper functions within the Textpattern source code that you can use as building blocks for your own plugins.

Before you start

If you're interested in writing plugins for Textpattern, you should first have an understanding of PHP and experience coding and testing PHP scripts. If you have experience programming in another language, PHP should be relatively easy to learn.

If you're looking for resources to begin learning PHP or just need to brush up on your skills, the following are good places to start:

- PHP Manual at www.php.net/manual/en/
- PHP Resources at www.friendsofed.com/book.html?isbn=1590597311

You should also have some familiarity with the MySQL database engine. Most plugins use data stored in the Textpattern database in some fashion, which means that you need to be familiar with SQL query syntax. While there are helper functions within the Textpattern code that can be used instead of writing all your queries from scratch, a basic understanding of SQL is necessary.

Digging in to the core code that drives Textpattern also helps you to gain an understanding of some of the functions and global variables you have at your disposal. Although you'll learn more about these subjects later in the chapter, here are some online resources that you'll find useful:

- Browse the Textpattern source code and revision history at http://dev.textpattern.com/browser and http://dev.textpattern.com/timeline.
- PHPXref generates source code documentation in an easily searchable HTML format at www.phpxref.com/xref/textpattern.

Finally, before spending time writing your own plugin, make sure that someone else hasn't already done the job. The Textpattern Forum at http://forum.textpattern.com and the Textpattern Resources site at www.textpattern.org are the best places to find details about previously released plugins. Reading through the code of plugins that others have developed can also help you to become familiar with different coding techniques.

Getting started

The first step of writing your own plugins is to set up a local development environment. In Chapter 2, you learned how to set up a local Textpattern installation, which gives you a testing ground for your new plugins. If you haven't already completed your local

Textpattern install, you should do that before reading any further. After you have a local Textpattern install up and running, it's time to start setting up your plugin development environment.

Textpattern plugin template

The Textpattern plugin template is the first building block to put in place. You can find the latest version in the Textpattern subversion repository at http://svn.textpattern.com/development/4.0-plugin-template/. You can also find the latest download package and discussion on the Textpattern forum at http://forum.textpattern.com/viewtopic.php?id=10330. Download the template files to the computer you'll be developing on.

The template actually includes three files:

- zem_plugin.php is the actual template you use to create the plugins. The file has been commented so that you can see where to place your PHP code, Textile-formatted help, and plugin metadata.

- zem_plugin_example.php contains examples of public and admin plugins. It isn't needed to create new plugins, but can be used for reference.

- zem_tpl.php is the plugin compiler that you use to build the plugins for installation into Textpattern. The compiler converts raw PHP code and help to a base64-encoded string that will be pasted into the Admin ➤ Plugins tab. It will be used when you're ready to release the plugins to the Textpattern community.

You'll dig in to the details of the plugin template files after you complete the local setup.

Local workspace setup

Once the plugin template has been downloaded locally, create a new directory that you'll use as the plugin-development workspace. For the rest of this chapter, c:\txp is used as the directory name. If you're working on an operating system other than Windows, just replace the directory name with the one you created. Now that you have a new empty directory, it is time to pull in the files you need to develop:

1. Copy the zem_tpl.php file into your c:\txp directory.
2. Copy the classTextile.php file from the texpattern/lib directory of the Textpattern installation into your c:\txp directory. This file enables you to create Textile-formatted help that will be included in the compiled plugin.

That's all you need to compile the plugins. Next, you configure the local Textpattern install so that you can start developing and testing the plugins.

Local Textpattern setup

There are several helpful features built in to Textpattern that make life easier for plugin developers. These features help you save time while you develop, test, and debug the plugins.

14

The first feature is the Plugin cache directory. When configured, Textpattern looks in this directory for plugin files and loads them as pages are built. This saves you from having to reinstall the plugin each time you need to test new functionality. To set up the directory, follow these steps:

1. Create a new directory within your Textpattern installation. (Create a new directory called plugins in the textpattern directory of the install.)

2. In the Textpattern admin interface, navigate to the Admin ➤ Preferences ➤ Advanced page.

3. Find the preference called Plugin cache directory path in the Admin section, as shown in Figure 14-1.

4. Copy the full path of the directory you just created into that field. For example, my local path is c:\apache\htdocs\textpattern\plugins.

5. Save your preferences.

Figure 14-1. Setting the Plugin cache directory path on the Advanced Preferences page

Next, you want to make sure that Textpattern is running in debug mode. Debug mode gives you more-detailed error messages on the screen, which can help you fully test the plugins and ensure that no errors are hidden.

1. In the Textpattern admin interface, navigate to the Admin ➤ Preferences ➤ Basic page.

2. Find the preference called Production Status in the Publish section.

3. Set the value to Debugging, as shown in Figure 14-2.

4. Save your preferences.

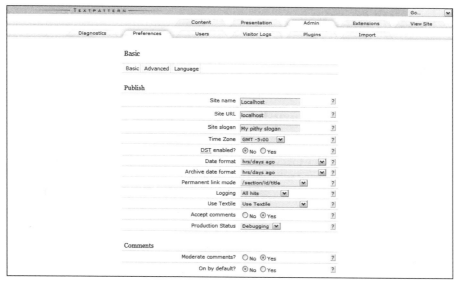

Figure 14-2. Setting the Production Status on the Basic Preferences page

Plugin loading

Before you jump in and start coding the plugins, it is helpful to understand how Textpattern loads and uses plugins.

When plugins are installed in the Textpattern admin interface on the Admin ➤ Plugins tab, they are stored in the txp_plugin table in the Textpattern MySQL database. Each time Textpattern renders a public-side or admin-side page, plugin code is loaded from the database and evaluated. In the same way, plugin files that you place in the Plugin cache directory are loaded as pages are built. You can think of plugin loading as being analogous to the PHP include function. All the plugin code is simply included along with the base Textpattern code.

Plugins are loaded using the load_plugins() function that can be found in /textpattern/ lib/txplib_misc.php. The specific point where plugins are loaded during the page-rendering process can be found on line 99 of /textpattern/publish.php for public-side plugins and line 89 of /textpattern/index.php for admin-side plugins. If you track down those lines of code, notice that there's a difference in the way the function is called.

As you'll see as you start working through the Textpattern plugin template, each plugin has a type. A type code of 0 indicates a public-side only plugin, while a plugin with a type code of 1 also includes admin-side code. Therefore, when the load_plugins() function is called during admin-side plugin loading, a parameter of 1 is passed in so that plugins used on the public side only are not loaded.

14

Basic plugin topics

The next section covers all the basics needed to write, test, compile, and release a simple Textpattern plugin. For that, turn back to the local development environment and use the zem_plugin.php file as the start to the plugin.

Textpattern plugin template explained

The zem_plugin.php file is the basis for all the plugins you create. The file contains several explanatory comments. In the following code, I removed the comments to shorten the size of the file. Once you're familiar with how the template functions, you can do the same. I'll start by stepping through this file to explain how it should be used.

```php
1   <?php
2   # $plugin['name'] = 'abc_plugin';
3   # $plugin['allow_html_help'] = 0;
4
5   $plugin['version'] = '0.1';
6   $plugin['author'] = 'Alex Shiels';
7   $plugin['author_uri'] = 'http://thresholdstate.com/';
8   $plugin['description'] = 'Short description';
9   $plugin['type'] = 0;
10
11  if (!defined('txpinterface'))
12    @include_once('zem_tpl.php');
13
14  if (0) {
15  ?>
16  # --- BEGIN PLUGIN HELP ---
17  h1. Textile-formatted help goes here
18
19  # --- END PLUGIN HELP ---
20  <?php
21  }
22
23  # --- BEGIN PLUGIN CODE ---
24
25  // Plugin code goes here.  No need to escape quotes.
26
27  # --- END PLUGIN CODE ---
28  ?>
```

The first construct you notice throughout the file is an array called plugin. You'll set several different values on this array in the plugin template. These values correspond directly to values in the txp_plugin table and will be shown when the plugin is installed on the Admin ➤ Plugins tab.

Your work starts on line 2 with the $plugin['name'] field. By default, the plugin name is taken from the plugin file name. For example, if the plugin file is named myplugin.php, the plugin name is myplugin when installed into Textpattern. To maintain control over the plugin name, I recommend uncommenting line 2 and setting your plugin name specifically. Doing so enables you to maintain different versions of the file while keeping the same plugin name.

On line 3, you can change the format for plugin help. By default, the help text you write is passed through the Textile engine for formatting. By uncommenting line 3, the plugin help is interpreted as raw HTML and is not parsed by Textile before display. But per the comment in the plugin template, this is not a recommended setting. It is easiest to remove this line from your plugin unless you have a need to change the setting.

Lines 5–9 contain specific details about the plugin, including the plugin name and description, the plugin type, and the plugin author's name and website address. The first 4 lines of this section should be easy enough for you to determine, and line 9 refers to the plugin type covered earlier. Again, per the comments in the plugin template, the valid types are the following:

- 0 is used for a regular plugin. The plugin is loaded on the public side only.
- 1 is used for an admin plugin. The plugin is loaded on both the public and admin sides.
- 2 is used for a plugin library. The plugin is loaded only when include_plugin() or require_plugin() is called.

The bulk of the work you do in the plugin template occurs between lines 16 and 27 in the template file. All the help text goes between the lines that read # --- BEGIN PLUGIN HELP --- and # --- END PLUGIN HELP --- on lines 16 and 19. All the plugin code goes between the lines that read # --- BEGIN PLUGIN CODE --- and # --- END PLUGIN CODE --- on lines 23 and 27. Be sure you don't alter any of these lines because they are used by the plugin compiler.

Now that the plugin template has been reviewed, you can move on to creating the first basic plugin.

Writing a basic plugin

The first step of writing the plugin is to copy the plugin template into the Plugin cache directory. Once you copy the template, start by renaming the file so that you can identify your plugin and its version. In this case, name the file rss_hello_world-0.1.php so that you can easily tell that this is version 0.1 of the rss_hello_world plugin.

Notice that the name of the plugin is preceded by a three-character code. To easily identify the author of plugins and to prevent name collisions, each plugin author selects a unique three-character prefix that precedes the name of the plugins. Typically, the code is an author's initials or nickname, but that's up to you. For all the plugin examples in this chapter, I'll be using my standard prefix of rss, which represents my initials. Before you

14

begin writing your own plugins, search through the list of existing plugins on the Textpattern Resources website at www.textpattern.org to ensure that the prefix you want to use hasn't been taken.

Now that you have the plugin template file set up, it is time to start coding. Here's the code for the first basic plugin. When called from a page template or form, the <txp:rss_hello_world /> tag displays the text Hello Textpattern World, my name is Anonymous on the page.

```php
<?php
$plugin['name'] = 'rss_hello_world';
$plugin['version'] = '0.1';
$plugin['author'] = 'Rob Sable';
$plugin['author_uri'] = 'http://www.wilshireone.com/';
$plugin['description'] = 'A basic Textpattern plugin.';
$plugin['type'] = 0;

if (!defined('txpinterface'))
  @include_once('zem_tpl.php');

if (0) {
?>
# --- BEGIN PLUGIN HELP ---

h1. Hello, Textpattern World

This is a basic Textpattern plugin.

# --- END PLUGIN HELP ---
<?php
}
# --- BEGIN PLUGIN CODE ---

function rss_hello_world($atts) {
  extract(lAtts(array(
    'name' => 'Anonymous',
  ),$atts));

  return 'Hello Textpattern World, my name is '.$name;
}

# --- END PLUGIN CODE ---
?>
```

Starting from the top of the file, you see that the basic plugin metadata has been defined based on the name and version of the plugin, along with my name and website URL. Some basic help has been defined, but for now, skip down to the plugin code.

Plugins as tags

Each function you write in your plugin code corresponds to a tag that can be used on your Textpattern page templates and forms. In the first example, since a function called rss_hello_world was created, you can call the plugin from Textpattern pages using the tag <txp:rss_hello_world/>.

Self-closing vs. enclosing plugin tags

Just as with standard Textpattern tags, you have the ability to create a self-closing plugin tag or an enclosing plugin tag. In the example already begun, you are creating a self-closing tag. You can easily discern a self-closing tag from an enclosing tag based on the tag function's signature. If you attempt to use a self-closing tag as an enclosing tag, you receive a tag_error notification on the screen.

A **self-closing** tag accepts only an array of variables as a parameter. All self-closing plugins are called as follows:

```
<txp:rss_self_closing_tag />
```

An **enclosing tag** accepts an array of variables along with the addition of a second parameter to the function. The second parameter holds the content you'll display between the opening and closing tags of the plugin. That content can include plain text, HTML, core Textpattern tags, or plugin tags.

```
<txp:rss_enclosing_tag>
Content
</txp:rss_enclosing_tag>
```

You'll see an example of an enclosing plugin tag later in this chapter, but for now continue through the self-closing plugin example.

Plugin attributes

The first construct you see in the plugin code is as follows:

```
extract(lAtts(array(
  'name' => 'Anonymous',
),$atts));
```

Although just a few lines, the preceding code is used to initialize the local variables used in the plugin and to do some basic validation of the attributes specified on the tag. The lAtts() function can be found in /textpattern/lib/txplib_misc.php if you want to step through the source.

The first thing to notice is the definition of a name/value pair. Typically, plugins have several of these pairs defined. These pairs enumerate the valid attributes that can be specified when calling the plugin and the default values for those attributes if they are not specified.

14

For example, the preceding code defined a local variable called name that has a default value of Anonymous. When the plugin is called, if an attribute called name is specified, the value passed in to the plugin is assigned to the name variable. However, if the plugin is called without specifying the name attribute, the name variable is assigned a default value of Anonymous. Each name specified in the array translates to a local variable by the same name.

The preceding code also verifies that the attributes specified when calling the plugin are valid. In this example, an attribute called name is the only valid attribute that can be passed into the plugin. The array of name/value pairs that I specified for the plugin will be compared against the $atts array that is passed in to the plugin code from Textpattern. This array contains all plugin attributes and their values as specified when the plugin tag is called. So if I attempt to call the plugin using the call <txp:rss_hello_world firstname="Rob" />, I receive an error message to let me know that firstname is not a valid attribute of the plugin.

Once this code has been executed, you are left with a collection of local variables that can be used in the plugin. The values were determined either by those passed in when calling the plugin or by the defaults that you specified.

Plugin output

Each tag handler plugin can return output to the Textpattern page. In the example, you see this in the following line of code:

```
return 'Hello Textpattern World, my name is '.$name;
```

The output of the plugin is displayed as a string, so you should ensure that the value returned is a string, not a PHP object. Using the return statement is a must because it places the string within the flow of the page as it is built. If you were to use a PHP output function such as echo or print_r, the output would be placed outside of the Textpattern page and appear at the top of your browser window.

Testing the first basic plugin

Because you placed the plugin file in the Plugin cache directory, it is now available to be used within Textpattern. At this point, you add the plugin tag to a Textpattern page for testing.

1. Start by creating a new page on the Content ➤ Pages tab called plugin-test. Copy the existing default page and remove the HTML within the <body> tags, which leaves you with the shell of a basic Textpattern HTML page.

```
<!DOCTYPE html PUBLIC "-//W3C//DTD XHTML 1.0 Transitional//EN"
        "http://www.w3.org/TR/xhtml1/DTD/xhtml1-transitional.dtd">
<html xmlns="http://www.w3.org/1999/xhtml" xml:lang="en" lang="en">
<head>
  <meta http-equiv="content-type" ➥
content="text/html; charset=utf-8" />
```

```
    <link rel="stylesheet" href="<txp:css />" ➥
type="text/css" media="screen" />
    <title><txp:page_title /></title>
</head>
<body>

</body>
</html>
```

2. Next, create a new section on the Content ➤ Sections tab called plugin-test and assign the new plugin-test page to the section. The configured section is shown in Figure 14-3.

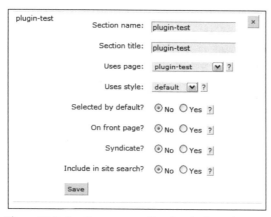

Figure 14-3. Creating a new section for plugin testing

3. Finally, add a call to the plugin within the <body> tags of the page and test the output. You can call the plugin in its simplest form as follows: <txp:rss_hello_world/>.

```
<!DOCTYPE html PUBLIC "-//W3C//DTD XHTML 1.0 Transitional//EN"
        "http://www.w3.org/TR/xhtml1/DTD/xhtml1-transitional.dtd">
<html xmlns="http://www.w3.org/1999/xhtml" xml:lang="en" lang="en">
<head>
    <meta http-equiv="content-type" ➥
content="text/html; charset=utf-8" />
    <link rel="stylesheet" href="<txp:css />" ➥
type="text/css" media="screen" />
    <title><txp:page_title /></title>
</head>
<body>
<txp:rss_hello_world />
</body>
</html>
```

This code gives you the HTML output shown in Figure 14-4.

14

297

Figure 14-4. Basic plugin output with no attributes specified

The plugin call did not specify the name attribute, so the output includes the default value of Anonymous. At this point, you've created and used a new Textpattern plugin.

Calling the plugin with attributes

Next, you'll update the plugin call to pass in a name attribute. The code in the page template changes as follows:

```
<!DOCTYPE html PUBLIC "-//W3C//DTD XHTML 1.0 Transitional//EN"
        "http://www.w3.org/TR/xhtml1/DTD/xhtml1-transitional.dtd">
<html xmlns="http://www.w3.org/1999/xhtml" xml:lang="en" lang="en">
<head>
  <meta http-equiv="content-type" ➡
content="text/html; charset=utf-8" />
  <link rel="stylesheet" href="<txp:css />" ➡

type="text/css" media="screen" />
  <title><txp:page_title /></title>
</head>
<body>
<txp:rss_hello_world name="Rob" />
</body>
</html>
```

This code results in a new page, as shown in Figure 14-5.

Figure 14-5. Basic plugin output with the name attribute specified

Since you now specified the name attribute, the default value has been overridden by the value you passed in when calling the plugin.

Calling the plugin with incorrect attributes

As discussed earlier, the plugin code validates the attributes passed in to the plugin. If an invalid attribute is used, an error is shown in your browser window. To demonstrate this, change the plugin to include an invalid attribute called firstname. The new page template code changes as follows:

```
<!DOCTYPE html PUBLIC "-//W3C//DTD XHTML 1.0 Transitional//EN"
        "http://www.w3.org/TR/xhtml1/DTD/xhtml1-transitional.dtd">
<html xmlns="http://www.w3.org/1999/xhtml" xml:lang="en" lang="en">
<head>
  <meta http-equiv="content-type" ➥
content="text/html; charset=utf-8" />
  <link rel="stylesheet" href="<txp:css />" ➥
type="text/css" media="screen" />
  <title><txp:page_title /></title>
</head>
<body>
<txp:rss_hello_world firstname="Rob" />
</body>
</html>
```

This code results in a new page, as shown in Figure 14-6.

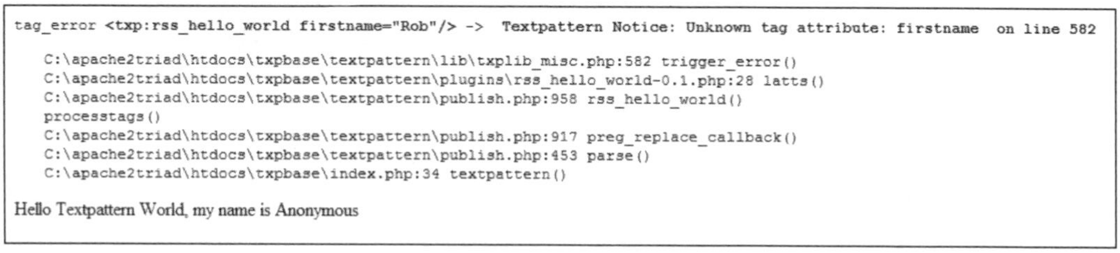

```
tag_error <txp:rss_hello_world firstname="Rob"/> ->  Textpattern Notice: Unknown tag attribute: firstname  on line 582

  C:\apache2triad\htdocs\txpbase\textpattern\lib\txplib_misc.php:582 trigger_error()
  C:\apache2triad\htdocs\txpbase\textpattern\plugins\rss_hello_world-0.1.php:28 latts()
  C:\apache2triad\htdocs\txpbase\textpattern\publish.php:958 rss_hello_world()
  processtags()
  C:\apache2triad\htdocs\txpbase\textpattern\publish.php:917 preg_replace_callback()
  C:\apache2triad\htdocs\txpbase\textpattern\publish.php:453 parse()
  C:\apache2triad\htdocs\txpbase\index.php:34 textpattern()

Hello Textpattern World, my name is Anonymous
```

Figure 14-6. Basic plugin output with the invalid firstname attribute specified

In this case, the error message displayed is very clear. You have specified an unknown tag attribute called firstname when calling the plugin. The rest of the page traces the error back to its origin. The important part of this message is the second line, which tells you that the error occurred on line 28 of the rss_hello_world plugin when calling the lAtts() function. The error messages displayed by Textpattern are very helpful when debugging and testing plugins.

Plugin errors

Aside from the error message you just received, any error you encounter in your plugin code is displayed in your browser window. For example, if you hadn't properly ended a line of code with a semicolon, you would see an error similar to the one shown in Figure 14-7.

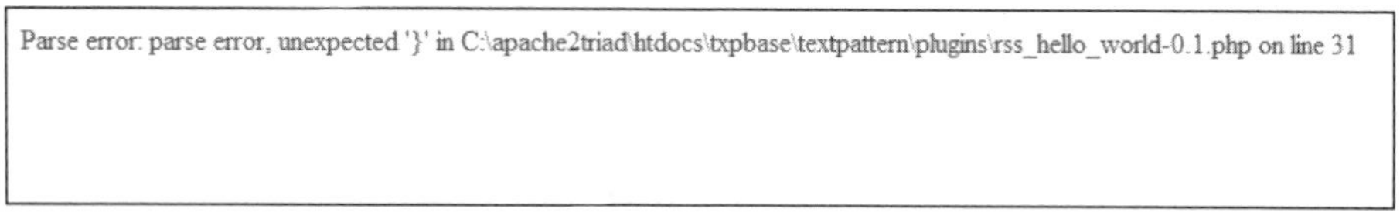

```
Parse error: parse error, unexpected '}' in C:\apache2triad\htdocs\txpbase\textpattern\plugins\rss_hello_world-0.1.php on line 31
```

Figure 14-7. A plugin parse error from a plugin in the Plugin cache directory

14

299

The benefit of coding and testing the plugin while it is in the Plugin cache directory instead of installed into Textpattern as a standard plugin is that you receive a much clearer error message. If you were to install the plugin, instead of leaving it in the Plugin cache directory, the error would look as shown in Figure 14-8.

```
Parse error: parse error, unexpected '}' in C:\apache2triad\htdocs\txpbase\textpattern\lib\txplib_misc.php(512) : eval()'d code on line 7 The above errors were caused
by the plugin:rss_hello_world

tag_error <txp:rss_hello_world name="Rob"/> -> Textpattern Warning: unknown_tag: rss_hello_world  on line 968

    C:\apache2triad\htdocs\txpbase\textpattern\publish.php:968 trigger_error()
    processtags()
    C:\apache2triad\htdocs\txpbase\textpattern\publish.php:917 preg_replace_callback()
    C:\apache2triad\htdocs\txpbase\textpattern\publish.php:453 parse()
    C:\apache2triad\htdocs\txpbase\index.php:34 textpattern()
```

Figure 14-8. A plugin parse error from an installed plugin

As you can see, you no longer have the same level of visibility in the error message. While the first message gave you the exact line number where the error occurred, the most you learn from the second message is that the error came from somewhere within the rss_hello_world plugin. The second message is much less specific than the first message you received because the plugin is being loaded from the database instead of the file system.

Debugging

During the course of development, it is probably necessary to inspect the contents of variables within the code that would not normally be part of the plugin's output. Textpattern makes this easy with the convenient dmp() function. Based on the plugin code you wrote earlier, you could dump the attributes passed in to the plugin to the screen by using the following code:

```
dmp($atts);
```

That code results in the following output:

```
array (
  'name' => 'Rob',
)
```

Compiling and releasing the plugin

Now that the plugin is successfully written and tested in the Plugin cache directory, it is time to make it available for others to download. There are two ways in which most plugins are made available to others in the Textpattern community.

Since you've been working on the plugin in the Plugin cache directory, start by copying the rss_hello_world-0.1.php file back into the workspace at c:\txp. You now have three files in the directory: zem_tpl.php, classTextile.php, and rss_hello_world-0.1.php. The easiest way to make the new plugin available for download is to copy all the plugin files in the local workspace directory to a public directory on a website. Once the files are there, point the browser to the plugin file. The output in the browser window is the compiled plugin, as shown in Figure 14-9.

```
# rss_hello_world v0.1
# A basic Textpattern plugin.
# Rob Sable
# http://www.wilshireone.com/

# .................................................................
# This is a plugin for Textpattern - http://textpattern.com/
# To install: textpattern > admin > plugins
# Paste the following text into the 'Install plugin' box:
# .................................................................

H4sIAAAAAAAAA3VRW2vCMBR+bn5FCEIVpBcvtaZO8G3P22CPkqbpGmibkKTrRPzvO1EHuzDI
w7l+1xNG05SeLV1R0rNOkMLSdE2JsfbYiLZVx1GZtvL1DSXvwlipep8tKUmi1EcZJWxwjTI+
2VLypEr8zMr2hpV8dY+Dkb6yAJzGOU3jeBzHaJStbaQRqhcRV118XUopqYT1Rmp3p/NbB1wy
Kz1+ER9OM+eE6bFuhzfZR34EHLiTB1ZJE0hzSgBPG2EtKUqa3sSBJ338Pra61TxADr5RsGvS
/aN3Pv9B9OrPsIuhiWBG718aaTE89r+oXaxhGCF8V8dVdb/vAojqoefeHf516ukEUOwMn1EA
kIZxN20PUJkyY9hpioIg9B8V4oc9Dg+96k+dGmw4R8FsfludFcCJjXADaAmvXv5amePuhD2Q
NxFGEx8W6ILuf9tV62sESpNsK+pN1fN6y1NRL9ciE1nNqyVjiyzJYe7yCX80dIFFAgAA
```

Figure 14-9. The compiled plugin in a browser window

At this point, anyone can copy the contents of the browser window, paste them into the Install plugin textarea on the Admin ➤ Plugins tab, and click the Upload button to start the plugin install process. After uploading the plugin, the plugin code and Textiled help text can be previewed, as shown in Figure 14-10. Complete the plugin install process to see how the new plugin will look when it is installed in Textpattern.

Figure 14-10. Plugin preview while installing the rss_hello_world plugin

14

After completing the install, the plugin must be activated. Once the plugin is active, it is now available for use.

New plugin installed in Textpattern

Now that you installed the new plugin, it is shown on the Admin ➤ Plugins tab. In Figure 14-11, you can see that rss_hello_world is the only installed plugin.

Figure 14-11. The rss_hello_world plugin after installation

The metadata you defined in the plugin template—including the plugin name, description, version, and author—translates directly to the information you see on this tab. The author name has also been hyperlinked using the URL that you provided in the template.

Viewing plugin help

The help text that you entered into the plugin template can be viewed (see Figure 14-12) by clicking the View link in the Help column.

Figure 14-12. The rss_hello_world plugin help

While the rss_hello_world plugin doesn't have extensive help, you have the ability to add as much as you need to your plugin help. You also have the ability to add any HTML formatting necessary to make your help text easy to read and understand.

A basic enclosing plugin

Now that you created the first self-closing plugin tag, adapt the example to become an enclosing tag. In addition to converting rss_hello_world to an enclosing plugin, you can keep its capability to be a self-closing plugin as well. Here's the new code:

```
function rss_hello_world($atts, $thing = NULL) {
  extract(lAtts(array(
    'name' => 'Anonymous',
    'message' => 'Hello Textpattern World, my name is',
    'wraptag' => 'p',
  ),$atts));

  if ($thing === NULL) {
    return doTag($message.' '.$name, $wraptag);
  }

  return doTag(parse($thing).' '.$name, $wraptag);
}
```

The first change is to add the second parameter, called $thing, to the function. The addition of this second parameter is needed to make the plugin an enclosing tag. When a page is rendered, Textpattern assigns the content between the opening and closing tags of the plugin to the $thing variable.

Notice a few other additions to the plugin. You now have two additional attributes available when calling the plugin. The first is called message and is used to display default text when the tag is called as a self-closing tag. The second is called wraptag and is used to wrap the message in an HTML tag.

If you want to force the plugin to be called as an enclosing plugin, you can return an error message when the $thing variable is NULL. But to demonstrate both the self-closing and enclosing varieties of the plugin, update the page code as follows:

```
<!DOCTYPE html PUBLIC "-//W3C//DTD XHTML 1.0 Transitional//EN"
        "http://www.w3.org/TR/xhtml1/DTD/xhtml1-transitional.dtd">
<html xmlns="http://www.w3.org/1999/xhtml" xml:lang="en" lang="en">
<head>
  <meta http-equiv="content-type" ➥
content="text/html; charset=utf-8" />
  <link rel="stylesheet" href="<txp:css />" ➥
type="text/css" media="screen" />
  <title><txp:page_title /></title>
</head>
<body>
<txp:rss_hello_world wraptag="strong"/>
<br/>
<txp:rss_hello_world name="Rob">
What's up world, I'm
</txp:rss_hello_world>
</body>
</html>
```

14

The updated page template generates output as shown in Figure 14-13.

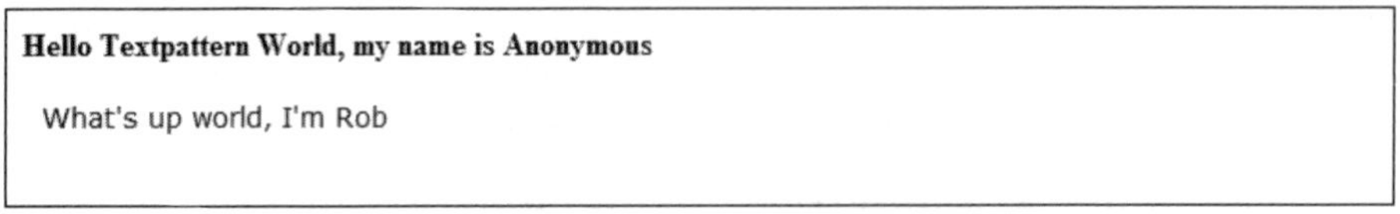

Hello Textpattern World, my name is Anonymous

What's up world, I'm Rob

Figure 14-13. Plugin output as both a self-closing and an enclosing tag

In the first call to the plugin, you use a self-closing tag and specify the wraptag attribute, which gives you the default message wrapped with <strong> tags. In the second call to the plugin, you use enclosing tags and specify the name attribute. In this case, the name and message specified are displayed wrapped with the default <p> tags.

Advanced plugin topics

Now that you know the basics of writing plugins, you can move on to some more-advanced topics. You'll learn that there are endless ways in which you can enhance and extend Textpattern's core. You'll explore some examples with the concepts covered in this section.

Conditional tags

A **conditional tag** is a more-advanced form of enclosing tag because it enables you to control the execution of one piece of code when the condition is true and another piece of code when a condition is false. You can think of a conditional Textpattern tag as a typical if/else programming statement. There is a variety of conditional tags built in to the Textpattern core. You can easily find these tags as they will begin with <txp:if.

To demonstrate a simple conditional tag, create the rss_if_positive tag, which accepts a number as a parameter and performs a conditional check to determine whether the number is positive. The code for the tag is the following:

```
function rss_if_positive($atts, $thing) {
  extract(lAtts(array(
    'number' => 0,
  ),$atts));

  $condition = ($number > 0) true : false;
  return parse(EvalElse($thing, $condition));
}
```

The magic here happens in the EvalElse() function, which you can find in the /textpattern/lib/txplib_misc.php file. After evaluating the condition, you let Textpattern know whether it was true or false so the appropriate output can be parsed and displayed. Call the plugin as follows:

```
<txp:rss_if_positive number="1">
It's positive!
<txp:else />
It's negative!
</txp:rss_if_positive>
```

In this case, the phrase It's positive! is included in the page output because the condition is true. If, however, you changed the tag call as follows, the output would change to It's negative! because the condition would be false:

```
<txp:rss_if_positive number="-1">
It's positive!
<txp:else />
It's negative!
</txp:rss_if_positive>
```

Callback functions

A **callback function** is a function that is passed as an argument to another function. The callback function is then executed at some point by the function it was passed to. This powerful concept enables plugin authors to write code that will be executed by Textpattern based on certain events. There are several callback functions available on the public side and even more available on the admin side.

The register_callback($func, $event, $step='', $pre=0) function is located in the /textpattern/lib/txplib_misc.php file. The $func and $event arguments are required, while $step and $pre are optional for admin-side callbacks. The functions arguments are used as follows:

- $func is the function you want Textpattern to call. This will be where the bulk of your plugin code is located.
- $event is the Textpattern event that will call back into your function.
- $step. On the admin side, an event might have multiple steps. You can target specific steps within an event for a finer level of control.
- $pre. On the admin side, if $pre is set to 1, the callback function will be called before the page is rendered instead of after.

When you register a callback function, you have the opportunity to completely override base Textpattern functionality or add your own features on top of the Textpattern core.

Public-side callback events

Public-side events are not as easy to recognize as admin-side events because they are buried in the Textpattern source code. The callback events currently available on the public side are these:

14

- pretext is called at the beginning of the pretext() function, which parses the URL to initialize variables used to build the page.

- textpattern is called at the beginning of the textpattern() function, which builds the pages based on values set in the pretext() function.

- comment.form is called before the comment form is added to a page.

- comment.save is called before a comment is saved to the database.

- rss_entry is appended to the end of each entry in the Rich Site Summary (RSS) feed.

- atom_entry is appended to the end of each entry in your Atom feed.

The pretext and textpattern callback events can be used to override the standard processing in the pretext() and/or textpattern() functions. This process is commonly used to override Textpattern's built-in URL handling to enable additional URL schemes to be supported. For example, the rss_suparchive plugin uses this technique to support date-based archives, and the rss_unlimited_categories plugin uses it to support /section/ category/title URL schemes.

The comment.form and comment.save events are primarily used to combat comment spam. For example, the mrw_spamkeywords_urlcount plugin analyzes keywords and link patterns in comment text to prevent spam from being posted and saved to the database.

To register a callback function with one of these public-side events, you need to add the following to your plugin code:

```
register_callback('rss_my_function', 'pretext');
```

Just replace the first argument with your function name and the second argument with the event to which you want to attach your callback. You typically find callbacks declared at the top of plugin's code, where they're easy to spot.

Admin-side callback events

The events and steps available on the admin side are much easier to find. In fact, you've been looking at them since the first time you logged into the admin interface, but you might not have known it. For example, take the URL of the Content ➤ Write tab, which ends in textpattern/index.php?event=article. You can clearly see from the URL that the article event is being used to identify this tab. If you pull up an article that you already saved in order to make changes, notice a URL ending in /textpattern/index. php?event=article&step=edit&ID=nnn. Again, you can see that the article event is being used, but you now have the addition of the edit step.

To register a callback function to be executed when you edit an existing article, make a call as follows:

```
register_callback('rss_my_admin_function', 'article', 'edit');
```

In addition to the step name that can be determined from looking at the URL, you can also determine step names by inspecting the admin interface source code. Each admin-side event is handled by a PHP script located at /textpattern/include/txp_EventNameGoesHere.php. For example, the article event is handled by a script located at /textpattern/ include/txp_article.php. If you look at the top of that script, you'll find the following switch statement:

```
switch(strtolower($step)) {
    case "":          article_edit();    break;
    case "create":    article_edit();    break;
    case "publish":   article_post();    break;
    case "edit":      article_edit();    break;
    case "save":      article_save();    break;
}
```

By reading through the switch statement on the $step variable, you can see that there are steps called create, publish, edit, and save that are handled by the article_edit(), article_post(), and article_save() functions (also located in the txp_article.php file). To have a callback function executed when a new article is posted, the following call should be made:

```
register_callback('rss_my_admin_function', 'article', 'publish');
```

This type of call is used by the rss_unlimited_categories plugin to save and retrieve categories from the database when articles are posted and edited. You'll learn more about that plugin later in this chapter.

All admin-side events and steps can be used to register callback functions with the exception of the plugin event. The plugin event is used to handle the Admin ➤ Plugins tab and does not load plugins and therefore register for callbacks. This was done to allow for the deactivation of any plugins that might be misbehaving.

Admin-side tab registration

In addition to adding your own callback functions on the admin side, you also have the ability to add new tabs to the admin interface that will appear under the extensions menu (see Figure 14-14).

The new tabs can be used for any number of purposes, including setting preferences for a public-side plugin, managing and backing up your MySQL database, manipulating images, and customizing the look and feel of the admin interface.

14

Figure 14-14. Admin plugins that have registered new tabs under the Extensions tab

To register a new tab, call another function in the /textpattern/lib/txplib_misc.php file called register_tab($area, $event, $title). After registering your new tab, you then register a callback function to handle the event for the new tab. The code that creates the tabs for the rss_admin_db_manager plugin (refer to Figure 14-14) is as follows:

```
if (@txpinterface == 'admin') {
  register_tab("extensions", "rss_db_man", "DB Manager");
  register_callback("rss_db_man", "rss_db_man");

  register_tab("extensions", "rss_sql_run", "Run SQL");
  register_callback("rss_sql_run", "rss_sql_run");

  register_tab("extensions", "rss_db_bk", "DB Backup");
  register_callback("rss_db_bk", "rss_db_bk");
}
```

The code is wrapped by an if statement, which ensures that the code is executed only within the admin interface. The arguments passed in to the register_tab() function are used as follows:

- $area is the top-level tab under which your new tab will be created. Plugins are typically added under the Extensions tab.
- $event is the new event that will be used for your tab.
- $title is the display name for the new tab.

After registering the new tab for a particular event, a callback is registered to handle that event.

Helper functions and global variables

In the examples presented throughout this chapter, you used several functions from the Textpattern source code. As plugins are loaded and executed, you'll have access to any and all functions and global variables that have been defined in the Textpattern source.

There is a variety of common functions that can be used for anything from querying the Textpattern database to generating HTML output. The more time you spend familiarizing yourself with the code that others have already written, the less time you'll spend writing your own code.

As your pages and forms are parsed and rendered, you'll also have access to global variables that can be used to generate custom output. Global variables are used to hold everything from general site preferences and configurations to page and form specific settings.

Appendix B contains a detailed listing of commonly used helper functions from the Textpattern source and the global variables that you'll have access to.

Real-world examples

Now that you know how to create Textpattern plugins, it is time to take a look at a few actual plugins to show how they can be used to enhance your Textpattern sites. One of the best ways to learn how to write plugins is to examine and learn the techniques of other plugin developers. The plugins listed cover a wide range of possibilities to get you started. All the plugins can be found on the Textpattern Resources site at www.textpattern.org or at the address noted in the following sections.

rss_unlimited_categories

This plugin contains examples of all the concepts covered in this chapter. It creates and uses its own database table, which enables you to attach an unlimited number of categories to an article above and beyond the standard two categories that Textpattern provides.

On the admin side, the plugin uses callbacks to enable you to set and edit article categories. It also registers its own admin-side tab that enables you to set preferences for the plugin.

On the public side, the plugin also uses a callback to support the /section/category and /section/category/title URL patterns. There is a collection of public-side tags of the self-closing, enclosing, and conditional variety.

www.wilshireone.com/textpattern-plugins/rss-unlimited-categories

14

rss_thumbpop

This plugin generates several different image gallery formats. The typical layout includes a listing of image thumbnails that display a full-size image when clicked. The gallery includes configurations that enable it to display the full images in a pop-up window, with or without a caption, or on the same page using JavaScript.

www.wilshireone.com/textpattern-plugins/rss-thumbpop

rss_auto_excerpt

This plugin automatically generates an article excerpt based on the number of characters, words, sentences, or paragraphs that you specify.

www.wilshireone.com/textpattern-plugins/rss_auto_excerpt

rss_admin_db_manager

This admin-side plugin adds three tabs to the admin interface that enable you to manage database backups, maintain your database tables, and execute SQL queries.

www.wilshireone.com/textpattern-plugins/rss_admin_db_manager

glx_admin_image

This admin-side plugin adds a wealth of helpful features to the Content ➤ Images tab, including the ability to rotate images and automatically create thumbnails.

http://grauhirn.org/txp/12/glx_admin_image_resize

ajw_if_comment_owner

This plugin enables you to generate different output if the current comment was posted by the owner of the site. It is commonly used by site owners to style their comments differently from others.

http://compooter.org/2005/03/textpattern-plugin-ajw-if-comment-owner

zem_contact_reborn

This plugin is one of the most widely used and can help you create anything from a simple contact form to a complex registration form.

http://thebombsite.com/txpplugins/408

Summary

This chapter covered everything you need to know to start writing your own Textpattern plugins. While the Textpattern core offers a great set of basic features, the plugin framework enables you to extend its functionality for whatever you need. If you're interested in writing your own plugins, make sure that you start from the basics. Getting an appropriate workspace set up and learning how best to use the helper functions and global variables that Textpattern offers will save you time in the long run. And don't forget to check the Textpattern Resources site at www.textpattern.org to find other plugins that you can learn from.

Now that all the building blocks that make up the Textpattern system have been discussed, the next three chapters explore the creation of professional websites that were built with Textpattern. All the sites are completely different and demonstrate how flexible Textpattern really is.

14

PART FIVE TEXTPATTERN SITE
EXAMPLES

15 MULTIAUTHOR WEBLOG

This chapter looks at what goes into building a multiauthor weblog of moderate complexity. The case study in this chapter involves a site that is already functioning in the wild and is live on the Internet. You'll look at the Godbit Project website, which has been online in its current state for a little more than a year now (see Figure 15-1).

Figure 15-1. A resource for churches to better use the Web: Godbit Project

You looked briefly at the hierarchical template structure of this site in Chapter 5, but for the sake of easy reference, the diagram makes an appearance again in this chapter (see Figure 15-2).

The purpose of Godbit is to help churches catch up with the rest of the world in adherence to the recommendations given by the World Wide Web Consortium (W3C).[1] This set of regulations has become known as **Web Standards** and is advocated by the Web Standards Project.[2] Godbit exists to do away with church websites that use nested tables and font tags, which are typically adorned with a variety of tacky clip art. Sites are featured that are both visually appealing and also well-coded (because the two need not be mutually exclusive).

---

1. www.w3.org
2. www.webstandards.org

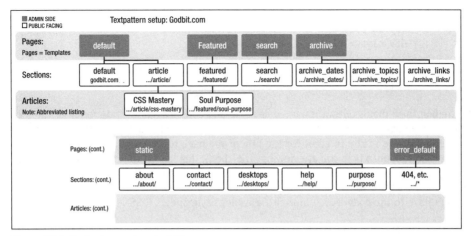

Figure 15-2. Textpattern setup: Godbit.com

As far as multiple authors go, those involved with the Godbit Project all share Managing Editor privileges (with a single Publisher-level user) and do a round-table vote on bringing on new contributors. This ensures that everyone is treated with mutual respect. If you are running a site and need varying levels of user permissions, be sure to adjust them accordingly. You might need to do this if you have several users submitting articles and others are working as editors, while also accommodating access to the site's presentational aspects for web designers. User permissions are covered further in Chapter 3.

Pages

This chapter first covers the Pages templates and then discusses the code snippets for Forms. It should be pretty clear from the diagram which sections use which page templates, so that topic is not talked about a great deal. One thing to note is that the only sections that are syndicated are article and featured because the rest do not change often enough to warrant Atom or Rich Site Summary (RSS) syndication.

static

First off, let's start with one of the more simple aspects of building a Textpattern site: setting up a template for static sections. The static page template for Godbit looks like this:

```
<txp:output_form form="doctype" />
<title><txp:sitename /> | <txp:section title="1" /></title>
</head>
<body id="godbit_com">
<div id="container">
  <txp:output_form form="sidebar_left" />
  <div id="content">
    <txp:article limit="1" form="single" />
```

15

```
      </div>
      <txp:output_form form="sidebar_right" />
      <div class="clear"> </div>
    </div>
  </body>
</html>
```

The first form that is output is named doctype and contains all the code required for each and every page in the site. That form also includes the beginning tag for head, which concludes after the title, to allow for the title of the page to change dynamically depending on which section/article you are viewing. The <body> tag has an id attribute with the value godbit_com, enabling users to override the stylesheet on a per-site basis. This is not essential for the site to function, but it is a nice courtesy to provide for your visitors, so they don't have to use body {...} in their Cascading Style Sheets (CSS), which affects all sites.

The two other forms pulled into the template are sidebar_left and sidebar_right. Note that the Form that is being used on the <txp:article /> tag is single. This is an easy way to build static pages with URLs structured like this: www.example.com/section.

default

The default page template differs only slightly from the static template, in that it has a little bit of conditional logic to allow for changes based on whether the user is on the main index page or an individual article. By default, the default section uses the default page template (hopefully that wasn't an abuse of the word *default*). The code for the default page template looks like this:

```
<txp:output_form form="doctype" />
<title>
  <txp:if_article_list>
    <txp:sitename />
    <txp:else />
    <txp:page_title separator=" | " />
  </txp:if_article_list>
</title>
</head>
<body id="godbit_com">
<div id="container">
  <txp:output_form form="sidebar_left" />
  <div id="content">
    <txp:if_article_list>
      <txp:article limit="5" form="excerpt" />
      <txp:else />
      <txp:article form="default" />
    </txp:if_article_list>
  </div>
  <txp:output_form form="sidebar_right" />
  <div class="clear"> </div>
```

```
      </div>
    </body>
  </html>
```

Notice that the following tags are used: `<txp:if_article_list>`...`<txp:else />`... `</txp:if_article_list>`. They are used once in the `<title>` and again in the content div. If the page that the user is looking at is an article list, a la the main page, only the name of the site is displayed. Otherwise, if the user is on an individual article's page, the page title is displayed with the designated separator (it looks like "Godbit Project | Name of Article"). Likewise, on the main page, a listing of five articles is output with the form of excerpt, showing an abbreviated bit of text from each one. Otherwise, the full article is shown via the default form.

featured

This page template is probably the most complicated because it serves up individual articles for the *featured* section and doubles as a gallery with pagination. Here is the code that comprises this template:

```
<txp:output_form form="doctype" />
<title>
  <txp:if_article_list>
    <txp:sitename /> | <txp:section title="1" />
    <txp:else />
    <txp:page_title separator=" | " />
  </txp:if_article_list>
</title>
</head>
<body id="godbit_com">
<div id="container">
  <txp:output_form form="sidebar_left" />
  <div id="content">
    <txp:if_article_list>
      <h1>Featured Sites</h1>
      <txp:article pgonly="1" offset="2" limit ="8" />
      <p class="pagination">
        <txp:older showalways="1">&laquo; Older</txp:older> /
        <txp:newer showalways="1">Newer &raquo;</txp:newer>
      </p>
      <p id="featured_gallery">
        <txp:article form="featured_gallery" offset="2" limit="8" />
      </p>
      <p class="pagination">
        <txp:older showalways="1">&laquo; Older</txp:older> /
        <txp:newer showalways="1">Newer &raquo;</txp:newer>
      </p>
    </txp:if_article_list>
    <txp:if_individual_article>
      <txp:article limit="1" form="featured_article" />
```

15

317

```
      </txp:if_individual_article>
    </div>
    <txp:output_form form="sidebar_right" />
    <div class="clear"> </div>
  </div>
  </body>
  </html>
```

Much of the conditional logic should already be familiar to you because of the previous examples, so you'll concentrate on what makes this template unique. Take note of the `<txp:article pgonly="1" />` tag, which causes a counter to be incremented, but does not actually output any content. This is necessary for the `<txp:older>...</txp:older>` and `<txp:newer>...</txp:newer>` tags to function (if they appear before your main article tag), along with the article tag that has the attribute and value `limit="8"`. This builds a gallery of eight featured site images per page, which can be navigated through via the Older/Newer links. If the user is on an individual article's page, only one is displayed and is formatted with the form named `featured_article`.

archive

This page template is not as complicated as it seems. Despite there being quite a bit of code, it is actually easier to understand than the featured template. Take a look at it and then you'll walk through the parts:

```
<txp:output_form form="doctype" />
<title><txp:sitename /> | archive</title>
</head>
<body id="godbit_com" class="archive_page">
<div id="container">
<txp:output_form form="sidebar_left" />
  <div id="content">
    <h1>Archive</h1>
    <txp:if_section name="archive_dates">
      <p class="info">
        Browse by: Dates |
        <a href="/archive_topics/">Topics</a> |
        <a href="/archive_links/">Links</a>
         </p>
      <txp:rss_suparchive section="article,featured" dateformat="F Y" ➥
        showsubdate="1" />
    </txp:if_section>
    <txp:if_section name="archive_topics">
      <p class="info">
        Browse by: <a href="/archive_dates/">Dates</a> |
        Topics |
        <a href="/archive_links/">Links</a>
      </p>
      <h2>Book Reviews</h2>
```

```
    <ul>
      <txp:article_custom limit="999" form="headlines" ➥
        section="article" category="books" sort="title asc" />
    </ul>
    <h2>Featured Sites</h2>
    <ul>
      <txp:article_custom limit="999" form="headlines" ➥
        section="featured" sort="title asc" />
    </ul>
    <h2>General</h2>
    <ul>
      <txp:article_custom limit="999" form="headlines" ➥
        section="article" category="general" sort="title asc" />
    </ul>
    <h2>Interviews</h2>
    <ul>
      <txp:article_custom limit="999" form="headlines" ➥
        section="article" category="interviews" sort="title asc" />
    </ul>
    <h2>Tutorials</h2>
    <ul>
      <txp:article_custom limit="999" form="headlines" ➥
        section="article" category="tutorials" sort="title asc" />
    </ul>
  </txp:if_section>
  <txp:if_section name="archive_links">
    <p class="info">
      Browse by: <a href="/archive_dates/">Dates</a> |
      <a href="/archive_topics/">Topics</a> |
      Links
    </p>
    <ul id="archive_links">
      <txp:linklist form="Links" sort="title asc" />
    </ul>
  </txp:if_section>
  </div>
  <txp:output_form form="sidebar_right" />
  <div class="clear"> </div>
</div>
</body>
</html>
```

As seen in Figure 15-1, this page template powers three sections: archive_dates, archive_topics, and archive_links. The archive_dates section is quite simple because I am using a plugin created by Robert Sable: rss_superarchive[3] (rss_ refers to his initials, not to RSS as in syndication). This tag contains two attribute/value pairs: dateformat="F" and showsubdate="1". The date format "F" outputs the full month name, and "Y" pro-

15

_____

3.   www.wilshireone.com/textpattern-plugins/rss-suparchive

duces a four-digit year. The other attribute controls whether the day of the month is displayed alongside the article title, or whether only the titles themselves are used.

If the user is viewing the archive_topics section, a simple list is output using the <txp:article_custom /> tag. The limit is set to 999 simply because the default is 10. At the point where any of these categories actually had that many entries, the limit could be set higher to accommodate the growth. They appear in ascending order by title, which is just a fancy way of saying that they are alphabetized for easier scanning. This just offers the user a different way to see the same data: topically versus chronologically.

For the archive_links section, it is basically just a gigantic listing of all links that have appeared in the left sidebar of the site. The links are output alphabetically and are floated left via CSS, using the hook of id="archive_links". This simulates a two-column layout for the listing.

search

This page template contains a <txp:article /> tag with the pgonly attribute, as did the featured template. This increments a counter of returned search results, so that it can be displayed visibly with <txp:search_result_count /> (assuming that it comes before your main article tag). You'll notice the same sort of pagination as was used in the featured page template. The newer and older tags do not pertain to chronology as with the featured sites gallery, but simply navigate through the most search results to the least.

```
<txp:output_form form="doctype" />
<title><txp:sitename /> | <txp:section title="1" /></title>
</head>
<body id="godbit_com">
<div id="container">
  <txp:output_form form="sidebar_left" />
  <div id="content">
    <txp:article pgonly="1" />
    <h1><txp:search_result_count />:</h1>
    <p class="pagination">
      <txp:newer showalways="1">&laquo; Prev</txp:newer> /
      <txp:older showalways="1">Next &raquo;</txp:older>
    </p>
    <txp:article form="search_results" limit="10" />
    <hr />
    <p class="pagination">
      <txp:newer showalways="1">&laquo; Prev</txp:newer> /
      <txp:older showalways="1">Next &raquo;</txp:older>
    </p>
  </div>
  <txp:output_form form="sidebar_right" />
  <div class="clear"> </div>
</div>
</body>
</html>
```

error_404

This page is very straightforward. It has a unique template because it is not necessary to show the entirety of the site content to convey to the user that they have reached a destination that does not exist. While this page still retains some distinctive branding, it is far simpler than the rest of the site, as seen in Figure 15-3.

Figure 15-3. Godbit error page

The code for this page is as follows and is purely XHTML without any Textpattern tags:

```
<!DOCTYPE html PUBLIC "-//W3C//DTD XHTML 1.0 Strict//EN"
  "http://www.w3.org/TR/xhtml1/DTD/xhtml1-strict.dtd">
<html xmlns="http://www.w3.org/1999/xhtml" xml:lang="en-us" ➥
  lang="en-us">
<head>
<meta http-equiv="content-type" content="text/html; charset=utf-8" />
<meta http-equiv="imagetoolbar" content="false" />
<meta name="mssmarttagspreventparsing" content="true" />
<meta name="robots" content="none" />
<link rel="shortcut icon" href="/favicon.ico" type="image/x-icon" />
<link rel="stylesheet" href='/css/godbit_error.css' type="t
  media="screen, projection" />
<title>Godbit Project | error</title>
</head>
<body id="godbit_com">
<h1>404 Error</h1>
```

15

```
<p>
   The file you are attempting to access cannot be found. It has either
   been moved, renamed or deleted. You might want to try the
   <a href="/">Homepage</a> or <a href="/archive_topics/">Archive</a> to
   find what you are looking for. If you are still having trouble, then
   feel free to <a href="/contact/">Contact Us</a>.
</p>
</body>
</html>
```

Forms

Now that we have looked at all the page templates involved in this site, let's turn our attention to the TXP forms used to house all the code snippets. Note that some forms call other forms, and this is perfectly allowable as far as Textpattern is concerned. Also, some forms control the output of articles and other dynamic content, while several forms simply contain large chunks of code.

comments (type: comment)

This form controls the output of comments. Notice that I am using a title attribute on a span to display more information in a tooltip about the date when each comment was posted. This is nice if someone really cares, but does not clutter up the page for those who just want to read the comments sequentially. The `<txp:comment_permlink>`... `</txp:comment_permlink>` (or `<txp:comment_permlink />`) is essential to have on a page because it allows for an anchor to jump directly to the comment when it has been posted. The `<txp:ajw_comment_num />` is a plugin that outputs the numerical value of each comment in the list, written by Andrew Waer.[4] This is helpful if you want the comments to be numbered, but are not necessarily using a typical ordered list. The self-closing `<txp:comment_name />` and `<txp:comment_message />` tags output the commenter's name and message, respectively.

```
<p>
   <span class="comment_num" title="Posted: <txp:comment_time />">
      <txp:comment_permlink><txp:ajw_comment_num /> ➡
        </txp:comment_permlink>
   </span>
   <span class="comment_name">
      <txp:comment_name />
   </span>
</p>
<txp:comment_message />
<txp:comment_form />
```

---

4. http://compooter.org/article/109/textpattern-plugin-ajw-comment-num

comments_display (type: article)

Like comments, this form is built in and cannot be removed. It is used to format the output of comments. Here, it is outputting all the accumulated comments via <txp:comments />. Note the use of the conditional tags to present a comments_preview form, if indeed a comment is being previewed. Likewise, if comments are allowed, the comment form is produced.

```
<h2 id="discuss">Discuss This Topic</h2>
<txp:comments />
<txp:if_comments_preview>
  <txp:comments_preview form="comments_preview" />
</txp:if_comments_preview>
<txp:if_comments_allowed>
  <txp:comments_form />
  <txp:else />
  <p id="txpCommentInputForm">Commenting has expired.</p>
</txp:if_comments_allowed>
```

comment_form (type: comment)

This form controls the formatting for the XHTML <form>...</form> itself. So this is the one and only instance in which the word *form* is actually being used the way it should be—to describe the XHTML tag. The code is pretty understandable. There is a label for each input, appropriately named for each corresponding TXP tag. The reason for this is for accessibility—to directly associate the text within the <label>...</label> tags with their respective input/fields.

```
<txp:comments_error wraptag="ul" break="li" />
<p>
  <label for="name">Name</label>
  <txp:comment_name_input />
</p>
<p>
  <label for="email">Email</label> - optional
  <txp:comment_email_input />
</p>
<p>
  <label for="web">Website</label> - optional
  <txp:comment_web_input /></p>
<p>
  <label for="message">Message</label> - ➥
  <a href="http://textile.thresholdstate.com/help-lite/?lang=en-en"> ➥
      help</a>
  <txp:comment_message_input />
</p>
<p id="publish">
```

15

```
<txp:comment_preview />
<txp:comment_submit />
</p>
```

Note that I have an ID added to the paragraph containing the Preview and Submit buttons, though it is not entirely necessary. This is to make it easier, via an interpage anchor link, for people to jump from their preview directly to submitting their comment. This helps for accessibility as well, and just better interaction in general if someone writes a long comment. (I also renamed the Submit button to Publish because I think it sounds better.) You can do this by downloading and editing your respective language file,[5] uploading it to /textpattern/lang/, and choosing Install from File via Admin ➤ Preferences ➤ Language.

comments_preview (type: comment)

This is essentially the same look and feel as a regular comment, except that it's a <div> styled to look like the <li> that contains all the other comments. It also has a nice message that informs the end user that this is in fact just a preview, not the final product. There is a link to #publish, so that users are directed to where they can actually press the Publish (Submit) button to post the comment once they are satisfied with it.

```
<div id="cpreview">
  <p>
    <span class="comment_num" title="Posted: <txp:comment_time />">
      <txp:comment_permlink><txp:ajw_comment_num /> ➥
        </txp:comment_permlink>
    </span>
    <span class="comment_name">
      <txp:comment_name />
    </span>
  </p>
  <div class="clear"> </div>
  <p class="announcement">
    <strong>Note:</strong> The following is a Preview of what your ➥
      comment will look like.
    Please do not forget to scroll back down and actually hit the
    <strong><a href="#publish">Publish</a></strong> button. Thanks!
  </p>
  <txp:comment_message />
</div>
```

default (type: article)

This is the form used for anything posted to the article section. Notice the conditional tags, which incorporate a variety of JavaScript files if the article has the category of "Code" chosen from the second drop-down menu in the Write interface. The nice thing about

---

5. http://rpc.textpattern.com/lang

JavaScript files, as opposed to CSS, is that they can be called from anywhere in a document, not just the <head>. If the article contains code examples, this brings in the files that run and add appropriate code highlighting. This JavaScript is provided free of charge by Dan Webb,[6] based on the initial work done by Dean Edwards.[7]

Following that, there is another set of conditional comments, which outputs the number of comments per article. One minor irritation for me is when there is only one comment, websites still read 1 comments. It should be singular, so I have written a short PHP snippet that uses raw PHP to determine the number of comments. If the number is not equal to 1, (0 or 2+), it reads "X comments" because of echo 's'. This is a roundabout way of fixing a small problem, but hey—I am picky.

```
<txp:if_article_category name="Code" number="2">
  <script type="text/javascript" src="/js/codehighlighter.js"></script>
  <script type="text/javascript" src="/js/css.js"></script>
  <script type="text/javascript" src="/js/html.js"></script>
  <script type="text/javascript" src="/js/javascript.js"></script>
  <script type="text/javascript" src="/js/ruby.js"></script>
</txp:if_article_category>
<h1><txp:title /></h1>
  <p class="info">
  <a href="#discuss">
    <txp:comments_count />
      comment<txp:php>
      if ($GLOBALS['thisarticle']['comments_count'] != 1)
      {
        echo 's';
      }
      </txp:php>
  </a> | Posted:
  <txp:posted /> in <em><txp:category1 /></em>, by <txp:author />
</p>
<txp:body />
```

doctype (type: misc)

When setting up Textpattern sites, one of the things I almost always do is make a TXP form named doctype that is of the type misc. In this, I place all the code that I typically need to appear on each and every page of the site. For Godbit, the doctype TXP form looks like this:

```
<!DOCTYPE html PUBLIC "-//W3C//DTD XHTML 1.0 Strict//EN"
  "http://www.w3.org/TR/xhtml1/DTD/xhtml1-strict.dtd">
<html xmlns="http://www.w3.org/1999/xhtml" xml:lang="en-us" ➥
  lang="en-us">
```

15

---

6. http://projects.danwebb.net/wiki/CodeHighlighter
7. http://dean.edwards.name/star-light

```
<head>
<meta http-equiv="content-type" content="text/html; charset=utf-8" />
<meta http-equiv="imagetoolbar" content="false" />
<meta name="author" content="Godbit Contributors" />
<meta name="copyright" content="Copyright 2005-<txp:php>
  echo date("Y"); </txp:php> Respective Authors" />
<meta name="description" content="Christian CSS Showcase + Web
  Development Resource" />
<meta name="keywords" content="christian, css, design, development,
  interface, javascript, standards, user, web, xhtml" />
<meta name="mssmarttagspreventparsing" content="true" />
<meta name="robots" content="all" />
<link rel="search" type="application/opensearchdescription+xml"
  href="http://godbit.com/opensearch_desc.xml"
  title="Godbit Project" />
<link rel="alternate" href="/rss/" type="application/rss+xml"
  title="RSS" />
<link rel="shortcut icon" href="/favicon.ico" type="image/x-icon" />
<link rel="stylesheet" href='/css/godbit_main.css' type="text/css"
  media="screen, projection" />
<!--[if IE]>
  <link rel="stylesheet" href='/css/godbit_ie.css' type="text/css"
    media="screen, projection" />
<![endif]-->
<link rel="stylesheet" href='/css/print.css' type="text/css"
  media="print" />
<script src=http://www.google-analytics.com/urchin.js
  type="text/javascript"></script>
<script type="text/javascript">
  _uacct = "UA-167104-1";
  urchinTracker();
</script>
```

I do not cover all of this in great depth because most of it is fairly standard XHTML, but I emphasize a few things that make this type of code snippet helpful. As an astute reader who is familiar with XHTML, you are no doubt wondering, "Why is there an opening <head> tag, but not a closing one?" The answer is that the doctype TXP form is merely the first portion of the beginning of the document—the portion that is repetitive across multiple pages. There is one key ingredient in <head>...</head> that needs to be dynamic and change with every page. This is, of course, the <title>, included in the Pages templates themselves.

PHP date()

You might also have noticed this bit of code among the metainformation for the site's copyright: <txp:php>echo date("Y");</txp:php>. You might recall from Chapter 3 that the regular PHP tags such as <?php ... ?> are not supposed to be used. Instead, the TXP syntax allows for use of <txp:php>...</txp:php> instead. These tags do exactly the same thing, indicating that raw PHP code is contained therein.

The code in this template simply produces the current year, according to the server on which Textpattern is installed. When it is passed to the browser, it reads Copyright 2005-XXXX Respective Authors" (XXXX = current year). That way, the copyright is always kept up to date, no matter how long since the site went live. This bit of code is invisible to the end user, but is read by automated site crawlers such as Google. This same technique is also used visibly elsewhere on the Godbit site.

External CSS

I link directly to CSS files instead of storing and calling them from within the Textpattern database. As mentioned in Chapter 5, the reason why is twofold:

- It is far easier to write CSS using a bona fide text-editing program with code highlighting and proper indentation.

- Using static files reduces strain on the server during periods of heavy traffic (that is, if you are *not* using site caching—which Godbit does not because of needing the forum feed pulled in un-cached to stay up-to-date). If you *are* using site caching, you can serve CSS via Textpattern just fine. Since a few of my articles, as well as those from other Godbit authors, have landed on the front page of Digg.com, it is imperative to do everything possible to squeeze the most performance out of the hosting environment.

OpenSearch

The link tag that points to opensearch_desc.xml is a way for you to add browser search functionality to your website for browsers such as Firefox 2 or Internet Explorer 7. If you are familiar with these browsers, you have used the search box in the upper-right corner of the window (it looks something like Figure 15-4 for Firefox). By placing a file by this name at the root of your domain, when visitors hit your site with a browser that supports this newer technology, the search box changes color, which indicates that a search engine is detected. Users can then click the down arrow and add your site's search engine to their browser.

Figure 15-4. Search box in Firefox 2

15

A screenshot of this being done in Internet Explorer 7 can be seen in Figure 15-5.

Figure 15-5. Adding a search engine in Internet Explorer 7

As far as the actual code that belongs in the opensearch_desc.xml file, it should look like the following example. You should, of course, swap out godbit.com with the actual URL for your particular website. Note that this is contingent on having a TXP section named search.

```
<OpenSearchDescription>
  <ShortName>Godbit Project</ShortName>
  <Description>Godbit Project - Article Search</Description>
  <Image height="16" width="16" type="image/x-icon"> ➡
    http://godbit.com/favicon.ico</Image>
  <Url type="text/html" method
    template="http://godbit.com/search?q={searchTerms}" />
</OpenSearchDescription>
```

OpenSearch was made possible by an initiative from A9.com, which was started by Amazon.com. More information on the actual XML specification can be found at its official website: www.opensearch.org.

Google Analytics

The last little bit of code that might look unfamiliar is simply the JavaScript necessary to track visitors with Google's statistics service called Analytics.[8] It was formerly provided by a company named Urchin Software Corporation, which was acquired by Google in April 2005. Now Google offers this service free to anyone who wants to sign up. I use it on Godbit because it enables multiple authors to log in and check site stats, as well as offloading the server overhead for stat recording and number-crunching to Google instead.

---

8. www.google.com/analytics

excerpt (type: article)

This form is responsible for the abbreviated bit of text that gives a glimpse into each article. Notice that I am using the `<txp:permlink />` as a self-closing tag instead of `<txp:permlink>...</txp:permlink>`. This is because using the opening and closing tags creates the title attribute with the message "Permanent link to this article", which is sort of redundant, considering that the name of the article is typically the text within the link. Not to mention that accessibility-wise, those using assistive technologies will hear "Permanent link to this article" needlessly repeated. (This snafu will most likely be removed in future releases beyond 4.0.4, so this bit of advice may indeed be a moot point by the time you read these words.)

The truncated text itself is handled by the kgr_safe_excerpt plugin,[9] which enables you to specify the number of words that will be displayed before a Read more type of link appears. The nice thing about this tag is that it does not cut off in the middle of a word and it also strips out all tags, so you do not accidentally have a starting tag with no ending.

```
<h1><a href="<txp:permlink />"><txp:title /></a></h1>
<p class="info">
  <a href="<txp:permlink />#discuss">
    <txp:if_comments>
      <txp:comments_count />
      <txp:else />
      0
    </txp:if_comments> comment<txp:php>
      if ($GLOBALS['thisarticle']['comments_count'] != 1)
      {
        echo 's';
      }
    </txp:php>
  </a> | Posted:
  <txp:posted /> in <em><txp:category1 /></em>, by <txp:author />
</p>
<p class="excerpt">
  <txp:kgr_safe_excerpt words="50" linktext="&bull; Read More" />
</p>
```

featured_article (type: article)

This is much like the default TXP form, with the exception that there is no conditional logic to include the code-highlighting JavaScript, and it also has the additional `<txp:article_image />`, which is specified in the Write area of the Textpattern interface.

15

---

9. www.textpattern.org/plugins/334/kgr_safe_excerpt

```
<h1><txp:title /></h1>
<p class="info">
  <a href="<txp:permlink />#discuss">
    <txp:if_comments>
      <txp:comments_count />
      <txp:else />
      0
    </txp:if_comments> comment<txp:php>
      if ($GLOBALS['thisarticle']['comments_count'] != 1)
      {
        echo 's';
      }
    </txp:php>
  </a> | Posted:
  <txp:posted /> in <em>Featured</em>, by <txp:author />
</p>
<p class="featured"><txp:article_image /></p>
<txp:body />
```

featured_gallery (type: article)

This is used to output the image for the featured sites as they are added to the gallery. They are floated left in the site design, creating a simulated two-column layout.

```
<a href="<txp:permlink />" title="<txp:title />"> ➡
  <txp:article_image /></a>
```

featured_preview (type: article)

This is identical to the previous TXP form, except it has a paragraph tag around it for inclusion in the sidebar_right template. When looking at the site design (refer to Figure 15-1), you can see the two images on the right side, using this form's code snippet.

```
<p><a href="<txp:permlink />" title="<txp:title />"> ➡
  <txp:article_image /></a></p>
```

headlines (type: article)

This is used to pull in lists of articles in both the sidebar_left and sidebar_right TXP forms.

```
<li><a href="<txp:permlink />"><txp:title /></a></li>
```

search_results (type: article)

This is the formatting used for search results in conjunction with the search page template. The `limit="3"` for the `<txp:search_result_excerpt />` refers to how many instances of the search term will be shown before the excerpt ends. It can be set to accommodate whatever number you like, but a few context clues should be enough to help people gauge whether the article is relevant.

```
<hr />
<p><a href="<txp:permlink />"><txp:title /></a></p>
<p class="search_results"><txp:search_result_excerpt limit="3" /></p>
```

single (type: article)

This form is used only with the `static` page template. It just outputs the title of the article and the article text.

```
<h1><txp:title /></h1>
<txp:body />
```

Links (type: link)

This is used to output a list of links in the `sidebar_left` form, as well as in the `archive_links` page template.

```
<li><txp:linkdesctitle /></li>
```

sidebar_left (type: misc)

This template contains the site branding, navigation, and links to the latest posts on the discussion forum. Notice the somewhat quizzical `<txp:if_section name="">`, followed by an XHTML comment, and `<txp:else />`. Essentially, it fills the logo `<div>` with ` ` if the name of the current section is blank (or "default"), which is the TXP way of identifying the default section. This keeps the dimensions of the `<div>` because something is inside it, but makes it just hold its place. If the end user is visiting any other section of the site, a link back to the main page appears since it comes after `<txp:else />`.

The code contained within `<txp:php>...</txp:php>` simply asks the database that drives the site's discussion forum to pull the four latest topic titles and link to the most recently updated posting in each one. The forum runs on PunBB,[10] but that is beyond the scope of this book. (However, I figured I should leave that bit of code in, just in case people wonder where it came from on the XHTML side of things.) The article titles for Book Reviews are sorted by `rand()`, which randomizes the listing. This way, older book reviews are cycled through every time the page loads. The same is true of the Tutorials and Interviews in the `sidebar_right` form, which helps circulate articles that might not otherwise get noticed.

15

---

10. www.punbb.org

```
<div id="sidebar_left">
  <a href="#content" id="skip">Skip to Content</a>
  <div id="logo">
    <txp:if_section name="">
      <!--   -->
      <txp:else />
      <a href="/" title="Go Home" accesskey="1">Go Home</a>
    </txp:if_section>
  </div>
  <ul id="menu">
    <li><a href="/forum/" accesskey="2">Discussion Forum</a></li>
    <li><a href="/purpose/" accesskey="3">Purpose + Vision</a></li>
    <li><a href="/about/" accesskey="4">About the Authors</a></li>
    <li><a href="/archive_dates/" accesskey="5">Article Archive</a></li>
    <li><a href="/desktops/" accesskey="6">Desktop Wallpaper</a></li>
    <li><a href="/help/" accesskey="7">Help + Questions</a></li>
    <li><a href="/contact/" accesskey="8">Contact Us</a></li>
  </ul>
  <h2>Forum Buzz:</h2>
  <ul class="links">
    <txp:php>
      $ch = curl_init("http://godbit.com/forum/extern.php? ➥
        action=active&show=4");
      curl_exec($ch);
      curl_close($ch);
    </txp:php>
  </ul>
  <h2>External Links: // <a href="/archive_links/">View all</a></h2>
  <ul class="links">
    <txp:linklist form="links" limit="4" sort="date desc" />
  </ul>
  <h2>Book Reviews:</h2>
  <ul class="links">
    <txp:article_custom limit="4" section="article" form="headlines" ➥
      category="books" sortby="rand()" />
  </ul>
</div>
```

sidebar_right (type: misc)

This is the form for the other side of the page. Notice that there are syndication links provided for comments. It is not native to Textpattern and is being done with a plugin called ajw_comments_feed.[11] Aside from that caveat, the rest of the TXP tags should be old hat by now.

---

11. www.compooter.org/article/140/textpattern-plugin-ajw-comments-feed

```
<div id="sidebar_right">
  <a href="http://www.9rules.com/" id="rules9">9rules Network</a>
  <form method="get" action="/search">
  <p>
    <input type="text" name="q" id="search_field" ➡
      value="Search Articles&#8230;" alt="search" ➡
      onfocus="this.value = '';" onblur="if(this.value == '') ➡
      {this.value = 'Search Articles&#8230;'}" />
  </p>
  </form>
  <p id="feed">
    <acronym title="Rich Site Summary">RSS</acronym>: ➡
      <a href="/rss/">Main</a>,
    <a href="http://godbit.com/?atom=1&amp;area=comments">Comments</a>,
    <a href="/forum/extern.php?action=active&amp;type=rss">Forum</a>,
    <a href="/?rss=1&amp;area=link">Links</a>
  </p>
  <h2>Featured Sites: // <a href="/featured/">View all</a></h2>
  <txp:article_custom form="featured_preview" limit="2" ➡
    section="featured" sortby="posted" sortdir="desc" pageby="8" />
  <h2>Tutorials:</h2>
  <ul class="links">
    <txp:article_custom limit="4" section="article" form="headlines" ➡
      category="tutorials" sortby="rand()" />
  </ul>
  <h2>Interviews:</h2>
  <ul class="links">
    <txp:article_custom limit="4" section="article" form="headlines" ➡
      category="interviews" sortby="rand()" />
  </ul>
  <h2>Site Mechanics:</h2>
  <p>
    This site is maintained using the
    <acronym title="Content Management System">CMS</acronym>
    <a href="http://www.textpattern.com/">Textpattern</a>, and adheres
      to valid <a href="http://validator.w3.org/check/referer"> ➡
      XHTML</a>,
    <a href="http://jigsaw.w3.org/css-validator/check/referer">CSS</a>
      and <a href="http://www.contentquality.com/mynewtester/cynthia ➡
      .exe?Url1=http://www.godbit.com/">508</a> accessibility
      requirements. The forum uses <a href="http://www.punbb.org/"> ➡
      PunBB</a>. Articles ➡
      <a href="http://creativecommons.org/licenses/by-nc-sa/2.5/"> ➡
      &copy; 2005-<txp:php>echo date('y');</txp:php></a>
      original authors.
  </p>
</div>
```

15

zem_contact_form (type: misc)

This form makes use of the zem_contact_reborn[12] and zem_contact_lang[13] plugins, which were originally written by Alex Shiels (known as Zem to the greater Textpattern community). These plugins have since been built upon and extended by a variety of users.[14] Basically, they enable you to build an email contact form in which the recipient's email is kept encrypted and hidden from public view. They also enable you to specify a form to be displayed after the email is sent. I have appropriately named mine zem_contact_thanks.

It should be noted that Godbit also makes use of one last plugin, pap_contact_cleaner,[15] which is designed to work with the zem_contact_reborn API to prevent comment form spam. While perpetrators might not know your actual address, it does not stop them from writing spam bots that go hunting for contact forms and bombard you with silly ads for imitation Gucci clothing and accessories. To combat this problem, simply install the pap_contact_cleaner plugin. It creates two hidden form fields, which you can name something similar to phone and mail (to not conflict with email), and spam bots will be savvy enough to fill them out with a number and address. The trick is this: if these hidden fields *are* filled out, the plugin keeps the form from actually sending the message. Human users can't see them and cannot fill them out, so the only way it can happen is via automated spam. Ta da! Problem solved.

```
<txp:zem_contact to="godbit.com@gmail.com" ➡
  thanks_form="zem_contact_thanks">
  <p>
    <txp:zem_contact_text label="Name" />
  </p>
  <p>
    <txp:zem_contact_email />
  </p>
  <p>
    <txp:zem_contact_text label="Website" />
  </p>
  <p>
    <txp:zem_contact_textarea />
  </p>
  <p id="publish">
    <input type="submit" class="button" value="Fire Away" ➡
      name="zem_contact_submit" />
  </p>
</txp:zem_contact>
```

---

12. www.textpattern.org/plugins/701/zem_contact_reborn
13. www.textpattern.org/plugins/702/zem_contact_lang
14. http://forum.textpattern.com/viewtopic.php?id=13416
15. www.textpattern.org/plugins/703/pap_contact_cleaner

zem_contact_thanks (type: misc)

This is displayed after someone sends an email via the Godbit contact form.

```
<p class="announcement">
  Thank you for your interest in our website. Your letter is on its way
  to the post office, and we should be recieving it within a few days.
  Please allow some time for us to review it and get back to you. We
  look forward to the conversation!
</p>
```

Summary

I hope that this chapter proved beneficial to you and showed some of the varieties of things that can be done with Textpattern, from building an image gallery to randomizing article content—making a blog into a site that is more community- and news-oriented. If you have any questions or want to get involved in our discussions about Web Standards, feel free to check out the Godbit forum. Once you have had a chance to digest the information you just read, get ready to roll up your sleeves because in the next chapter you will crank your skills up yet one more notch and learn how to use Textpattern to build sites for e-commerce.

15

16 CASE STUDY: POPULARWEDDINGFAVORS.COM

In the last chapter, you saw a multiauthor weblog that was built with Textpattern. While that may be the most common use of Textpattern, a weblog is certainly not the only type of site that will benefit from using it. This chapter explores the use of Textpattern to build the PopularWeddingFavors.com ecommerce store, including a product catalog, shopping cart, and payment system integration.

Why use Textpattern for ecommerce?

When I first set out to build an ecommerce site, I searched far and wide for an open-source, PHP-based ecommerce package that I could use. I quickly found that most of the available packages were either incomplete and bug-ridden, or monolithic and difficult to understand. Instead of being faced with learning a complex new website platform from scratch, I continued to search for an alternative.

The more I researched the subject, the more problems I found with the scripts that were readily available on the Internet. I had already built several Textpattern sites and authored many plugins, so I wondered how much easier it would be if I could build an ecommerce site using Textpattern. I started to capture my basic requirements for an ecommerce site framework and found that I could easily satisfy most of them with Textpattern. Here's the list that I started with, which included the features I was looking for:

- Have the ability to use a Web Standards–based design
- Have the ability to maintain a separation of content and presentation
- Use a web-based content entry system for text and images
- Use the same software to maintain static site pages and the product catalog
- Easily employ standard Search Engine Optimization (SEO) tactics
- Use clean URLs
- Use keywords in URLs
- Maintain a shopping cart on the site to be passed to a payment processor
- Handle payments through PayPal

When I reviewed this list along with all my options, it was no contest in the end. With some custom coding, Textpattern would enable me to satisfy all these requirements. Several new Textpattern plugins and a custom shopping cart later, my first ecommerce site, FavorableDesigns.com, was launched in November of 2005. The site, pictured in Figure 16-1, was well-received, and much of the custom coding done for the site has since been released to the Textpattern community.

After the site launched, I monitored search engine results for critical keywords and found that the site was well-indexed by all major search engines. This was the icing on the cake for me, and at that point I decided that Textpattern would be my ecommerce platform of choice.

Figure 16-1. FavorableDesigns.com was my first integrated Textpattern ecommerce website.

Building PopularWeddingFavors.com

After the success of the original FavorableDesigns.com website, I was given the task of creating a new ecommerce site called PopularWeddingFavors.com. The first thing I did was contact Claudia Baggiani and Brian Buschmann to help me with the site design. Claudia created all the illustrations and the overall site layout, and Brian helped with the information architecture and some of the finer details. My job was to bring the site to life in Textpattern. The result of our hard work is shown in Figure 16-2.

Figure 16-2. PopularWeddingFavors.com was illustrated and designed by Claudia Baggiani and Brian Buschmann, and implemented in Textpattern by Rob Sable.

The rest of this chapter shows you how the PopularWeddingFavors.com website was built using Textpattern.

## 16

Site structure

The PopularWeddingFavors.com site is a mix of dynamic pages used for product listings and static pages used for general information. All of the content for the site is managed through Textpattern. The entire site consists of the following pages:

- Home is used for highlighted products, general information, and search results.
- Catalog is used for listing products by category and to display individual products.
- Policies is used to display static information regarding company policies.
- About is used to display static information about the company.
- Contact is used to display contact information including a contact form.
- Sitemap has quick links to all sections and products on the site.
- Cart is used to display products that users have added to their shopping cart.
- Checkout is used to finalize and complete order details before making a payment.
- Order is used for confirmation of order after purchase.
- 404 error is used to handle any page not found errors.

Because the focus of the site is on the products being sold, there aren't very many pages used. Many of the pages listed previously will end up being implemented using a single Textpattern page template.

To manage products, I considered each product to be an article, so I could use the Textpattern admin interface to enter product content and many of the standard Textpattern tags to display the content. The biggest problem I saw was that I was limited to only two categories per product. Because I was in need of more, I developed the rss_unlimited_ categories plugin[1] (refer to Chapter 14), which is used to display all the article and category listings throughout the site.

Textpattern's custom fields also play a large role in this site. Detailed information about each product—including pricing, colors, size, personalized messages, and minimum order quantities—are stored in the custom fields. To pack even more information into the custom fields, I used the sed_pcf plugin,[2] which enabled me to fit multiple prices into a single custom field for products that offer quantity-based discounts.

With a mix of core Textpattern functions, several Textpattern plugins, and some custom coding, I was ready to begin building PopularWeddingFavors.com.

Page structure

The construction of the site started when I received a series of page layout templates from Claudia and Brian. My first job was to turn the pages into valid HTML and CSS code. Once the pages went through a series of cross-browser and cross-platform tests, they were ready to be broken down into Textpattern pages and forms.

---

1. www.wilshireone.com/textpattern-plugins/rss-unlimited-categories
2. http://txp-plugins.netcarving.com/plugins/packed-custom-fields

Page header and footer

As with most websites, the PopularWeddingFavors.com site has a common header, footer, and sidebar on all pages. For the sake of simplicity, all the common code is first broken out into two distinct forms in Textpattern. I like to add a prefix to the forms that I create so that I can easily distinguish my forms from the base Textpattern forms. So my two new forms are called pwf_header and pwf_footer.

The pwf_header form contains everything from the <DOCTYPE> declaration down through the <head> element, including all metadata for the site. The header also includes the beginning of the <body> tag code along with the logo, top menu, and search bar. With the source ordered so that the main content elements come before the sidebar menu, the pwf_footer form can hold all the code for the sidebar and footer menus. Figure 16-3 illustrates the areas covered by the pwf_header and pwf_footer forms.

By moving all the common code into two forms, the definition of each individual page becomes much simpler. Using the <txp:output_form/> tag, I can include those two forms in a page template and generate the appropriate content in-between. My default page template looks as follows:

```
<txp:output_form form="pwf_header" />
<txp:output_form form="pwf_home" />
<txp:output_form form="pwf_footer" />
```

The form included between the pwf_header and pwf_footer forms, called pwf_home, includes all content in Figure 16-3 that doesn't appear in the highlighted areas labeled pwf_header and pwf_footer. While I could have included this directly in my page template, I chose to move it to a separate form to keep my default page code clean when I start to enhance the page in order to display search results.

Home page

After defining my page header and footer and moving my home page content into the pwf_home form, I add additional code to the default page to enable it to handle and display search results:

```
<txp:output_form form="pwf_header" />
<txp:if_search>
  <txp:article pgonly="1" />
  <txp:rss_if_search_results>
    <h2>Search Results</h2>
    <txp:article />
  <txp:else />
    <txp:article_custom id="503" form="pwf_static" />
  </txp:rss_if_search_results>
<txp:else/>
  <txp:output_form form="pwf_home" />
</txp:if_search>
<txp:output_form form="pwf_footer" />
```

Figure 16-3. The areas covered by the pwf_header and pwf_footer forms on PopularWeddingFavors.com

I start by wrapping the pwf_home form in <txp:if_search/> tags, which enables me to display search results if a search was executed; otherwise, the pwf_home form is displayed. Within the <txp:if_search/> tag, I then use the rss_if_search_results plugin[3] to enable me to display search results when they are found or display an alternate message when no results are found. Figure 16-4 demonstrates the home page when a search is executed and results are found.

---

3. www.wilshireone.com/textpattern-plugins/rss-if-search-results

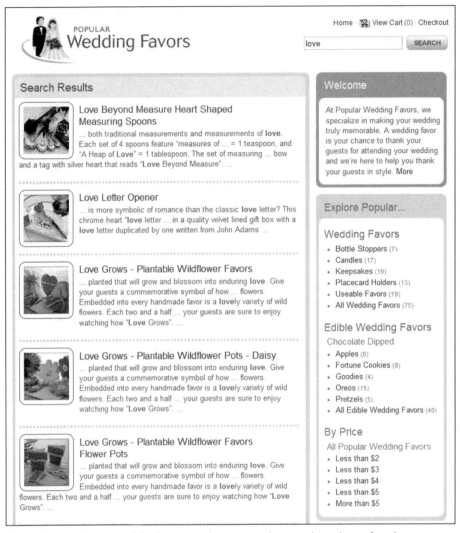

Figure 16-4. The PopularWeddingFavors.com home page when search results are found

In the case of a search that returns no results, the code after the `<txp:else/>` tag is used, and I display a specific article (# 503) that contains the no results found message. That page can be seen in Figure 16-5.

Figure 16-5. The PopularWeddingFavors.com home page showing no search results found

The last part of the page template is a line of code that doesn't generate any output:

```
<txp:article pgonly="1" />
```

The use of the `<txp:article/>` tag with the `pgonly` attribute set enables the `<txp:rss_if_search_results/>` tag to function properly. Until the `<txp:article/>` tag is called, I can't tell whether there are any search results. But by that point, it's too late for me to alter the page display the way I want to. Although adding the `pgonly` attribute to the call to the `<txp:article/>` tag hides it from display in the browser, Textpattern still parses the tag and provides me with the information I need to know—whether a search has returned results or not.

With fewer than 15 lines of code in my default page template, I can handle my normal home page view, a search results view, and a no search results found view. The home page serves as a launching point for the rest of the site.

Static pages

All the static content pages on the site use the same page template. These pages include Policies, About Us, Contact Us, and Sitemap. The code for the static page is very simple:

```
<txp:output_form form="pwf_header" />
<txp:article form="pwf_static" limit="1" />
<txp:output_form form="pwf_footer" />
```

The page displays one article from the current section between the header and footer. The layout of all four pages is the same, so the only part that differs is the article that is displayed.

Catalog page

The catalog page is used to display product listings by category and by price as well as individual products:

```
<txp:output_form form="pwf_header" />

<txp:if_article_list>

  <txp:if_category>
    <h2><txp:category title="1" /></h2>
  <txp:else />
    <h2>All Wedding Favors</h2>
  </txp:if_category>

  <txp:if_category>
    <txp:rss_unlimited_categories_article_list section="catalog"
    usechildren="1" limit="999" form="pwf_prodlist"
    sortby="(custom_6+0)" />
  <txp:else />
    <h3>Wedding Favors</h3>
    <ul>
      <txp:rss_unlimited_categories_article_list section="catalog"
      category="wedding-favors" usechildren="1" limit="999"
      form="pwf_byprice" filter="1" filterfield="custom_6"
      filtername="byprice" sortby="(custom_6+0)" />
    </ul>
    <h3>Edible Wedding Favors</h3>
      <ul>
```

```
      <txp:rss_unlimited_categories_article_list section="catalog"
       category="edible-wedding-favors" usechildren="1" limit="999"
       form="pwf_byprice" filter="1" filterfield="custom_6"
       filtername="byprice" sortby="(custom_6+0)" />
      </ul>
   </txp:if_category>

 <txp:else />
   <txp:article form="pwf_product" />
 </txp:if_article_list>

 <txp:output_form form="pwf_footer" />
```

The page again begins with the pwf_header form and ends with the pwf_footer form, as all pages do. In between, I started by adding the <txp:if_article_list/> tag so that the page can handle the display of article lists and individual articles. The code before the <txp:else/> tag is used for product listings, and the code after is used for individual products.

In the case of an article-listing page, there are two types of pages that can be built. The <txp:if_category/> tag is used to alter the display when there is a global category set within Textpattern. The existence of a global category is determined by the rss_unlimited_categories plugin as it evaluates the page URL and set for later use while building the page. When there is a global category set, the page shows a list of all products in that category and displays the category title at the top of the page. This type of page is shown in Figure 16-6.

The other type of product listing that this page can handle is listing by price. The URL is parsed by the rss_unlimited_categories plugin to produce a filtered listing. Here's the code again from the catalog page template that produces the listing by price:

```
      <txp:rss_unlimited_categories_article_list section="catalog"
       category="wedding-favors" usechildren="1" limit="999"
       form="pwf_byprice" filter="1" filterfield="custom_6"
       filtername="byprice" sortby="(custom_6+0)" />
```

The last four plugin attributes being specified in this case are the ones doing all the work. The filter parameter tells the plugin that I want to build a filtered list. The filterfield parameter declares custom_6 as the field I'll be filtering on. The filtername parameter defines byprice as the name of the filter in the URL. Finally, by using a sortby value of (custom_6+0), I force the list to be ordered numerically by price (which is stored in the custom_6 custom field).

Figure 16-6. A product category listing page on PopularWeddingFavors.com

For example, a URL of www.popularweddingfavors.com/catalog/byprice/lt/2 would be used to generate a product listing from the catalog that includes all products from the catalog with a price less than $2. The third part of the URL (/lt) is used to tell the plugin that it should use a less-than (<) comparison, and the fourth part of the URL (2) is the number to filter on. This URL gives a product listing as shown in Figure 16-7.

Figure 16-7. Product listing by price page on PopularWeddingFavors.com

The products are shown in this type of listing with a different article form—highlighting just the name and price of the product.

The remaining part of the page code simply displays the individual product page, as shown in Figure 16-8.

Figure 16-8. Individual product page on PopularWeddingFavors.com

Each product page includes the product's picture, detailed information on the product, and an order form. The product shown in Figure 16-8 demonstrates the tiered pricing that was implemented using the sed_pcf plugin. All the prices are stored in a single custom field. For example, the pricing field for this product looks as follows:

```
prices(1=3.00;23=2.40;47=2.20;96=2.00)
```

The data from that field is evaluated as the page loads to display the proper pricing on the page. When the item is added to the shopping cart, the correct price is calculated based on the price levels and the quantity purchased.

Another product example is shown in Figure 16-9.

Figure 16-9. Individual product page on PopularWeddingFavors.com

This page shows a few additions from the previous page. First, the order form contains two additional options. The options and their choices are again stored in custom fields. Each product can have up to three customizable options.

A message noting that the product is nonreturnable is added to this page. This message is displayed only for products that have been assigned to the nonreturnable category through the use of the `<txp:rss_if_article_unlimited_category/>` tag, which is part of the `rss_if_article_unlimited_categories` plugin.

Cart and checkout pages

The shopping cart and checkout pages on PopularWeddingFavors.com are driven by a shopping cart system that I developed. The basic functionality was based on the wfCart free PHP shopping cart class, which can be found at www.webforcecart.com. I adapted the cart class to work within Textpattern and implemented some special rules that I needed to enforce minimum order quantities, calculate quantity-based pricing, and display the contents of the cart. A full shopping cart is shown in Figure 16-10.

Figure 16-10. The shopping cart with products on PopularWeddingFavors.com

Each product that is added to a shopper's cart is displayed, along with information on quantity ordered and price paid. The shopping cart screen is used to enable shoppers to confirm their orders before completing their orders and choosing a form of payment. Once all of the desired products are added to the cart, it's time to proceed to the checkout page, which is shown in Figure 16-11.

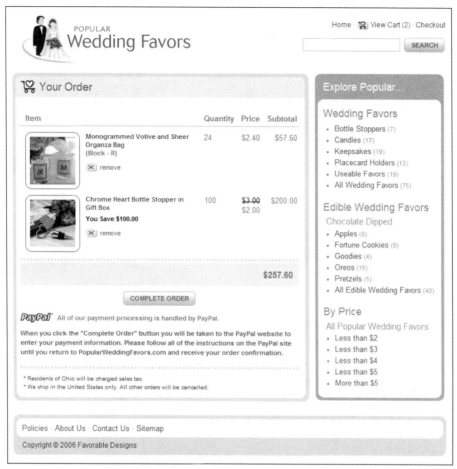

Figure 16-11. Checkout page on PopularWeddingFavors.com

The checkout page is essentially the same as the shopping cart page, with minor differences in the options available. This is the final confirmation step before beginning the payment process. Once the Complete Order button is clicked, shoppers are taken to the PayPal site to pay for their purchases. After making payment, shoppers are returned to PopularWeddingFavors.com and shown an order confirmation.

Order confirmation page

The information on the order confirmation page shown in Figure 16-12 is returned to PopularWeddingFavors.com using the PayPal Instant Payment Notification (IPN) service. The IPN service returns payment information, including the payee's name and address, from PayPal back to the PopularWeddingFavors.com site immediately after orders are completed. This gives customers a nice order confirmation in case they have questions in the future.

Figure 16-12. Order confirmation page on PopularWeddingFavors.com

Error page

The standard Textpattern error_default page has been customized to use the same header and footer as the rest of the site. The error message is still displayed (see Figure 16-13), along with some helpful information to help the user proceed in the right direction.

Figure 16-13. 404 error page on PopularWeddingFavors.com

Plugins used

The following plugins were used in the creation of PopularWeddingFavors.com (the custom shopping cart code and payment system integration have not been publicly released as of the time of this writing):

- rss_unlimited_categories is used to assign multiple categories to an article. All the product and category listings on the site are generated by this plugin.

- rss_if_search_results is used to display different messages on the search results page based on the existence of search results.

- rss_admin_db_manager is used to manage database backups and maintain the Textpattern database.

- rss_admin_show_adv_opts serves an essential purpose with the extensive use of custom fields. It automatically expands the Advanced Options menu on the Write tab.

- rss_admin_quikpik is used to create a custom color scheme in the admin interface and provides a series of time-saving drop-down menus.

- rss_article_edit enables the addition of a link on public-side article forms that takes an authorized user directly into article-editing mode for that article.
- sed_pcf is used to manage product pricing in custom fields.
- ied_hide_in_admin is used to hide fields on the Write tab that aren't used.
- zem_contact_reborn is used for the contact form.
- pap_contact_cleaner prevents spam from the contact form.

Summary

This chapter demonstrated how Textpattern can be used to manage and run an ecommerce business. Although Textpattern is commonly used for weblogs, it can be used for virtually any type of site. While many open-source shopping cart systems can be difficult to work with and modify, Textpattern is an excellent platform for building a Web Standards–compliant ecommerce store.

The PopularWeddingFavors.com site is a great example of the flexibility and extensibility of Textpattern. By managing products as articles and using the rss_unlimited_categories plugin, the site's product catalog and static content are both easily controlled within Textpattern. And the addition of a custom shopping cart and payment system integration demonstrates the limitless opportunity to extend the core functionality of Textpattern. In the end, the features that attracted me to Textpattern as a basic web publishing platform are the same ones that make it a great platform for developing more complex websites such as the PopularWeddingFavors.com ecommerce store.

I live in a small city called Boise, located in the great state of Idaho (U.S.A.). I imagine that my city is small to some, but big to others. At any rate, the city is not unlike most cities. As such, there are numerous places and types of foods to eat in Boise. All too often, however, because of the amount of choices available in Boise, I forget about places that have outstanding food. This forgetting would typically happen when I was trying to decide where to eat on Friday night after a long week of work. Not only that—if I did manage to remember a few of the great places to eat around Boise, I found it difficult to make a selection. So I decided to create BoiseCityEats.com (scheduled for launch in 2007).

What is BoiseCityEats.com?

BoiseCityEats.com is a place to find and review local places to eat. More specifically, BoiseCityEats.com enables you to search for a dining establishment by name, description, or keywords (tags). After searching for and finding a place to eat, BoiseCityEats.com provides several features (driving directions, reviews, ratings, contact information, price, and so on) to help the user select the perfect meal outside of the home, or maybe even via delivery at home.

At this point I could continue describing what BoiseCityEats.com is, but a good look at the visual comps is better than any additional words I might say. So before reading on, you might find it helpful to review the comps in Figure 17-1.

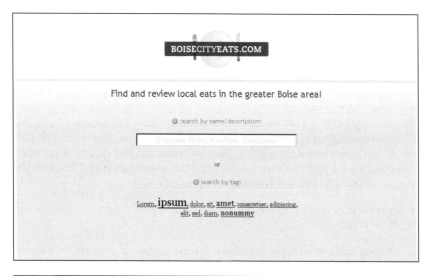

Figure 17-1. Visual comps for the up-and-coming BoiseCityEats.com website

Why look at BoiseCityEats.com?

Normally, a website such as BoiseCityEats.com would require the assistance of a web programmer to construct. That is, someone who is versed in creating a database and using a sever-side programming language (ASP.NET, PHP, Python, ColdFusion, Perl, Java, Ruby) to pull information from that database for display on a website. However, since I decided to use Textpattern to build BoiseCityEats.com, the majority of the work typically done by a web programmer to build a site has already been done. Using TXP, almost anyone who has a basic understanding of HTML and can set up the default installation of TXP (refer to Chapter 2) can create and deploy a site. From this point on, this chapter is about exactly that. Together, we'll create the base functionality that drives BoiseCityEats.com. The site will be called CityEats.com, which is shown in Figure 17-2.

This chapter focuses on re-creating the prototype I originally developed when building BoiseCityEats.com.

Before jumping straight into the prototype, I want to take a moment to explain why CityEats.com (refer to Figure 17-2) looks so plain when compared with BoiseCityEats.com (refer to Figure 17-1). For the most part, the CityEats.com site that will be built in this chapter lacks a visual layer. If you are familiar with the term **prototype** in reference to a web application, this probably makes complete sense. If you are not familiar with the purpose of a prototype, you might not know that the lack of a visual layer is deliberate. In general, a prototype is constructed to concentrate on the functionality (logic) of the application, not the visual aspect associated with BoiseCityEats.com.

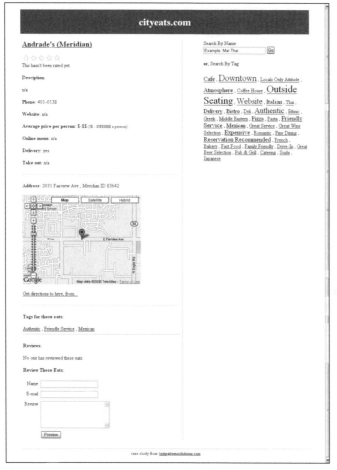

Figure 17-2. Screenshot for CityEats.com prototype

CityEats.com on textpatternsolutions.com

This book has an accompanying website, and the prototype site CityEats.com can be viewed on the textpatternsolutions.com domain at the following subdomain: http://cityeats.textpatternsolutions.com. Given that you are mostly concerned with the TXP tool itself, a live version of the CityEats.com site is available so that you can log in to the CityEats.com TXP installation and poke around all you want. To do so, simply tack on /textpattern/ (http://cityeats.textpatternsolutions.com/textpattern/) to the URL I just gave you and log in using the following use name and password:

- Username: Guest
- Password: h8d945

Certain functionality has been disabled to retain the same settings for all who log in to the CityEats.com TXP installation, so no changes can be made to the CityEats.com site found at http://cityeats.textpatternsolutions.com using these login credentials.

Preparing TXP for CityEats.com

To get under way, all you need to do is have a fresh install of TXP awaiting you. This means you should have a workable version of the default installation of TXP live and functioning on a domain you have admin rights to. It's crucial that you start with a default installation of TXP so that many of the instructions that follow make sense.

I have taken the liberty of assuming that you have read a good portion of this book, so I have forgone any lengthy explanations about certain aspects of the TXP system that can be found in other chapters in this book. I'll diligently attempt to indicate when and where additional information on a particular topic can be found outside of this chapter and in which chapter it can be further studied.

Setting Site Preferences

If you have been reading this book in numerical order, starting with Chapter 1, you are already familiar with the Admin tab. This is where you will start (and where I typically begin when creating any TXP site).

Under the Admin tab, select the subtab Preferences. Under Site Prefences ➤ Publish, locate the following field labels: Site name, Date format, Site slogan, Permanent link mode, Use Textile, and Production Status. Starting with Site name, change the default values to the following (don't change anything else in this panel unless told to do so):

- Site name: cityeats.com
- Date format: DD/MM/YYYY (defaults to the current date in the drop-down menu)
- Site slogan: Find and review local eats!
- Permanent link mode: /section/title
- Use Textile: Leave text untouched
- Production Status: Live

Under the Comments section on the same page, locate the following field labels: Moderate comments?, On by default?, Default invite, Disabled after, and Automatically append comments to articles?. Change the default values as follows:

- Moderate comments?: No

- On by default?: Yes

- Default invite: Review These Eats

- Disabled after: never

- Automatically append comments to articles?: No

Although most of these configuration changes are self-explanatory, the Automatically append comments to articles? setting needs a brief explanation. This setting turns off the default TXP rules that help automate the addition of comments to article pages by injecting TXP tags into forms automatically. It is turned off here so the comments can be added by manually adding TXP tags where you want them, not where the system would place them.

This completes the changes to Site Preferences. Before moving on to Advanced Preferences, make sure that you scroll to the bottom of the page and press Save.

Setting Advanced Preferences

The only settings in Advanced Preferences of interest are the Custom Fields settings, which add custom inputs to an article (viewable on the Content ➤ Write tab) that have no specific, predefined purpose. You can find detailed information about Custom Fields in Chapter 12.

Locate the ten custom fields on the Advanced Preferences page and change the default values to the values shown as follows (and yes, case matters):

- Custom field 1 name: Address

- Custom field 2 name: City

- Custom field 3 name: State

- Custom field 4 name: Zip

- Custom field 5 name: Website

- Custom field 6 name: Phone

- Custom field 7 name: Price

- Custom field 8 name: OnlineMenu

- Custom field 9 name: TakeOut

- Custom field 10 name: Delivery

This completes the changes to Advanced Preferences. Make sure that you scroll to the bottom of the page and press Save before leaving this page.

Adding the right plugins

If you are a TXP veteran, you already know that its plugin architecture is one of its most powerful features. If you are a TXP newbie, you'll soon come to appreciate the functionality enhancements that a plugin can deliver to TXP without having to change the base code. This is especially important when it comes to upgrading TXP because using a plugin (versus hacking the base code) can mean seamless upgrades to future releases of TXP. Modified versions of TXP are not supported by the developers of TXP, so if you break something you are on your own. More information about plugins can be found in Chapters 13 and 14. The CityEats.com prototype site uses the plugins shown in Figure 17-3.

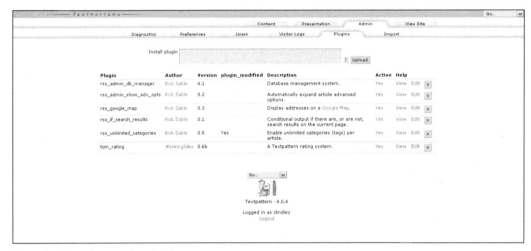

Figure 17-3. Plugins page for CityEats.com

If you are familiar with installing plugins, you can navigate to the Plugins page (Admin ➤ Plugins) and install the plugins shown in Figure 17-3 using the plugin text files that are available when you download the source code for this book. If you have never installed a TXP plugin, I suggest reading Chapters 13 and 14 before proceeding.

The plugin text files for CityEats.com can be found in the Chapter 17 folder and are named according to the name of the plugin. Simply cut and paste the contents from each plugin text file into the TXP Plugins interface and upload. Don't activate the plugins until you have uploaded them all.

My suggestion is to use the files that accompany this chapter because of the possible changes to the plugins that might have transpired during the writing of this book. But you can find all the plugins for CityEats.com on the websites shown here:

- www.wilshireone.com/textpattern-plugins
  - rss_admin_db_manager
  - rss_admin_show_adv_opts
  - rss_google_map
  - rss_if_search_results
  - rss_unlimited_categories

- http://forum.textpattern.com/viewtopic.php?id=14218
  - tcm_rating

Once each plugin is installed, make sure to click No in the Active column to enable the use of the TXP plugin. When the plugin is active, No changes to Yes.

In most cases, that's all it takes to install plugins. However, since one of the plugins will add an additional tab to the TXP interface at the main navigation level, there is some additional work to do.

17

After you install any plugin, a quick read of the help text associated with it is usually necessary and helpful. You can view any help/documentation associated with a plugin by clicking the View link. So do that now. Click the View link for the tcm_rating plugin. The installation instructions show that a trip to the Extensions tab is required for the tcm_plugin to function.

Go to the Extensions tab by first clicking the Admin tab (it is located to the right of the Admin tab). Click the Admin tab first because the Extensions tab is not available when you are on the Plugins tab. Open this tab to complete the installation of the tcm_rating plugin.

Now that you have completed adding the necessary plugins, you are done with the Admin section of TXP. If you are curious about the functionality of each plugin you just uploaded, hold tight; I'll explain the plugins as you use them.

Building a foundation with sections, categories, and content

The foundation for a TXP site can be found in the manipulation and creation of sections and categories. Because the default TXP install comes with a foundation already in place, you need to mold and add to what is already there to support CityEats.com.

Removing default settings, and adding one section

To begin, navigate to the Images tab (Content ➤ Images). You'll remove the only image being managed by TXP. Click the gray x button to remove the divider.gif image.

Next, navigate to the Articles tab (Content ➤ Articles) and remove the only article in the TXP system (First Post). Here you must select the article with the checkbox. Then, from the drop-down menu labeled With selected, select Delete and click the Go button.

From here, navigate to the Categories tab (Content ➤ Categories). Locate Link Categories, which should be showing the default link category Textpattern. Select this category with the checkbox and then delete the Textpattern category by using the drop-down menu. Next, select all the article categories that are included in the default installation and delete them. The only category that should be left on the page at this point should be the Site Design category, which is an image category.

Next, navigate to the Sections tab (Presentation ➤ Sections). Here you remove the default sections and add the single section (besides the section called default, which can't be removed) that is used on CityEats.com. Simply clicking the x button associated with the default sections removes the sections from the system. Once this is complete, enter a section called the-eats by placing the text into the box by the button labeled Create and then click the Create button. After creating this section, notice several settings associated with the-eats section. You'll come back to configure this section momentarily.

Creating categories

Article categories are used inside TXP for organizing articles by the nature of their content, not by their location in the navigation structure. That is what sections are used for. CityEats.com uses article categories as a way of classifying each dining establishment. Some might call this tagging or metadata. The default installation of TXP allows only two article categories for any given article, but the rss_unlimited_categories plugin gives the capability to add an unlimited number of article categories to an article. Before an article/dining establishment can be tagged with categories/tags, all the appropriate article categories for CityEats.com must be added into the TXP system.

Since CityEats.com has more than just a couple of categories, and adding them all by hand is somewhat time-intensive, I'll show you two ways to add the appropriate article categories: the long way and a shortcut for those willing to get their hands a little bit dirty with SQL.

The first method of adding all the necessary categories for CityEats.com is to do so by hand. That is, you can enter each category in the Article Categories text field and click Create. Now navigate to the Categories tab (Content ➤ Categories). Open up the categories.txt text file that was provided with this chapter and enter each of the categories into TXP using the article categories found in the text file.

A less-laborious way of adding the categories is to use the rss_admin_db_manager plugin, which was installed earlier. What I am about to demonstrate is not a TXP-supported method for adding categories; it's a shortcut for adding a bunch of categories to the database. It isn't usually possible with the default installation of TXP, but the rss_admin_db_manager plugin enables running SQL statements through the TXP interface.

Navigate to the run sql tab (Extensions ➤ run sql). Open up the text file called categoriesSql.txt in the supporting materials for this chapter. Cut and paste the contents of the categoriesSql.txt file into the text field on the run sql tab and click the red Run button. This should return the SQL statements (70 of them) in green below the text field. You have one last thing to do before the sections are correctly added: Navigate to the Categories tab (Content ➤ Categories) and enter a dummy article category called AAA. Click the Create button; after the page reloads, all the categories inserted with SQL now show up. Remove the AAA article category—and that's it!

Entering content

With the categories all set up and ready to go, navigate to the Write tab (Content ➤ Write). This is where you'll enter each of the dining establishments on the CityEats.com prototype site. Before you enter any articles, however, have a look around the user interface. Because of the rss_admin_show_adv_opts plugin installed earlier the custom fields, shown in Figure 17-4, are by default showing up in the left column. If this plugin were not installed, by default these fields would be hidden behind an Advanced Options link.

Figure 17-4. Custom fields for CityEats.com

Additionally, changes made earlier in Preferences that are not in the default install include having comments set to on by default (click More in the right column to view the comment settings) and not allowing Textile to parse any of the markup entered in the Title, Body, or Excerpt text inputs. While it might not be labeled as such, the (X)HTML text field and textarea inputs in the middle of the page (refer to Figure 17-4) are considered the Title and Body inputs.

Notice also that the additional input form, Categorize, is filled with all the article categories that were entered and is shown in the right column under Sort and Display (see Figure 17-5). This is an additional field added by the rss_unlimited_categories plugin. This form input enables you to select multiple article categorizes for each article/dining establishment entered into the system.

Figure 17-5. Screenshot showing the Categorize input

Before actually entering any content, it might be a good idea to visit the completed CityEats.com website and view an article/dining page. To do so, enter the following URL: http://cityeats.textpatternsolutions.com/the-eats/asiagos.

The content found on this page pertaining to Asiago's restaurant is the same type of content that needs to be entered for each dining establishment in the CityEats.com site. Let's take the Asiago's content as example data and enter it into the version of CityEats.com that has been developed in this chapter. If you are not already there, navigate to the Write tab (Content ➤ Write) of TXP and enter the following content (see Figure 17-6):

- Title: Asiago's
- Body: Walking into Asiago's takes you away to simpler times. The dining room has rustic, handmade tables, hand troweled walls with fieldstone, wooden doors along the patio that open for warm weather dining, and a rugged wooden pergola twined with grapevines standing over all. The unpretentious setting invites you to relax and escape from the worries of the day, catch up with friends, or gather the family.
- Excerpt: 11am-10pm M-F, 4pm-11pm Sa-Su
- Categorize: Italian, Outside Seating, Website (you can select multiple items by using the Ctrl key)
- Address: 3423 N. Cole Rd
- City: Boise
- State: ID
- Zip: 83704
- Website: http://www.asiagos.com
- Phone: 323 -1469
- OnlineMenu: yes
- TakeOut: yes

Maybe you noticed (and maybe you didn't), but no data was entered for the custom fields called Price and Delivery. Leaving the Price and Delivery custom fields blank tells TXP that this information is not available for this specific dining entry (this will make a little more sense in a bit).

Figure 17-6. Asiago's data

After you enter the Asiago's data into TXP, make sure that you click Save to save the data.

Now there is only one article/dining entry in the TXP system. For the purpose of this case study, it's highly recommended that you enter a couple more article/dining entries. You can use the data from the CityEats.com website located at http://cityeats. textpatternsolutions.com as dummy data, which you need to enter by hand, or you can always enter a few dining establishments that are local to your own home town.

Alternatively, if you feel comfortable with SQL and can live with a few database inconsistencies for the sake of this exercise, you can add the content from the http://cityeats. textpatternsolutions.com site to your own version of CityEats.com by using SQL statements. To do this, open the data.txt file included with the files for this chapter and run the SQL statements in the run sql tab in TXP (Extensions ➤ run sql). This is very similar to the way you added the article categories. Next, you'll build the presentation of the site.

Preparing the presentation

If the sections and categories are the foundation, the presentation is the visual structure built on top of the foundation. Thus far, a great deal of time has been spent building the foundation to the CityEats.com website. Next you'll begin to create the presentation for CityEats.com by removing the default styles and adding styles of your own.

Adding new styles and removing the default styles

Navigate to the Style tab (Presentation ➤ Style). By default, the styles that are part of the default installation are loaded onto the page here. Replace the default styles with the following Cascading Style Sheet (CSS) declarations. These styles have also been included with the support files (css-default.txt), so you can simply cut and paste these styles into the text input.

```
body {
background-color:#fff;
color:#333333;
margin: 20px 50px;
}

/*base links*/
a:link {color: #990000;}
a:visited {color: #990000;}
a:hover {color: #990000;text-decoration: none;}
a:active {color: #990000;}

hr{
border: 0;
color: #ccc;
background-color: #ccc;
height: 1px;
}

#head, #footer{
text-align:center;
}

#footer{
clear:both;
}

h1{
background-color:#716844;
padding:20px 20px;
color: #fff;
}
```

```css
h1 a:link, h1 a:visited, h1 a:active{
color: #fff;
text-decoration: none;
display:block;
}

#leftCol{
float:left;
width:56%;
padding:0 2% 0 1%;
border-right:1px solid #ccc;
min-height:500px;
}

#rightCol{
float:right;
width:37%;
padding:0 2% 0 1%;
min-height:500px;
}

.comments{
list-style:none;
padding-left:0;
}

small{
color:#666;
}

#cpreview{
background-color:#FFFFCC;
padding:10px;
margin:20px 0;
}

.reviewError, .comments_error {
color: red;
}
```

If you are not familiar with CSS declarations and their use in TXP, refer to Chapter 11 or grab a book on the topic (I recommend *CSS Mastery* by Friends of ED).

Once these styles are added, make sure to click Save. Besides the default styles, one additional stylesheet needs to be added. Click the Create or load new style link in the left column of the Style tab. The name of the stylesheet is css-rating. These styles are the associating styles necessary to use the tcm_rating plugin, which is a simple star rating system. Enter the following styles into the input box and click Save (these styles can also be found in a text file called css-rating.txt):

```css
/*             styles for the star rater             */

.star-rating{
list-style:none;
margin: 0px;
padding:0px;
width: 125px;
height: 25px;
position: relative;
background: url(add image path here) top left repeat-x;
}

.star-rating li{
padding:0px;
margin:0px;
/*\*/
float: left;
/* */
}

.star-rating li a{
border: 0;
display:block;
width:25px;
height: 25px;
text-decoration: none;
text-indent: -9000px;
z-index: 20;
position: absolute;
padding: 0px;
}

.star-rating li a:hover{
background: url(add image path here) left bottom;
z-index: 2;
left: 0px;
}

.star-rating a.one-star{
left: 0px;
}

.star-rating a.one-star:hover{
width:25px;
}

.star-rating a.two-stars{
left:25px;
}
```

```
.star-rating a.two-stars:hover{
width: 50px;
}

.star-rating a.three-stars{
left: 50px;
}

.star-rating a.three-stars:hover{
width: 75px;
}

.star-rating a.four-stars{
left: 75px;
}

.star-rating a.four-stars:hover{
width: 100px;
}

.star-rating a.five-stars{
left: 100px;
}

.star-rating a.five-stars:hover{
width: 125px;
}

.star-rating li.current-rating{
background: url(add image path here) left center;
position: absolute;
height: 25px;
display: block;
text-indent: -9000px;
z-index: 1;
}

.ratingerror {
color: red;
}
```

The css-rating styles just entered require an image—a star image, to be exact. Locate the ratingStar.gif file that is part of the supporting files for this chapter. Next, navigate to the Images tab (Content ➤ Images) and add the ratingStar.gif image to TXP by browsing for the file, selecting it, and then clicking the upload button. Locate the input on the page labeled Category, select the site-design category, and click Save. On the screen that follows, take notice of the ID of the newly added image (it is probably 2). Next, you need to find the path to the newly added image.

If you do not know the path to the images directory, it's fairly easy to figure out. Navigate to the Preferences tab (Admin ➤ Preferences) and locate the label Site URL. Simply take the Site URL value and add on /images/ to the end of it—you'll have the path to the images directory that is used by TXP. For example, the path looks like this:

Site URL/images/

Once you have figured out the path to the images directory, add on the name of the image to the end of the path. The name of the image in this case is the ID including the file extension. Unless you have deviated from the default installation of TXP the image is 2.gif. The full path to the image is this:

Site URL/images/2.gif

Now make sure you add it to the css-rating styles where indicated by the add image path here text. As usual, make sure that you save the changes before leaving the Styles tab.

Adding a new page and removing default pages

With the stylesheets squared away, you can now begin to build the actual pages of the website by beginning to use sections, pages, and forms together to set in place the actual web pages that make up CityEats.com. Navigate to the Pages tab (Presentation ➤ Pages). The first thing you need to do is to delete the archive page (it should be the top page in the right column). Click the gray button to the right of the archive text, which deletes this page from the TXP system. (You will not be using an archive for CityEats.com.)

The CityEats.com website uses only four pages: default, error_default, and two pages that you need to create: one called the-eats and the other called error_404. At the bottom of the middle column, you see the Save button. With the default page open, enter the name the-eats in the text input to the right of the Save button and click the Copy button. You have now created the the-eats page by duplicating the default page and renaming it the-eats. Now do the same process for the error_404 page.

With all the pages created for CityEats.com, you now need to remove the default markup for each of these four pages and wipe the slate clean, so to speak. One by one, select each of the four pages, remove all markup associated with the page, and click Save. At this point, you should not have any markup associated with the four pages.

Because you have finally created a page called the-eats, you need to return to the Sections tab where you added the section called the-eats and tell this section to use the page named the-eats. Navigate to the Sections tab (Presentation ➤ Sections), locate the input called Uses page that is associated with the the-eats section, and select the the-eats page from the drop-down menu.

Before you save, however, you need to make one additional configuration to the the-eats section—you have to make sure that when you create a new article/dining entry, by default the entry will be in the the-eats section. To do this, simply check the Yes radio button for Selected by default?. Save the changes by clicking the Save button associated with the the-eats section. Only one section can be selected by default, so the choice was easy since you created only one section.

Removing default forms and adding new forms

Navigate to the Forms tab (Presentation ➤ Forms). Take a quick inventory of the forms already created and displayed in the right column of the page. Notice that certain forms are selectable by using a checkbox, and certain forms inherent to the TXP system are unselectable (they can't be deleted; they can only be changed). Let's clean this up a bit by getting rid of the forms that are not needed. Using the checkbox, select the lofi, noted, plainlinks, single, search_results, and popup_comments forms. All the forms that are selectable will be deleted. With these forms selected, choose Delete from the drop-down menu and click the Go button to delete them.

Now that the forms you don't need are gone, add the forms you do need. In the right column above the list of forms, you see a link that says Create new form. Using this link, add the six new forms exactly as they appear in Table 17-1 (make sure that you click Create new form each time).

Table 17-1. Name and type of forms to be added

Name	Type
comment_preview	comment
comment_form_preview	comment
master_foot	misc
master_head	misc
search_results	misc
search_UI	misc

Building the presentation using Pages and Forms

With the presentational preparation efforts complete, you can now begin to actually build the presentation using Pages and Forms as the containers for the (X)HTML and TXP tags.

Creating the home page and error page

From here on, you'll jump back and forth between the Pages tab and the Forms tab. Keep in mind that while the CityEats.com site is made up of only two TXP pages (default and the-eats), the pages themselves can have multiple uses depending upon how the TXP system uses the page and interprets the TXP tags on the page. For example, the default page is used as both the home page and the search results page. Also, the the-eats page is used by the system as an article list page and individual article page. If this does not make sense yet, it will shortly as you begin to add markup to our pages and forms.

Navigate to the Pages tab (Presentation ➤ Pages). On each of the pages in the right column you'll add the following comments: (X)HTML and TXP tags. Make sure that you open each page (default, error_404, error_default, and the-eats), add the following code, and then press Save:

```
<!-- master head -->
<txp:output_form form="master_head" />

<!-- content head -->
<div id="head">
</div>

<!-- content-->
<div id="content">
</div>

<!-- master footer -->
<txp:output_form form="master_foot" />
```

The code added to each page has two TXP tags (shown in bold) that simply output the contents of a form to a page. Currently, there is nothing in either the master_head or master_foot form. So jump over to the Forms tab and add the code you want to output on each of the pages you added the <txp:output_form /> tag to. Select the master_head form and add the following comments in the input: (X)HTML and TXP tags. Make sure to click Save so the TXP system will add the markup to the form.

```
<!DOCTYPE html PUBLIC "-//W3C//DTD XHTML 1.0 Strict//EN" ➡
"http://www.w3.org/TR/xhtml1/DTD/xhtml1-strict.dtd">
<html xmlns="http://www.w3.org/1999/xhtml" xml:lang="en" lang="en" >

<head>
<meta http-equiv="Content-Type" content="text/html; charset=utf-8" />

<meta name="author" content="cityeats.com © " />
<meta name="description" content="<txp:site_slogan />" />

<!-- microsoft handlers -->
<meta name="mssmarttagspreventparsing" content="true" />
<meta http-equiv="imagetoolbar" content="false" />

<!-- styles -->
<style type="text/css" media="all">
@import "<txp:css n="default" />";
<txp:if_individual_article>
@import "<txp:css n="css-rating" />";
</txp:if_individual_article>
</style>
```

```
<!-- javascript -->
<script type="text/javascript" src="<txp:css n="js-global" />" >➡
</script>
<txp:if_individual_article>
<txp:tcm_rating_js_tag />
<txp:rss_google_map_js apikey="ABQIAAAAFYzfBwvqscQO15Y4Cyim7hS3- ➡
4ZtJuCaT8RY8Z5dhg1xKhWE2hSmt1dyzBphVEf4lRNHZFwLnXERWg" />
</txp:if_individual_article>

<title><txp:page_title separator=" - " /></title>

</head>

<body>
```

You should recognize the bold code as TXP tags. Starting from the top, the first TXP tag in the code simply outputs the site slogan. I'm using it here to provide content for the description meta element. Next, the `<txp:css />` tag is used twice to load the correct stylesheet, depending upon whether the current page using this form is an individual article. I make this distinction by wrapping the link to the css-rating stylesheet inside the `<txp:if_individual_article>` tag.

The next block of TXP tags uses the same if statement tag to include links to JavaScript files. If the page being viewed is an individual article, the JavaScript is included on this page. And finally there is a TXP title tag that is used to create a unique title for each page that uses this form. Keep in mind that all the pages (every dining article page) use this form, and it's the TXP tags that enable you to make unique choices and output unique content based on where you are in the CityEats.com website.

Before proceeding, and if you are following along and constructing this site on your own server, you need to visit www.google.com/apis/maps/signup.html and get your own Google Maps API key. Visit the link, read the instructions, and (once you have your own key) make sure that you update `<txp:rss_google_map_js />` with your own API key.

Now open the master_footer form and add the following (X)HTML (make sure to click Save so the TXP system adds the markup):

```
<hr />
<div id="footer"><small>case study from: <a title="Textpattern ➡
Solutions"
href="http://www.textpatternsolutions.com">textpatternsolutions.com
</a></small></div>
</body>
</html>
```

All you have done here is create two templates (forms) that are included on each and every page (default, error_404, error_default, and the-eats) used by TXP.

Jump back to the Pages tab (Presentation ➤ Pages) and select the default page. Locate the `<div>` element with an id of head. You'll place an if else TXP statement here, but first let me explain why. By default, and in consideration of our current TXP configuration, TXP uses the default page as the home page as well as the page that word search results will be returned to. So you need to use an if search tag to determine when the page is being used as the home page or the word search results page. The tags necessary to create this type of functionality are highlighted in bold:

```
<!-- content head -->
<div id="head">

<txp:if_search>
<h1><txp:link_to_home><txp:sitename /></txp:link_to_home></h1>
<txp:else />
<h1><txp:sitename /></h1>
<p><txp:site_slogan /></p>
</txp:if_search>

</div>
```

If the default page is being used as a search results page, you must make the site name link back to the home page. I accomplished this by using the TXP tags <txp:link_to_home> and <txp:sitename />. Now, if the page is not being used as the search results page, it's obviously being used as the home page. If that's the case, output the site name without it linking and then add the site slogan. Before you move on, make sure that you have added that last bit of code to the default page inside the <div> element with an id attribute of head.

The other three pages (error_404, error_default, and the-eats) also need to have the site name added to them without the use of the <txp:if_search> tag. Open the error_404, error_default, and the-eats pages and add the following (X)HTML and TXP tags *inside* the <div> element with an id of head:

```
<!-- content head -->
<div id="head">

<h1><txp:link_to_home><txp:sitename /></txp:link_to_home></h1>

</div>
```

Before you start filling out the default page, fix up the error_404 and error_default pages. Open the error_404 page and *replace* the <div> element with an id of content with the following markup (make sure that you click Save to save the changes):

```
<div id="content" style="text-align:center;">

<h3>Sorry, but these eats are gone. Please return to the ➡
<txp:link_to_home>homepage</txp:link_to_home> to find more eats.</h3>

</div>
```

If you like, change the error message to anything you want. Just remember that this is the page that users see when there is a 404 server error.

Next, open the error_default page and *replace* the <div> element with an id of content with the following markup:

```
<div id="content">

<h3><txp:error_status /><h3>
<p><txp:error_message /></p>

</div>
```

Return to the default page and locate the <div> element with an id of content. Since the content of the default page is different depending upon whether the page is being used as a search page or home page, you need to add an if else statement to fork the markup. Inside the content <div>, add the following markup:

```
<!-- /////////////// Search Page //////////////// -->
<txp:if_search>

<txp:else />

<!-- /////////////// Homepage //////////////// -->

</txp:if_search>
```

Below the Homepage comment and before the closing <txp:if_search> tag, add a new <div> element with a style attribute. The style attribute has a value of text-align: center. Inside the <div> element, you'll add a <txp:output_form /> tag to output the search_UI form. In all, the markup should look as follows:

```
<div style="text-align:center;">
<txp:output_form form="search_UI" />
</div>
```

Don't forget to save the page after you do this.

Right now, the search_UI form does nothing. If you have visited the CityEats.com website, however, you know that all the pages on the site include searching functionality (by name or by tag). The search_UI form is basically what you see on the home page of CityEats.com. This same functionality can be found on a search results page, a tag search results page, and an article page (or in this case, a page with a restaurant entry on it). Let's go add some markup to the search_UI form.

Navigate to the Forms tab (Presentation ➤ Pages) and select the search_UI form. Here we are going to add the markup that creates the searching functionality on CityEats.com. Enter the following markup and make sure to click Save:

17

```
<form action=" <txp:site_url />" method="get">
<label for="q">Search By Name:</label><br />
<input type="text" onblur="if(this.value == ''){this.value = ➥
'Them eats are awaiting ya!'}" onfocus="this.value = '';" alt="search" ➥
value="Example: Mai Thai" style="width:200px" name="q" />
<input  type="submit" value="Go" />
</form>
<p><strong>or</strong>, Search By Tag:</p>
<txp:rss_unlimited_categories_cloud section="the-eats" ➥
linktosection="the-eats" break="," />
```

The TXP tag `<txp:search_input />` usually suffices, but for CityEats.com I wanted access to the (X)HTML that is generated by the `<txp:search_input />` tag. I have done so to add a bit of JavaScript to the `<input>` element, which is shown in bold. This JavaScript removes the default text inside the `<input>` element upon focus, and upon blur it adds text back into the `<input>` element. Replacing the `<txp:search_input />` tag with your own markup is as simple as making sure that the `<input>` has an attribute with a value of q, and the `<form>` element has an action attribute with a value of `<txp:site_url />`.

The next section of bold code is a plugin tag. Remember that you installed a plugin to alter how TXP categories work. The rss_unlimited_categories plugin creates multiple categories to be used as a tagging system. Here you use a custom tag from the rss_unlimited_ categories plugin that outputs a tag cloud. If you look closely at the tag, the attributes should be self-explanatory since you use only one section for the CityEats.com website (the-eats).

If you are reconstructing CityEats.com as you are reading this chapter, you can now visit the home page and should see the same exact home page found at the CityEats. textpatternsolutions.com site (see Figure 17-7). Of course, nothing functions correctly yet because you have not yet added the all-powerful `<txp:article>` tag.

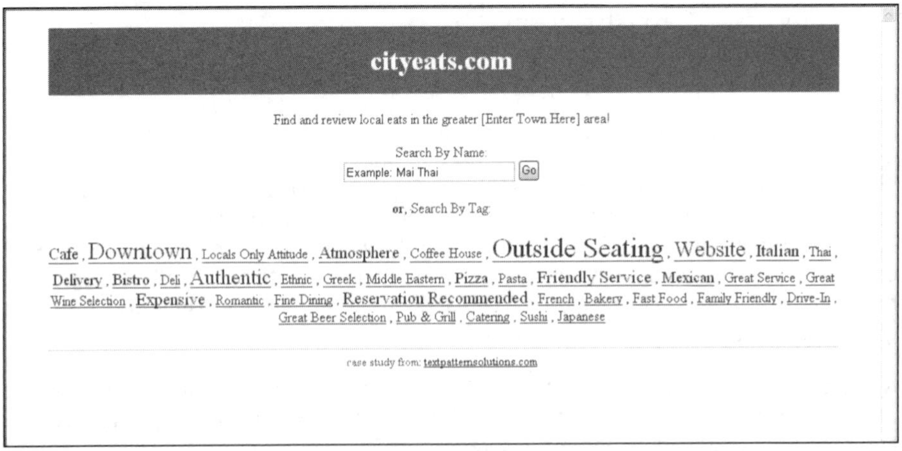

Figure 17-7. The home page

Navigate back to the Pages tab and start editing the default page again. After the search page comment and directly after the `<txp:if_search>` tag, add the following markup (make sure that you click Save to save the changes):

```
<div id="rightCol">
<txp:output_form form="search_UI" />
</div>
<div id="leftCol">
<h3>Name search results:</h3>
<hr />
<txp:article />
<txp:rss_if_no_search_results>
<p>Your search returned 0 results.</p>
</txp:rss_if_no_search_results>
</div>
```

The code that you added to the default page shows only on a word search results page because it's encapsulated inside a `<txp:if_search>` tag. Notice two new `<div>` elements that will divide the page in two columns. In the right column, you output the same search_UI form that is output on the home page. In the left column, you find the all-powerful `<txp:article>` tag. In this context, the tag is being used to output search results. Inside this column you make use of another handy plugin from Rob Sable called rss_if_no_search_results, which is simply an if tag that outputs its contents into the page if in fact the word search returns no results.

With this code added to the default page, you now need to jump back to the Forms tab and add markup for the form that is used to produce search results. Open the search_results form and add the following markup (make sure that you click Save to add the markup to the search_results form):

```
<h4><txp:permlink><txp:search_result_title /></txp:permlink></h4>
<p><txp:search_result_excerpt /></p>
<hr />
```

The markup you just added is the template used to produce the word search results. With this coded added, the word search (or in this case, the restaurant name search) should now be functioning. You can test it out by viewing the version of CityEats.com (home page) you have been developing in this chapter and using the Search By Name input form to do a site search. You might try searching the site for the word Food.

Believe it or not, you are now done with the default page and the forms that depend on it. Next, you will deal with the the-eats page.

Creating the article list and individual article

Before you begin adding markup to the the-eats page, note that this page is associated with the the-eats section. So when you visit this section of the site, the system uses the the-eats page to output all articles (restaurants) in a list that are associated with the the-eats section. Once one of these articles (restaurants) has been selected, the same exact page (the-eats) is used to output an individual article view. So the the-eats page functions as an article list template as well as an individual article template.

Navigate to the Pages tab and open the the-eats page. Locate the <div> element that has an attribute id value of content. Inside the content <div> add the following code (make sure to click Save to add the markup to the the-eats page):

```
<!-- /////////////// Tag List /////////////// -->
<txp:if_article_list>
<div id="rightCol">
<txp:output_form form="search_UI" />
</div>
<div id="leftCol">
<h3>Tag search results for <span style="font-weight:normal;"> ➥
<txp:category /></span>:</h3>
<hr />
<txp:rss_unlimited_categories_article_list />
</div>
</txp:if_article_list>
```

I have labeled this block of code Tag List (instead of article list) because when a tag is clicked in the tag cloud, the TXP system returns a list of all the articles (restaurants) that have been categorized with that word. Essentially, it's a list of restaurants that contain a particular tag (category). Since you use the rss_unlimited_categories plugin to mimic the concept of tagging, the list page requires the <txp:rss_unlimited_categories_article_list /> tag instead of the normal <txp:article />. If it's not obvious, I am using the idea of a list of articles to fuel the Search By tag functionality. In reality, the Search By tag functionality is simply a view of the the-eats page that lists all the articles (restaurants) assigned to a single category.

As mentioned earlier, since the the-eats page is used for both the list view and individual article view, you also need to add markup to the the-eats page that handles the individual article view. You can do this by providing a <txp:article /> tag when the the-eats page is in an individual article view. Place the following markup after the tag list chunk of markup you just added (make sure to click Save to add the markup to the the-eats page):

```
<!-- /////////////// Individual Restaurant /////////////// -->
<txp:if_individual_article>
<div id="rightCol">
<txp:output_form form="search_UI" />
</div>
<div id="leftCol">
<txp:article />
</div>
</txp:if_individual_article>
```

If you study both chunks of markup just added, you might conclude that it is a bit verbose. I could have optimized this markup down to less code by using an <txp:else /> tag, but for the sake of readability I have completely separated the two chunks of markup. In that last chunk of markup, the <txp:article /> tag is used instead of the <txp:rss_unlimited_categories_article_list /> tag, which is necessary for the individual article view to function correctly.

Next you'll edit the default article form, which is used by both the `<txp:rss_unlimited_categories_article_list />` and the `<txp:article />` tags. Navigate to the Forms tab and open the default article form. Remove the default markup found in this form and add the markup that will be used by the `<txp:rss_unlimited_categories_article_list />` tag. Add the following markup to the default article form (make sure to click Save to add the markup to the default article form):

```
<txp:if_article_list>
<h4><txp:permlink><txp:title /></txp:permlink></h4>
<hr />
</txp:if_article_list>
```

Here you are checking to see what view is needed; if it's the article list view used by the `<txp:rss_unlimited_categories_article_list />` tag, output its title and a permanent link to an individual page. With this code added, the tag functionality should now be enabled. You can test this out by viewing the version of CityEats.com you have been developing in this chapter and clicking a word in the tag cloud.

In the default article form, you'll add all the content that appears on a individual article view *wrapped* by an `<txp:if_individual_article>` tag. Start by adding the following markup after the ending `</txp:if_article_list>` tag:

```
<txp:if_individual_article>

</txp:if_individual_article>
```

Inside the `<txp:if_individual_article>` add several lines of markup that produce an individual article view (a single restaurant view):

```
<h2><txp:permlink><txp:title /></txp:permlink></h2>
<txp:tcm_rating_form /><txp:tcm_rating_num noratings="" />

<p><strong>Desciption:</strong></p>
<p><txp:body /></p>

<txp:if_excerpt>
<p><strong>Hours: </strong><txp:excerpt /></p>
</txp:if_excerpt>
```

This chunk of code outputs the title of the article/restaurant, the star rating plugin that appears below the title, the body of the article, or the description of the restaurant, and the excerpt if an excerpt was entered for the restaurant. (Remember that the excerpt is the input field you used to hold the hours associated with a restaurant.)

Below the markup just added, add all the custom field data for each entry:

```
<p><strong>Phone: </strong>
<txp:if_custom_field name="Phone">
<txp:custom_field name="Phone" />
<txp:else />
n/a
```

```
</txp:if_custom_field>
</p>

<p><strong>Website: </strong>
<txp:if_custom_field name="Website">
<a href="<txp:custom_field name="Website" />">➡
<txp:custom_field name="Website" /></a>
<txp:else />
n/a
</txp:if_custom_field></p>

<p><strong>Average price per person: </strong>
<txp:if_custom_field name="Price">
<txp:custom_field name="Price" /><small> (5$ - 30$$$$$ a person) ➡
</small><br />
<txp:else />
n/a
</txp:if_custom_field></p>

<p><strong>Online menu: </strong>
<txp:if_custom_field name="OnlineMenu">
<txp:custom_field name="OnlineMenu" />
<txp:else />
n/a
</txp:if_custom_field></p>

<p><strong>Delivery: </strong>
<txp:if_custom_field name="TakeOut">
<txp:custom_field name="TakeOut" />
<txp:else />
n/a
</txp:if_custom_field></p>

<p><strong>Take out: </strong>
<txp:if_custom_field name="Delivery">
<txp:custom_field name="Delivery" />
<txp:else />
n/a
</txp:if_custom_field></p>

<hr />
```

Note that each if else statement in the code could be shortened by using the default attribute of the custom_field tag. Using this attribute, it functions similar to an if else statement (if the custom field is blank, the default value is used). For example:

```
<txp:custom_field name="Phone" default="n/a" />
```

Doing things this way shortens the code.

The section of markup just added outputs the custom field data entered into the Write tab for each restaurant. If the field is left blank, the text n/a is outputted. Next, add the markup for the address, the Google map, and the link to the Google map:

```
<p><strong>Address: </strong><txp:custom_field name="Address" />, ➥
<txp:custom_field name="City" /> <txp:custom_field name="State" />➥
 <txp:custom_field name="Zip" /></p>

<txp:rss_google_map section="the-eats" addfield="Address" ➥
cityfield="City" statefield="State" zipfield="Zip"➥
width="380" height="280" zoom="3" usearticle="1" />

<p><a href="http://maps.google.com/maps?f=d&hl=en&saddr=&daddr=➥
<txp:custom_field name="Address" /> ➥
<txp:custom_field name="City" /> ➥
<txp:custom_field name="State" /> <txp:custom_field name="Zip" />">➥
Get directions to here, from...</a></p>

<hr />
```

Notice the use of the custom field's tags. I use the custom fields in this markup to output the address of the restaurant for use with the rss_google_map plugin, to output the address, and to create a link to Google Maps with the address in a query string (shown in bold).

After the `<hr />`, add the following markup:

```
<p><strong>Tags for these eats:</strong></p>
<txp:rss_unlimited_categories_filedunder section="*"
linktosection="the-eats" />

<hr />
```

This chunk of markup outputs all the tags (really categories) that are associated with a particular restaurant. Notice the use of the custom tag rss_unlimited_categories_filedunder.

Finally you add the commenting system to the page for a specific restaurant. In the context of CityEats.com, you can consider the commenting system to be a review system that enables the user to leave a review of the restaurants. After the last chunk of code added, add the following code:

```
<txp:if_comments>
<txp:comments />
<txp:else />
<p class="reviewError">No one has reviewed these eats.</p>
</txp:if_comments>

<p><strong><txp:comments_invite textonly="1" showalways="1" ➥
showcount="0" />:</strong></p>
```

```
<txp:if_comments_preview>
 <div id="cpreview"><strong>Comment Preview</strong>
<hr />
<txp:comments_preview form="comment_preview" />
</div>
<txp:comments_form preview="1" form="comment_form_preview" />
<txp:else />
<txp:comments_form />
</txp:if_comments_preview>
```

You are first checking to see whether there are any comments; if there are, output the comments to the page. If there are no comments, let the user know that no one has reviewed this restaurant as of yet. After that, add the appropriate TXP tags to output the commenting system.

At this point, save the default article form and open up the comment_form. Add the following markup to this form and click Save:

```
<txp:comments_error wraptag="ul" break="li" />
<txp:comments_error />
<table cellpadding="4" cellspacing="0" border="0">
  <tr>
    <td align="right" valign="top"><label for="name">
      <txp:text item="name" />
      </label>
    </td>
    <td valign="top"><txp:comment_name_input />
    </td>
  </tr>
  <tr>
    <td align="right" valign="top"><label for="email">
      <txp:text item="email" />
      </label>
    </td>
    <td valign="top" colspan="2"><txp:comment_email_input />
    </td>
  </tr>
  <tr>
    <td valign="top" align="right"><label for="message">
      <txp:text item="Review" />
      </label>
    </td>
    <td valign="top" colspan="2"><txp:comment_message_input />
    </td>
  </tr>
  <tr>
    <td> </td>
    <td><txp:comment_preview />
    </td>
  </tr>
</table>
```

Next, open up the comment_form_preview and add the following markup (make sure that you click Save):

```
<txp:comments_error />
<table cellpadding="4" cellspacing="0" border="0">
  <tr>
    <td align="right" valign="top"><label for="name">
      <txp:text item="name" />
      </label>
    </td>
    <td valign="top"><txp:comment_name_input />
    </td>
  </tr>
  <tr>
    <td align="right" valign="top"><label for="email">
      <txp:text item="email" />
      </label>
    </td>
    <td valign="top" colspan="2"><txp:comment_email_input />
    </td>
  </tr>
  <tr>
    <td valign="top" align="right"><label for="message">
      <txp:text item="Review" />
      </label>
    </td>
    <td valign="top" colspan="2"><txp:comment_message_input />
    </td>
  </tr>
  <tr>
    <td> </td>
    <td><txp:comment_preview />
      <txp:comment_submit />
    </td>
  </tr>
</table>
```

Open up the comment_preview, add the following markup, and click Save:

```
<txp:message />
```

And finally, open the comments form (not to be confused with the comment_form) and add the last piece of markup that follows:

```
<txp:message />

<p class="small">&#8212; <txp:comment_name /> &#183; <txp:comment_ ➡
time /> &#183; <txp:comment_permlink>#</txp:comment_permlink></p>
```

Click Save. You have completed the CityEats.com prototype. You can now view the site in its fully functional state. By the way, if you are wondering about the comments_display form (or files and links form), it is not used. I would delete it, but it's inherent to the system and deleting it would blow up the world.

Summary

While the visual appearance of the site has much to be desired, it is a strong base of functionality to build around. If you think about it, the CityEats.com prototype could be shaped into any sort of review site imaginable. Change the content and the custom form fields a bit, and you can create a site about popular mountain biking destinations or the best places to visit while in Texas. The possibilities are endless.

I hope this case study has demonstrated the simplicity of TXP and the power of the robust plugin architecture.

PART SIX **APPENDIXES**

A TAG REFERENCE

Before you dive into the list of Textpattern tags (in alphabetical order), take a moment to become acquainted with the tag entry template:

<txp:tag_name /> Ⓢ Ⓒ Ⓟ Ⓕ

To help you see at a glance where and how tags can be used, this reference makes use of four different icons, which you can see next to each tag reference entry heading. They represent (from left to right): single tags, container tags, page tags, and form tags.

Single tags are used by themselves:

    <txp:tag_name />

Container tags are wrapped around something else (other Textpattern tags, plain text, or XHTML):

    <txp:tag_name>contents</txp:tag_name>

In addition, each tag name heading is formatted accordingly. For tags that can be used as either single tags or container tags, the tag name heading reflects the format most commonly used.

Description

A general description of the tag.

Attributes (in alphabetical order)

attribute_name="[value],[value]" (specific values you can choose from)

attribute_name=" " (custom value)

Examples

See Chapter *XX*.

<txp:article /> Ⓢ Ⓟ

Description

One or more articles from the currently viewed section or, if viewing the default section (front page), from all sections set to display On front page? in the Sections tab.

Attributes

allowoverride="[1],[0]"

Whether to allow and use Override form for the current article.

- *Available values:* 1 (yes) or 0 (no)
- *Default value:* When viewing search results: 0; otherwise: 1

customfieldname=" "

Restrict to articles with specified value for specified custom field name. Replace customfieldname with the name of the custom field.

- *Available values:* Any custom field values to which you want to restrict your article list
- *Default value:* unset

form=" "

See "Common tag attributes" section. When used with listform, form is used for display of individual articles only.

- *Default value:* default

limit=" "

See "Common tag attributes" section.

listform=" "

Form used to format articles when viewing articles as a list.

- *Available values:* Any article type form name
- *Default value:* unset (form value is used)

keywords=" "

Restrict to articles with specified keywords.

- *Available values:* Single keyword or comma-separated list of keywords
- *Default value:* unset

offset=" "

Number of articles to exclude from the beginning of the list.

- *Available values:* Any number
- *Default value:* 0

pageby=" "

Split article list into several chunks by using article multiple times on a page, without messing up older or newer navigation links. It tells article how many articles to jump forward or back when an older or newer link is clicked.

- *Available values:* Any number
- *Default value:* unset

pgonly="[1],[0]"

Increment the article count, but do not display anything. Used when you want to show the number of search results or article navigation tags before the list of articles. Make sure that other than pgonly, both article tags are identical.

- *Available values:* 1 (yes) or 0 (no)
- *Default value:* 0

searchall="[1],[0]"

Whether all searchable sections are displayed in search results. This attribute does not override the Is searchable? setting in the Sections tab.

- *Available values:* 1 (yes) or 0 (no, search only currently viewed section)
- *Default value:* 1

searchform=" "

Form to format content when displaying as search results.

- *Available values:* Any article type form name
- *Default value:* search_results

searchsticky="[1],[0]"

Whether to include Sticky status articles in search results.

- *Available values:* 1 (yes) or 0 (no)
- *Default value:* 0

sort

See "Common tag attributes" section.

- *Available values:* ID (article ID number), AuthorID (author login name), LastMod (date and time last modified), LastModID (author of last modification login name), Posted (date and time created), Title, Category1, Category2, comments_count (number of publicly visible comments), Status, Section, Body, Excerpt, Keywords, Image (article image), url_title, and custom_1 through custom_10, ascending (asc) or descending (desc)
- *Default value:* For search results, score desc (keyword relevancy score); otherwise, Posted desc

status="[draft],[hidden],[pending],[live],[sticky]"

Restrict to articles with specified status.

- *Default value:* live

time="[past],[future],[any]"

Restrict to articles published within specified time frame.

- *Default value:* past

Examples

See Chapters 6–11 and 15–17.

<txp:article_custom /> Ⓢ Ⓟ

Description

One or more articles with a variety of custom options.

Unlike article, article_custom always returns articles as a list and is not context-sensitive. This means that although article can see articles only within the currently viewed section/category/author and so on, article_custom can see all articles from all sections/categories/authors and so on (unless you restrict it via the following attributes).

Attributes

allowoverride="[1],[0]"

Whether to allow and use Override form for the current article.

- *Available values:* 1 (yes) or 0 (no)
- *Default value:* 0

author=" "

Restrict to articles by specified author.

- *Available values:* Any user login name
- *Default value:* unset

category=" "

Restrict to articles within specified category.

- *Available values:* Any article category name
- *Default value:* unset

customfieldname=" "

Restrict to articles with specified value for specified custom field name. Replace customfieldname with the name of the custom field.

- ■ *Available values:* Any custom field name
- ■ *Default value:* unset

excerpted="[y],[n]"

Restrict to articles with excerpts.

- ■ *Available values:* y (containing an excerpt) or n (not containing an excerpt)
- ■ *Default value:* unset

id=" "

Restrict to specified article. Other attributes, such as status, are still taken into account.

- ■ *Available values:* Any article ID number
- ■ *Default value:* unset

form=" "

See "Common tag attributes" section.

- ■ *Default value:* default

limit=" "

See "Common tag attributes" section.

keywords=" "

Restrict to articles with specified keywords.

- ■ *Available values:* Single keyword or comma-separated list of keywords
- ■ *Default value:* unset

month=" "

Restrict to articles from the specified month.

- ■ *Available values:* Any year and month in the format *yyyy-mm*
- ■ *Default value:* unset

offset=" "

The number of articles to exclude from the beginning of the list.

- ■ *Available values:* Any number
- ■ *Default value:* 0

section=" "

Restrict to articles within specified section.

- *Available values:* Any section name
- *Default value:* unset

sort=" "

See "Common tag attributes" section.

- *Available values:* ID (article ID number), AuthorID (author login name), LastMod (date and time last modified), LastModID (author of last modification login name), Posted (date and time created), Title, Category1, Category2, comments_count (number of publicly visible comments), Status, Section, Body, Excerpt, Keywords, Image (article image), url_title, and custom_1 through custom_10, ascending (asc) or descending (desc)
- *Default value:* For search results, score desc (keyword relevancy score); otherwise Posted desc

status="[draft],[hidden],[pending],[live],[sticky]"

Restrict to articles with specified status.

- *Default value:* live

time="[past],[future],[any]"

Restrict to articles published within specified time frame.

- *Default value:* past

Examples

See Chapters 7, 8, 12, 15, and 16.

<txp:article_id /> Ⓢ Ⓕ

Description

Article ID number. Its context is an article type form. Can also be used within a page if it is wrapped within an if_individual_article tag.

Attributes

None.

(Add a full stop.)

Examples

None.

(Add a full stop.)

<txp:article_image /> Ⓢ Ⓕ

Description

Article image. Its context is an article type form. Can also be used within a page if it is wrapped within an if_individual_article tag.

Attributes

class=" "

See "Common tag attributes" section.

- *Default value:* unset

escape="[html]"

See "Common tag attributes" section.

html_id=" "

See "Common tag attributes" section.

thumbnail="[1],[0]"

Whether to display the image's thumbnail.

- *Available values:* 1 (yes) or 0 (no, display full-sized image)
- *Default value:* 0

wraptag=" "

See "Common tag attributes" section.

Examples

See Chapter 15.

<txp:author /> Ⓢ Ⓕ

Description

Author of the current article. Its context is an article type form. Can also be used within a page if it is wrapped within an if_individual_article tag.

Attributes

link="[1],[0]"

See "Common tag attributes" section. Links to listing of articles by the author.

```
section=" "
```

Used with the `link` attribute, restricts author request to specified section. This attribute conflicts with `this_section`; only one or the other should be used.

- *Available values:* Any section name
- *Default value:* unset (include from all sections)

```
this_section="[1],[0]"
```

See "Common tag attributes" section. Used with the `link` attribute, restricts author request to the current section. This attribute conflicts with `section`; only one or the other should be used.

Examples

See Chapter 15.

<txp:body /> Ⓢ Ⓕ

Description

Body, or main content, of the current article. Its context is an article type form. Can also be used within a page if is wrapped within an `if_individual_article` tag.

Attributes

None.

Examples

See Chapters 8–10, 12, 15, and 17.

<txp:breadcrumb /> Ⓢ Ⓟ Ⓕ

Description

Breadcrumb navigation, either hyperlinked or plain text. Displays any time you are not on the home page.

Attributes

```
class=" "
```

See "Common tag attributes" section.

```
label=" "
```

See "Common tag attributes" section. Text displayed as the first breadcrumb.

- *Default value:* Site name preference

`linkclass=" "`

(X)HTML class attribute applied to each link.

- *Available values:* Any valid CSS class name
- *Default value:* noline

`link="[y],[n]"`

See "Common tag attributes" section. Hyperlinks breadcrumbs to sections/categories.

- *Available values:* y (yes) or n (no)
- *Default value:* y

`sep=" "`

Text to use as the breadcrumb separator.

- *Default value:* » (renders as »)

`title="[y],[n]"`

Whether to display section/category titles.

- *Available values:* y (yes) or n (no, display names)
- *Default value:* n

`wraptag=" "`

See "Common tag attributes" section.

- *Default value:* p

Examples

None.

<txp:category /> Ⓢ Ⓒ Ⓟ Ⓕ

Description

Currently viewed category.

Attributes

`class=" "`

See "Common tag attributes" section.

- *Default value:* unset

`link="[1],[0]"`

See "Common tag attributes" section. Links to listing of articles in the category.

`name=" "`

Override to specified category.

- *Available values:* Any article category name
- *Default value:* unset

`section=" "`

Used with `link` attribute, restricts category request to named section. This attribute conflicts with `this_section`; only one or the other can be used.

- *Available values:* Any section name
- *Default value:* unset

`this_section=" "`

See "Common tag attributes" section. Used with `link` attribute, restricts category request to current section. This attribute conflicts with `section`; only one or the other can be used.

`title="[1],[0]"`

Whether to display category Title.

- *Available values:* 1 (yes) or 0 (no, display name)
- *Default value:* 0

`type="[article],[link],[image],[file]"`

Category type.

- *Default value:* `article`

`wraptag=" "`

See "Common tag attributes" section.

Examples

See Chapters 7, 16, and 17.

<txp:category_list /> Ⓢ Ⓟ Ⓕ

Description

Linked list of categories.

Attributes

active_class=" "

See "Common tag attributes" section.

break=" "

See "Common tag attributes" section.

categories=" "

Restrict to specified category. This attribute conflicts with exclude and parent; only this or the other(s) can be used.

- *Available values:* Single category name or comma-separated list of category names
- *Default value:* unset

class=" "

See "Common tag attributes" section.

- *Default value:* category_list

exclude=" "

Exclude specified categories. This attribute conflicts with categories; only one or the other can be used.

- *Available values:* Single category name or comma-separated list of category names
- *Default value:* unset

label=" "

See "Common tag attributes" section.

labeltag=" "

See "Common tag attributes" section.

parent=" "

Restrict to categories under specified parent category. This attribute conflicts with categories; only one or the other should be used.

section=" "

See "Common tag attributes" section.

this_section="[1],[0]"

See "Common tag attributes" section.

type="[article],[image],[link],[file]"

- *Default value:* article

wraptag=" "

See "Common tag attributes" section.

Examples

None.

<txp:category1 /> Ⓢ Ⓒ Ⓕ

Description

Category1 of the current article. Its context is an article type form. Can also be used within a page if it is wrapped within an if_individual_article tag.

Attributes

class=" "

See "Common tag attributes" section.

link="[1],[0]"

See "Common tag attributes" section. Links to listing of articles in the category.

section=" "

Used with link attribute, links to specified section.

- *Available values:* Any section name
- *Default value:* unset

this_section="[1],[0]"

See "Common tag attributes" section.

title="[1],[0]"

Whether to display category Title.

- *Available values:* 1 (yes) or 0 (no, display name)
- *Default value:* 0

wraptag=" "

See "Common tag attributes" section.

Examples

See Chapters 8–10 and 15.

<txp:category2 /> Ⓢ Ⓒ Ⓕ

Description

Category2 of the current article. Its context is an article type form. Can also be used within a page if it is wrapped within an if_individual_article tag.

Attributes

class=" "

See "Common tag attributes" section.

link="[1],[0]"

See "Common tag attributes" section. Links to listing of articles in the category.

section=" "

Used with link attribute, links to specified section. This attribute conflicts with this_section; only one or the other can be used.

- *Available values:* Any existing section name
- *Default value:* unset

this_section="[1],[0]"

See "Common tag attributes" section. Used with link attribute, links to current section. This attribute conflicts with section; only one or the other can be used.

title="[1],[0]"

Whether to display category Title.

- *Available values:* 1 (yes) or 0 (no, display name)
- *Default value:* 0

wraptag=" "

See "Common tag attributes" section.

Examples

None.

<txp:comment_anchor /> Ⓢ Ⓕ

Description

Empty comment anchor of current comment. Its context is a comment type form.

Attributes

None.

Examples

None.

<txp:comment_email /> Ⓢ Ⓕ

Description

Comment author's email address (E-mail). Its context is a comment type form.

Attributes

None.

Examples

None.

<txp:comment_email_input /> Ⓢ Ⓕ

Description

Comment form email address input field. Its context is a comment type form.

Attributes

None.

Examples

See Chapters 5, 15, and 17.

<txp:comment_id /> Ⓢ Ⓕ

Description

Comment ID number. Its context is a comment type form.

Attributes

None.

Examples

None.

<txp:comment_message /> Ⓢ Ⓕ

Description

Comment Message. Its context is a comment type form.

Attributes

None.

Examples

See Chapters 10 and 15.

<txp:comment_message_input /> Ⓢ Ⓕ

Description

Comment form message input field. Its context is a comment type form.

Attributes

None.

Examples

See Chapters 5, 15, and 17.

<txp:comment_name /> Ⓢ Ⓕ

Description

Comment author's Name. Its context is a comment type form.

Attributes

link="[1],[0]"

Whether the author's name will be linked to the author's website (if entered) or the author's email address (if entered and Never display e-mail address? preference is set to Yes).

- *Available values:* 1 (yes) or 0 (no)
- *Default value:* 1

Examples

See Chapters 10, 15, and 17.

<txp:comment_name_input /> Ⓢ Ⓕ

Description

Comment form name input field. Its context is a comment type form.

Attributes

None.

Examples

See Chapters 5, 10, 15, and 17.

<txp:comment_permlink> Ⓢ Ⓒ Ⓕ

Description

Comment link. Its context is a comment type form.

Attributes

anchor="[1],[0]"

Whether to apply the comment's ID number to the link as an XHTML id attribute, setting this link as the comment's page anchor.

- *Available values:* 1 (yes) or 0 (no)
- *Default value:* If you have not yet used comment_anchor in your form: 1; otherwise: 0

Examples

See Chapter 10, 15, and 17.

\<txp:comment_preview />

Description

Comment form preview button. Clicking the button displays a preview of the visitor's comment. Its context is a comment type form.

Attributes

None.

Examples

See Chapters 15 and 17.

\<txp:comment_remember />

Description

Comment form checkbox input field. If checked, visitors' details are remembered by the system the next time they view a comment form. Checked by default. Its context is a comment type form.

Attributes

None.

Examples

None.

\<txp:comment_submit />

Description

Comment form submit button. Not displayed until visitor has previewed the comment. Clicking the Submit button adds the comment information to the database. Its context is a comment type form.

Attributes

None.

Examples

See Chapters 15 and 17.

<txp:comment_time /> Ⓢ Ⓕ

Description

Comment date/time (Date). Its context is a comment type form.

Attributes

format=" "

Date/time format.

- *Available values:* See "Common date format strings" section
- *Default value:* unset, Comments date format preference is used

gmt="[1],[0]"

See "Common tag attributes" section.

lang=" "

See "Common tag attributes" section.

Examples

See Chapters 10, 15, and 17.

<txp:comment_web /> Ⓢ Ⓕ

Description

Comment author's Website URL, if provided. Its context is a comment type form.

Attributes

None.

Examples

None.

<txp:comment_web_input /> Ⓢ Ⓕ

Description

Comment form website URL input field. Its context is a comment type form.

Attributes

None.

Examples

See Chapters 5 and 10.

<txp:comments /> Ⓢ Ⓕ

Description

One or more comments.

Attributes

break=" "

See "Common tag attributes" section.

- *Default value:* If Present comments as a numbered list? preference is set to Yes: li; otherwise: div

breakclass=" "

See "Common tag attributes" section.

class=" "

See "Common tag attributes" section.

- *Default value:* comments

form=" "

See "Common tag attributes" section.

- *Default value:* comments

id=" "

Display comments for specified article; works only on nonindividual article pages.

- *Available values:* Any article ID number
- *Default value:* unset

wraptag=" "

See "Common tag attributes" section.

- *Default value:* If Present comments as a numbered list? preference is set to Yes: ol; otherwise: unset.

Examples

See Chapters 10, 15, and 17.

<txp:comments_count /> ⓢ ⓕ

Description

The number of comments associated with the current article. Its context is an article type form.

Attributes

None.

Examples

See Chapter 15.

<txp:comments_error /> ⓢ ⓕ

Description

Comment error list. Displays if visitor's comment does not meet required criteria, listing the fields that need correction.

Attributes

break=" "

See "Common tag attributes" section.

class=" "

See "Common tag attributes" section.

wraptag=" "

See "Common tag attributes" section.

■ *Default value:* div

Examples

See Chapter 15.

<txp:comments_form /> ⓢ ⓕ

Description

Comment form.

Attributes

class=" "

See "Common tag attributes" section.

form=" "

See "Common tag attributes" section.

- *Default value:* comment_form

id=" "

Override article to add comments to; this attribute works only on nonindividual article pages.

- *Available values:* Any article ID number
- *Default value:* unset

isize=" "

XHTML size attribute applied to the comment form input fields.

- *Available values:* Any number
- *Default value:* 25

msgcols=" "

XHTML size attribute applied to the comment form message input field.

- *Available values:* Any number
- *Default value:* 25

msg_rows=" "

XHTML rows attribute applied to the comment form message input field.

- *Available values:* Any number
- *Default value:* 5

wraptag=" "

See "Common tag attributes" section.

Examples

See Chapters 10, 15, and 17.

<txp:comments_help /> Ⓢ Ⓟ Ⓕ

Description

Textile help link that includes examples of Textile formatting allowed within comments.

Attributes

None.

Examples

None.

<txp:comments_invite /> Ⓢ Ⓕ

Description

Comment invitation link, with link text taken from Invitation contents in the Comments area of the Write tab. Its context is an article type form. Can also be used within a page if it is wrapped within an if_individual_article tag.

Attributes

class=" "

See "Common tag attributes" section.

showcount="[1],[0]"

Whether to display comment count.

- *Available values:* 1 (yes) or 0 (no)
- *Default value:* 1

showalways="[1],[0]"

Whether to display invite on individual article page.

- *Available values:* 1 (yes) or 0 (no)
- *Default value:* 0

textonly="[1],[0]"

Whether to display invite as plain text instead of a link.

- *Available values:* 1 (yes) or 0 (no, display as a link)
- *Default value:* 0

wraptag=" "

See "Common tag attributes" section.

Examples

See Chapter 17.

<txp:comments_preview /> Ⓢ ⓕ

Description

Visitor comment preview.

Attributes

class=" "

See "Common tag attributes" section.

form=" "

See "Common tag attributes" section.

- *Default value:* comments

id=" "

Override the article to add comments to. This attribute works only when not viewing an individual article page.

- *Available values:* Any article ID number.
- *Default value:* unset

wraptag=" "

See "Common tag attributes" section.

Examples

See Chapters 15 and 17.

<txp:custom_field /> Ⓢ ⓕ

Description

Article custom field.

Attributes

escape="[html]"

See "Common tag attributes" section.

default=" "

Text to display when custom field is empty.

- *Default value:* unset

name=" "

Custom field to display.

- *Available values:* Name of any one of the ten custom fields, as defined in Advanced Preferences
- *Default value:* First custom field name

Examples

See Chapters 8, 11, 12, and 17.

<txp:css /> Ⓢ Ⓟ Ⓕ

Description

Link to one or more Styles (CSS, or Cascading Style Sheets) within a page. (See the "Style" and "Sections" sections in Chapter 5.)

Attributes

format="[url],[link] "

How to format output.

- *Available values:* url (URL of Style) or link (complete XHTML link with all necessary attributes)
- *Default value:* url

media=" "

Used with link format, XHTML media attribute value.

- *Default value:* screen

n=" "

Override Style to link to.

- *Available values:* Any Style name
- *Default value:* unset

rel=" "

Used with link format, XHTML rel attribute.

- *Default value:* stylesheet

title=" "

Used with link format, XHTML title attribute.

- *Default value:* unset

Examples

See Chapters 5, 11, 14, and 17.

<txp:else /> ⓢ ⓟ ⓕ

Description

Used within a conditional tag to define alternative behavior when the condition set in the conditional tag is not met.

Attributes

None.

Examples

See Chapters 8–10, 12, and 15–17.

<txp:email /> ⓢ ⓟ ⓕ

Description

Email hyperlink.

Attributes

email=" "

Email address to link to.

- *Default value:* unset

linktext=" "

Link text.

- *Default value:* Contact

title=" "

Link XHTML title attribute.

- *Default value:* unset

Examples

See Chapter 5.

\<txp:error_message /> Ⓢ Ⓟ Ⓕ

Description

HTTP error status message.

Attributes

None.

Examples

See Chapters 11 and 17.

\<txp:error_status /> Ⓢ Ⓟ Ⓕ

Description

HTTP error status code. See "Common HTTP status codes" section.

Attributes

None.

Examples

See Chapters 11 and 17.

\<txp:excerpt /> Ⓢ Ⓕ

Description

Article Excerpt. Its context is an article type form. Can also be used within a page if it is wrapped within an if_individual_article tag.

Attributes

None.

Examples

See Chapters 8, 9, 11, and 17.

\<txp:feed_link /> Ⓢ Ⓟ Ⓕ

Description

Link to Atom or Really Simple Syndication (RSS) feed of articles.

Attributes

category=" "

Restrict to specified category.

- *Available values:* Any article category name
- *Default value:* Current category

flavor="[rss],[atom]"

Syndication feed format.

- *Available values:* rss (RSS 2.0) or atom (Atom 1.0)
- *Default value:* rss

format="[a],[link]"

Output format.

- *Available values:* a (XHTML a tag, for <body>) or link (XHTML link tag, for <head>)
- *Default value:* a

label=" "

Used with a format, link text.

- *Default value:* unset

limit=" "

See "Common tag attributes" section. Number of recent articles shown in feed.

section=" "

Restrict to specified section.

- *Available value:* Any section name
- *Default value:* Current section

title=" "

XHTML title attribute.

- *Default value:* for "rss" format: RSS Feed; for "atom" format: Atom feed

wraptag=" "

Used with a format. See "Common tag attributes" section.

Examples

None.

<txp:file_download /> Ⓢ Ⓟ Ⓕ

Description

File download formatted with file type form.

Attributes

filename=" "

Filename of the file to link to. This attribute conflicts with id; only one or the other can be used.

- *Available values:* Any filename
- *Default value:* unset

form=" "

See "Common tag attributes" section.

- *Default value:* files

id=" "

File download to link to. This attribute conflicts with filename; only one or the other can be used.

- *Available values:* Any file ID number
- *Default value:* unset

Examples

None.

<txp:file_download_category /> Ⓢ Ⓕ

Description

File Category. Its context is a file type form.

Attributes

class=" "

See "Common tag attributes" section.

- *Default value:* unset

`wraptag=" "`

See "Common tag attributes" section.

Examples

None.

<txp:file_download_created /> Ⓢ Ⓕ

Description

File creation date and time. Its context is a file type form.

Attributes

`format=" "`

Date and time format.

- *Available values:* See "Common date format values" section
- *Default value:* Archive date format **preference**

Examples

None.

<txp:file_download_description /> Ⓢ Ⓕ

Description

File Description. Its context is a file type form.

Attributes

`class=" "`

See "Common tag attributes" section.

- *Default value:* unset

`escape="[html]"`

See "Common tag attributes" section.

`wraptag=" "`

See "Common tag attributes" section.

Examples

None.

\<txp:file_download_downloads /> Ⓢ Ⓕ

Description

The number of times the current file has been downloaded. Its context is a file type form.

Attributes

None.

Examples

None.

\<txp:file_download_id /> Ⓢ Ⓕ

Description

File ID number. Its context is a file type form.

Attributes

None.

Examples

None.

\<txp:file_download_link> Ⓢ Ⓒ Ⓟ Ⓕ

Description

File download link. When used as a single tag file, URL is returned. When used as a container tag, links contents to file URL.

Attributes

filename=" "

Filename of the file to link to. This attribute conflicts with id; only one or the other can be used.

- *Available values:* Any filename
- *Default value:* unset

form=" "

See "Common tag attributes" section.

- *Default value:* files

id=" "

File download to link to. This attribute conflicts with filename; only one or the other can be used.

- *Available values:* Any file ID number
- *Default value:* unset

Examples

See Chapter 5.

<txp:file_download_list /> Ⓢ Ⓟ Ⓕ

Description

List of file downloads.

Attributes

break=" "

See "Common tag attributes" section.

category=" "

Restrict to specified category.

- *Available values:* Any file category name
- *Default value:* unset

class=" "

See "Common tag attributes" section.

form=" "

See "Common tag attributes" section.

- *Default value:* files

label=" "

See "Common tag attributes" section.

labeltag=" "

See "Common tag attributes" section.

limit=" "

See "Common tag attributes" section.

offset=" "

Number of files to exclude, starting from the first in the list.

- *Available values:* Any number
- *Default value:* unset

sort=" "

See "Common tag attributes" section.

- *Available values:* id (file ID number), filename, category, description, downloads or rand() (random)
- *Default value:* filename asc

wraptag=" "

See "Common tag attributes" section.

Examples

None.

<txp:file_download_modified /> Ⓢ Ⓕ

Description

File last modified date and time. Its context is a file type form.

Attributes

format=" "

Date and time format.

- *Available values:* See "Common date format values" section.
- *Default value:* Archive date format preference

Examples

None.

<txp:file_download_name /> Ⓢ Ⓕ

Description

File name. Its context is a file type form.

Attributes

None.

Examples

See Chapter 5.

<txp:file_download_size /> Ⓢ Ⓕ

Description

File size. Its context is a file type form.

Attributes

decimals=" "

Number of decimal places.

- *Available values:* Any number
- *Default value:* 2

format=" "

Filesize format.

- *Available values:* B (bytes), KB (kilobytes/kibibytes), MB (megabytes/mebibytes), GB (gigabytes/gibibytes), PB (petabytes/pebibytes)
- *Default value:* B

Examples

None.

<txp:if_article_author> Ⓒ Ⓕ

Description

Render contents if current article author matches specified conditions. Its context is an article type form. Can also be used within a page if it is wrapped within an if_individual_ article tag.

Attributes

name=" "

Render contents only if specified author matches author of current article.

- *Available values:* Single user login name or comma-separated list of user login names
- *Default value:* unset

Examples

None.

<txp:if_article_category> ⓒ ⓕ

Description

Render contents if specified category is assigned to the current article. Can also be used within a page if it is wrapped within an if_individual_article tag.

Attributes

name=" "

Render contents if specified category is assigned to current article.

- *Available values:* Any article category name
- *Default value:* unset

number="[1],[2]"

Render contents if specified category number is assigned to current article. When used with name attribute, renders contents only if both specified category number and name are assigned to the current article.

- *Available values:* 1 (Category1) or 2 (Category2)
- *Default value:* unset, matches either number

Examples

See Chapter 15.

<txp:if_article_id> ⓒ ⓕ

Description

Render contents if specified article ID number matches the current article ID number. Can also be used within a page if it is wrapped within an if_individual_article tag.

Attributes

id=" "

Article ID number

- *Available values:* Single article ID number or comma-separated list of article ID numbers
- *Default value:* unset

Examples

None.

<txp:if_article_list> Ⓒ Ⓟ

Description

Render contents if an article list is being displayed.

Attributes

None.

Examples

See Chapters 15–17.

<txp:if_article_section> Ⓒ Ⓕ

Description

Render contents if current article is from within specified section. Its context is an article type form. Can also be used within a page if it is wrapped within an if_individual_ article tag.

Attributes

name=" "

- *Available values:* Single section name or comma-separated list of section names
- *Default value:* unset

Examples

None.

`<txp:if_author>` C P F

Description

Render contents if author article listing is being viewed.

Attributes

name=" "

Render contents only if specified author matches author listing being viewed.

- *Available values:* Single user login name or comma-separated list of user login names
- *Default value:* unset

Examples

None.

`<txp:if_category>` S P F

Description

Render contents if category article listing is being viewed.

Attributes

name=" "

Render contents only if specified category matches category listing being viewed.

- *Available values:* Single category name or comma-separated category names
- *Default value:* unset

Examples

See Chapter 16.

`<txp:if_comments>` C F

Description

Render contents if current article has one or more public comments. Its context is an article type form. Can also be used within a page if it is wrapped within an if_individual_ article tag.

Attributes

None.

Examples

See Chapters 15 and 17.

<txp:if_comments_allowed> Ⓒ Ⓕ

Description

Render contents if commenting is permitted for current article. Its context is an article type form. Can also be used within a page if it is wrapped within an if_individual_ article tag.

Attributes

id=" "

Override article to check. This attribute works only on nonindividual article pages.

- *Available values:* Any article ID number
- *Default value:* unset

Examples

See Chapters 10 and 15.

<txp:if_comments_disallowed> Ⓒ Ⓕ

Description

Render contents if commenting is not permitted for the current article. Its context is an article type form. Can also be used within a page if it is wrapped within an if_individual_ article tag.

Attributes

id=" "

Override article to check. This attribute works only on nonindividual article pages.

- *Available values:* Any article ID number
- *Default value:* unset

Examples

See Chapter 10.

<txp:if_comments_error> Ⓒ Ⓕ

Description

Render contents if a comments error condition has been set.

Possible error causes include the following: if the user did not supply all required fields, if an installed spam protection plugin detects spam, or if the comment form has expired. Comment forms expire as one of the Txp antispam measures. When that happens, you simply need to click the Preview button once more.

Attributes

None.

Examples

See Chapter 17.

<txp:if_comments_preview> Ⓒ Ⓟ Ⓕ

Description

Render contents if a visitor is previewing their comment.

Attributes

None.

Examples

See Chapters 15 and 17.

<txp:if_custom_field> Ⓒ Ⓕ

Description

Render contents if specified custom field of the current article has content. Its context is an article type form. Can also be used within a page if it is wrapped within an if_individual_article tag.

Attributes

name=" "

- *Available values:* Name of any one of the ten custom fields, as defined in Advanced Preferences
- *Default value:* First custom field

val=" "

Render contents only if custom field contents matches specified value.

- *Default value:* unset

Examples

See Chapters 12 and 17.

<txp:if_different> Ⓒ Ⓕ

Description

Render contents if the value of the contents differs from the preceding value. This is useful for a list in which there is more than one item or in which there might be more items in the future. On an individual article, the contents would always be rendered because there is no previous value to compare to. Its context is any type of form.

Attributes

None.

Examples

None.

<txp:if_excerpt> Ⓒ Ⓕ

Description

Render contents if an excerpt exists for the current article. Its context is an article type form. Can also be used within a page if it is wrapped within an if_individual_article tag.

Attributes

None.

Examples

See Chapter 17.

<txp:if_first_article> Ⓒ Ⓕ

Description

Render contents if the current article is first in the displayed list. This is useful for a list in which there is more than one item or in which there might be more items in the future. On an individual article, the contents would always be rendered because there are no other articles being displayed. Its context is an article type form.

Attributes

None.

Examples

None.

\<txp:if_individual_article\> Ⓒ Ⓟ Ⓕ

Description

Render contents if an individual article is being displayed.

Attributes

None.

Examples

See Chapters 6, 8–10, and 17.

\<txp:if_last_article\> Ⓒ Ⓕ

Description

Render contents if the current article is last in the currently displayed list. This is useful for a list in which there is more than one item or in which there might be more items in the future. On an individual article, the contents would always be rendered because there are no other articles being displayed. Its context is an article type of form.

Attributes

None.

Examples

None.

\<txp:if_plugin\> Ⓒ Ⓟ Ⓕ

Description

Render contents if specified plugin is installed and enabled.

Attributes

name=" "

Plugin to search for.

■ *Default value:* unset

ver=" "

Restrict to plugins with version numbers equal to or higher than specified.

■ *Default value:* unset

Examples

None.

<txp:if_search> Ⓒ Ⓟ Ⓕ

Description

Render contents if current page is a search results listing.

Attributes

None.

Examples

See Chapters 16 and 17.

<txp:if_section> Ⓒ Ⓟ Ⓕ

Description

Render contents if specified section matches current section.

Attributes

name=" "

Section name.

■ *Available values:* Single section name or comma-separated list of section names
■ *Default value:* unset

Examples

See Chapters 11 and 15.

<txp:if_status> Ⓒ Ⓟ Ⓕ

Description

Render contents if current HTTP status matches specified condition.

Attributes

status="[200],[301],[302],[304],[307],[401],[403],[404],[410],[414],[500],[501],[503]"

HTTP status code number. See "Common HTTP status codes" section.

- *Default value:* 200

Examples

See Chapter 11.

<txp:image /> Ⓢ Ⓟ Ⓕ

Description

Full-size image.

Attributes

class=" "

See "Common tag attributes" section.

- *Default value:* unset

escape="[html]"

See "Common tag attributes" section.

html_id=" "

See "Common tag attributes" section.

id=" "

Image to display. This attribute conflicts with name; only one or the other can be used.

- *Available values:* Any image ID number
- *Default value:* unset

name=" "

Image to display. This attribute conflicts with id; only one or the other can be used.

- *Available values:* Any image name
- *Default value:* unset

wraptag=" "

See "Common tag attributes" section.

Examples

See Chapter 7.

<txp:image_display /> Ⓢ Ⓟ Ⓕ

Description

Used in tandem with image_index, displays requested full-size image.

Attributes

None.

Examples

None.

<txp:image_index /> Ⓢ Ⓟ Ⓕ

Description

Used in tandem with category_list and image_display, displays a linked list of image thumbnails for requested category.

Attributes

break=" "

See "Common tag attributes" section.

class=" "

See "Common tag attributes" section.

label=" "

See "Common tag attributes" section.

labeltag=" "

See "Common tag attributes" section.

wraptag=" "

See "Common tag attributes" section.

Examples

None.

\<txp:keywords />

Description

Article Keywords. Its context is an article type form. Can also be used within a page if it is wrapped within an `if_individual_article` tag.

Attributes

None.

Examples

See Chapters 7 and 11.

\<txp:lang /> Ⓢ Ⓟ Ⓕ

Description

Four-letter code per ISO 639 (language) and ISO 3166 (region) of the Language preference.

Attributes

None.

Examples

See Chapter 5.

\<txp:link /> Ⓢ Ⓕ

Description

Link, as defined in Links tab, using Title as the link text. Its context is a link type form.

Attributes

`rel=" "`

XHTML `rel` attribute.

- *Default value:* unset

Examples

None.

A

437

<txp:link_category /> Ⓢ Ⓕ

Description

Link Category.

Attributes

class=" "

See "Common tag attributes" section.

label=" "

See "Common tag attributes" section.

labeltag=" "

See "Common tag attributes" section.

title="[1],[0]"

Whether to display category Title.

- *Available values:* 1 (yes) or 0 (no, display category name)
- *Default value:* 0

wraptag=" "

See "Common tag attributes" section.

Examples

None.

<txp:link_date /> Ⓢ Ⓕ

Description

Link Date.

Attributes

format=" "

Date format.

- *Available values:* See "Common date format values" section.
- *Default value:* Date format preference

gmt="[1],[0]"

See "Common tag attributes" section.

lang=" "

See "Common tag attributes" section.

Examples

None.

<txp:link_description /> Ⓢ Ⓕ

Description

Link Description. Its context is a link type form.

Attributes

class=" "

See "Common tag attributes" section.

- *Default value:* unset

escape="[html]"

See "Common tag attributes" section.

label=" "

See "Common tag attributes" section.

labeltag=" "

See "Common tag attributes" section.

wraptag=" "

See "Common tag attributes" section.

Examples

None.

<txp:link_feed_link /> Ⓢ Ⓟ Ⓕ

Description

Link to Atom or RSS syndication feed of links.

Attributes

category=" "

Restrict to specified category.

- *Available values:* Any article category name
- *Default value:* Current category

flavor="[rss],[atom]"

Syndication feed format.

- *Available values:* rss (RSS 2.0) or atom (Atom 1.0)
- *Default value:* rss

format="[a],[link]"

Output format.

- *Available values:* a (XHTML a tag, for <body>) or link (XHTML link tag, for <head>)
- *Default value:* a

label=" "

Used with a format, link text.

- *Available values:* Any text
- *Default value:* unset

title=" "

XHTML title attribute.

- *Available values:* Any text
- *Default value:* for "rss" format: RSS Feed; for "atom" format: Atom feed

wraptag=" "

Used with "a" format. See "Common tag attributes" section.

Examples

None.

<txp:link_name /> Ⓢ Ⓕ

Description

Link Title.

Attributes

```
escape="[html]"
```

See "Common tag attributes" section.

Examples

None.

<txp:link_to_home> Ⓢ Ⓒ Ⓟ Ⓕ

Description

Link to the site's home page. When used as a single tag, returns URL (same as site_url). When used as a container tag, contents are linked.

Attributes

```
class=" "
```

See "Common tag attributes" section.

- *Default value:* unset

Examples

See Chapter 17.

<txp:link_to_next> Ⓢ Ⓒ Ⓟ Ⓕ

Description

Next article link. When used as a single tag, returns URL. When used as a container tag, contents are linked.

Attributes

```
showalways="[1],[0]"
```

Show container contents when no next article exists.

- *Available values:* 1 (yes) or 0 (no)
- *Default value:* 0

Examples

None.

<txp:link_to_prev> Ⓢ Ⓒ Ⓟ Ⓕ

Description

Previous article link. When used as a single tag, returns URL. When used as a container tag, contents are linked.

Attributes

showalways="[1],[0]"

Show container contents when no previous article exists.

- *Available values:* 1 (yes) or 0 (no)
- *Default value:* 0

Examples

None.

<txp:link_url /> Ⓢ Ⓕ

Description

Link URL.

Attributes

None.

Examples

None.

<txp:linkdesctitle /> Ⓢ Ⓕ

Description

Link, as defined in the Links tab, using Title as the link text and Description as the XHTML title attribute. Its context is a link type form.

Attributes

rel=" "

XHTML rel attribute.

- *Default value:* unset

Examples

See Chapters 7 and 15.

<txp:linklist /> Ⓢ Ⓟ Ⓕ

Description

List of links.

Attributes

break=" "

See "Common tag attributes" section.

- *Default value:* unset

category=" "

Restrict to category.

- *Available values:* Any link category name
- *Default value:* unset

class=" "

See "Common tag attributes" section.

form=" "

See "Common tag attributes" section.

- *Default value:* plainlinks

label=" "

See "Common tag attributes" section.

labeltag=" "

See "Common tag attributes" section.

limit=" "

See "Common tag attributes" section.

- *Default value:* unset

sort=" "

See "Common tag attributes" section.

- *Available values:* id (link ID number), linkname, url, category, description, date, linksort (Sort Value), or rand() (random)
- *Default value:* linksort asc

wraptag=" "

See "Common tag attributes" section.

Examples

See Chapters 7 and 15.

<txp:meta_keywords /> Ⓢ Ⓟ Ⓕ

Description

Individual article Keywords as XHTML Keyword META element (used in <head>).

Attributes

None.

Examples

See Chapter 7.

<txp:meta_author /> Ⓢ Ⓟ Ⓕ

Description

Individual article author as XHTML Author META element (used in <head>).

Attributes

None.

Examples

None.

<txp:newer> Ⓢ Ⓒ Ⓟ Ⓕ

Description

Used in tandem with article (does not work with article_custom), links to the next page in the list of articles. When used as a single tag, returns URL. When used as a container tag, contents are linked.

Attributes

showalways="[1],[0]"

Whether to render contents, even when no newer page exists.

- *Available values:* 1 (yes) or 0 (no)
- *Default value:* 0

Examples

See Chapter 15.

<txp:next_title /> Ⓢ Ⓟ Ⓕ

Description

Next article's title.

Attributes

None.

Examples

None.

<txp:older> Ⓢ Ⓒ Ⓟ Ⓕ

Description

Used in tandem with article (does not work with article_custom), links to the previous page in the list of articles. When used as a single tag, returns URL. When used as a container tag, contents are linked.

Attributes

showalways="[1],[0]"

Whether to render contents, even when no newer page exists.

- *Available values:* 1 (yes) or 0 (no)
- *Default value:* 0

Examples

See Chapter 15.

<txp:output_form /> Ⓢ Ⓟ Ⓕ

Description

Render misc type form contents. Can be used to easily use and manage often reused portions of text, Textpattern tags, XHTML tags, or combinations of each.

Attributes

form=" "

Form to render.

- ■ *Available values:* Any misc type form name
- ■ *Default value:* unset

Examples

See Chapters 8, 9, 11, and 15–17.

<txp:page_title /> Ⓢ Ⓟ Ⓕ

Description

Page title. Output depends upon the context in which it is being used. Results appear as follows:

Context	Output
Front page	Site name
Page two or more	Site name **separator** Page number
Section listing	Site name **separator** Section Title
Category listing	Site name **separator** Category Title
Search results	Site name **separator** Search results for: search term
Individual article	Site name **separator** Article Title
Popup comments	Site name **separator** Comments on: Article Title

Attributes

separator=" "

Text to use as a separator between items.

- ■ *Default value:* :

Examples

See Chapters 11, 14, 15, and 17.

<txp:page_url />

Description

Current page URL.

Attributes

type=" "

The component of the current URL to display.

- *Available values:* id (current article ID request), s (current section request), c (current category request), q (search query terms), pg (current page number request), month (current month request), author (current author request), request_uri (URL path, relative to domain), status (HTTP status code number, see "Common HTTP status codes" section)
- *Default value:* request_uri

Examples

None.

<txp:password_protect />

Description

Prompt visitor for username and password. If response does not match, terminate render of page, and display error page with message Authorization required.

This tag works only for websites on an Apache web server, running PHP as a module (does not work when running PHP as CGI or on non-Apache servers.

Attributes

login=" "

Username

- *Default value:* unset

pass=" "

Password

- *Default value:* unset

Examples

None.

<txp:permlink> Ⓢ Ⓒ Ⓟ Ⓕ

Description

Article link. When used as a single tag, URL is returned. When used as a container tag, content is linked.

Its context is an article type form. Can also be used within a page if it is wrapped within an if_individual_article tag.

Attributes

id=" "

Override link to specific article. When this attribute is used, the tag can be used anywhere (article, page, form, and so on).

- *Available values:* Any article ID number
- *Default value:* unset

Examples

See Chapters 5, 7–9, 15, and 17.

<txp:php> Ⓒ Ⓟ Ⓕ

Description

Run custom PHP code. Enter code without starting (<?php) and ending (?>) PHP tags, using this tag as a container instead.

For example, in a regular PHP script, you can write this:

```
<?php echo 'Hello world!'; ?>
```

To do the same in Textpattern, enter this:

```
<txp:php>echo 'Hello world!';</txp:php>
```

This feature can be switched on and off in Advanced Preferences.

Attributes

None.

Examples

See Chapter 15.

<txp:popup /> Ⓢ Ⓟ Ⓕ

Description

Pop-up or drop-down menus for browsing by section or category.

Attributes

label=" "

See "Common tag attributes" section.

- *Default value:* Browse

section=" "

Used with c type, jump to the selected category for the specified section. This attribute conflicts with this_section; only one or the other can be used.

this_section="[1],[0]"

Used with c type, jump to the selected category for the current section. This attribute conflicts with section; only one or the other can be used.

- *Available values:* 1 (yes) or 0 (no)
- *Default value:* 0

type="[s],[c]"

Type of list to output.

- *Available values:* s (sections) or c (categories)
- *Default value:* c

wraptag=" "

See "Common tag attributes" section.

Examples

None.

<txp:posted /> Ⓢ Ⓕ

Description

Article creation date and time (Timestamp). Its context is an article type form. Can also be used within a page if it is wrapped within an if_individual_article tag.

Attributes

format=" "

Date format.

- *Available values:* See "Common date format values" section
- *Default value:* If individual article, category, or page listing: Archive date format **preference**; otherwise: Date format **preference**

gmt="[1],[0]"

See "Common tag attributes" section.

lang=" "

See "Common tag attributes" section.

Examples

See Chapters 7–10 and 15.

<txp:prev_title /> Ⓢ Ⓟ Ⓕ

Description

Previous article title.

Attributes

None.

Examples

None.

<txp:recent_articles /> Ⓢ Ⓟ Ⓕ

Description

List of links to recently published articles.

Attributes

`break=" "`

See "Common tag attributes" section.

`category=" "`

Restrict to specified category.

- *Available values:* Any article category name
- *Default value:* unset

`class=" "`

See "Common tag attributes" section.

`label=" "`

See "Common tag attributes" section.

- *Default value:* `Recent Articles`

`labeltag=" "`

See "Common tag attributes" section.

`limit=" "`

See "Common tag attributes" section.

`section=" "`

Restrict to specified section.

- *Available values:* Any section name
- *Default value:* unset

`sort=" "`

See "Common tag attributes" section.

- *Available values:* ID (article ID number), AuthorID (author login name), LastMod (date and time last modified), LastModID (author of last modification login name), Posted (date and time created), Title, Category1, Category2, comments_count (number of publicly visible comments), Status, Section, Body, Excerpt, Keywords, Image (article image), url_title, and custom_1 through custom_10, ascending (asc) or descending (desc)
- *Default value:* `Posted desc`

`wraptag=" "`

See "Common tag attributes" section.

Examples

None.

<txp:recent_comments /> Ⓢ Ⓟ Ⓕ

Description

List of recent comments.

Attributes

break=" "

See "Common tag attributes" section.

class=" "

See "Common tag attributes" section.

label=" "

See "Common tag attributes" section.

labeltag=" "

See "Common tag attributes" section.

limit=" "

See "Common tag attributes" section.

sort=" "

See "Common tag attributes" section.

- *Available values:* discussid (comment ID number), parentid (parent article ID number), name (comment author name), email (comment author email), web (comment author website), ip (comment author IP address), posted (comment creation date and time), message
- *Default value:* posted desc

wraptag=" "

See "Common tag attributes" section.

Examples

None.

\<txp:related_articles /> Ⓢ Ⓕ

Description

List of links to articles related (matching specified categories) to current article. Its context is an article form. Can also be used within a page if it is wrapped within an if_individual_ article tag.

Attributes

break=" "

See "Common tag attributes" section.

class=" "

See "Common tag attributes" section.

label=" "

See "Common tag attributes" section.

labeltag=" "

See "Common tag attributes" section.

limit=" "

See "Common tag attributes" section.

match="[Category1],[Category2],[Category1,Category2]"

Which of the current article's categories to match.

- *Default value:* Category1, Category2

section=" "

Restrict to specified section.

- *Available values:* Any section name
- *Default value:* unset

sort=" "

See "Common tag attributes" section.

- *Available values:* ID (article ID number), AuthorID (author login name), LastMod (date and time last modified), LastModID (author of last modification login name), Posted (date and time created), Title, Category1, Category2, comments_count (number of publicly visible comments), Status, Section, Body, Excerpt, Keywords, Image (article image), url_title, and custom_1 through custom_10, ascending (asc) or descending (desc)
- *Default value:* posted desc

wraptag=" "

See "Common tag attributes" section.

Examples

None.

<txp:search_input /> Ⓢ Ⓟ Ⓕ

Description

Article search form.

Attributes

button=" "

Creates and labels a form submit button.

- *Available values:* Any text
- *Default value:* unset, no button is created

form=" "

See "Common tag attributes" section.

- *Default value:* search_input

label=" "

See "Common tag attributes" section.

- *Default value:* search

section=" "

Use the specified section as the destination page that will display the search results.

- *Available values:* Any section name
- *Default value:* unset, front page is used

size=" "

button XHTML size attribute

- *Available values:* Any number
- *Default value:* 15

wraptag=" "

See "Common tag attributes" section.

- *Default value:* p

Examples

See Chapter 11.

<txp:search_result_count /> Ⓢ Ⓟ Ⓕ

Description

Number of search results found.

Attributes

text=" "

Inline text to label count.

- *Default value:* For one article: article found; otherwise: articles found

Examples

See Chapter 15.

<txp:search_result_date /> Ⓢ Ⓕ

Description

Search result article creation date and time (Timestamp). Its context is an article type form.

Attributes

format=" "

Date format

- *Available values:* See "Common date format values" section
- *Default value:* If viewing first page of search results, Date format preference; otherwise, Archive date format preference

Examples

See Chapter 11.

<txp:search_result_excerpt /> Ⓢ Ⓕ

Description

Highlighted occurrences of the search term with some surrounding context. Its context is an article type form.

Attributes

hilight=" "

XHTML tag (without brackets) to be used to highlight search terms.

- *Default value:* strong

limit=" "

Maximum number of occurrences to highlight.

- *Available values:* Any number
- *Default value:* 5

Examples

See Chapters 11, 15, and 17.

<txp:search_result_title /> Ⓢ Ⓕ

Description

Linked title of article search result. Its context is an article type form.

Attributes

None.

Examples

See Chapters 11 and 17.

<txp:search_result_url /> Ⓢ Ⓕ

Description

Linked URL of article search result. Its context is an article type form.

Attributes

None.

Examples

See Chapter 11.

<txp:section /> Ⓢ Ⓒ Ⓟ Ⓕ

Description

Currently viewed section. When used in an article form or on an individual article page, returns article section (same as article_section).

A

Attributes

class=" "

See "Common tag attributes" section.

- *Default value:* unset

link="[1],[0]"

See "Common tag attributes" section. Links to listing of articles in the section.

name=" "

Override to specified section.

- *Available values:* Any section name
- *Default value:* unset

title="[1],[0]"

Whether to display section Title.

- *Available values:* 1 (yes) or 0 (no, display section name)
- *Default value:* 0

wraptag=" "

See "Common tag attributes" section.

Examples

See Chapters 8 and 15.

<txp:section_list /> Ⓢ Ⓟ Ⓕ

Description

Linked section list.

Attributes

active_class=" "

See "Common tag attributes" section.

break=" "

See "Common tag attributes" section.

class=" "

See "Common tag attributes" section.

default_title=""

Used with include_default, text used for the default section (front page).

- *Available values:* Any text
- *Default value:* Site name preference

exclude=" "

Exclude specified sections. This attribute conflicts with include_sections; only one or the other can be used.

- Available values: Single section name or comma-separated list of section names
- Default value: unset

include_default="[1],[0]"

Whether to include default section (front page) in list.

- *Available values:* 1 (yes) or 0 (no)
- *Default value:* 0

label=" "

See "Common tag attributes" section.

labeltag=" "

See "Common tag attributes" section.

sections=" "

Restrict to specified sections. Also determines the list's sort order. This attribute conflicts with exclude; only one or the other can be used.

- *Available values:* Single section name or comma-separated list of section names
- *Default value:* unset

```
wraptag=" "
```

See "Common tag attributes" section.

Examples

None.

<txp:sitename /> Ⓢ Ⓟ Ⓕ

Description

Site name preference.

Attributes

None.

Examples

See Chapters 15 and 17.

<txp:site_slogan /> Ⓢ Ⓟ Ⓕ

Description

Site slogan preference.

Attributes

None.

Examples

See Chapter 17.

<txp:site_url /> Ⓢ Ⓟ Ⓕ

Description

Site URL preference.

Attributes

None.

Examples

See Chapter 17.

<txp:text />

Description

Predefined text according to Language preference. Examples of this tag can be seen in the default pages and forms distributed with Textpattern.

Attributes

item=" "

Language string.

- *Available values:* Too many to list here
- *Default value:* unset

Examples

See Chapter 17.

<txp:thumbnail />

Description

Image thumbnail.

Attributes

class=" "

See "Common tag attributes" section.

- *Default value:* unset

escape="[html]"

See "Common tag attributes" section.

html_id=" "

See "Common tag attributes" section.

id=" "

Image to display. This attribute conflicts with name; only one or the other can be used.

- *Available values:* Any image ID number
- *Default value:* unset

name=" "

Image to display. This attribute conflicts with id; only one or the other can be used.

- *Available values:* Any image name
- *Default value:* unset

poplink="[1],[0]"

Whether to link to pop-up window containing full-size image.

- *Available values:* 1 (yes) or 0 (no)
- *Default value:* 0

wraptag=" "

See "Common tag attributes" section.

Examples

None.

<txp:title /> Ⓢ Ⓕ

Description

Article title. Its context is an article type form. Can also be used within a page if it is wrapped within an if_individual_article tag.

Attributes

no_widow="[1],[0]"

Inhibit line breaks that would leave a single word (*widow*) on the last line.

- *Available values:* 1 (yes) or 0 (no)
- *Default value:* Prevent widowed words in article titles? preference

Examples

See Chapters 5, 7–10, 12, 15, and 17.

<txp:txp_die /> Ⓢ Ⓟ

Description

Terminate normal page rendition, display an error page, and return the specified status to the user agent (browser, search engine crawler, feed aggregator).

Attributes

msg=" "

Error message.

- *Default value:* unset

status="[200],[301],[302],[304],[307],[401],[403],[404],[410],[414],[500],[501],[503]"

HTTP status code number.

- *Available values:* See "Common HTTP status codes" section.
- *Default value:* 503

Examples

None.

Common tag attributes

Here is a list of several attributes, supported by a large number of Textpattern tags, which always carry the same meaning.

active_class

XHTML class attribute applied to the "active" or current link in a list.

- *Available values:* Any valid CSS class name
- *Default value:* unset

break

XHTML tag (without brackets) or string used to separate list items. Suggested values include br and hr for presentational markup, or li if semantic markup is preferred. Textpattern cares for the correct nesting of tags in either case.

- *Available values:* Any XHTML tag name
- *Default value:* br, unless otherwise stated

breakclass

XHTML class attribute to be applied to break (when value supplied is a tag).

- *Available values:* Any CSS class name
- *Default value:* unset

class

XHTML class attribute to be applied to the specified wraptag. Images will have the class applied to the image itself if no wraptag is specified.

- *Available values:* Any CSS class name
- *Default value:* Textpattern tag name (without brackets)

escape

Whether to escape XHTML entities within output.

- *Available values:* html (convert < and > into their named entity equivalents)
- *Default value:* unset

form

Form used to format content for display.

- *Available values:* Any existing form of the relevant type (for example, for articles an article type form)

A

gmt

Whether to output date/time according to Greenwich Mean Time.

- *Available values:* 1 (yes) or 0 (no)
- *Default value:* 0

html_id

XHTML id attribute to be applied to the wraptag. Images will have the class applied to the image itself if no wraptag is specified.

- *Available values:* Any XHTML id attribute name
- *Default value:* unset

label

This string will be prepended to the output. When using a wraptag value of either ol or ul, label will be the first list item.

- *Available values:* Any desired text
- *Default value:* unset, unless otherwise stated

labeltag

XHTML tag (without brackets) to wrap around label.

- *Available values:* Any valid XHTML tag name
- *Default value:* unset

lang

The language (locale) to use to output date/time.

- *Available values:* Four-letter code of the language [ISO 639 (language) and ISO 3166 (region)]
- *Default value:* Locale for the Language preference

limit

The number of items of data (articles, search term occurrences, links, and so on) to display.

- *Available values:* Any positive number
- *Default value:* 10, unless otherwise stated

link

Whether to link the output to the relevant URL.

- *Available values:* 1 (yes) or 0 (no), unless otherwise stated
- *Default value:* 0 (no), unless otherwise stated

sort

How the resulting list of data (articles, links, and so on) should be sorted before being displayed. Available values include any comma-separated combination of column field names from that content's database table, ascending (first to last, the default) or descending (last to first).

this_section

Whether to link the output to the current section.

- *Available values:* 1 (yes) or 0 (no)
- *Default value:* 0 (no)

wraptag

XHTML tag (without brackets) to wrap around output. Suggested values can include p, ol, or ul.

- *Available values:* Any XHTML tag name
- *Default value:* unset, unless otherwise stated

Common date format values

Here is a list of the most commonly used date format values. You can see the other options listed in the PHP manual: http://php.net/strftime.

Value	Output
since	Textpattern-specific format, outputs the time elapsed since published date/time
%d	day of the month (range: 01–31)

Value	Output
%A	weekday name
%a	weekday name abbreviated
%m	month (range: 01–12)
%B	month name
%b	month name abbreviated
%y	year without the century (range: 00–99)
%Y	year including the century (range: 0000–9999)
%H	hour using a 24-hour clock (range: 00–23)
%I	hour using a 12-hour clock (range: 01–12)
%M	minute
%S	second
%p	either am or pm
%%	a literal % character

A

Common HTTP status codes

Here is a list of some common HTTP status codes.

Number	Message
201	OK
301	Moved Permanently
302	Found
304	Not Modified
307	Temporary Redirect
401	Unauthorized
403	Forbidden

Continued

Number	Message
404	Not Found
410	Gone
414	Request-URI Too Long
500	Internal Server Error
501	Not Implemented
503	Service Unavailable

See the other options in the HTTP Status Code Registry: www.iana.org/assignments/ http-status-codes.

Index

A

A

469

A

B PLUGIN DEVELOPER RESOURCES

This appendix contains a detailed listing of commonly used helper functions from the Textpattern source and the global variables that you have access to when writing plugins. While you can dig through all of the Textpattern source code to locate every function and variable, this reference contains those that are most commonly used.

Helper functions

When writing plugins, all the libraries in the Textpattern core are at your disposal. The libraries contain a wide range of functions that can be reused to save time when writing your own plugin code. The following sections highlight some of the most helpful functions that you'll find in the scripts within the /textpattern/lib/ directory.

txplib_db.php

The txplib_db.php file contains functions that help you interact with the Textpattern database. All the functions are "safe" because they automatically attach a table prefix to the table name if necessary.

- safe_query() executes a SQL query
- safe_delete() executes a SQL DELETE query
- safe_update() executes a SQL UPDATE query
- safe_insert() executes a SQL INSERT query
- safe_upsert() attempts to execute a SQL UPDATE query; if it fails, a SQL INSERT query is executed
- safe_field() retrieves the value of a single field in a table
- safe_column() retrieves an array of values from a single column in a table
- safe_row() retrieves a single row from a table
- safe_rows() retrieves an array of rows from a table
- safe_count() retrieves a count of the number of rows in a table

txplib_forms.php

The txplib_forms.php file contains functions that help you build HTML forms and form elements.

- yesnoRadio() creates yes/no radio button input elements
- onoffRadio() creates on/off radio button input elements
- selectInput() creates a select list
- fInput() creates a form input element
- hInput() creates a hidden form input element
- sInput() creates a hidden step input element for the admin interface

- eInput() creates a hidden event input element for the admin interface
- checkbox() creates a checkbox input element
- form() creates a form
- text_area() creates a textarea

txplib_html.php

The txplib_html.php file contains functions that help you build HTML code. The functions in this file can be used so that you don't have to embed HTML in your plugin code.

- startTable() creates an opening table tag
- endTable() creates a closing table tag
- tr() creates a table row
- hcell() creates a table header cell
- td() creates a table cell
- assRow() creates a table row from an array of data
- assHead() creates a table header row from an array of data
- tag() creates an HTML tag of your choice
- graf() wraps text in <p> tags
- hed() creates a heading element
- href() creates a hyperlink
- sLink() creates a step link for the admin interface
- strong() wraps text in <strong> tags
- htmlPre() wraps text in <pre> and <code> tags
- comment() wraps text in an HTML comment
- dom_attach() creates a new element and attaches it to the DOM
- script_js() wraps JavaScript code in <script> tags

txplib_misc.php

The txplib_misc.php file contains a variety of miscellaneous helper functions.

- gTxt() returns a translated string from the language file
- dmp() dumps variables to the screen
- gps() checks for GET and POST variables
- gpsa() checks for GET and POST variables in an array
- ps() checks for a POST variable
- psa() checks for a POST variable in an array
- cs() checks for a COOKIE variable

B

- load_plugin() loads a plugin from the database or plugin cache directory
- require_plugin() attempts to load a plugin and returns an error if not found
- include_plugin() attempts to load a plugin and returns a warning if not found
- register_callback() registers a callback function
- register_tab() registers a new tab in the admin interface
- lAtts() confirms that attributes passed to a function are valid
- is_valid_email() checks a string for a valid email address
- safe_strftime() formats time and respects the locale set in Textpattern
- EvalElse() is used for conditional tags to display appropriate output based on a condition
- fetch_form() retrieves a form from the database
- fetch_category_title() retrieves a category name's title
- fetch_section_title() retrieves a section name's title
- get_lastmod() retrieves the date an article on a site was last modified
- set_pref() inserts or updates a preference in the database

Global variables

As Textpattern pages and forms are parsed to render your completed web page, you can access a wealth of global variables in your plugin code. The following are lists of global variable names and descriptions.

$prefs

The $prefs array contains general values for site-wide settings, as shown in Table B-1. Most of the preferences contained in the array can be set within the Admin ➤ Preferences tab. Their specific location in the admin interface is noted in Table B-1. You can refer to Chapter 3 for details on those preferences. Preferences that cannot be changed in the admin interface are also listed. This array is available on all pages.

You can dump all global variables to the screen in a sorted list by using the following code on any Textpattern page:

```
<txp:php>
global $prefs;
ksort($prefs);
dmp($prefs);
</txp:php>
```

Table B-1. Site preferences global variable names and corresponding locations in the admin interface

Variable Name	Preference Location
`$prefs['admin_side_plugins']`	Advanced—Publish—Use admin side plugins?
`$prefs['allow_article_php_scripting']`	Advanced—Publish—Allow PHP in articles?
`$prefs['allow_form_override']`	Advanced—Publish—Allow form override?
`$prefs['allow_page_php_scripting']`	Advanced—Publish—Allow PHP in pages?
`$prefs['allow_raw_php_scripting']`	Advanced—Publish—Allow raw php?
`$prefs['archive_dateformat']`	Basic—Publish—Archive date format
`$prefs['article_list_pageby']`	Content ➤ Articles
`$prefs['articles_use_excerpts']`	Advanced—Publish—Articles use excerpts?
`$prefs['attach_titles_to_permalinks']`	Advanced—Publish—Attach titles to permalinks?
`$prefs['blog_mail_uid']`	Set by Textpattern; first admin user's email address used if the use_mail_on_feeds_id preference is true
`$prefs['blog_time_uid']`	Set by Textpattern; year used to create the blog_uid
`$prefs['blog_uid']`	Set by Textpattern; a unique ID for the site
`$prefs['comment_list_pageby']`	Content ➤ Comments
`$prefs['comment_means_site_updated']`	Advanced—Publish—New comment means site updated?
`$prefs['comment_nofollow']`	Advanced—Publish—Apply rel="nofollow" to commenters' website URL?
`$prefs['comments_are_ol']`	Basic—Comments—Present comments as a numbered list?
`$prefs['comments_auto_append']`	Basic—Comments—On by default?

Continued

B

Table B-1. Site preferences global variable names and corresponding locations in the admin interface *(Continued)*

Variable Name	Preference Location
$prefs['comments_dateformat']	Basic—Comments—Comments date format
$prefs['comments_default_invite']	Basic—Comments—Default invite
$prefs['comments_disabled_after']	Basic—Comments—Disabled after (never, 1 week, 2 weeks, 3 weeks, 4 weeks, 5 weeks, **or** 6 weeks)
$prefs['comments_disallow_images']	Basic—Comments—Disallow user images?
$prefs['comments_mode']	Basic—Comments—Comments mode (nopopup **or** popup)
$prefs['comments_moderate']	Basic—Comments—Moderate comments?
$prefs['comments_on_default']	Basic—Comments—On by default?
$prefs['comments_require_email']	Advanced—Comments—Require user's e-mail address?
$prefs['comments_require_name']	Advanced—Comments—Require user's name?
$prefs['comments_sendmail']	Basic—Comments—Mail comments to author?
$prefs['custom_1_set']	Advanced—Custom Fields—Custom field 1 name
$prefs['custom_10_set']	Advanced—Custom Fields—Custom field 10 name
$prefs['custom_2_set']	Advanced—Custom Fields—Custom field 2 name
$prefs['custom_3_set']	Advanced—Custom Fields—Custom field 3 name
$prefs['custom_4_set']	Advanced—Custom Fields—Custom field 4 name
$prefs['custom_5_set']	Advanced—Custom Fields—Custom field 5 name

Variable Name	Preference Location
$prefs['custom_6_set']	Advanced—Custom Fields—Custom field 6 name
$prefs['custom_7_set']	Advanced—Custom Fields—Custom field 7 name
$prefs['custom_8_set']	Advanced—Custom Fields—Custom field 8 name
$prefs['custom_9_set']	Advanced—Custom Fields—Custom field 9 name
$prefs['dateformat']	Basic—Publish—Date format
$prefs['dbupdatetime']	Set by Textpattern; the date the database was last updated
$prefs['edit_raw_css_by_default']	Advanced—Style—Use raw editing mode by default?
$prefs['expire_logs_after']	Advanced—Publish—Logs expire after how many days?
$prefs['file_base_path']	Advanced—Admin—File directory path
$prefs['file_list_pageby']	Content ➤ Files
$prefs['file_max_upload_size']	Advanced—Admin—Max Upload File Size (in bytes)
$prefs['gmtoffset']	Basic—Publish—Time Zone
$prefs['image_list_pageby']	Content ➤ Images
$prefs['img_dir']	Advanced—Admin—Image directory
$prefs['include_email_atom']	Advanced—Publish—Include e-mail in Atom feeds?
$prefs['is_dst']	Basic—Publish—DST enabled?
$prefs['language']	Language—Currently active language
$prefs['lastmod']	Set by Textpattern; the date your site was last changed
$prefs['link_list_pageby']	Content ➤ Links

Continued

B

479

Table B-1. Site preferences global variable names and corresponding locations in the admin interface *(Continued)*

Variable Name	Preference Location
$prefs['locale']	Language—Currently active language
$prefs['log_list_pageby']	Admin ➤ Visitor Logs
$prefs['logging']	Basic—Publish—Logging
$prefs['max_url_len']	Advanced—Publish—Use e-mail address to construct feed ids? (Default is site URL)
$prefs['never_display_email']	Advanced—Publish—Never display e-mail address?
$prefs['override_emailcharset']	Advanced—Admin—Use ISO-8859-1 encoding in e-mails sent? (Default is UTF-8)
$prefs['path_from_root']	Deprecated
$prefs['path_to_site']	From config.php; the absolute path to the site on the web server
$prefs['permalink_title_format']	Advanced—Publish—Permalink title-like-this? (Default is TitleLikeThis)
$prefs['permlink_mode']	Basic—Publish—Permanent link mode
$prefs['ping_textpattern_com']	Advanced—Publish—Ping textpattern.com?
$prefs['ping_weblogsdotcom']	Advanced—Publish—Ping ping-o-matic.com?
$prefs['plugin_cache_dir']	Advanced—Admin—Plugin cache directory path
$prefs[prefs_id]	Cannot be changed; no known use
$prefs['production_status']	Basic—Publish—Production Status
$prefs['rss_how_many']	Advanced—Admin—How many articles should be included in feeds?
$prefs['send_lastmod']	Advanced—Admin—Send Last-Modified header
$prefs['show_article_category_count']	No longer used; remains for backward compatibility

Variable Name	Preference Location
`$prefs['show_comment_count_in_feed']`	Advanced—Publish—Show comment count in feeds?
`$prefs['site_slogan']`	Basic—Publish—Site slogan
`$prefs['sitename']`	Basic—Publish—Site name
`$prefs['siteurl']`	Basic—Publish—Site URL
`$prefs['spam_blacklists']`	Advanced—Publish—Use e-mail address to construct feed ids? (Default is site URL)
`$prefs['syndicate_body_or_excerpt']`	Advanced—Publish—Syndicate article excerpt? (Default is article body)
`$prefs['tempdir']`	Advanced—Admin—Temporary directory path
`$prefs['textile_links']`	Advanced—link—Textile link descriptions by default?
`$prefs['textile_updated']`	Cannot be changed; no known use
`$prefs['timeoffset']`	Basic—Publish—Time Zone
`$prefs['title_no_widow']`	Advanced—Publish—Prevent widowed words in article titles?
`$prefs['url_mode']`	Basic—Publish—Permanent link mode
`$prefs['use_categories']`	No longer used; remains for backward compatibility
`$prefs['use_comments']`	Basic—Publish—Accept Comments
`$prefs['use_dns']`	Advanced—Publish—Use DNS?
`$prefs['use_mail_on_feeds_id']`	Advanced—Publish—Use e-mail address to construct feed ids? (Default is site URL)
`$prefs['use_plugins']`	Advanced—Publish—Use plugins?
`$prefs['use_sections']`	No longer used; remains for backward compatibility
`$prefs['use_textile']`	Basic—Publish—Use Textile
`$prefs['version']`	Set by Textpattern; the current Textpattern version

B

$txpcfg

The $txpcfg array contains general settings for the Textpattern installation, as shown in Table B-2. This array is available on all pages.

Table B-2. General site configuration global variables

Variable Name	Description
$txpcfg['db']	The MySQL database used by Textpattern
$txpcfg['dbcharset']	The character set used in the MySQL database
$txpcfg['doc_root']	The web server's document root
$txpcfg['host']	The database server hostname
$txpcfg['pass']	The password used to connect to the database
$txpcfg['table_prefix']	The table prefix for all Textpattern tables (if applicable)
$txpcfg['txpath']	The full path to the /textpattern directory
$txpcfg['user']	The username used to connect to the database

$pretext

The $pretext array contains values that are set by Textpattern after parsing the URL but before building pages, as shown in Table B-3. The values in this array can be read or altered for various purposes, including the capability to support different URL schemes. Some of the variables in this array are consistent across a site, some change based on the current page, and some are available only on article listing pages. This array is available on all pages.

Table B-3. Global variables generated after URL parsing but before pages are built

Variable Name	Description
$pretext['author']	The current author when browsing by author
$pretext['c']	The current category when browsing by category
$pretext['id']	The current article's ID (only on article listings)
$pretext['id_author']	The current article's author (only on article listings)
$pretext['id_keywords']	The current article's keywords (only on article listings)

Variable Name	Description
$pretext['month']	The current month when browsing by month
$pretext['next_id']	The ID of the next article in the listing (only on article listings)
$pretext['next_posted']	The posted date of the next article in the listing (only on article listings)
$pretext['next_title']	The title of the next article in the listing (only on article listings)
$pretext['next_utitle']	The URL title of the next article in the listing (only on article listings)
$pretext['p']	The current image used by the image_display tag
$pretext['page']	The page template used to build the page
$pretext['path_from_root']	Deprecated
$pretext['path_to_site']	From config.php; the absolute path to the site on the web server
$pretext['permlink_mode']	The current permanent link mode as set in Admin ➤ Preferences
$pretext['pfr']	Deprecated
$pretext['pg']	The current page number when browsing by page
$pretext['prev_id']	The ID of the previous article in the listing (only on article listings)
$pretext['prev_posted']	The posted date of the previous article in the listing (only on article listings)
$pretext['prev_title']	The title of the previous article in the listing (only on article listings)
$pretext['prev_utitle']	The URL title of the previous article in the listing (only on article listings)
$pretext['q']	The search string when executing a site search
$pretext['qs']	The query string for the page
$pretext['req']	The request URI without the subdirectory path

Continued

B

Table B-3. Global variables generated after URL parsing but before pages are built *(Continued)*

Variable Name	Description
$pretext['request_uri']	The request URI for the page
$pretext['s']	The current section
$pretext['secondpass']	Indicates whether the Textpattern parser is on its first or second pass through the page code
$pretext['sitename']	The site name as set in Admin ➤ Preferences
$pretext['status']	The HTTP page status
$pretext['subpath']	The subdirectory path for the site

$thispage

The $thispage array contains values about the current page, as shown in Table B-4. This array is available on pages that contain an article listing tag.

Table B-4. Global variables used on article listing pages

Variable Name	Description
$thispage [c]	The current category when browsing by category
$thispage ['grand_total']	The total number of articles not including the offset
$thispage ['numpages']	The total number of pages
$thispage['pg']	The current page number
$thispage ['s']	The current section
$thispage ['total']	The total number of articles minus the page offset

$thisarticle

The $thisarticle array contains values about the current article, as shown in Table B-5. This array is available on article forms and is prepopulated when requesting an individual article page, unless otherwise noted.

Table B-5. Global variables used on article forms

Variable Name	Description	Textpattern Tag
$thisarticle ['annotate']	When true, commenting is open for the article	<txp:if_comments_allowed />
$thisarticle ['article_image']	The image ID assigned to the article	<txp:article_image />
$thisarticle ['authorid']	The author of the article	<txp:author />
$thisarticle ['body']	The body of the article	<txp:body />
$thisarticle ['category1']	The article's first category	<txp:category1 />
$thisarticle ['category2']	The article's second category	<txp:category2 />
$thisarticle ['comments_count']	The number of comments posted on the article	<txp:comments_count />
$thisarticle ['comments_invite']	The comment invite text for the article	<txp:comments_invite />
$thisarticle ['excerpt']	The article's excerpt	<txp:excerpt />
$thisarticle ['is_first']	Indicates if the current article is first in the article list (populated only after the article tag has been used within the page)	<txp:if_first_article />
$thisarticle ['is_last']	Indicates if the current article is last in the article list (populated only after the article tag has been used within the page)	<txp:if_last_article />
$thisarticle ['keywords']	The keywords assigned to the article	<txp:keywords />

Continued

485

Table B-5. Global variables used on article forms *(Continued)*

Variable Name	Description	Textpattern Tag
$thisarticle ['override_form']	The override form assigned to the article (if applicable)	
$thisarticle ['posted']	The date the article was posted	<txp:posted />
$thisarticle ['section']	The article's section	<txp:section />
$thisarticle ['thisid']	The ID number of the article	<txp:article_id />
$thisarticle ['title']	The title of the article	<txp:title />
$thisarticle ['url_title']	The URL title of the article	

$thiscomment

The $thiscomment array contains values about the current comment, as shown in Table B-6. This array is available on comment forms.

Table B-6. Global variables used on comment forms

Variable Name	Description	Textpattern Tag
$thiscomment ['discussid']	The comment ID	<txp:comment_id />
$thiscomment ['email']	The comment's email address	<txp:comment_email />
$thiscomment ['ip']	The IP address the comment was posted from	
$thiscomment ['message']	The comment message	<txp:comment_message />
$thiscomment ['name']	The commenter's name	<txp:comment_name />

Variable Name	Description	Textpattern Tag
$thiscomment ['parentid']	The article ID to which the comment is attached	
$thiscomment ['posted']	The date and time the comment was posted	`<txp:comment_time />`
$thiscomment ['time']	The Unix timestamp indicating when the comment was posted	`<txp:comment_time />`
$thiscomment ['visible']	Indicates whether the comment should be displayed on the public site	
$thiscomment ['web']	The commenter's website address	`<txp:comment_web />`

B

$thislink

The $thislink array contains values about the current link, as shown in Table B-7. This array is available on link forms.

Table B-7. Global variables used on link forms

Variable Name	Description	Textpattern Tag
$thislink ['category']	The link category assigned to the link	`<txp:link_category />`
$thislink ['date']	The date the link was posted	`<txp:link_date />`
$thislink ['description']	The link description	`<txp:link_description />`
$thislink['linkname']	The link name	`<txp:link_name />`
$thislink ['url']	The link URL	`<txp:link_url />`

$thisfile

The $thisfile array contains values about the current file, as shown in Table B-8. This array is available on file forms.

Table B-8. Global variables used on file forms

Variable Name	Description	Textpattern Tag
$thisfile ['category']	The file category assigned to the file	`<txp:file_download_category />`
$thisfile ['created']	The date the file was originally uploaded	`<txp:file_download_created />`
$thisfile ['description']	The file description	`<txp:file_download_description />`
$thisfile ['downloads']	The number of times the file has been downloaded	`<txp:file_download_downloads />`
$thisfile ['filename']	The file name	`<txp:file_download_name />`
$thisfile ['id']	The file ID	`<txp:file_download_id />`
$thisfile ['modified']	The date the file was last uploaded	`<txp:file_download_modified />`
$thisfile ['size']	The size of the file	`<txp:file_download_size />`

Miscellaneous

There are several global variables available besides those in the arrays previously mentioned (see Table B-9). The variables are available on all pages.

Table B-9. Miscellaneous global variables

Variable Name	Description
$has_article_tag	Indicates whether the current page has a valid Textpattern article tag
$is_article_list	Indicates whether the current page is an article listing page

Variable Name	Description
$plugin_callback	An array containing all active plugin callbacks
$plugins	An array containing the names of active public-side plugins
$plugins_ver	An array containing the version numbers of active public-side plugins
$txptrace	The Textpattern tag trace detailing all tags and queries used to build the page
$txp_error_code	The HTTP error code (if applicable)
$txp_current_tag	The Textpattern tag currently being parsed
$qcount	The number of database queries used to build the page
$qtime	The amount of time (in seconds) taken to build the page

B

INDEX

friendsofed.com/forums

Join the friends of ED forums to find out more about our books, discover useful technology tips and tricks, or get a helping hand on a challenging project. *Designer to Designer*™ is what it's all about—our community sharing ideas and inspiring each other. In the friends of ED forums, you'll find a wide range of topics to discuss, so look around, find a forum, and dive right in!

- **Books and Information**

  Chat about friends of ED books, gossip about the community, or even tell us some bad jokes!

- **Flash**

  Discuss design issues, ActionScript, dynamic content, and video and sound.

- **Web Design**

  From front-end frustrations to back-end blight, share your problems and your knowledge here.

- **Site Check**

  Show off your work or get new ideas.

- **Digital Imagery**

  Create eye candy with Photoshop, Fireworks, Illustrator, and FreeHand.

- **ArchivED**

  Browse through an archive of old questions and answers.

HOW TO PARTICIPATE

Go to the friends of ED forums at **www.friendsofed.com/forums**.

Visit **www.friendsofed.com** to get the latest on our books, find out what's going on in the community, and discover some of the slickest sites online today!

friendsof ™

DESIGNER TO DESIGNER™

an Apress® company